Mass Media, Politics and Democracy

Mass Media, Politics and Democracy

2nd Edition

John Street

First published 2011 by
RED GLOBE PRESS

Red Globe Press in the UK is an imprint of Springer Nature Limited,
registered in England, company number 785998, of 4 Crinan Street,
London, N1 9XW.

Red Globe Press® is a registered trademark in the United States,
the United Kingdom, Europe and other countries.

ISBN 978–1–4039–4734–5   ISBN 978–1–137–01555–6 (eBook)

A catalogue record for this book is available from the British Library.

A catalog record for this book is available from the Library of Congress.

For Marian, Alex, Jack and Tom

Contents

Acknowledgements

I owe thanks to a wide variety of people who have, sometimes unwittingly, contributed to both this edition and its predecessor: Nick Anstead, Sigrid Baringhorst, Michael Billig, Marian Brandon, Valentina Cardo, Stephen Coleman, John Corner, Ian Forbes, Marion Forsyth, Steve Foster, Simon Frith, Peter Golding, Andy Grantham, John Greenaway, Shaun Hargreaves Heap, Michael Harker, Sanna Inthorn, Mark Jancovich, Brian Loader, Lee Marsden, Anne Martin, Carla Moore, Alastair Mullis, Kate Nash, Keith Negus, Pippa Norris, Keith Povey, Alex Rousso, Roberta Sassatelli, Heather Savigny, Mike Saward, Alan Scott, Martin Scott, David Sinclair, Steve Smith, Mike Stephens, Hazel Taylor, Liesbet Van Zoonen, Frank Webster, Sally-Ann Wilson, Scott Wright, several anonymous reviewers and many generations of students at the University of East Anglia. I owe a particular debt to Steven Kennedy, Stephen Wenham and Helen Caunce at Palgrave Macmillan for their patience, persistence and wise advice, and to Susan Curran at Curran Publishing Services for copy editing. My family – Marian, Alex, Jack and Tom – have continued to provide the best possible distraction. The book is dedicated to them – again.

John Street

This book draws in places on some earlier articles by the author: 'In praise of packaging', *Harvard International Journal of Press/Politics*, 1(2), 1996, pp. 43–55; 'Remote control? Politics, technology and "electronic democracy"', *European Journal of Communication*, 12(1), 1997, pp. 27–42; 'Prime time politics: popular culture and politicians in the UK', *The Public/Javnost*, 7(2), 2000, pp. 75–90; (with Alan Scott) 'From media politics to e-protest: the use of popular culture and new media in parties and social movements', *Information, Communication and Society*, 3(2), 2000, pp. 215–40; 'Celebrity politicians: popular culture and political representation', *British Journal of Politics and International Relations*, 6(4), 2004, pp. 435–52; and 'Politics lost, politics transformed, politics colonised? Theories of the impact of mass media', *Political Studies Review*, 3, 2005, pp. 17–33.

Introduction

When the first edition of this book was published in 2001, none of us owned an iPod or an iPhone; there were no social networking sites like Facebook or video streaming sites like YouTube to occupy our time; we had not heard of Twitter or Wikipedia. Back then Barack Obama was teaching constitutional law at the University of Chicago. Yet by the decade's end, Obama was living constitutional law, having won the US presidency on the back of a campaign that deployed Facebook, YouTube and many of the other communications innovations that have become part of everyday life for many – but significantly, not all – citizens of the modern world.

The first edition of this book began with an anecdote about the musical tastes of the then candidates for the US presidency. George W. Bush, it transpired, liked Van Morrison, while his rival for the Republican nomination was a Frank Sinatra fan. Their Democrat opponent, Al Gore, went for Shania Twain. These apparently trivial choices were treated by the media as significant markers of character and style, and could be seen, in turn, as providing a telling insight into the way politics was changing; in particular, how the line between popular entertainment and political communication were becoming increasingly blurred. Few, though, would have predicted that Bush's successor as president would have one of his speeches reworked to a hip-hop beat, with guest vocal performances from the good and the great of the film, music and sports worlds, and that the resulting video would secure over 25 million hits. Few might also have anticipated that Arnold Schwarzenegger, star of Hollywood blockbusters like *The Terminator* and *Total Recall*, would be elected as governor of California; or that the rock musicians Bono and Bob Geldof would come to lead political movements which, they claimed subsequently, forced the world's most powerful figures to change their policy on third world debt; or that one of those world leaders would take time out to pose with a Fender Stratocaster guitar as part of a photo-opportunity, as

1

Tony Blair did. In this new world order, the rock and film stars played at being politicians, while the politicians pretended to be rock stars.

As such phenomena become increasingly familiar, we hardly notice them, let alone examine them. But only three decades earlier, no politician, and certainly no prime minister, would have allowed themselves to be pictured as the British prime minister was; and the only reason for a rock star to be on the front page of the newspaper would have been because they had died from a drug overdose or done something shocking (like swearing on television).

What the new order symbolizes is the way in which politics and modern mass media (in all its forms) have become ever more closely linked, with the result that it sometimes seems as if the form and content of politics are now dictated by those with media power and media skills. Why else would a moderately successful pop singer like Geldof come to be treated as the source of wisdom and insight on the plight of Africa? Why else would David Cameron, as the then newly elected leader of the British Conservative Party, allow himself to be cross-examined on Jonathan Ross's popular night-time chat show about whether, as a young man, he had entertained sexual fantasies about one of his predecessors, Margaret Thatcher?

There is, of course, much debate about what exactly is going on in such a 'mediatized' world, but the main focus of the discussion is whether politics is being 'transformed' by its contact with mass media. The traditional forms of political communication and the traditional sources of political power, it is widely suggested, are being reconstituted and reshaped. For some, it is for the worse (Lloyd, 2004); for others, it is for the better (Temple, 2006). For others, what we are witnessing is the emergence of 'post-democracy', in which the transformation of the media–politics relationship is but one element of a much wider set of changes. 'Post-democracy' is defined as a situation in which, according to Colin Crouch (2004: 6), 'while the forms of democracy remain fully in place ... politics and government are increasingly slipping back into the control of privileged elites in the manner characteristic of pre-democratic times'. In such a world, says Crouch, there is frequent 'recourse to show business for ideas of how to attract interest in politics', and political communication is increasingly simplified and sensationalized (2004: 28).

This book is an attempt to trace, explore and assess this alleged process of transformation of politics and the media's role in it. There is a lot at stake. The 'transformation' is held to affect not just what we are told and what we know, but how we think and act. In later chapters, I will look in detail at the various dimensions and aspects of politics' complicated relationship with mass media. But before this, it is worth recalling how we got here, how the idea emerged that media and politics were indeed connected and interdependent.

Politics and mass media: the emerging agenda

In recent years, we have seen a proliferation of textbooks and monographs, articles and journals, that acknowledge the importance of the politics–media relationship. This now vast literature stands in marked contrast to the situation two or three decades ago. The change can be detected in the content of textbooks. Only very gradually were mass media acknowledged as important to understanding political processes. But through the 1980s, they came to assume ever greater prominence in political studies. It was then that the leading US journal *Political Communication* was founded, although it was not until 1996 that the *Harvard International Journal of Press/Politics* joined it. Key monographs on the topic also emerged slowly (for example, Lippman, 1922; Klapper, 1960; Blumler and McQuail, 1968; Habermas, 1989/1962), and it was not until the late 1980s and early 1990s that the subject came into its own. Now publishers' catalogues have pages devoted to books on political communication and the mass media, not to mention the many undergraduate and postgraduate courses that they serve.

Historically, mass media's relationship to politics has been framed by the idea of 'propaganda' and fear for its effect on 'mass society' (anxieties most vividly captured in George Orwell's *Nineteen Eighty-Four*). This vision of a mass manipulated society was fuelled in particular by the rise of Nazism. Joseph Schumpeter, writing in the 1940s, warned of how 'Newspaper readers, radio audiences, members of a party even if not physically gathered together are terribly easy to work up into a psychological crowd and a state of frenzy in which attempt at rational argument only spurs the animal spirits' (1976: 257).

Schumpeter, like most of the early writers on the media–politics link, was less interested in media content, and more concerned with its effects as a medium on political rationality and behaviour. This perspective came to dominate the literature, and found expression in later studies of media's effects on voting and elections (for example, Miller, 1991).

But there have been those for whom the content has been crucial to the story of media's power. The political messages contained within mass media have been scrutinized by a range of writers and researchers from a diversity of disciplines – from linguistics, sociology, media studies and political science, to name but a few (Aarts and Semetko, 2003; Chilton, 2003; Fowler, 1991; Herman and Chomsky, 1988; Glasgow University Media Group 1976, 1980, 1993; Norris et al., 2003). An early example is Jacques Ellul's *The Political Illusion*, published in France in 1965. In this unusual book, Ellul foreshadows many of the complaints that are now associated with the accusation of 'dumbing down' in media coverage. He writes of how the form and content of 'news' represents a 'stupefying lack of continuity' (Ellul, 1972: 57), which effectively reduces the individual's capacity to act as a responsible citizen. Instead of producing wise and informed citizens, the news produces ignorant ones, capable of 'pseudodecisions' only (ibid.: 59–63). This past study of the political content of media messages connects to a more recent interest in changes in political communication and the impact of media on these developments (see for example Stanyer, 2007; Negrine, 2008; Washbourne, 2010).

These later writers have perhaps been less concerned with the impact of media on mass behaviour, and more with how ideas are conveyed by politicians and parties (Kavanagh, 1995; Rosenbaum, 1997; Wring and Horrocks, 2001). Much of its attention has been – like much of the effects literature – on elections (Bartle and Griffiths, 2001; Bartle et al, 2002; Crewe et al., 1998), but it has also addressed government communication (Davis, 2002; Lees-Marshment, 2004; Scammell, 1995). While this research has tended to concentrate on the way organizations have used media to communicate their message and to persuade audiences to support their cause, we have also seen a growth in research into how media has shaped the behaviour of organizations. This is captured in the idea of the 'CNN effect', where it is claimed that governments' foreign policies have been led by media coverage. It turns out that the CNN effect is more a matter of appearance than reality (Robinson, 2002), but there remains good reason for taking a close interest in how elites – as much as 'masses' – respond to media (Davis, 2003).

There is one final area in which the link between politics and media has come to prominence. Besides the impact of media on policy, there has been the impact of policy on media. The political economy of mass media is arguably the most important work in the field. It is here that media's capacity to shape politics is determined or moderated. This research has focused on the particular public policy issues raised by the regulation of media, especially broadcasting policy in both country specific and comparative perspective (Baker, 2007; Collins and Murroni, 1996; Dyson and Humphreys, 1988; Hallin and Mancini, 2004; Hardy, 2008; Humphreys, 1996; Levy, 1999; Freedman, 2008; Tunstall, 2008). This work has been supplemented by studies of the broader political economy of media and culture industries (see, for example, Baker, 2002; Hesmondhalgh, 2007; Tunstall and Machin, 1999).

So, to summarize, we have seen the study of media's relationship to politics move from an exclusive concern with propaganda and its mass effects, to mapping changes in political communication, to studying elite effects, to tracing the contours of media policy and the political economy of communications. But while much has changed, much remains the same. The agenda that drives our curiosity remains rooted in questions of power and democracy. What power do media exercise? On whose behalf? With what consequences? These persist as the dominant concerns. Discussion of media's place in politics is animated by the powers imputed to them and the judgements made of them. These same questions continue to occupy us as we contemplate the rise of new media and their deployment in election campaigns and in government policy-making. New media may bring the question of 'transformation' into sharper focus, but the question itself is not new. It has always been there. Indeed, I would argue that it is not a question of technology, but of politics, of how we understand what it is that is being transformed, as much as it is about what is doing the transforming.

Defining terms

There a few exercises more boring – and, indeed, frequently unhelpful – than the defining of key terms, but the claims above do require a brief justification, and this is best achieved through a short account of what we mean by 'media' and 'politics'.

Media

There is a temptation – a perfectly understandable one – to think of media as 'things': the flatscreen television set, the mp3 player, the radio, the mobile phone, and so on. And to an extent, these *are* what we mean by media, but they have this identity because of what they allow us to do, which is to communicate. But, at the same time, media are not to be associated with all forms of communication. As John Thompson (1988) has pointed out, mass media deal with communication of particular types, ones that are to be distinguished from personal communications as it is traditionally understood. Mass media are distinguished by, among other things, the fact that communication is at a distance with an undefined audience; that the substance of the communication can be stored, can be reproduced and can be sold. Furthermore, while they are shaped by technology – phones allow for a different form of communication from that of television, as Marshall McLuhan (1964) famously argued – the conditions of communication are not simply dictated by technology. They are the product of politics, economics and law. The opportunity to communicate is structured by decisions about the allocation of access to systems of communication, about the rights (copyright, intellectual property) and constraints (libel, secrecy) attaching to communication; it is determined by the distribution of resources in both the production and consumption of communication. Put simply, while the same basic technologies of communication are used the world over, we all communicate in different ways because of the different regimes and systems of communication that operate. These variations owe much to the political values and interests that inform regulatory decisions.

Politics

Politics too is more complicated and more encompassing than is sometimes assumed.

One implication of the transformation of both media and politics is that the traditional boundaries, which mark where politics ends and, say, entertainment begins, no longer apply. This is not just because politicians now communicate through the world of entertainment, telling us about their favourite records or their family, but because politics has, in part, to be understood as 'entertainment': its language and conventions are often drawn from the pop video, the advert and the chat show host. But the political use of such things reminds us that entertainment is itself 'political'. When politicians tell us about their favourite items of popular culture, this is not an innocent exercise. They are deliberately selecting – as maybe we all do – the images and associations of those films and stars in order to enhance their chosen image. 'Entertainment' is often looked down on or ignored in the study of mass media. As James Curran notes, entertainment is not thought to involve 'rational exchange' and therefore 'not [to] belong to the political arena' (2000: 139). But entertainment is intimately linked to politics through the values it articulates and the passions it generates: think of the films of Oliver Stone or Michael Moore or the music of Rage Against the Machine or Public Enemy; think of the way that every state censors and regulates access to media and culture. Understanding politics' relationship to the media cannot be confined to analysis only of news and current affairs; it has to take account of entertainment too. Game shows, situation comedies, films and music, all of these are bearers of meaning, making sense of our world and our responses to it – structuring our feelings, as Raymond Williams (1981) put it. Media output, whether in the form of news or of soaps, acts upon our emotions and our reason. So when we talk of the power of mass media to transform politics we are talking about many, complex relationships. But we are not talking about all relationships. Colin Hay (2007: 65) offers what he calls 'a differentiated yet inclusive conception of politics'. Politics, by this account (Hay, 2007: 65–70), refers to situations in which people face a choice, the result of which will cause change. Politics is also defined by the presence of deliberation and social interaction. Government, parties, politicians and social movements are all implicated in these aspects of politics, because they are all implicated in the business of shaping and making choices, of articulating deliberations and organizing social interaction. All of these dimensions of Hay's definition, furthermore, are directly connected to the role played by media.

Transforming politics?

One of the shorthand ways that the transformation of politics is identified is to talk of 'dumbing down'. Serious debate and discussion, it is argued, has been replaced by cynically crafted sound bites and photo-opportunities; politics has been trivialized and democracy has been damaged. If this is right, it is an important and worrying charge; but if things are to be changed for the better we need to do more than to bemoan the latest stunt or gimmick of this or that politician. We need to ask why it is happening. This question cannot be directed just to the politicians, with their entourage of media consultants, advertising executives and spin doctors. It needs also to be addressed to the media which print the spin and broadcast the images. After all, the media could (and in some countries they do) ignore all the razzmatazz. If we want to understand the character of political communications, obviously we need to look at the changing incentives and practices of the modern politician, but equally obviously we need to note changes in the contemporary media corporation. The two are linked.

Politicians are adapting to the medium upon which they have come to rely. They design their campaigns and their approach to fit the media. Their schedules are timed to coincide with journalists' deadlines; their public performances are intended to look good on the screen. They are in the 'popularity' business and they seek out the populism that the world of entertainment offers. Politics is moulded to fit the medium. But the medium is not just an instrument of the politicians' will. It creates the rules and sets the agendas for the coverage of politics. And as politicians embrace the world of celebrity politics, they also pay the price it demands. Flaws in their personality become flaws in their political standing, as President Bill Clinton found when his relationship with White House intern Monica Lewinsky became national news. Suddenly the president's sex life was not only a matter of legitimate media concern, it was also a matter of constitutional importance. This did not just happen because of what Clinton did – some other presidents, it would seem, have behaved little better. It happened because of what counted as news and how politics was to be covered. These were linked to the way politicians were campaigning, but they were also connected to increasing media concern with 'human interest' stories, with gossip and celebrities, rather than with traditional political news. It is as important to explain the incentives at work in the media – increasing competition for audiences and advertisers – as it is to explain those acting on politicians.

This raises the important subject of what people are being told about the 'world' in their papers and programmes. What story is being conveyed in reports of natural disasters and election results, in gossip columns and soap stories? One way of giving an answer is to talk in terms of the 'truthfulness' or 'fairness' of the picture. Media content is to be described and judged by the accuracy of its account, and one of the key ideas in this analysis is that of 'bias'. It is common to hear politicians and political activists complaining that their case and their claims have been misrepresented, or that there is a systematic bias against their view of the world. These complaints come from the left and the right, from Russian and US presidential candidates. They refer to a bias in favour of one point of view over another, or of one group over another; they refer to the way women or gays or ethnic groups are portrayed; they refer to the fact that some parts of the globe are ignored and others receive favoured treatment.

Political content can be analysed in terms of these 'biases', by the way one perspective is given preference over another. But 'bias' is just one possible criterion for analysing media content. Another is to focus on the narrative; to be less concerned with the events and details, and more with the way they are linked to tell a story. Stories create a causal chain: this happened because she did that, he responded by doing this. They identify notions of responsibility and blame; they make sense of the chaos of events 'out there', and in doing so steer the audience's response towards one view of the world rather than another.

However media texts are understood, their content matters because it is assumed that we believe what we see or read and that, in believing it, we change the way we think and act. Sometimes study of the relationship between politics and the media is left here, with the focus on media content and its assumed effects. But this omits other, equally pressing concerns: why, for example, does the content take one form rather than another; who or what decides the coverage and character of the media? Equally important is the question of whether, in fact, we are influenced by what we see and read.

At its heart, the relationship between politics and mass media is a power relationship. There are two dimensions to this: there is the power *over* the media – what gets shown or reported – and there is power *of* the media – what gets changed by the media. In respect of the first dimension, if the media does not simply mirror or distil reality, if it imposes particular biases or stories upon the world, we need to ask who is to blame for the result. One obvious response is to look to those with a direct interest in the outcome, those with most to gain: the governments, parties and politicians. This is the assumption behind the interest in the use of spin doctors, sound bites and photo-opportunities, all intended to produce the images and ideas that keep these politicians in power. It is the spin doctor whose job it is to pre-empt unfavourable bias, or to introduce a favourable one, enabling the politically powerful to manipulate and distort the democratic process. Such claims deserve careful analysis because they go to the heart of media's relationship with politics, but the focus on political devices – on spin doctors and sound bites – can obscure the other interests involved in this relationship. These include the journalists who produce the copy and the programmes, and the corporations who employ them. In understanding media content, we need to understand the politics of journalistic practice: why *this* story, why *that* image? And perhaps more importantly, we need to understand corporate politics, and the interests and influences that circulate within the global multimedia empires. To what extent is the 'news' and its coverage a product of the ambitions and designs of the companies that produce the papers and programmes? Organizations like News Corporation, with its newspapers, television stations, film studios and book publishers, are sometimes portrayed as using their media outlets to advance their own political cause; this is why the coverage takes the form it does. No attempt to make sense of the relationship between politics and mass media can afford to ignore such possibilities.

But equally, if not more, important is what impact the media have on the world they report. This is the second dimension of media power: the media's power over people and events. Politicians' desperation to appear on television (and to create the right image) is matched by the capacity of the media to make or break political careers. It sometimes seems that 'politics' is what appears on TV or in the press, that appearance is everything in political life: those who control the image control the reality; we no longer have real politics, we have virtual politics. This idea was taken to its logical extreme by the Hollywood film *The Matrix* (1999). 'Perception: our day-in, day-out world is real,' read the blurb on the posters for the movie, 'Reality: The world is a hoax, an elaborate deception spun by all-powerful machines of artificial intelligence that control us.' The film played with the proposition that our 'reality' was the product of someone else's will, exercised through their power over the means of communication. *The Matrix* may have occupied the dystopian end of views about political manipulation, but it tapped into a conventional wisdom about the power of the media and those who wield it; this is why the media seem to matter: they appear to determine who wins and loses, what we think and say. But do they?

Power is rarely exercised directly through the use of brute force. Typically, people obey rules and regulations, not because the authorities stand over them waving a baton or pointing a gun (though, of course, this does happen), but because they already recognize the right of those authorities to direct their actions. Insofar as coercion is involved, the threat of it is usually enough, and threats depend on words and impressions as well as actual deeds. Power relies on our 'common sense' view of how the world is and how it works; threats and authority depend on how we perceive those who make those threats or claim that authority. These thoughts, the unexamined assumptions of our routines, help us to know our place and our identity. And they are daily disseminated through news and current affairs, situation comedies and blockbuster movies.

It is no surprise that, when political coups take place, the rebels head first for the radio and television stations in order to secure their victory. It is also obvious that one device for subsequently maintaining control is to manage strictly the flow of information. Hence the Chinese authorities' obsessive concern to monitor the content and use of the internet. Secrecy is a key weapon of the powerful; they hold the information that is denied to the rest. When NATO bombers began attacking his country in 1998, President Milosevic of Yugoslavia responded by removing the head of Belgrade's independent radio station B92. And when Milosevic was deposed in 2000, demonstrators set fire to the state television station and attacked its director. The writer Gabriel Garcia Marquez claimed that, in Venezuela, a shift in political power turned on the skill with which rival leaders made use of the country's television studios (*Guardian*, 2 September 2000).

Just as media can serve authority, they can also subvert it. Challenges to 'common sense' can find expression in the same media that reinforce it. The power of the media is not just measured by the way citizens may be controlled. That power can be used to unsettle and even unseat the powerful. The media have tried (and sometimes succeeded) in humbling many politicians, whether US presidents (Richard Nixon, Bill Clinton), Italian prime ministers (Silvio Berlusconi) or British cabinet ministers (David Blunkett, Peter Mandelson, David Mellor, John Prescott and Jacqui Smith). These politicians suffered because their reputation, as John Thompson (1997) points out, is a key political resource, and it is one that is, to a large extent, supplied by and through mass media. In destroying political careers (or at least, in being the catalyst for their destruction), the mass media often style themselves as the 'voice of the people'. It is this role that entitles them to interrogate public figures and to scrutinize the actions of public institutions. Indeed, there are commentators, such as Andrew Marr (1996), the BBC's former political editor, who claim that the media are more effective at ensuring democratic accountability than the arrangements formally designated for this purpose. It is a thought that echoes in John Keane's (2009) suggestion that the current mode of democracy is 'monitory democracy', in which media provide ubiquitous scrutiny of both public and private realms.

Certainly, in Western liberal democracies, the mass media have claimed the right to represent the people and to uphold democracy, and the consumers of newspapers and television have come to treat these media sources as the basis on which to think and act in the world. We need only to recall public behaviour during scares about fuel shortages or about genetically modified food, or to witness the extraordinary generosity that follows reports of earthquakes or hurricanes in other parts of the world, to see how media seem to influence thought and action. But things are, of course, not this simple. Not every piece of news has the same effect. Not only do people discriminate between the origin of news and the credibility they attach to it, but in different parts of the world television and newspapers perform quite different functions from those fulfilled in the West. The media are not automatically and inevitably treated as sources of information which is blindly acted upon. Endless reports have appeared on the dangers of smoking, but people continue to buy cigarettes. The argument still rages about the consequences of media portrayals of violence or pornography. One side contends that media content actually alters the levels of violence in society or that it changes for the worse the relations between men and women. Others argue that such claims are entirely unproven, and that media content is, at most, a reflection (rather than a cause) of social attitudes.

Similar arguments emerge in discussion of political behaviour. There is the familiar debate between those who see biased media coverage as winning elections for one side or the other. There are others who worry about the divide between those who are information rich and those who are information poor, because the first has the power which the other lacks. For some, the cause of this social chasm is television itself (Putnam, 1995, 2000). Others note the uneven distribution of people's capacity to control, or be controlled by, the media they consume. Interpreting media is a skill, a skill that is dependent upon social and educational background (Bourdieu, 1986; Norris, 2000).

Whatever side you take, the argument about mass media's power – whether as the power over media or the power of media – cannot be resolved easily. This is hardly surprising. As Nicholas Garnham has pointed out, studying media means engaging with issues that have troubled social scientists for a very long while:

> it can be argued that the central question underlying all debates about the media and how we study them concerns the way in which and the extent to which humans learn and thus how through time identities are formed and actions motivated.
>
> (Garnham, 2000: 5)

When and where do people act freely, as the authors of their own fate; when and where do they act at the behest of others? These persistent questions pervade the study of the media–politics relationship, and derive from the desire to know how the world is organized. But accompanying them is another set of related questions. As well as wanting to know how things *are*, we are also concerned about how they *ought* to be. What sort of control over media is acceptable or necessary in a democracy?

This question tends to divide people along political lines, between those, on the one hand, who advocate public regulation, either provided by the terms of media ownership or by the rules which apply to journalists and editors, and those, on the other, who advocate complete deregulation, leaving the market to arbitrate. This crude divide is, of course, more complex than it appears here. It is more complex because there are many competing notions of 'democracy' in circulation; it is also made more complex by the rapidly changing context in which the argument takes place. The emergence of the internet and digital television transforms the means of communication as well as the balance of power. It is suggested, for example, that blogging and Twitter create the conditions for the rise of the citizen journalist, and the decline of professional journalism. Assessing the political implications of any such shift in power depends on how we understand the role and responsibility of journalism in a democracy. Only then can we make sense of the debate about the political significance of the internet; only then can we compare the attempts of those, like China and Singapore, who aim to control internet use, with those on the other side who see the 'information superhighway' as the last truly free political forum, and who use it to advance an alternative democratic order. This debate is about how modem media should function in a democracy. It is an argument which extends from questions about what is meant by a 'free press' to ones about whether the internet can create an electronic democracy that recalls the republican glories of Ancient Greece. It is assumed that mass media contribute in some way to the political life of citizens, furnishing them with a means of representing themselves and their interests, and allowing them the space – a 'public sphere' – within which they can reflect on the conditions of their lives and how these might be changed for the better (Habermas, 1989, 1996). But can such an ideal coexist with commercialized media directed at consumers rather than citizens?

It should be evident by now that there are a large number of issues and areas that come together in the relationship between politics and mass media. This book is an attempt to bring some order to them and yet still reflect their complexity and interconnectedness. Making sense of the relationship between mass media and politics requires us to think about its ever-changing character and its cultural peculiarities. To take one obvious example: what is meant by 'political coverage' has varied over time and between places, as we can see by the way in which politicians have been treated, from the vicious satire directed at the politicians of the eighteenth century, to the deference of the mid-twentieth, to the cynicism of the twenty-first century; from the protection their privacy receives in France to the intrusive glare that they encounter in the United States and United Kingdom. Seeing the relationship historically and comparatively allows us to identify the forces that shape its current form, to realize that it has not always been like this and that it is unlikely to remain this way.

Equally, the relationship between politics and mass media has to be understood in terms of the institutions that manage the flow of power: the systems of regulation and patterns of control that organize the media. The history of the relationship between politics and mass media has to be understood as the product of particular institutional forms that shape the media. Comparison of national broadcasting systems reveals considerable variations in the role assigned to the state and the type of regulation to which media organizations are subject, whether measured in terms of control of content, opportunities for access to the airwaves or the strictures of libel legislation.

This book reflects the constantly changing nature of the relationship between politics and mass media, and draws attention to the institutional interests that shape the change. The discussion is divided into three parts. The first considers the ways in which politics is represented in the mass media and the debate about how this content affects thought and action. Part II deals with the institutional interests – whether those of the state or the commercial sector – that organize mass media and impose their politics upon them. If the first two parts are about how things are, then the final part is primarily about how they might be. This is partly an opportunity to reflect upon the future form of mass media's relationship to politics, but it is also a chance to debate the normative question of how that relationship ought to be organized.

Within these parts, individual chapters deal with specific issues and arguments. Chapter 1 begins the discussion of media content by looking at the idea of 'political bias', in particular at what sorts of biases are said to be contained in the press and television, and at how such bias is to be detected. Moving on from discussion of 'bias', the chapter introduces an alternative approach which stresses the 'framing' of politics, the way political stories are told. This provides the basis for the next chapter, which analyses how 'politics' is represented in mass media: the political institutions and actors that are included and excluded, the motives that are recognized and those that are marginalized. Chapter 3 continues the concern with the representation of politics, but moves the attention away from news and current affairs to look at the politics of entertainment, including satire, movies, soap operas and sport. Part I ends with a critical review of the debate about media influence, and the claims made for how media content shapes thought and action.

Part II begins with a chapter on the ways in which the state, through its legislative power and other resources, is able to shape the content of mass media. Chapter 6 turns attention to the equivalent power of the new multimedia conglomerates; Rupert Murdoch's empire is used as a case study of claims about corporate control of media. One of the arguments against placing too much emphasis on the power of people like Murdoch is that journalists and editors enjoy some relative autonomy, and any explanation of the particular character of media content must acknowledge their role. Looking in particular at the fate of investigative journalism, Chapter 7 examines the power of journalists by comparing different models of their behaviour, from those that see journalism as an independent activity to those that see it as a controlled process, and – as 'churnalism' – an increasingly irrelevant one. Chapter 8, which concludes Part II, considers the impact of globalization on the state, media corporations and journalism, to see how the emerging global political economy affects the ways in which media and politics are related.

In contemplating this emerging world, the final part of the book begins with a detailed discussion of the debate about the marketing of politics and the rise of the celebrity politician. The latter is increasingly seen to symbolize the transformation of political communication. Chapter 9 documents the emergence of celebrity politics, how it might be explained and indeed justified, and what effects it is having. It argues that we need to treat the phenomenon seriously, and that in doing so we can better appreciate the changing character of contemporary political communication. In a similar vein, Chapter 10 considers the thought that the internet – through blogging, Twitter, and user-generated content in general

– is providing the basis for a new 'e-democracy'. It argues for caution in the face of media hyperbole. The political uses of new media are not inscribed in the technology itself, but in the interplay with the political order into which they are introduced. The last two chapters tackle the themes that lie at the core of the book, and are constant features throughout it: power and democracy. Chapter 11 looks at competing claims, deriving from different ideological and analytical standpoints, about the transformative power of mass media, and their implications for some of the key concerns in this book. Are we seeing the emergence of a totalizing, network-based communication power, of the kind identified by Manuel Castells (2009)? Chapter 12 reviews the arguments for changing the organization of media in the name of democracy, and at the implications of these for the practice of journalism, public access and media ownership.

In summary, *Mass Media, Politics and Democracy* connects the many issues and arguments that are raised by any attempt to make sense of the relationship between politics and mass media. The book links the different aspects of that relationship: how the political use and content of mass media is shaped by the commercial and political incentives that drive the state and media conglomerates, how claims of media power are linked to media effects, how the 'celebritization' of politics and new media technologies are linked to the notion of democracy. Without understanding such things, we cannot hope to comprehend either the nature of modern media or modern politics, or offer a judgement on whether politics is being transformed by its relationship with modern forms of communication.

Part I

Representing Politics

Chapter 1

Political Bias

Words matter. They affect us in any number of different ways. They make us laugh and cry; they make us angry and they make us smile. Each year I do an experiment with my students. They are given a policy choice. It is the same for everyone in the class, but it is worded in two different ways. Invariably, students faced with one wording make a different decision from those with the other wording. The experiment is a variant on research (Fischoff et al., 1983) which shows that that how a risk is presented to us affects our willingness to accept or reject it. It serves to remind us of the impact of words – and by implication, of images and sounds. Put simply, they do things to us and hence to our world. It is this thought that lies behind the importance attached to media content and its politics, the topic of this and the next two chapters.

James Curran (2002) provides a vivid illustration of the ways in which mass media, through their use of words, images and sounds, do things to the world. He charts the different narratives that are used to tell media history. For example, he talks of how the emergence of the mass circulation newspaper gave a 'voice' to ordinary citizens, as opposed to the political elite. He argues too that mass media were instrumental in creating a tolerance for what was previously found intolerable – by making the unfamiliar commonplace. The mass media were, in other words, a force for a more libertarian society. In a similar way, mass media in the form of women's magazines gave recognition to the presence and capacities of women in a society that treated them as invisible, second-class citizens. And so on. These narratives, suggests Curran, appeal to the notion that the mass media made the world more equal, liberal and democratic. But as Curran also points out, there are media narratives that tell a less happy story. These report the media's role in thwarting popular power, in making society less equal and free; they are narratives in which media is used to repress, rather than liberate, people. What these different perspectives share is the view that media have real-world effects. Where they disagree is in discerning what these effects are. One way to address this dispute is to examine more closely media content, to see what it is 'saying'. Typically this discussion begins by asking whether media accurately represent the world or whether they offer partial or slanted views. Put simply, are media biased?

Humanitarian disasters happen with tragic regularity; earthquakes, floods and famines are persistent features of our world. They form, too, a regular part of our news coverage. Or so it may seem, until we look more closely. In 2005, two hurricanes hit the American continent. Both killed more than a thousand people, and both were the subject of media reports. But here the similarity ends. One of the hurricanes was mentioned 3,105 times in UK papers; the other was mentioned only 34 times. The first was Hurricane Katrina which hit New Orleans; the second was Hurricane Stanley which hit Guatemala (CARMA, 2006). For the authors of the report that documented this divergent coverage of very similar human disasters, this was a case of bias. The coverage was indicative of a greater sympathy for the people of the United States than of Guatemala; the former were represented as the more 'worthy' victims. The *Guardian* (4 February 2003) made such a point when it noted that on a single day seven astronauts died in the Space Shuttle, seven schoolchildren were killed on the Canadian ski slopes, and seven desperate migrants from Africa were washed up dead on a Spanish beach. Only one of these incidents of multiple deaths was reported in the UK press – that of the astronauts.

There are many other examples of what might be labelled selective reporting. In the United Kingdom, much more media attention was devoted to the deaths caused by swine flu in 2009–10, than was devoted to the deaths caused by other strains of flu. This follows a familiar pattern in the reporting of causes of death, whereby the relatively rare causes receive far more attention than the routine, but predominant, forms – like cancer, alcohol or road traffic accidents (Harrabin et al., 2003). The Islamic Human Rights Commission (2007) published a report in which it spoke of 'the unashamed bias' against Muslims to be found in mass media. Roy Greenslade's (2005: 23) report, *Seeking Scapegoats*, noted that in the period 2001–05, the newspaper columnist Richard Littlejohn made '88 disparaging references to asylum-seekers'. In a general condemnation of media reporting, David Edwards and David Cromwell (2006: 90) complain of a media system that 'strongly selects for ... certain beliefs, certain facts and certain crimes against humanity'.

Elections are often the source of many of the accusations of political bias. During the Russian presidential elections in 1996, Boris Yeltsin's rivals complained, with some justice, that they were being denied the favourable coverage that he received (Mickiewicz and Richter, 1996: 120–1). In Italy, Silvio Berlusconi's political opponents complain at their coverage relative to his (Ginsborg, 2005). In the United Kingdom, all the parties complain about their coverage and their treatment, including their treatment in drama as well in current affairs (the Conservative Party, for example, did not like the way they were portrayed in television plays about the miners' strike of 1984–5). In the United States, the same sense of injustice is echoed in arguments between liberals and the right, both of whom feel under- or mis-represented. The Australian Broadcasting Corporation had its funding cut by successive governments – of different political persuasions – each of which regarded the corporation's coverage as 'biased' (Schultz, 1998: 5–6).

Accusations of bias are not to be treated lightly. They strike at the core of journalists' self-image. Reporters see themselves as impartial observers of the world. It is a view that is reinforced by mechanisms that are designed to ensure that bias is expunged. Most media organizations, like the BBC or the *New York Times*, have complaints procedures in which accusations of bias – or failing to show due impartiality – can be heard and assessed. These 'in-house' regulations are supplemented by external ones. In 2004, Fox News was reported to the US Federal Trade Commission on the grounds that its claim to be 'fair and balanced' was fraudulent (MoveOn.Org, 19 July 2004). In the United Kingdom, the regulatory body Ofcom is charged with ensuring that broadcasters show due 'respect for the truth'. And following a story headlined 'Asylum seekers ate our donkey', the *Daily Star* was forced to apologise by the UK's Press Complaints Commission because the story was untrue. These regulatory regimes are themselves complemented by a wealth of research, commissioned by interested parties, into media coverage. Their aim is to monitor the accuracy and fairness of that coverage (Greenslade, 2005; Ofcom, 2005; Electoral Commission, 2005; Scott 2008, 2009).

Journalists report that they are constantly exercised by the need to appear fair. For example, Andrew Marr (BBC news online, 16 February 2005) explained how, as the BBC's political editor, he worried about being fair:

> at the back of my head I try to ensure that the main voices speaking in 'Labour airtime' or 'Tory airtime' really do represent the leading strand of thinking in these parties, while also ensuring that dissenting voices get a show, from time to time, too.

Failing to be seen to be fair can have serious consequences. In March 2000, South Africa's human rights commissioners demanded that 30 journalists appear before them. These journalists were to face charges of racial bias in their papers. The accusations against them were contained in a 200-page report which identified what it saw as 'media racism' in the use of language and imagery. The report became the focus of an intense political debate between those who derided its methods and conclusions, and those who saw its accusations as accurately describing media coverage of South Africa. If anyone needed proof that it matters how the media cover politics, then here it was. Failure to appear before the commissioners could incur a six-month prison sentence. There is no doubt, then, about the importance that attaches to the content of mass media, but the question that follows is how this content is to be analysed and judged. We need, first, to remind ourselves why bias matters – and how it came to be so.

Why does bias matter?

It was not always assumed that journalists would be, or indeed should be, unbiased. The notion of the journalist as impartial or objective observer of events is a relatively new one, and it is still not one that applies identically to all countries and all contexts. Michael Schudson (2001: 165) argues, for example, that the need to be objective is felt more strongly in the United States and the United Kingdom than it is in China or Germany. Equally, he suggests (2001: 164), the pressure to be objective is deemed more pressing in political coverage than in sports coverage, especially where the national or local team is involved. These observations aside, what most intrigues Schudson is why objectivity took hold as the defining feature of professional journalism in the 1920s in the United States.

For Schudson (2001: 162–3), the emergence of a journalistic code that valued objectivity was the consequence of a political process. One key factor was the rise of the public relations industry in the early years of the twentieth century. Journalism was forced to define itself against the overtly partisan practices of the PR professional. A further factor, according to Schudson, was the desire of editors to establish control over their workforce. 'Objectivity as ideology', he writes (Schudson, 2001: 162), 'was a kind of industrial discipline.' Requiring journalists to be objective meant that they were less free to act as autonomous individuals. Now, of course, the idea of unbiased journalism is internalised and unquestioned – as an article by a BBC journalist was headlined, 'Objectivity is our lifeblood' (*Guardian*, 9 September 2005)

Schudson's story has two lessons for us. The first is that the standard by which journalism is judged is not fixed in time, but is a product of historical and political circumstances. It is, for example, perfectly conceivable that, in the world of political blogs and tweets, new standards emerge. The second is that the principles that organize journalism are the result of the interplay of rival interests. But in acknowledging the contingency of journalistic standards, we do not diminish their importance. We still need to ask why bias matters, why it is so furiously condemned.

The answer lies, I would suggest, in the way in which bias is tied to fundamental assumptions about 'power' and 'democracy'. It is assumed that, in liberal democracy, no one group or set of interests is systematically preferred over another, and that the information available to citizens is accurate and impartial. Under these conditions, the principles of political equality and accountability can operate. What makes 'bias' a problem is the thought that the media can, if they distort the representation of the world, skew and thwart the democratic process. If the media systematically promote some interests and misinform the citizenry, the democratic process itself will not operate effectively. In identifying biases, critics of the media are voicing a fear that misrepresentation or partiality has important consequences for the way people regard themselves, for how they are regarded by others, for the outcome of political processes and for the practice of democracy.

Implicit in these concerns is a view about the power and effect of the media. Put another way, 'bias' will seem much less of a problem if you (a) adopt a different account of democracy and (b) do not think that representations of the world actually shape thoughts and practices within it. These are not arguments to be considered here; they are dealt with later. In this context, they serve merely to remind us that the extent to which 'bias' matters is a consequence of a set of underlying political assumptions. This chapter concentrates first on what 'bias' means, what sort of distortions it refers to; second, it looks at the way bias can be detected, at how it can be shown to exist.

Defining bias

The claim that the media are biased begins with the idea that the practices of journalists and editors result in articles and programmes that favour one view of the world over another, providing sustenance for one set of interests while undermining an alternative. These interests may be those of the particular corporations for which they work or they may be those of a particular ideology. The notion of bias is not confined to the battle between political parties. It applies equally to competing value systems, to the representation of women and men, to the portrayal of ethnic groups and to the priority accorded to whole countries and their peoples. 'Bias' refers to any systematic favouring of one position, but it has further implications. It entails a critical judgement. To call someone or some account 'biased' is to challenge its validity and to see it as failing to be 'truthful', 'impartial', 'objective' or 'balanced', terms that appeal to slightly different ideals. These implicit contrasts hint at the complexity of 'bias', and hence the need to look more closely at what it means.

While accusations of 'bias', of favouring one side or another, is typically viewed as a criticism, we do not regard all such behaviour as wrong. There are many occasions when we take up such a position in our relations with our friends and family, and in political arguments in informal settings. In these situations, bias is viewed as natural or reasonable. It is only on particular occasions in particular roles that such behaviour is liable to be criticized. Teachers, for example, are not expected to award high marks to only those essays that echo their own political prejudices. It is because journalists and broadcasters present themselves as unbiased, or are required to appear to be unbiased, that bias becomes a matter of political concern. A journalist can argue for any political cause in private, but if she were to do the same in reporting a story, this would be regarded as a dereliction of her responsibility as a reporter. This view is itself the product of a larger set of assumptions about the character of 'news'. Sometimes these assumptions form part of the rules governing broadcasting (that is, regulations laid down by such bodies as the Federal Communications Commission (FCC) in the United States or Ofcom in the United Kingdom); sometimes they are part of the law (libel legislation, for example); and sometimes they are a part of professional codes.

Whatever their source, these arrangements establish mechanisms by which 'journalism' is defined. Contained within this definition is the distinction between 'opinion' and 'fact', a distinction that is formally reproduced in the layout of papers or the format of programmes. Opinion is seen as the expression of a personal or partial view; it is biased and its bias is openly acknowledged. News reporting aspires to objectivity, to stating the facts; or it aspires to balance and impartiality in recording competing interpretations of an event, without favouring one view over another. These practices are enshrined in codes of conduct or in training manuals.

The fact that such rules exist does not mean, of course, that they are always followed, or indeed that they *can* be followed. The very terms themselves hide their contradictions and complications. It might be assumed that 'neutrality' is a simple enough idea. To be neutral you must just report the facts: 'The election was won by Barack Obama'; 'A British soldier was killed in Afghanistan'; 'Sydney won the right to host the Olympics in 2000'. As Ken Newton (1989: 131) notes, the ideal of neutrality can be stated easily: 'A neutral media will present a full and fair account of the facts.' It is, though, impossible to get even close to this notion of neutrality. Newton offers two sets of reasons for this. First, the practicalities of the media's daily routines mitigate against giving a 'full' account. The media are constituted as businesses that have to serve a market (audiences, advertisers), and this means tailoring the reporting to the needs of that market. Long, factual accounts may drive viewers or readers away; besides, there are deadlines to meet.

Beyond the practical and commercial pressures that compromise a complete, factual account, there is a second set of problems. These might be classed as the theoretical problems of neutrality. The first of them is that reporters cannot record *all* the facts. Any event contains an infinity of facts. The name of every individual who voted for Obama is a 'fact' involved in his election, as is the name of all those who did not vote for him. Facts have to be selected on some criterion of relevance, a judgement of what matters most. Second, the selected facts have to become part of a 'story' with a narrative that links them together. The death of a soldier in war can be a story of a casualty on the battlefield or a child and their grieving parents. The same basic event can generate quite different narratives. These processes of selection and interpretation obviously cause reporting to deviate from the ideal of simply recounting the facts.

The theoretical ambiguities identified by Newton are also part of journalistic practice. As Holli Semetko (1996) notes, 'objectivity' and 'balance' actually demand contradictory practices. To be objective is to let *news values* determine the coverage an event receives. News values are the working assumptions of journalists about the extent to which an event matters and what is significant about it. To be balanced, by contrast, is to give *equal coverage* to all the parties to an event, irrespective of the news value of their contributions. A reporter who is being objective may judge that it is appropriate to ignore certain views because they are marginal or inconsequential to the main story. A reporter who wants to provide balance may feel compelled to represent the full range of views. This sort of tension (and there are many others involved in the reporting of news) is resolved or managed through the routine practices of journalists, the codes and rules which evolve to make journalism possible. Together they form what Semetko labels 'journalistic culture'. Like the notion of objectivity itself, this is not a fixed entity, but varies with time and place. The way it operates can be illustrated by the way in which elections are covered on television. Essentially there are two dominant cultures. The first places the emphasis on balance, and tries to allocate equal time, as measured by a stopwatch, to all the leading contenders. The second places the emphasis on news values. Election coverage is determined by journalists' judgements about the importance of what each party is saying or doing. In the United States and in Germany, the news value approach dominates. For UK broadcasters the tendency is to use the stopwatch to measure balance (Semetko, 1996). Whatever strategy was adopted, these news organizations shared the same purpose: to establish a journalistic code of conduct that was defensible as 'unbiased' in the face of conflicting demands.

But if 'neutrality' cannot exist, and if balance and objectivity are incompatible, the notion of bias needs to be qualified. It cannot simply be treated as any 'deviation from reality'. It is not that bias is a meaningless term; it is just that a distinction has to be made between what is acceptable or reasonable and what is unacceptable and unreasonable. How these boundaries are drawn varies with forms and systems of communication. In the United Kingdom, terrestrial broadcasting is constrained to provide 'due impartiality' in ways that newspapers are not. In Italy, broadcasting institutions are assigned to different political interests. Countries differ in the extent to which political cleavages are recognized within the organization of their media system (Hallin and Mancini, 2004). What bias is and what significance attaches to it will, therefore, also vary. There is always a distinction drawn between where it is acceptable and where it should be condemned. This is not an argument for discounting bias as a viable concept in analysing media content. The fact that it is definitionally complex and institutionally mediated does not reduce it to an empty category. Quite the contrary, its continued usage in discussion of media, and its place in the idea of a legitimate political order, underline the need to give it attention.

Types of bias

Bias appears in a variety of (dis)guises. Denis McQuail (1992) identifies four types of bias. They are to be distinguished by their place in a two-dimensional matrix. The first dimension concerns the 'explicitness' of the bias – whether it is open or hidden; the second dimension concerns the intention behind it – whether the bias is a result of some deliberate policy or a product of some ingrained, unconscious process. These two dimensions yield a useful set of categories for thinking about bias.

Partisan bias

Here a cause is explicitly and deliberately promoted. Examples of this are editorial comments that recommend support for one political party or take sides in a policy controversy. It can take the form of explicit recommendations to vote for one party or another, or it can be identified in the blatant endorsement of a cause. There is little difficulty in detecting such examples.

Propaganda bias

This is involved where a story is reported with the deliberate intention of making the case for a particular party or policy or point of view, without explicitly stating this. So stories about high-living students or social security fraud or asylum seekers are reported as news, but in such a way as to make a particular point (about welfare 'scrounging' or immigrants 'swamping' a country). In the United Kingdom, the *Sunday Telegraph* reported a story that was headlined 'Hot cross banned: councils decree buns could be "offensive" to non-Christians'. It turned out the story was completely untrue, but its original intent was clear: to attack the 'politically correct' priorities of local councils and to give succour to critics of immigration (Greenslade, 2005: 27). The formal purpose of such stories is to report the details, but disguised within them are thinly veiled attacks upon local government or students or the unemployed or refugees. Readers are encouraged to generalize from the particular case and to see students or others in an unfavourable light. Racial imagery in the reporting of crime can express propagandist value judgements about ethnic groups (Gilliam et al., 1996). Propaganda can also be detected in the way that national media report the activities of other countries. This is revealed in the tendency to publish stories about corruption, scandal or disasters in the rest of the world, thereby reinforcing negative perceptions of political life in these 'foreign' places (Wallis and Baran, 1990; Seymour and Barnett, 2005).

Unwitting bias

Newspapers have a finite number of pages; news broadcasts have limited time slots in the schedule. Hard choices have to be made about what to include and what to exclude. These decisions are about the 'importance' to be given to a story, and they are reflected in the item's place in the running order or its place in the paper or on the (web) page. Inevitably these decisions involve a judgement about the issue and/or the people involved. The convention of journalism is that what appears on the front page is the most important of the day's news. The same implication is carried by the ordering of broadcast news: the main stories are dealt with first and at length. These judgements constitute a form of bias: X matters more than Y. Think of the treatment of death: some deaths and some forms of dying are regarded as worthy of front-page news; others are confined to the obituary pages. But though this bias is explicit (the decision to give a particular story one column inch on page 4), it is not conscious or deliberate. It is the product of ingrained routines about what is 'news' and a story's 'newsworthiness'; it is a product of journalistic culture. Detection of this type of bias involves looking at the standard operating procedures of papers and newsrooms, to see how these practices routinely create hierarchies of values.

Ideological bias

In McQuail's final category, the bias is hidden and unintended, and it can be detected only in a close reading of the text, where the hidden assumptions and value judgements can be extricated. The attention is upon the 'common sense' against which news is created. Incorporated in all reporting is some version of the 'norm': of what 'usually happens' or how people 'usually behave'. These are based on the assumption that something is 'newsworthy'; that is, it is both out of the ordinary and also part of a general framework of expectations (that is, it is a 'typical' news story). These assumptions are grounded in ideologies which seek to explain the way the world works, and these are themselves 'biased'. Think of the way in which women are repre-sented in papers (Herzog, 1998; Norris, 1997a). First, their activities receive less coverage than do men's; second, descrip-tions of them refer to their appearance or to the men in their lives (they are not accorded an independent existence). Such represen-tations articulate a particular ideological view about men and women.

One of the most vivid examples of this kind of bias is revealed in coverage of the developing world. In a series of reports (Pandania et al., 2006; Smith, et al., 2006; Scott, 2008, 2009), researchers have documented the increasingly narrow picture of the wider world provided by television. International coverage tends to be selective, with certain countries and continents (for example, North America) dominating world news. Where the developing world does appear, it is either in the guise of humanitarian disaster or of military conflict, or as the location for tourism and wildlife. To the extent that the coverage is dominated by such images, it can be seen to represent the wider world in general and the developing world in particular in a distinct, ideological form.

To identify different types of bias is a necessary task, but it does no more than to establish what biases might exist. To give substance to McQuail's categories poses two obvious methodological problems. The first relates to the way we detect bias, how we discover meanings that are 'submerged' within the text, as distinct from those that seem to sit on the surface. This is linked to the second methodological issue: how do we know what is intended? Think of the difficulty of discerning whether something is said 'ironically': when the rap star Eminem gives vent to aggressive attitudes to women or gay people, is he parodying those attitudes or does he really share them? It is clear that it is hard to 'prove' the existence of any particular bias, whether explicit or implicit, whether offered ironically or not. What one observer sees as unwitting bias another may see as propaganda and another as fair reporting. The problem stems, in part, from the difficulty in establishing agreed definitions of bias and agreed methods for identifying it. It is certainly not sufficient to rely on public perception, because readers and viewers make unreliable witnesses. Readers of newspapers tend to see them as reflecting their own prejudices, while they see television as being biased against their own views. Thus the same programme can be seen by left-wingers as having a right-wing bias, and by right-wingers as having a left-wing bias (Miller, 1991). Then again, there are people who appear to be oblivious to (or ignorant of) the bias in their papers. Such evidence tells us little about the fact of bias; it merely serves to indicate that detecting it is less simple than might at first appear.

Looking for bias is not just a matter of 'reading' the news or transcripts; it is about establishing a method that is able on the one hand to capture what is being said implicitly as well as explicitly, and on the other to provide a technique that can be used by others (or can persuade others of particular findings). For instance, in analysing coverage of the wider world, Martin Scott (2009: 26) studied the output of '19 digital and terrestrial TV bulletins and 6 online sources' over a period of two weeks; all the news stories were then coded for 'length, topic, principal country (or institution), story type, position, treatment and "who speaks"'. This dataset was used to map variations in international news coverage in the different outputs, and to draw the conclusion that, while there was evidence of diversity of coverage, 'most bulletins continue to report a fairly narrow range of international stories, dominated by stories about the USA' (Scott, 2009: 26). Here the claim to bias, to a partial representation of the world, is based upon a detailed content analysis of a range of news outputs.

Discerning the quantity of coverage is important in establishing bias, but it is not the only measure. There is also a matter of the type of coverage. The UK communications regulator commissioned research into the coverage of the 2005 general election (Ofcom, 2005). The question here was less about how much coverage each party was given, but how 'fair' was that coverage. This question was answered by asking a representative sample of viewers about their *perceptions* of the coverage. The conclusion reported was that the coverage was thought generally to be 'fair, accurate, balanced, informative and impartial' (Ofcom, 2005: 15). But viewer perceptions of coverage, while important, may not tell the whole story. Research commissioned by the Electoral Commission (2005) about the same election, but in which content analysis, rather than perception, was the main method, paints a rather different picture. It is one in which the election's absence is as important as its representation – '87% of tabloid front covers' did not mention the election at all (Electoral Commission, 2005: para 3.5), and where the election was discussed, the emphasis was on the electoral process rather than the parties' policies (ibid.: paras 3.9, 3.10). The Electoral Commission reveals too the gender gap in media coverage, with male politicians appearing ten times more often than female politicians (ibid.: para 3.24). And perhaps most tellingly, it reveals how the coverage tended to give the impression that politicians could not be trusted, by distinguishing between what a speech or pronouncement 'appeared' to be saying and what it was 'really' about (ibid.: paras 3.43–3.46). In short, the coverage was seen to be biased, not so much in terms of the quantity of coverage, but in terms of its focus and emphasis.

Another illustration of how quantity of coverage may tell only half the story is revealed in research into television reporting of the UK general election of 1987. Under the laws and regulations governing coverage, television felt obliged to give *exactly equal time* to the three main parties (Labour, Conservative and Alliance [now the Liberal Democrats]). This commitment was honoured, and would seem to suggest a complete absence of partiality or bias; it would seem to meet, at the very least, the conditions of what Semetko (1996) defines as 'balance'. But, as William Miller and his colleagues reveal (Miller, 1991; Miller et al., 1989), within this equal treatment there was considerable evidence of bias, if you look at the character of the coverage rather than the quantity alone. The researchers measured coverage in terms of time spent on camera and the message being conveyed. Close examination revealed that, although all three contending parties received equal screen time, the way that time was organized gave the impression that the contest was only between the Labour and Conservative parties. The Alliance was marginalized as an 'also ran'. This impression was created by covering the Alliance on its own, but covering the other two parties locked in controversy.

In order to demonstrate the existence of bias, Miller's team combined quantitative and qualitative research methods. The quantitative work employed a version of content analysis, in an attempt to provide a scientific method for recording the use of words and pictures. Such an approach focuses upon the frequency with which certain words are used to describe an event. It examines the space (in time or column length) devoted to different news items. It allows researchers to observe the frequency with which certain words are used and the way words are combined. Robert Entman (1996), for instance, shows how in the coverage of the environmental policy debate – to deregulate or not – the word 'extreme' is applied much more frequently to one side than the other, as are aggressive words like 'backlash', 'attack' and 'assault'. Qualitative work, by contrast, tends to draw on semiotics and the pioneering work of Roland Barthes (1967) and others. This approach is concerned with the way meaning is contained in what is not said as well as what is, in images and impressions as much as in words.

The way a sentence is structured is not merely a matter of grammar, but of meaning. John Thompson (1988) provides a neat summary of four different linguistic techniques that can be employed to favour one group, view or interest over others. A set of arrangements can be made *legitimate* by attributing popular support or expert authority to them. Second, the text may serve to *dissimulate*, to cover up the particular social relations, for example by attributing blame to identifiable individuals, rather than to underlying processes and systems ('The value of shares fell' versus 'Panic selling caused shares to fall' versus 'The actions of anxious stockbrokers led the value of shares to fall'). A third device is *fragmentation*: the media represent groups as opposed to each other, when in fact they may have a common cause (the treatment of refugees as an 'alien threat', for example, rather as contributing to a more diverse community). And finally, Thompson talks of *reification*, by which he means the ways in which the media present the world as naturally ordered and fixed, thereby marginalizing the claims of those who want to change that world. Together these devices, and many more besides, are seen as presenting a 'common sense' view of the world which actually serves to preserve particular interests. Thompson's focus is on the way images and words interact to suggest a meaning that goes beyond any literal reading of the text. This approach builds upon the idea that words do not simply describe an object or event but evoke an entire edifice of associated ideas and impressions.

Each of these techniques has strengths and weaknesses (for excellent overviews, see Deacon et al., 2007; Gillespie and Toynbee, 2006). The richness of interpretation provided by semiotic analysis is limited by the problem of comparability or replicability. Why should one reading of a text be preferred to another? Content analysis does at least allow for systematic comparison, but at the cost of reducing meaning to individual words. Most attempts to identify bias use both techniques (for example, Anderson and Weymouth, 1999; Entman, 1996; Norris, 1997a). It is important, therefore, in judging these attempts, to be aware, first, that bias cannot simply be 'seen', and second, that in detecting it, there is unlikely to be universal agreement about the 'right' interpretation.

Given the many attempts to deal with these problems of proving bias (although fewer than the attention to the subject would suggest), we cannot do justice to them all here. Instead, we shall concentrate on two, one concerned with bias on television and the other with bias in the press. Each has assumed the status of a 'classic' or 'pathbreaking' study.

The Bad News studies

In a series of very detailed, and much debated, studies of television reporting of news and current affairs, the Glasgow University Media Group (GUMG) has claimed to identify systematic ideological bias. The GUMG's central claim is that 'news is not a neutral and natural phenomenon; it is rather the manufactured production of ideology' (GUMG, 1980: xvii–xviii). Each study has taken a different topic – trade unions (*Bad News*), the economy (*More Bad News*), war (*War and Peace News*) and the Middle East (*Bad News from Israel*) – and examined the way in which TV news has covered them, and in each case they have revealed systematic distortion and the propagation of an ideological slant. The Glasgow researchers argue that, although the news may report facts, it nonetheless produces a skewed account. This is because of the particular way that the facts are presented:

> 'facts' are situated in dominant story themes ... such themes build upon basic frames of reference – basic assumptions about society viewed in particular ways – which often hinder the full and proper coverage of the events in question.
>
> (GUMG, 1976: 9)

To validate its claims, the GUMG deploys a wide variety of research tools, borrowing from semiotics, content analysis and reception studies. Not only do the researchers observe practice in a working newsroom, they also examine in minute detail the reports produced, and how subsequently they are received. They analyse the words, the camera angles, the presentation format, and the range and setting of the people interviewed. As one of the Group's founding figures explained, their research was concerned to reveal:

> the verbal and visual grammar ... the use of graphics and other symbolic expressions ... the use of headlines ... who is

interviewed ... in short, the way information is organized and the implicit and explicit explanations that are put before us.

(Eldridge, 1993: 5)

The media's presentation of the news is then set against alternative explanations of the situation being portrayed.

Take one example of this technique: *More Bad News* (1980). In this book, the GUMG focuses upon the reporting of the economy and upon the explanations given for its performance. It is hard to exaggerate the importance of the economy to politics, especially given recent studies of electoral behaviour (Sanders, 1996) that have demonstrated an intimate connection between perceptions of the economy (and of the relative economic competence of political parties) and the outcome of national elections. Mass media can play an important role in forming those impressions.

More Bad News begins by recording the different possible academic and political interpretations of the UK economy in the 1970s. It contrasts these with the single explanation that tends to dominate news coverage. The impression created by television, argues the GUMG, was that wage-led inflation was the root of the problem: 'Often the argument over whether inflation was in fact caused in this way was pre-empted by simply prefixing references to wage settlements with the word "inflationary"' (GUMG, 1980: 15). Attempts to promote an alternative explanation would be thwarted by the way interviewers set their questions or by the selection of those whom they interviewed (ibid.: 17–18). These conclusions were reached on the basis of examination of the words used in reports and in detailed analysis of the conduct of interviews. The GUMG sought to expose the assumptions that underlay the journalism.

Further evidence was acquired through examination of journalists' reliance upon official statistics and the presentation of those figures. Both served to reinforce a particular view of economic reality, a view that was challenged by other commentators and different statistical data (ibid.: 29–31). The GUMG argued that the evidence was selected to fit the underlying ideology:

> An essential feature of the television news coverage is that the figures were used invariably to suggest that wages were ahead of prices ... the predominant feature of this news coverage

therefore was the manner in which official figures from which a number of conclusions could have been drawn were used consistently to emphasise only one interpretation.

(GUMG, 1980: 48–9)

In the same way, a study of television coverage of the 1984/5 coal dispute strike revealed journalists' reliance on statistics produced by the Coal Board (Philo, 1990). These figures recorded the 'drift back to work', and were designed to give the impression that the strike was crumbling. Other figures (about the numbers staying home or about gestures of support for the strike) were absent or marginalized.

In *More Bad News*, the GUMG identified four competing political interpretations of the economy, and then examined the attention received by each. Attention was measured by the number of references made to the various interpretations and to the manner of the reference: whether it was positive or negative (GUMG, 1980: 57). Frequency measures of this kind were also used to analyse the words deployed to describe certain events. The team found that, overwhelmingly, industrial action was identified by the word 'strike', thereby shifting responsibility to the unions and appealing to the pejorative judgements associated with the word: the 'disruptions' caused by strike action, for example (ibid.: 180). These tests of the frequency and manner of references revealed a general disposition (albeit an unconscious one) to favour one interpretation of economic performance and to marginalize the other. The preferred explanation – wage-led inflation – had clear implications for the attribution of blame to trade unions. The way in which wage negotiations were reported also emphasized this allocation of blame: trade unions were presented as making 'demands', while the behaviour of employers was largely overlooked or presented as reasonable and legitimate (ibid.: 91).

In summary, the GUMG described its project as an attempt 'to reveal and analyse the linguistic designs' (ibid.: 121) that constitute news bulletins, and to show that these designs favoured particular interests and the world views that legitimated them: 'All descriptions close off or foreclose on sets of alternatives' (ibid.: 123). In its detailed examination of the way in which industrial news is reported, the GUMG argued that the stories were 'heavily weighted against the trade union and labour point of view' (ibid.: 129). Similar conclusions were reached in the

GUMG's parallel concern with the images used in news coverage. The Glasgow group painstakingly analysed the images on the screen, and the ways in which words and pictures were juxtaposed (ibid.: 193ff). Here too an ideological bias was found in that people's status, and the respect in which their position was held, was reflected in the way they were filmed (ibid.: 401). The authority and credibility of figures could even be conveyed in the choice of still photographs: one of the left-winger Tony Benn looking up to the camera was followed by another of Winston Churchill looking down (ibid.: 317–19).

One of the GUMG's (2004) more recent studies, *Bad News from Israel*, applies their approach to coverage of conflict in the Middle East. They draw attention to the immensely complex, competing accounts given for the current state of the region, and then go on to analyse the particular version given or assumed by mainstream television coverage and the understandings derived from this by audiences. They argue that the coverage rarely explains the events being covered and is devoted in large part to describing discrete outbursts of violence (ibid.: 102–4). When not concerned with violence, the reporting tends to be devoted to the attempt to establish peace in the region, but here again, they claim, the news rarely gives insights into the motives of the protagonists, particularly in respect of the Palestinians, and why a settlement proves so elusive (ibid.: 104–8). They conclude their study with the judgement that television coverage has tended to be biased and 'that it was Israeli perspectives which predominated in TV news' (ibid.: 251).

Through their analysis of all aspects of news coverage, and armed with the assumptions the researchers make about the way meaning is conveyed, the GUMG has concluded that television reporting contains a systematic bias. This bias has been primarily, in McQuail's terms, ideological and unwitting; that is, it is not explicit, and it is deliberate only in the sense that it is informed by routinized journalistic practices. The GUMG (1980: 138; 2004: 251) has argued that biased news reporting has been the result of habit and training, rather than conscious deliberation, and has been shaped by systems of public relations and lobbying for a particular point of view. This conclusion is not simply a result of the content analysis, but of observation of daily newsroom practice, interviews with editors and journalists, and reception analysis.

The GUMG research represents one approach to the problem of demonstrating the existence of political bias in the media. Using a variety of research tools they produce evidence of distortion, misrepresentation and omission which, when taken together, constitute a systematic promotion of one reading of the world over another. What the GUMG found in television, others have claimed to find in the press.

Manufacturing Consent

Like the GUMG, in their book *Manufacturing Consent* (1988) Edward Herman and Noam Chomsky conclude that the mainstream media provide a systematically biased worldview. But in their case this conclusion is reached through an analysis of the content of the US press. Their hypothesis is that the US press acts to sustain the US government's foreign policy interests, themselves the product of a particular ideology and particular material interests. The US media, they argue, act as propagandists for dominant corporate interests in the United States. They write (ibid.: xii): 'Most biased choices in the media arise from the pre-selection of right-thinking people, internalized preconceptions, and the adaptation of personnel to the constraints of ownership, organization, market, and political power.'

Herman and Chomsky examine the way in which the US media treated the same kind of event as it occurred in different contexts. One of their case studies involves the murder of religious leaders and other religious workers. They examine reports of the murder of Cardinal Popieluszko in Poland in 1984, and of religious workers killed in South America at various times. Two features of their analysis of these stories are worth noting here. The first is that the killing of the Polish priest received far more coverage – as measured by column inches and by position in the paper – than did the other murders. Second, in the reporting of these events, the US press dwelt upon the perpetrators in Poland, tracing responsibility back to the communist regime, whereas in the second case very little is said about the murderers. Herman and Chomsky explain this disparity in terms of the propaganda interests of the United States. Attributing blame to the authorities in Poland contributed to the US struggle with communism; close investigation of the Latin American case was likely to have revealed CIA involvement. Herman and Chomsky argue:

> A constant focus on victims of communism helps convince the public of enemy evil and sets the stage for intervention, subversion ... an endless arms race .... The public does not notice the silence on victims in client states, which is as important in supporting state policy as the concentrated focus on enemy victims.
>
> (Herman and Chomsky, 1988: xv)

Herman and Chomsky use similar techniques to those deployed by the GUMG. Their analysis of the murders, for instance, relies upon detailed documentation of the column inches allocated to various comparable cases, to the number of stories about each case, and to the prominence they were accorded in the paper or magazine (ibid.: 40–1). This is supplemented by an analysis of the words and narrative used to tell the various stories. The authors draw attention, for example, to the way in which sympathy is elicited or denied by the use of emotive or flat language, the first creating feelings of concern, the latter those of neutrality or indifference (ibid.: 43, 48, 63).

Their book *Manufacturing Consent* also compares the treatment of national elections in El Salvador, Guatemala and Nicaragua. They argue that the treatment given to each varies, from being taken seriously as exercises in democracy to being dismissed as cynical gestures, and that this treatment is itself directly correlated to the relationship between the state concerned and the United States. Where relations were friendly, the election was seen as 'democratic'; where they were unfriendly, the coverage was less sympathetic. In short, Herman and Chomsky claim that journalists operated double standards. To demonstrate this bias, they again analyse the texts, in terms of the space allocated, the tone used, the expertise referred to, and so on (ibid.: 132–6). Other cases – treatment of Indochina, for instance – are added to their claim that the media act as a propaganda tool.

Although Herman and Chomsky do not command the range of techniques and the sophistication of the GUMG, their use of a comparative approach provides a persuasive basis for their conclusions. Their main focus is on the language used and on the space allocated. The US media act, they contend:

to inculcate and defend the economic, social, and political agenda of privileged groups that dominate the domestic society and the state. The media serve this purpose in many ways: through selection of topics, distribution of concerns, framing of issues, filtering of information, emphasis and tone, and by keeping debate within the bounds of acceptable premises.

(Herman and Chomsky, 1988: 298)

In short, the US press demonstrates a systematic, political bias in its coverage of foreign affairs. This claim is sustained by revelations about the attention and language accorded to ostensibly similar events, and the correlation between this differential treatment and the foreign policy interests of the United States.

Critiques of bias research

Both *Manufacturing Consent* and the *Bad News* studies appear to provide evidence for the existence of systematic bias. Such bias is seen as undermining the claims of the United States or the United Kingdom to enjoy the benefits of a 'free press'. In the United States, the freedom is compromised by the thought that the media act as instruments of propaganda; in the United Kingdom, it is the impartiality of public service broadcasting that is called into question. Other, more recent studies, have continued to find evidence for the same claims. David Edwards and David Cromwell (2006: 178), for instance, maintain that 'media performance overwhelmingly promotes the views and interests of established power'. Evidence of systematic bias, if valid, has profound political implications for claims about media power and about the condition of democracy. It is not surprising, therefore, that such studies have been the object of intense debate. Criticisms have come from a number of different directions, from both the left and the right, from journalists and from academics.

Martin Harrison's *TV News: Whose Bias?* (1985) has provided the most detailed examination of the GUMG's research technique. He argues that, despite the vast edifice of formal analysis, the results are tainted by the prior assumptions of the researchers and do not make allowance for the conditions under which journalists work. The biases detected by the GUMG would not be seen as such by other observers. This view is echoed by the one-time editor of Independent Television News, who said: 'People will always find evidence of bias if they believe it's there' (quoted in the *Observer*, 23 July 2006). Harrison accuses the GUMG of being selective in their use of the data, picking out those features that served their general argument. He is not convinced that the GUMG had provided the kind of 'scientific' method which would reveal the same results whoever did the experiment. While the GUMG sees the word 'idle' as being used pejoratively, as a way of criticizing the (in)activity of the workers, Harrison claims that the word is actually used in just this sense by the strikers themselves. The Harrison critique can, in this respect, be seen as an attack on a particular research method; but Harrison is also sceptical about the existence of the 'dominant ideology' to which the GUMG relates media coverage. Certainly, if there is no such pervasive ideology, which systematically promotes the values and interests of one group, then the particular biases of the media cannot be explained in terms of a 'dominant ideology'.

Criticisms of bias research also focus on the assumptions that underlie the notion of 'bias' itself. The complaint here is that 'bias' assumes the possibility of a 'reality', against which media representations can be measured. But for the critics, there is no such reality, or not one that can be reached without some intervening mediation. The GUMG often compares the claims made by broadcasters with an 'independent reality': 'viewers were given a *misleading* portrayal of industrial disputes in the UK when measured against *the independent reality*' (GUMG, 1980: xiii; emphasis added). Herman and Chomsky presume a proper or fair distribution of coverage and use of language. It is these general assumptions that trouble other critics of the bias studies (see Bennett, 1982a; Hall, 1982). For them, the idea of an independent reality is not plausible. All events, indeed the notion of an 'event' itself, are the product of an ideological framework which creates order out of an infinite number of possible observations or impressions. As Stuart Hall points out, 'the event must become a "story" before it can become a *communicative event*' (1980: 129, original emphasis). This line of criticism builds from a general assumption that there is no independent truth against which media representations can be judged. Instead the suggestion is that there are competing interpretations, some of which reinforce the status quo, while others diverge from it. Media reporting is engaged in an attempt to establish a truth and the criteria for the validation of something as 'true'. In the case of TV news, it is seeking to claim that 'seeing is believing'. The criterion for truthfulness is to be found in pictures and eyewitnesses, and the reporting of expert or personal testimony. But, as all social scientists are aware, appearances are deceptive; personal testimony may be partial and witnesses may be mistaken. Hall is not claiming that there is a truth to be found through the use of the correct method; rather he is asserting that each interpretation is a product of a particular ideology.

A final line of criticism focuses on the explanation given for the bias that is found and its effect. Herman and Chomsky are accused of seeing media coverage as the product of a conspiracy by corporate elites, and of treating audiences as passive recipients of the dominant message (see Klaehn, 2002, for a review of these criticisms). While they have little to say on the latter criticism, they reject the former on the grounds that their model of media behaviour is a product, not of conspiracy, but of the routine operations of a market economy (Klaehn, 2002: 148–9). The debate about bias is an important one because of the strong intuitive associations of the idea. Biased reporting is seen as a real and damaging feature of media coverage. At the same time, it poses very awkward methodological and theoretical challenges. And for this reason, alternative approaches are explored.

Constructing reality?

Douglas Kellner provides one such alternative approach to media content, one which retains a notion of bias, but which tries to avoid the assumption of an independent reality. Kellner writes about media culture generally – *Beavis and Butt-head*, the *Rambo* movies – and not just news, and what makes him interesting is the way his analysis of news and popular culture uses the same approach. In his account of coverage of the 1991 Gulf War, Kellner treats the war as a 'media construct', by which he means its 'reality' was not located in the desert battlefields: 'In a sense, the 1990s war against Iraq was a cultural–political event as much as a military one' (Kellner, 1995: 198). Kellner is not prepared to take the extreme view attributed to Jean Baudrillard that the war existed only as a media spectacle, but he does suggest that the reporting of war entails a struggle to define its meaning and to chart its course. 'The war against Iraq,' he writes (ibid.: 199), 'can be read as a text produced by the Bush Administration, the Pentagon, and the media which utilized the images and discourse of the crisis and then the war to mobilize consent and support for the U.S. military intervention.' Kellner sees the media, not as covering the war, but as being used to create support for the US government's military strategy. News reports were not neutral observations of events on the battlefield but a product of a government public relations exercise.

The US government, argues Kellner, was able to control the images and information available to the press corps. The combined effect of government manipulation and journalistic practice (and prejudice) served to create conditions that legitimated the war and US policy. For Kellner, the media's version of the war and the crisis that preceded it are a product of US interests and can be understood in terms of these alone. But note that, in making these claims, he himself adopts an alternative perspective on the first Gulf War, against which he sets the dominant version. In talking about the 'disinformation' spread by the government, he is acknowledging another account of events. He refers, for example, to US media reports of Saddam Hussein's 'intransigence', when subsequent evidence revealed that he was willing to negotiate (ibid.: 201–2). In short, Kellner argues that there was another story to be told.

Kellner's emphasis on the textual formation of reality is not an invitation to relativism. In moving away from the idea of 'bias', he is not embracing an indiscriminate pluralism. Rather he is inviting a different approach to the analysis of media content, in which the debate does not focus on the bias/reality issue, but rather on the *quality* of the story. Kellner believes that there are alternative versions which represent a 'better' account of events, and that not all coverage is to be viewed as equally valid or invalid. What this suggestion raises, of course, is the problem of judging between different accounts. The selection cannot be based on accuracy alone, even though it does clearly matter that details of fact be correct. It must also be based on the credibility attributed to different sources of information. Kellner, for instance, relies upon contrary accounts of events in order to challenge the media version. In doing so, he is assuming these to be

more persuasive (if not more 'true'). He judges the minutes identifying Saddam Hussein's willingness to negotiate as more accurate
or reliable than the briefings given to the press corps. This view is,
though, a judgement of the relative veracity of accounts of events.
So Kellner's understanding of the reportage is informed by his
judgement of the possible interpretations. It also depends on who
is telling the story: he places trust in stories by papers like *In These
Times*; he mistrusts the *Washington Post*.

Kellner's approach moves us some way from the idea of 'bias'
as it is traditionally conceived. Instead, he suggests that we
confront competing truth claims, different interpretations of a
putative reality. He is not offering a simple dichotomy of truth
and lies, but rather a 'truth' that is constituted and conveyed
within different genres and narratives. His approach to interpreting the news and political coverage draws heavily on the
approach associated with cultural studies, in which interpretation
emerges through an understanding of the generic conventions
which order the text and the associations that are linked to it.
The implications of this approach are explored in the next two
chapters.

Conclusion

The Kellner approach, like Stuart Hall's, argues that all political
coverage is ideological and has to be understood and judged as
such. The implication of this is not that all perceptions of bias are
a result of personal prejudice and perspective, that bias is merely
in 'the eye of the beholder' and, therefore, an empty and useless
notion. Nor is the implication that, given the presence of an ideologically dominant group, bias is systematic and consistent. Such
conclusions are too comforting (there is nothing to worry about)
or too defeatist (there is nothing to be done). The picture is more
complicated. As writers like John Corner (1995) and Andrew
Goodwin (1990) argue, there is reason to retain some version of
'bias' in order to criticize and analyse competing accounts of the
world. Goodwin, for example, writes:

> It is quite plausible to believe that the media images are
> constructed and still maintain that some constructions are
> more truthful than others. Surely there are competing

explanations of social reality, and surely all factual statements are also statements of value. But none of this means that there are not real events in the actual world that do take place and unreal events in the minds of policemen, politicians and Coal Board officials that do not take place.

(Goodwin, 1990: 57)

This is an argument for shifting the terrain on which the debate is conducted and the criteria that distinguish the relative merits of competing accounts of media representation; it is not one for rejecting critical judgements altogether.

From the point of view of public policy for a democratic media, this conclusion has important consequences. As Newton (1989: 132) notes, it suggests the need for 'airing all opinions, including those which are unpopular, eccentric, or supported only by small minorities'. This leads to a further injunction: 'the media should be broadly, not narrowly selective; judgements should be open, not doctrinaire or party political; the emphasis should be on inclusion rather than exclusion, and in presenting all sides they should take no side' (ibid.: 133). In a similar vein, Corner writes:

> television news is inevitably the product of a 'point of view' and ... the best arrangement for television services is therefore to have a multiplicity of outlets (national and local) each of which is able to declare the broad political and social assumptions informing its news production.
>
> (Corner, 1995: 64–5)

We return to these policy issues later in this book. They are raised here because it is important to emphasize the possible implications of the debate about bias.

More immediately, the qualified notion of bias has important implications too for the way we analyse media content. It suggests, for instance, the need to be aware of the contradictory and complex content of a media text. News programmes do not tell one simple, consistent story, but reveal many different, conflicting dimensions to the way that politics is conveyed. From the point of view of analysis, this means introducing a more reflexive understanding of media representations of the world. Coverage of politics needs to be read not just in terms of 'bias', but as 'narratives', as stories about the world which call into play some actors (and marginalize others), which suppose some motivations and ignore others, and so on.

These stories, furthermore, are not flat reports, devoid of drama and sentiment, they are designed to capture the viewers' and the readers' attention and to engage their emotions. And just as we judge feature films and soap operas in terms of their 'authenticity' or 'truth', so we judge news reports. We do not 'know' whether a reporter is telling the truth; rather we judge the way they tell their story. How we respond to their words and pictures is not predetermined, but is a consequence of a complex set of factors, of which one is an aesthetic judgement. The criteria may not be identical when dealing with news and fiction, but the element of judgement is there in both cases. These judgements may not ever be settled, they may not be validated by 'hard data', but this does not make them any less important. For the analyst of media content, it follows that the texts under consideration should be studied not just as 'accurate' documents of real events, though this is clearly relevant, but also as works of imaginative reconstruction, as works intended to produce responses and feelings in viewers and readers.

Chapter 2

Telling Tales: The Reporting of Politics

When media report politics, they are telling stories about the world. They are not just holding up a mirror to events or pointing a telescope at them. They do not simply describe what happens; they create narratives with plots and actors. Just as they create a story for 'the Iraq War' or for the 'Obama victory', so they create the political process itself, the context in which such things take place. Movies use the artifice of cinema to tell a story, to create characters in a believable world; news does a similar job for the events that are its concern. News reporters are storytellers too. They recount the pursuit of political ambition, the rivalries and pacts, the human frailties and strengths. Political careers sometimes assume epic form, ending in tragedy or triumph; more often they take the guise of soap opera. This is not simply a metaphor; this is how news is told. 'News' is, in this sense, an art form and news reporting an art, and political coverage is one particular genre of this art, in which competing realities are constructed (Starkey, 2007). This is the central theme of this chapter, which looks at the various ways the story of politics is narrated.

In her book *Entertaining the Citizen*, Liesbet van Zoonen (2005: 105–20) identifies the four narratives that, she argues, dominate the recounting of the political story, whether in fact or in fiction. The four are the quest, the conspiracy, the bureaucracy and the soap. The quest represents politics as an individual's struggle for a goal – most obviously, elected office. The conspiracy pictures politics as the deliberate attempt by a covert organization to thwart the good intentions of others, while the bureaucracy narrative, in telling a similar story of frustrated ambition, attributes it to the operation of a political machine or system, one without intent or self-conscious operators. The final narrative is that of the soap, in which humans struggle together, for all their

49

weaknesses and faults, to realise some good intent. Van Zoonen suggests that all accounts of politics are dramatized using one of these narratives, or a combination of them. Her argument, though, is not just about the need for narratives in making sense of politics, but about how each narrative proffers an explanation of how politics works – why things happen the way they do and who or what is responsible for the outcome (bureaucrats or conspirators, individuals or teams). Van Zoonen's use of the idea of narrative to analyse how politics is recounted stands in contrast to the approach of those concerned with bias. Her question is less about whether the story is 'true', but rather how the truth is presented. The narrative approach is concerned with the question of how politics is framed by media.

Frames versus biases

The last chapter showed how the idea of bias was used to analyse media content, but it also revealed some of the dissatisfaction felt with this approach. In particular, there was the feeling that the focus on bias, with its emphasis on systematic misrepresentation, tended to obscure as much as it revealed. Instead of using the idea of ideology to analyse media content, most recent research has preferred the notion of the 'frame' and 'framing'. 'News' is a distilled form of the multiple 'events' taking place in the world. It not only selects particular events, it also has to make sense of them. It has to make them matter to the readers and viewers, and this entails setting them within a frame, which screens out certain events and perspectives, and emphasises others. Robert Entman offers this definition: 'A *frame* operates to select and highlight some features of reality and obscure others in a way that tells a consistent story about problems, their causes, moral implications, and remedies' (1996: 77–8; original emphasis).

The frame achieves its effects through the use of a variety of techniques. William Gamson and Andre Modigliani (1989: 3) list metaphors, historical examples, catchphrases, depictions and visual images as examples of the 'reasoning devices' that offer a view of the causes, effects and principles that animate the story. In the process, one account of the world is privileged over another. Entman, for example, uses a framing analysis to show how the US media gave a particular slant to the debate, which took place in the mid-1990s, over affirmative action and its value in promoting equality between black and white citizens:

> The most prominent elements of the message – the headlines, the visuals, the highlighted quotes, and the journalists' narrative emphases – framed the policy dispute as a zero-sum conflict of interest between whites and blacks in which only one group could win and one must lose.
>
> (Entman, 1997: 40)

More recently, Entman (2003) has applied the same approach to analyse media reporting of the aftermath of the 9/11 attacks. His analysis shows how the coverage largely reproduced the frame adopted by President Bush. The point is that the story did not have to be told like this; other frames could have produced a different account, and in the case of 9/11 this did occur when the journalists Seymour Hersh and Thomas Friedman offered an alternative perspective.

Frames are devices for seeing the world in a particular way; they differ from the notion of bias in the sense that they do not presume a single ideological position. The frame 'implies a range of positions' and 'should not be confused with positions for or against some policy measure' (Gamson and Modigliani, 1989: 3–4). Where analysing bias is associated with the *general* disposition of the newspaper or broadcaster, the framing approach makes no such assumption, treating each case on its merits. Entman offers this summary:

> A *bias* defines a tendency to frame different actors, events, and issues in the same way, to select and highlight the same sort of selective realities, thus crafting a similar tale across a range of potential news stories.
>
> (1996: 78; original emphasis)

The point is not that the word 'frame' replaces the word 'bias'; rather it is that, first, framing does not assume that all biases point in the same direction, and second, not all biases are *ideological* biases. In coverage of environmental policy in the United States, Entman (1996) identifies a variety of different biases: a 'popularity' bias, by which the media favour the popular view; a class bias, by which journalists adopt positions on environmental issues that serve their class interests; and a cynicism bias, by which policy is presented as exclusively self-interested or self-serving.

In focusing on ideological biases, argues Entman, media analysts are liable to overlook what he sees as the real biases:

> All of the concern with ideological bias has obscured the systematic, consistent biases that the media truly do impose on their narration of politics and policy. The real media biases favor simplicity over complexity, persons over institutional process, emotions over facts, and, most important, game over substance.
>
> (Entman, 1996: 78)

This version of the systematic biases, revealed through framing analysis, indicates a different approach to the study of media content. It suggests that we look at the way in which the media give life and form to the entire political process. It also suggests that we pay attention to the evaluative and rhetorical character of news. Entman (1997: 32) talks of 'emotion-arousing vocabulary'. This chapter draws heavily on the framing approach in discussing the ways in which 'politics' and the political process are represented within the media.

Producing news

As Entman, Gamson and others suggest, reporting is a form of rhetoric, it is about *persuading* us – the readers, the viewers – that something happened. Very few people actually witness the political events that are reported. We are not present at a president's inauguration; we are not among the crowds on the streets of Tehran; we are not on patrol with the troops in Helmand Province. And yet when we read or see news broadcasts about Obama becoming president, or about political dissent in Iran or about the Taliban attacks in Afghanistan, we do not just believe that they happened: we *know* they did. We are sure about these things, even though we have no direct corroborative evidence.

This belief cannot be explained simply by the claim that 'I read it in the papers' or 'I saw it on the news'. The mere fact of reading something does not make it true. Novels are not accounts of true events, and although they move us to tears or laughter, we are aware that we are reading stories that do not map directly onto a real world. This does not stop us saying that a film or novel is honest or truthful, but when we do we mean something different than when we talk about the accuracy of a news report. The point is, though, that in each case – in fiction or news – we are being *persuaded* of its truthfulness, and the difference between genres lies in the techniques they use to do this. The credibility of any story is undoubtedly enhanced by the fact that every other paper carries it too. But even if this is not the case, when the press boasts of an 'exclusive', we are still disposed to believe the report. It is, of course, the case that the level of credibility varies between sources: some papers or programmes are seen as more 'trustworthy' than others; and scandals about journalistic fabrication or faked documentaries do damage the trust people have in media sources. So when it was revealed that the *New York Times* journalist Jayson Blair had made up interviews and stories, he was sacked immediately in an attempt to protect the integrity of the paper (*New York Times*, 3 May 2003).

But despite such attempts to preserve the integrity of media outlets, popular trust has proved an allusive entity. In 2009, a Pew Research Center survey (http://people-press.org/report/ 543/) found that only 29 per cent of Americans thought that news organizations got the facts straight. Over 60 per cent viewed news as inaccurate. This represents a significant change from 20 years earlier when a majority considered the media to be reliable in their reporting of news. The key is that the decision to believe or to disbelieve rarely has anything to do with any direct knowledge of the events reported (Kohut and Toth, 1998). It is a matter of being persuaded that the journalist has not invented their story.

Engendering trust is not just an issue for the written word. Seeing something on the television – seeing pictures of refugees or peace negotiations – does not in itself provide proof that the event occurred. On either side of these images are soap operas, situation comedies and movies. We see events taking place in these too, and yet we do not believe they are picturing real moments in real people's lives. Or rather, when viewers come to believe that the characters are 'real', this is often seen as a symptom of some kind of failure on their part. Most viewers recognize that the characters in soaps are no more real than Homer, Bart and Marge Simpson. Whatever happens, we know that we will not end up living next door to them.

But what is important is that the 'reality' of the news, of the 'real' events that it describes, is not formally any different from the events in soaps. They are part of the same medium that carries the dramas or prints the fiction. The difference between what is true and what is invented is not something that can be 'seen'. It is something we learn, and it is something we are taught; making sense of media content requires skill, an ability to interpret clues. To apply this skill we have to be given guidance or signals that allow us to recognize what is truth and what is fiction.

One way of thinking about this is to imagine the conditions under which we might be persuaded *not* to believe the news. Imagine a world in which news reports are peppered with jokes, or are written in very florid language, and are delivered by the Hollywood actor Sacha Baron Cohen in the guise of his character Borat. Imagine that a news broadcast beginning with the newsreader saying: 'It seems to me that the president is up shit creek without a paddle' and that this announcement is accompanied by the sound of a studio audience cheering or booing. Imagine that the newscaster is dressed in jeans and a t-shirt, that the TV news programme uses a song by Jay-Z for its theme tune, or that the reporters are sponsored like football or tennis professionals and wear their sponsor's logo on their clothes. If the news was like this, we would not believe it; we would not be able to take it seriously as 'reality'. This is despite the fact that we would have no more or less direct evidence for the reported facts than we do when we believe the news in its current format. In other words, the format, the *style* of the news, does a great deal of work in establishing the status and significance of its content.

News reports tend to be written in a dry, impersonal language. Newscasters typically dress soberly and their broadcasts are introduced by music that is portentous. News reporters use film and photos, experts, eyewitnesses and official sources to validate their report. News stories, while formally committed to reporting the unusual or the untypical, actually stay firmly within strict conventions. They report fluctuations in the exchange rate, not the price of bread in the local supermarket. A whole range of signals and conventions establish that something is 'news' and serious, that it is about the real world. In the same way, other codes and devices tell us that something is fictional. These techniques are supplemented by the image of the professional journalist and the codes of conduct that attach to such an occupation, all of them designed to establish credibility and trust.

These methods for persuading us of the truth of particular stories and programmes are themselves built upon a larger edifice. First, there is the assumption that there exists something called 'news' which we need to know about and believe; and second, there is the idea that the mass media are legitimate providers of this product. We could, after all, manage with gossip exchanged in the street; the fact that people watch the news instead is a consequence of the operation of social conventions and the political interests underlying them. In other times and places, 'news' does not impose the same compulsive pressure (for example, news broadcasts are shorter and more infrequent on national holidays). Nor is the pressure felt equally by all; the desire for news correlates with the socio-economic position of the consumer: the poor feel less 'need' for news (Putnam, 1995). In other words, we have to be aware of the process both by which news is constituted and by which it comes to be important: how, that is, it becomes institutionalized.

'News' is, in one sense, a consequence of economics. It is a product of the need to trade. Where communities have no such need, where their actions do not depend on those of their neighbours, there is little reason or incentive to create news, save as a form of entertaining gossip. News is also a product of politics. In *The Structural Transformation of the Public Sphere,* Jürgen Habermas (1989) connects the rise of the press with the development of public political dialogue. This was itself a result of changes in the structure of power in industrializing countries, where a new political order was struggling into life, one in which the business class sought to control public policy. The press provided a means of articulating these political views. What was to emerge, through the publication of journals and magazines, was what became known as 'public opinion', the construction of views which had legitimacy through the fact that they were held by the 'people'. This was, as it continues to be, a construct of the system of communication. The 'public' is the product of mass media and their relationship to authority. The press and broadcasters represent themselves as the voice of the people. Public opinion is called into existence through the rhetoric of public communication. Opinion and information are products, on the one hand of the attempt to make political power accountable, and on the other of the rise of systems of communication that give shape to that process of accountability.

For Habermas, the emergence of a public sphere, created through the circulation of a political press and facilitated by coffee house society, was a significant moment in the process of modernization and democratization. But it was a moment that was contingent upon many factors, and as those factors changed, so did the public sphere. Habermas himself, and those who have followed him (Crouch, 2004; Garnham, 1986; Marquand, 2004), argue that the industrialized and commercialized media have effectively eliminated the public sphere. Nowadays, the citizen of the public sphere has been replaced by the consumer of the private sphere. The new order does not serve the need for public discourse about political goods; instead, it aims to link audiences and advertisers.

This shift has direct implications for news. Where news was used previously to constitute public opinion among active citizens, it has become increasingly geared to servicing the commercial market. In the United States, advertisers have begun to insist on control over the editorial content of magazines; editorial and advertising branches of newspapers have been amalgamated. This is captured in the concept of the 'total newspaper', described by Daniel Hallin (2000: 221) as 'the idea that circulation, sales and editorial efforts must be integrated, all directed towards the project of marketing news-information'. In the United Kingdom, News International titles have been accused of tailoring their coverage of China in order to accommodate their owner's commercial interests in that part of the world (Page, 2003). The very notion of 'news' itself has changed under the influence of commercial pressure. The move towards 'human interest' stories can be seen to accord with the desire to produce more consumer-friendly news. Hallin (2000: 221) talks of the change in the content of US papers: 'They include shorter stories, colour and graphics, and a shift in the news agenda away from traditional "public affairs" and towards lifestyle features and "news you can use".' The same trend may explain, for instance, the obsession with President Clinton's affairs (with, among others, Monica Lewinsky) in 1997–98, even as the world appeared to edge closer to another war in the Gulf. It might explain too why popular newspapers prefer to feature celebrities rather than politicians on their front pages. Newspapers do not, however, have to take this form. The press in Germany, for example, found space for lengthy and sophisticated debate of the war in Kosovo, with contributions by such academics as Ulrich Beck and Habermas (Scott, 1999). Steven Barnett and his colleagues (2000: 12) draw similar conclusions in their study of television news, where they argue that there is considerable variation between nations in the mix between hard and soft news. 'News' is a media product, and like all such products it is the result of a complex process and history.

To summarize: in presenting a version of the world, news has first to persuade us of its veracity through the use of various techniques, and second the character and role of that news have to be seen as circumscribed by wider commercial and political processes. These general points have a considerable significance for the way we then think about how news represents politics. The logic of the argument is that news has to be understood as another media product, like soap operas, chat shows, drama series, lifestyle magazines and so on. Each of these too has a particular history and is the result of a particular concatenation of interests. News is not an isolated example of media production, but just one among many such instances. What defines each of them is not simply, or even, their relationship to the truth, but rather the rules and conventions and interests with which they operate. The way to capture this is to say that 'news' is just a particular genre within the system of mass communications. And it is this aspect of it, as a genre, that has to be borne in mind as we consider the way it constitutes politics and the political realm.

Genres are defined by Steve Neale (1980: 19) 'as systems of orientations, expectations and conventions that circulate between industry, text and subject'. News reporting forms a genre of which 'political coverage' is a sub-genre. It is in working with these genres that journalists come to frame events. In this sense, the frames are the practical realization of the genre. As the journalist Sarah Benton (1997: 137) argues, political coverage is organized around pre-established story lines or frames. The plot is always the same: 'there are only old stories which we know already .... We know it all already because information about politics only becomes the news when it can be fitted into a story that we know already.' Thus, for example, coverage of the UK debate about the United Kingdom's relationship to the European Union was organized, in the 1990s, around two basic plots: the destruction of the Conservative Party or the end of national sovereignty (ibid.: 138). But the politics frame does not just work with particular plots, it also involves specific characters and predicaments. This is most obvious in the focus on leaders, and their representation as individuals motivated by the desire for power. The genre of political coverage creates 'the political process'; its conventions define politics and its narratives organize the plot lines of political stories.

Genres and political coverage

A genre, like the frames it gives rise to, is not fixed or universal; it institutes general regularities, establishing practices that allow the production of any particular cultural form. But genres do not emerge out of nowhere, nor do their rules or conventions provide absolute and unbreakable rules. Genres change and have histories. So it is that the genre of political coverage is a constantly evolving form, and the paths taken by the press and by broadcasting are different, not only between countries but within them too. Genre conventions are specific to their context. News genres differ, for example, according to their dependence on advertising or according to their regulatory regime. Such factors help explain, for instance, the different ways in which general elections and political leaders are covered in different countries (Hallin and Mancini, 2004; Masters et al., 1991; Negrine, 1996; Semetko, 1996).

In the same way, change in political coverage has to be understood in terms of the increasing competition for space between it and sports and lifestyle coverage, and the competition for readers and viewers with an ever-expanding range of media sources to choose from. Such processes lead to claims that news is being 'dumbed down', a charge that is supported by reference to the decline in column inches devoted to representative assemblies (Congress, Parliament) since the Second World War, and to the rise of the political sketch writer, for whom politics is a source of amusement (Franklin, 1992, 2004; Negrine, 1996; Tutt, 1992). There has been a move away from direct reporting of representatives' business, and a rise in *commentary* upon that business. The job of the political commentator is more akin to that of the television critic than to that of the reporter. Political commentators review performances and amuse their readers by dwelling on the quirky aspects of the political representatives.

Such commentary can be seen as framing politics as soap opera or situation comedy. This is one political commentator, Mathew Parris, writing about the then British Conservative Party leader, William Hague: 'We saw Big Chief Bald Eagle, the young warrior recently anointed leader of the Tory tribe, down on the reservation at Smith Square, spiritual homeland of his people' (*The Times*, 24 July 1997). In the Netherlands, politicians are framed within the conventions of gossip writing. Liesbet van Zoonen documents the ways in which Dutch magazines write about the marriages of politicians as well as about their alleged corrupt activities:

> Now that Elco Brinkman is no longer minister, he can give more attention to wife Janneke and their children Eduard, Christine and Henriette; 'SCANDAL! This is the way politicians fill their pockets with your tax money.
>
> (van Zoonen, 1998a: 57)

Such accounts invite ridicule and cynicism. The use of these styles of reporting politics shapes the way politics is seen, and marks the changing relationships between audiences, politics and their media. Readers are there to be amused rather than informed; they are expected to laugh and mock. But this form of political coverage, while increasingly common, is just one among many.

Karen Sanders (2009: 210–16) distinguishes between the roles and styles in the coverage of politics, each with their own histories and incentive structures. There is, she says, the 'chronicler', who simply documents the business of politics. Such a role stands in contrast to the 'news reporter', who aims to highlight or investigate select features of the political process. These reporting styles are to be contrasted with that of the 'critic', for whom politics is all about performance, who is, in turn, to be distinguished from the more impartial, less engaged, role of 'pundit or commentator' and that of 'interrogator', cross-examining politicians on their values and claims. These roles are not discrete; they overlap, and the same person may occupy several of them. The point is, however, that each of them constructs and frames politics in different guises, and invites different perceptions of what 'politics' means.

The different perspectives and frames are not given or pre-determined. They are products of commercial and political processes. They have their own histories. Furthermore, political coverage does not just change within a particular medium, but across media. Where the press began as a highly politicized form, broadcasting in the United Kingdom began as an apparently apolitical one. The Post Office's management of the then British Broadcasting Company in the early 1920s required that the company avoid controversy and comment. This constraint was reinforced by the BBC's competitors. Lord Reith, the BBC's first director-general, tried to develop a news service, but was frustrated by the press, who saw broadcasting as a dangerous rival. It was only in 1927 that the BBC was allowed to broadcast news during the daytime. Until then it could only report news after 7 pm, and it still had to confine itself to copy supplied by the Reuters news agency. After 1927, it began to rely on its own sources. It remained tied by the rule that forbade it to editorialize, but gradually the bar on controversy was lifted. In 1944, the 'Fourteen day rule' was introduced, preventing the BBC from mentioning any issue that was due to be discussed in Parliament in the next two weeks. Elections also were not covered.

This cautious distance between politicians and broadcasters began to break down with the founding of commercial television. The Fourteen day rule was scrapped and the 1959 general election was the first to be subject to direct coverage by the broadcasting media. Slowly, too, the deference which broadcasters accorded politicians was eroded, helped by the so-called 'satire boom' of the early 1960s. Nonetheless, representative politics still enjoyed a protected existence. The first election phone-ins did not take place until 1974; radio microphones were not installed in Parliament until two years later; and cameras were not introduced in the House of Commons until 1990.

In Australia, news and political coverage changed in response to technical development. With the laying of coaxial cables in the 1960s, it was no longer necessary to fly news film to the broadcaster; it could be sent instantaneously. Prior to this, coverage of the government in Canberra was largely ignored, with preference given to local (accessible) news. Full-time coverage of Parliament, therefore, did not occur until the 1970s. In the same way, satellite television gave an increased incentive to cover world politics. Political coverage changed for other reasons too. As in the United

Kingdom, there was a gradual shift from deferential, descriptive reporting of politics to a more assertive, irreverent approach. This shift owed something to changes in broadcasting rules and to a growing professionalization of journalists (Tiffen, 1989: 25–8).

If the coverage of politics changes in response to political and technical drivers, it also changes in response to economic ones. James Hamilton's (2004) book, *All the News That's Fit to Sell,* has as its subtitle, 'How the market transforms information into news'. He identifies two news genres – hard news and soft news – measured by the quantity of public information they contain. The presence of either, he argues (2004: 15ff), is determined by the coalition of media outlet and advertiser interests.

These stories of the changing nature of political coverage are not confined to liberal democracies. They can also be told about authoritarian regimes. Writing of China, Jeremy Tunstall (2008: 194) suggests that the televised trial in 1980 of Madame Mao (Jiang Qing), wife of the late Chinese leader Mao Zedong, 'dramatized the combined political and entertainment potential of television.' Prior to this, media served primarily to deliver propaganda rather than report politics. Major events – like the famine of 1960 – were not reported (Tunstall, 2008: 198, 203–4). The continuing reluctance to allow critical reporting of issues such as Tiananmen Square, Tibet or Taiwan suggests that the representation of politics remains highly constrained, but there are signs of change, as media report shortcomings in the system and new programme formats are developed for doing so (Tunstall, 2008: 22). Even in regimes in which there is extensive top-down control over media, the character of political coverage is susceptible to change.

The point of these different histories is to establish the context within which the broadcast form of political coverage emerged. Where the reporting of politics is organized by the political elite, the coverage reflects this distribution of power. Where commercial interests are pre-eminent in forming the generic type, another set of rules apply (Hallin and Mancini, 2004: 55ff). Chapter 6 looks in more detail at the ways in which corporate considerations influence the shape of the genre. What needs to be discussed here is how existing genres, in fact, represent or constitute the political realm. With this in mind, we look now at the frames that currently distinguish the way politics is presented to readers, viewers and listeners. It is not intended to offer a comprehensive picture, but rather to identify some of the most salient aspects. The question is straightforward: in the framing of politics, which aspects of the political process are organized into political coverage and which are organized out?

Telling political stories

If all political coverage, as van Zoonen argues, involves telling a story, then the choice of narrative frame is key to how politics is represented. For example, a news story can tell how actors cause events (how Henry Kissinger and Richard Nixon covered up the bombing of Cambodia; how Western political leaders decided to intervene in the former Yugoslavia). Equally, news stories can tell how those same political actors are driven by events, how they were the victims of circumstance. The way the story is told, the narrative devices used, will determine the way the political process is imagined. To illustrate this, let us consider how elections are covered (Lichter and Smith, 1996). The political motives of all politicians are commonly understood in terms of their desire to win elections, and their actions are interpreted in relation to this dominant concern.

Elections are typically represented as the culmination of titanic struggles in which leaders battle for supremacy. The right to rule is secured by the power won as a result of a heroic victory, in which a leader puts his or her rivals to the sword. These rivals are not simply the leaders of other parties. They also inhabit the leader's own party. As Sarah Benton caricatures it:

> Behind every leader there are dark forces; if the leader is weak, the dark forces are really in control .... A great leader is hampered and surrounded by buffoons .... Leaders are always beset by conspiracies .... The job of the *young* leader is to wake the inert people from their long sleep.
>
> (Benton, 1997: 146–7)

These rivals exist first within their own party; they have to win the battle to lead the party. In the United States, the primaries and the party conventions provide the formal setting for the playing out of these rivalries, whereas in the United Kingdom leadership elections and annual party congresses provide the theatre. The successful leader is then engaged in a battle with their opponent, which is resolved in the head-to-head that is the national election.

One metaphor that is typically associated with the account of these electoral struggles is the horse race (Gitlin, 1991; Lichter and Smith, 1996; Strömbäck and Dimitrova, 2006; Zhao and Bleske, 1998). If representative assemblies are covered as if part of the world of light entertainment, elections are covered as if they are sporting encounters. Opinion pollsters act as bookies and Election Day is the winning post. Commentary on them is driven by poll data and by other estimates of the parties' chance of success; each day's campaigning is seen as an opportunity to comment upon the relative performances of the parties: who is ahead, who has just fallen, and so on. But the horse race is just one of the many metaphors deployed. Another is the idea of armed conflict, with talk of battle zones and war rooms. More recently, elections have been represented as a talent contest. When it was announced that, for the 2010 UK general election, the leaders of the three largest parties would take part in televised debates, the BBC's Nick Robinson likened these contests to a political version of *The X Factor* ('Nick Robinson's Newslog', BBC Online, 21 December 2009). Whatever the allusion, the story of the election is narrated through words and images, themselves constituted by an overarching frame. Together they construct a particular vision of the political process. The presence of this general narrative structure is evident in the way leaders dominate the coverage of politics. 'Parties' do not exist as a chorus of different voices, but of one: that of their designated leaders. The political position of the Social Democrat, the Republican, or the Conservative party is assumed to be contained in the speeches and pronouncements of its leader. Or put another way, the story is told in terms of a leader who seeks to control their party and who is constantly fighting off rivals. Leaders tend to dominate election campaigns.

Research (Billig et al., 1993; Deacon et al., 1998; Norris, 2001a; Electoral Commission, 2005) into coverage of UK general elections over the last two decades has revealed that the party leaders were greatly in evidence. In 1992, where the Conservative leader (John Major) appeared 175 times, his chancellor, Norman Lamont, appeared a mere 62 times (indeed the grand total for appearances by other members of the party was 247). In 1997, the pattern was much the same. Tony Blair appeared 531 times, while his deputy, John Prescott, mustered only 56 appearances. Little if anything had changed by 2005, when the Electoral Commission (2005: para 3.16) reported that: 'The leaders of the three main political parties accounted for more than one-third of all politicians identified in coverage,' and that in the tabloid papers they provided nearly two-thirds of quotations from politicians. However much this imbalance is the product of party management, the media tend to collude in this arrangement and thereby generate a picture of politics in which competition between leaders (and aspiring leaders) defines the game. This is not a peculiarity of UK media coverage. Research into news coverage in France, the United States and Germany reveals that in these countries as well leaders occupy a great deal of the available screen time (Masters et al., 1991). And in the United States at least, the typical tone of the coverage has been negative, with the leaders being framed in such a way as to make them appear as 'scoundrels' (Farnsworth and Lichter, 2003: 107, 148).

This emphasis on leadership is underpinned by a (largely unarticulated) social theory which holds that collective action needs to be explained by the actions of leaders (hence the references to the existence of 'ringleaders' or 'militants' in discussion of unofficial or illegal activities). The media favour an explanation of political action that follows the formal contours of the bureaucratic/democratic hierarchy. There is a reluctance to attribute behaviour to spontaneity or to social forces or processes. Politics is framed as the product of the activity of key individuals; ordinary people are essentially passive followers (either portrayed positively as 'supporters' or negatively as 'sheep' or 'dupes'). In such a worldview, there is no space for structural factors to shape the course of events.

Another feature of this coverage of leaders, according to Joshua Meyrowitz (1985), is the way those leaders are viewed. For Meyrowitz, television treats leaders as 'people like us'. This is as much a consequence of the medium's technical character, its use of the intimate close-up, as of a choice on the part of programme makers. Leaders are portrayed (and judged) by their performance as human beings under pressure (the interview) or in conversation (the chat show), rather than as leaders in the traditional sense (Meyrowitz has in mind Churchill and Roosevelt). Under the glare of the studio lights, leaders are seen as personalities. This is a topic to which we return when considering new forms of political communication (Chapter 9). For the moment it is sufficient to note that, in thinking about the way politics is portrayed, we need to be mindful of style as well as content.

The concentration on individuals and events, on personalities and ambitions, inevitably marginalizes an alternative account of political change. Such an alternative might draw attention to the social forces or structures that drive change, and which make events the contingent result of these larger processes. To return to the case of the election: the extensive media treatment it receives reinforces the idea that the outcome is decided in this period. Much of the research on voting behaviour indicates, however, that this emphasis may be misplaced (Curtice and Semetko, 1994; Newton and Brynin, 2001). Sociological accounts, which place emphasis on class, see patterns of voting changing more gradually and over longer periods of time than is allowed by election campaigns. Even those theories that dwell upon the impact of political factors also see votes as being determined over time and in advance of the election campaign (Heath et al., 1991). Certainly, the appearance of major shifts in popular support or of dramatic changes of electoral strategy, both of which feature in the reporting of elections across the world, may owe more to the nature of media routines than to actual political change.

Telling the election story in this way also plays down the part played by parties (as collective bodies). Other collectivities are also identified through their leaders: companies by the chief executive; the European Union by its president. Even where there is no formal organization, the media will still seek a leader. So it is that the media will expect 'community leaders' to talk on behalf of some putative 'community'.

In portraying leaders as the key actors and elections as the key political event, there then comes the question of the motivation: what is it that drives the actors engaged in the election? Cappella and Jamieson (1997) identify two competing sets of motives: one is marked by a devotion to some principle that determines what policy is to be offered or advocated, the other by a strategic calculation which produces policies according to their vote-winning potential. In ascribing these different motives to politicians, journalists are establishing different frames through which to view political action. The frame is constructed by the ways that language, phraseology and imagery are used to paint a picture of the political process as animated by particular kinds of politician with particular kinds of motivation.

The motives attributed to leading actors are not applied universally, or without concession to who they are. This is most apparent in foreign coverage, in the way the world is drawn and reported. The portrait of the world is marked by a process of inclusion and exclusion: certain countries share in the narrative, others do not. And those that are part of the story may themselves be narrated in a particular way – hence the emphasis on scandal and corruption (Wallis and Baran, 1990). Chris Paterson gives this account of the problem of persuading Western news agencies to carry stories about Africa:

> All they want out of Africa is death, blood, famine, corruption, and all that. We've got plenty of that in Africa – there's no shortage of that. But we've also got a hell of a lot of other stuff in Africa which is much more important to the continent than just the various wars that go on.
>
> (Paterson, 1998: 91–2)

By this account, Africa is framed as a site of struggle and dependence (where the United States is framed as a site of power and autonomy). But more recent research suggests that the balance is shifting towards a concern with 'politics' and 'international relations', rather than 'violence' and disasters (Scott, 2009: 17). Nonetheless, this later research also concludes that coverage of developing countries are not framed by a continuing news story, but as a one-off snapshot, which in turn creates the impression 'that nothing ever changes' (ibid.: 18).

The conventions that demarcate the world also affect the people included within it. Pippa Norris (1997b), for example, has explored the narratives that frame accounts of women in politics. Her concern has been to examine the conventional wisdom that women leaders receive less attention than their male equivalents, and that the coverage they receive is based on female stereotypes. Norris's research examined the treatment of 20 world leaders, of whom ten were women (for instance, Margaret Thatcher, Benazir Bhutto and Indira Gandhi). The coverage included both print and broadcast media, and was analysed both quantitatively and qualitatively. Over 130,000 stories were examined. The evidence revealed that male leaders (1,600 stories per year) did indeed receive more coverage than female leaders (1,400 stories per year). Perhaps extraordinarily, this meant that 'the gray John Major receives more daily news coverage than the remarkable Mrs Thatcher' (Norris, 1997b: 158). On the other hand, though there is some evidence of sex role stereotyping, it is less than might be expected. There are occasional references to appearances or other irrelevant personal details in coverage of women, but says Norris (ibid.: 159), these remarks are 'exceptional'. Men and women are described in broadly similar terms.

There is, however, evidence of the use of different framing devices for the reporting of men and women. These frames have both positive and negative effects. Norris reveals how women often appear within a 'breakthrough' frame: they are seen as the first of their sex to achieve a particular goal. A second frame treats them as 'outsiders', and in doing so denies them credit for their experience and qualifications. A final frame detected by Norris treats women as 'agents of change, most especially in sweeping away corruption' (ibid.: 163).

The idea of the 'frame' then complements the idea of the genre. Both serve to draw attention to the ways in which coverage of politics gives prominence, first to individual actors, and second to the particular kinds of motives and expectations that guide their actions. But representations of politics are not couched only in terms of leaders. Indeed the activities of these leaders have to be understood through the generic convention that attaches them to some other representative body – a parliament, assembly or congress. The role accorded by the media to elected representative bodies is shaped by a number of factors. One of these is the formal constitutional reading of the role of the elected assembly. Where, as in the United States, the elected assembly is accorded distinct separate powers, it is able to claim more media space against the rival claims of the executive. Different constitutional arrangements produce different pictures. Roger Masters and his colleagues (1991: 386) noted that the attention given to a leader tends to 'mirror [the] constitutional and political structure' of their country. A second factor shaping reportage is the means by which information is disseminated: codes of secrecy or rights to freedom of information, as well as other informal systems of news management, determine what appears in papers and in broadcasts. See, for example, the difference between the practices of the Washington lobby and the Westminster lobby. A third factor is the use of sources. In his study of the affirmative action debate, Entman (1997: 36) notes: 'Journalists, it seems, built their frame on claims by elite sources with an interest in promoting the impression of white arousal.' A similar lesson derives from Kellner's (1995) account of coverage of the first Gulf War.

A fourth, related factor involves the way in which the sourcing of news is financed and the balance of power between journalists and their sources. David Miller (1993), for instance, argues that the reporting of Northern Ireland is a product of the control exercised by the Northern Ireland Office and the Northern Ireland Information Service. Using its considerable resources – 58 staff, £7 million (in 1991–92) – the NIIS produced thrice-daily press releases, which, says Miller (ibid.: 76), 'present its view of the conflict as the legitimate and rational perspective in opposition to that of the paramilitaries and other "extremists".' The increasing prominence of PR agencies in all aspects of public life, it is suggested (Davies, 2008), continues to shape the representation of politics. A fifth factor shaping media portrayal of representative institutions is the standing of the relevant institution. In the mid 1980s, for example, Blumler and Gurevitch (1995: 89) talked of UK press treatment of Parliament as 'sacerdotal', placing it just below the monarchy and the Church; today, the attitude is less respectful and this is reflected in the coverage and prominence accorded to Parliament (Franklin, 1992; Negrine, 1996). This, though, is not a simple fact of all political coverage, but of the peculiarities of a particular system. In other constitutional settings, with other party structures, leaders still feature, but their motives and actions will be framed differently.

What this teaches us is that, in looking at the coverage of politics, we need to focus upon who is viewed as the key political actor and what motives drive them. We have seen how there is a general tendency to focus on leaders, but the treatment of them varies between systems. Whatever the coverage accorded to leaders, such attention will tend to overlook the role played by 'ordinary' participants, or by participants outside the political mainstream, by principle or wider political forces. Indeed, this is a necessary result: making elected leaders the focus of attention also accords them legitimacy which is denied to others; making liberal democratic assumptions about the normal order of politics makes other kinds of political assumption 'extreme'. Insofar as politics is presented as an electoral game in which individual political ambition is the core motivating force, the media engage in a process of constituting and legitimating a version of the political process. In telling the story of politics this way, the media are also engaged in other important cultural processes. They are constructing a citizenry and a political realm, and distributing social and cultural capital – the ability to contribute to that society – in accordance with the picture they paint.

We the people

Contained in every news story is an implied audience or readership. Stories are written for a particular group, and the way they are written assumes a particular set of responses or values. There is an assumption about what 'we' are interested in, what we do, care about and know. Gamson and Modigliani (1989: 9) quote a newscaster reporting on the Chernobyl accident: 'Is there anyone out there not thinking about this nightmare of the nuclear age, talking about it, learning from it?' The everyday conversation of editorial offices is about whether 'our readers' or 'our audience' are interested in X or Y. The ex-BBC political editor, John Cole, recalls how his colleagues made assumptions about the political interests of their audiences:

> Editors, even on more spacious programmes than the news bulletins for which I used to work, judge that viewers' and listeners' attention span in political matters is very limited; that they cannot listen to an uninterrupted speech; that their tastes must be titillated by confrontational studio discussion.
>
> (*Guardian*, 4 March 1996)

A measure of a paper's success is its ability to deliver a product that is appreciated by its target audience. Different papers and programmes work in different markets. This process is not simply a matter of responding to economic forces; the market is being created in the commercial process.

Readers and viewers are themselves constructed through the stories they see or read or hear; their concerns and worries are shaped and constituted by the way they are addressed by their papers and programmes. Journalists and editors may think of themselves as reflecting their audience, but actually they are imagining and constituting them. Fear of genetically modified foods did not spring spontaneously from the public. Concern was orchestrated by the interaction of journalists, lobbyists, scientists and so on. Reporters have very limited access to the public, and what access they have is often mediated by other media and other interests. This means that they have, in a sense, to invent or create their audience. News values, what counts as an important issue, are attempts to establish a particular kind of audience/readership. They are ways of saying 'this is what matters to you'. Brian McNair writes of the British press:

> The *Sun* claims to 'speak' for the conservative working class, making it frequently racist, sexist and anti-socialist, while at the same time irreverential and critical of the establishment, whether it be in the form of Royal 'scroungers', gay judges, or two-timing Tory politicians.
>
> (McNair, 1995: 69)

What is involved in this process is the creation of 'them' and 'us'. This is particularly noticeable in the framing of terrorism (Norris et al., 2003). The magazine *Index on Censorship* (2000) devoted a special issue to the creation of 'them'. It was entitled 'Manufacturing monsters', and described how 'they' are created in different media for different audiences, as 'refugees' or 'Arabs' or 'gypsies'. Franklin Gilliam and his colleagues (1996) have shown how in the United States the media create the fear of crime: of 'them' attacking 'us', and the way 'they' are configured as 'black'. These constructions of an audience, a particular 'we', is achieved through a series of contrasts and oppositions, through the implicit and explicit orchestration of 'us' and 'them'. National borders are drawn and redrawn this way, as are norms of sexuality and of political behaviour. At a trivial level, this can be discerned in sports commentary for international competitions where it is assumed that the audience is on one side or another; at a more serious level, it is involved in the construction of an enemy in the prelude to, and conduct of, war (Carruthers, 2000).

Interviews are conducted with a similar ethos in mind. Interviewers legitimize themselves by reference to their audience.

Their claim is that they ask the questions that the public want answered; they are part of some democratic process. This understanding is reinforced by the way in which the interview is presented. Typically, only the interviewer addresses the camera directly; the politician addresses the interviewer. The audience only has access to the interviewee via the interviewer. The style of the interview also affects the relationship to the audience. It can be aggressively combative or informally gossipy. These conventions are wittily exposed by satirists like Sacha Baron Cohen and Chris Morris who engineer interviews that mock their interviewees' pomposity or ignorance or gullibility. The formal rules and expectations of interviews are revealed as they are parodied.

More subtly, if more pervasively, 'the people' are also constructed through other aspects of the media, from a mode of address, or a tone of voice, to the setting of a schedule. Radio stations, like papers and TV programmes, are concerned with creating specific audiences. They do this through the style of programme and choice of presenter. When the BBC began broadcasting, there was only one channel, and it sought to create the conditions for a particular general public, that of a family gathered round the hearth (Frith, 1988). By contrast, the early days of US radio saw the emergence of stations which created regional, taste-specific audiences. With the proliferation of channels, the audiences have become ever more variegated, but the same principle holds. All forms of communication involve creating audiences and making certain assumptions. The 'people' are constituted in the process, and their existence is confirmed through the artifice of public opinion polls and market research, or of tweets and smart mobs. Individual answers to pollsters' questions are aggregated into 'public opinion'; crowds are created via internet traffic. The creation of these phenomena allows them to become tools for legitimizing partisan opinion or media agendas. The media's definition of the people (through the use of news values, editorials and interviews) and representation of them (through opinion polls and phone-ins) construct a particular version of the people. Opinion polls represent the aggregation of individual opinions expressed at particular times in particular settings. Using other techniques, or asking different questions, could create a different picture. Reality television has introduced new forms of popular participation and new versions of 'the people' (Cardo, 2009).

Consider the techniques that can be used to create other images of the people. Editorials could work from different assumptions; interviews could be staged in different ways. Current news values work with an assumption that what matters is our immediate well-being (itself defined by the assumption that 'we' are nuclear family house owners). Imagine, though, a newspaper, not written from the perspective of families in a single country, but from the point of view of the world's population of poor and destitute. Would the 'news' be the same? Would fluctuations in the mortgage rate matter? Would not market speculation on the price of grain count for a great deal more? The point of this argument is not to suggest that there is, in fact, a single 'people', or that one account of who 'we' are is necessarily more accurate than any other, but that different forms of address create different versions of the people. In creating one version, the media marginalize another.

In constituting the people (or, in fact, many different peoples), the media also constitute politics. First, and most obviously, this is achieved by the contrast between the 'us' who are reading and watching, and the 'they' who perform the political acts. This simple move constitutes 'politics' as a distinct realm. But there is more to this process. Borders are also drawn round the realm in which politics takes place. Politics is defined as the activities of public agencies (parliaments, public utilities and so on), of politicians and political parties, and of pressure groups. The activities of all of these are treated as being directed to the exercise of power and as being legitimized by a set of constitutional rules. 'Politics' is the topic of news pages or current affairs programmes; it does not appear on sports pages, nor is it typically part of entertainment programmes. There are, of course, exceptions in each case: political dramas, protest songs and satire.

If media representations organize themselves around the picture of politics described so far, what is left out? What stories are not told, what forms of politics are marginalized or overlooked? Apart from the way a focus on leaders omits the ordinary members, and the focus on parties and Parliament omits the administrative structures of the state, the account of politics offered by the media also tends to exclude the pervasive influence of commercial interests. 'Business' is treated as separate from politics; it occupies its own part of the paper, it has its own programmes. The financial markets are seen as autonomous and strangely unpredictable creatures that rise and fall on whim, and are reported in terms similar to those accorded the weather forecast: rises in the Dow Jones index are spoken of as if they resembled the movement of high-pressure zones.

It is not just business and the financial markets that may be missing from politics. It is everything that appears under a different heading in newspapers or in broadcasting that is excluded: entertainment, lifestyle, travel, and sport. These are not – apparently – part of 'politics'. But there is another level to what is excluded. Definitions of politics are primarily about the 'public' realm, the world of political debate and policy. This is not to say, of course, that the private realm is ignored. The media devoted huge effort to reporting allegations about the sex lives of Presidents Clinton and Sarkozy, or Prime Ministers Berlusconi and Major. The media's interest in these matters is, however, primarily occasioned by the view that these private matters are of direct relevance to the performance of the protagonists' public duties. Political coverage is not interested in sexual relations or family decisions as *politics*, but only as they relate to conventional understandings of politics. Such matters are, of course, the dominant concern of much else in the media, and the politics of soaps (and the polity they construct) should not be overlooked.

Explaining political stories

It should be clear by now that the reasons for the stories of politics presented by mass media do not lie simply in the values and perceptions of individual journalists and editors, though these no doubt play a part. Rather, they lie in the processes which organize the daily practices of these individuals, the way genres and frames are produced by commercial, professional and political pressures. This is a theme that is developed later in this book, but it is worth just illustrating briefly the kind of factors that shape (and misshape) the portrayal of politics. Sreberny-Mohammadi (1990) argues that the West failed to anticipate the demise of the shah of Iran and the rise to power of Ayatollah Khomeini because of *systemic* features of media organization. The revolution of 1979 was largely unanticipated by the Western press, who saw the shah's position as unassailable and the Ayatollah as a religious extremist of no great consequence. The popular forces behind the Ayatollah were ignored. As Sreberny-Mohammadi observes:

> Almost no attention was paid to the living conditions of ordinary rural people, the bulk of Iran's population .... Almost no attention was paid to the fast and ungainly growth of Tehran, its traffic, pollution, and inflation .... Almost no attention was paid to human rights abuses.
>
> (Sreberny-Mohammadi, 1990: 300)

The Western media not only failed to report these things, they also failed to note the disaffection that was being organized around each of these issues, and the predictions of those who thought that a revolution was possible. Instead, the press reported on the stability of the shah's regime. Little serious credibility or legitimacy was given to the Shi'ite opposition, which was seen as 'fanatical' (ibid.: 302). As a result the Western media failed to account for the processes that led to the revolution in 1979, just as later they failed to anticipate the collapse of apartheid in South Africa or the Soviet regime. When the media subsequently try to make sense of the process, they tend to resort to vague and unhelpful metaphors drawn from nature, such as the idea of 'winds of change'. In the case of the financial crisis of 2009, which the media – together with many economists – failed also to anticipate, the preferred explanation owed less to nature than to the greed and short-sightedness of bankers. Most of the coverage failed to identify the systemic and regulatory causes (Lanchester, 2010).

A similar failure of understanding is evident in reporting of political 'extremism'. So it is that Philip Schlesinger and others (1983: 37) write of the reporting of terrorism in Northern Ireland: 'The coverage of Northern Irish affairs in the British media has tended to simplify violent incidents, to avoid historical background, to concentrate on human-interest stories.' Twenty years later, researchers (Liebes and First, 2003; Norris et al., 2003) report that little has changed in the representation of terrorism. The effect of such coverage, says Carruthers (2000: 192), is that terrorism appears as nothing more than 'psychotic behaviour'. Enemies of the state tend to be demonized in ways that reinforce their illegitimacy and deny rationality to their actions. So it was that Saddam Hussein was portrayed as a modern 'Hitler' (ibid.: 42; Said, 2000).

Conclusion

Media coverage of politics differs between countries and political systems. This simple observation contains some important lessons. The first is the assumption that, however this coverage differs, it is about the same thing: creating a narrative of the political process, bound by the genre conventions, and moulded by the frames, which journalism deploys. Second, the picture produced is not a mirror image of the political system, but a creation shaped by political and media processes. It may be true that the mass media are obsessively interested in the minutiae of campaign tactics, or in the private lives of political leaders, but this is not some sort of universal media fact. It is the product of a system of news reporting, itself shaped by commercial, political, professional and other factors.

Why reporters tend to ignore processes and favour personalities is not to be explained by the prejudices of journalists and their editors. The phenomenon is too pervasive to be reduced to the personal foibles of lone actors. Rather, the answer lies in the structure and organization of the media, in the need to deal with events in a limited space and under the demands of tight deadlines. But these constraints are themselves the product of the larger pressures and interests to which the media have to respond. They have to sell their product, and lengthy explorations of the background to events (or refusal to make much of news events) may be very unattractive to readers or viewers.

Covering politics means creating a believable story about actors and agencies deemed to be important. First, it entails convincing those who read, listen or hear news reports that they are getting the truth. Second, it involves identifying a particular terrain as 'politics'. As we have seen, these ends are achieved in a variety of ways. Reportage is made credible through the use of various rhetorical devices, and in the process, the media create a mode of address that, in turn, establishes an audience. What is 'covered' by these techniques is itself defined as politics. As a result, certain aspects of the story and other audiences are excluded. Other techniques would result in different coverage. The representing of politics is itself part of a political process.

One feature of that politics, as we have noted, is the way in which the boundaries of the political realm are themselves drawn. The media's coverage of politics is confined to particular pages and programmes, to particular practices and places, but this does not mean that politics itself remains confined within these borders. The next chapter explores the way politics is constituted elsewhere in the media, away from the news pages and the current affairs programmes, in the world of entertainment.

Chapter 3

It's Just for Fun: Politics and Entertainment

In a candid description of News Corporation, Rupert Murdoch once remarked: 'We are in the entertainment business' (quoted in Shawcross, 1992: 261). With this aside, Murdoch called into question an assumption that lurks in much analysis of the politics of the media: that any such discussion should be confined to news and current affairs. Television schedules and newspaper layouts draw seemingly neat boundaries around what is 'politics' and what is 'entertainment'. These boundaries are marked in a variety of ways: by a tone of voice and a style of writing, by format and layout. As viewers and readers, we are given clues as to how to respond to what is before us, whether we should take it seriously as information or political debate, or whether we should be amused by it. In thinking about the representation of politics in mass media, there is a strong temptation to reproduce this distinction, and to concentrate exclusively upon those areas of mass media that deal with what is formally designated 'politics' (that is, news, documentaries and current affairs). But this formal distinction between what is and what is not 'important' is mistaken. As Jonathan Burston (2003: 165) argues, it assumes that only information changes the world, when in fact fun and pleasure may do so too. Or as James Curran and Colin Sparks (1991: 216) observe, 'entertainment has an important ideological dimension'. Such claims have far-reaching implications. If we want to understand how politics is represented in mass media, we need to look at the full range of media, and at the full range of broadcasting and newspaper content.

Some people watch news as 'entertainment', admiring the clothes of the newsreaders, mocking the pomposity of politicians (Taylor and Mullan, 1986). Others watch entertainment, and draw political conclusions from it. Reflecting, in a rather jaundiced way on this, the ex-Mayor of London, Ken Livingstone (quoted in the *Guardian G2*, 5 March 2008), once remarked: 'This isn't a world of ideology any more – it's a world where people watch *Big Brother* and *Strictly Come Dancing*. People vote for someone because they feel comfortable with them.' Things may be more complicated then this, but there is little doubting that the line between politics and entertainment is a very fuzzy one. There is, for example, a long list of Hollywood movies that have dealt with serious issues, from war (*From Here to Eternity*, 1953, *Saving Private Ryan*, 1998, *The Hurt Locker*, 2009), to nuclear deterrence and the Cold War (*Dr Strangelove*, 1964), to ecological disaster (*The Road*, 2009, *The Day After Tomorrow*, 2004). And then there are the entertainers who take a political stand, from Woody Guthrie to Bob Dylan to Sting to Rage Against the Machine. Events like Live8 in 2005, when the musicians Bono and Bob Geldof led a campaign to reduce developing country debt, become just another instance of the blurring of the line between politics and entertainment.

But even as the line becomes fuzzier, organizations such as the BBC, mindful of their duty of political impartiality, become increasingly sensitive to the politics lurking within entertainment. When the BBC carried the Hyde Park Live8 concert, one of several such shows staged across the world, it refused to broadcast the videos arguing the case for reducing developing country debt that were shown between the musical performances. They were deemed to compromise the BBC's obligation to 'due impartiality', and indeed the BBC Trust later voiced concern that the corporation was become too closely allied with political causes of the kind that Live8 represented. As a result, it cancelled a planned, celebrity-led climate change day (http://entertainment.timesonline.co.uk/, 6 September 2007). What the BBC's anxiousness revealed, among other things, was that treating entertainment and politics as discrete worlds is difficult at best, and more likely impossible. Politics does not disappear from the television as the newscaster bids us 'goodnight'. From sports matches to satires, from conspiracy films to chat shows, political values and views are being produced and reproduced, just as they are in news coverage and current affairs.

This idea, that politics is contained and constituted within non-political arenas like entertainment, is of course a familiar one. In his study of the world of the US slave, Eugene Genovese (1976) tells how the oppressed workers used songs to articulate their defiance, just as E. P. Thompson (1968) recounts how the emergent industrial working class of eighteenth-century England challenged their masters in song and poetry. In generalizing from such examples, James Scott (1990) talks of the 'hidden transcripts' within popular culture that express the experience and frustration of the poor and the downtrodden. Seeing popular culture as 'political' remains a feature of the modern world. From the birth of rock'n'roll in the 1950s, through flower power in the 1960s and punk in the 1970s, on into rap and dance culture in the 1980s and 1990s, pop music has been both a vehicle for radical sentiments and the object of conservative anger. Political values, ideas and arguments feature constantly in popular culture, and perhaps what is most perverse about the world of entertainment is how infrequently it acknowledges this connection. For all their desire to reflect the realities of everyday life, soap operas, as Stephen Coleman (2007) points out, almost never refer to politics or politicians.

This chapter draws out more fully the politics contained within various forms of mass entertainment. This is an increasingly important task as the boundary between the two realms, between conventional politics and popular culture, becomes ever more porous. Increasingly politicians are drawing upon the language, icons and expertise of popular culture (see Chapter 9), just as news producers appear to rely upon the repertoire of gestures and styles traditionally associated with entertainment – dramatic reconstructions, vivid graphics and soundtrack music – to report the news. At the same time, and perhaps more significantly, entertainment and the world of the celebrity have come to dominate the news.

This latter trend began some time ago. In the early 1990s, James Curran and Colin Sparks (1991: 215) noted that 'less than 20% of the editorial content of the popular national press is devoted to news and comment about political, social and economic affairs'. The rest was given over to human interest stories, celebrity gossip and the like. The same thought is expressed rather more graphically by Kelvin McKenzie, who as editor of the *Sun* was reported to have said to the paper's political editor: 'Forget all this crap about politicians – who's interested, eh? … the readers don't give a fuck about politicians … why don't you get a story for them, eh? One with people they've heard of for a change?' (quoted in Marr, 1996: 135). Such thinking lies behind the attention that the press devotes to the activities of film, television, sports and pop stars. It also lies behind the reporting of the private misdemeanours and sexual adventures of politicians rather than of their public, political deeds. More generally, it is the logic that helps to account for the spread of lifestyle and culture sections in newspapers.

What is important is how, in the reporting and coverage of stories that appear to have nothing to do with politics and everything to do with human interest or entertainment, we find politics present nonetheless. Curran and Sparks (1991: 228–9) illustrate this with their analysis of two stories, each apparently devoid of political content. The first tells how an Irish international footballer punched a taxi driver; the second is about a 39 year-old woman who leaves the family home and has an affair with a 19 year-old man. These are just two of a multitude of different stories that jostle for our attention in our daily papers. These stories do not just tell us anecdotes about our world, they are not just gossip; they are reinforcing wider norms. 'Entertainment features,' write Curran and Sparks (ibid.: 231), 'promote social integration within a "model" of society in which the existence of fundamental differences of interest is tacitly denied and a commonality of interest and identity is regularly affirmed.' The news items may not appear to be about politics, but they each tell a political story, and they serve to reinforce the status quo. Curran and Sparks conclude:

> the popular press foregrounds stories that do not pose a challenge or problem to the social order. Its perspective on the world – with its focus on individuals, its 'commonsense' frameworks of explanation, its moral rather than its political solutions – also provides tacit support for existing power relations.
>
> (Curran and Sparks, 1991: 231–2)

In a similar way, Brett Mills argues, in his analysis of the situation comedy *Peep Show,* that:

> the programme is ... informed by the concept of the 'surveillance society' in the sense that it uses for comic effect the characters' constant concern over what they can say or do, and the policing of their potential 'deviancy' through the fear of being 'laughed at'.
>
> (Mills, 2008: 4, 14)

In this chapter, the idea that politics is not confined to the explicitly political is developed by looking at how forms of entertainment construct an account of politics and power relations. We begin by examining forms of entertainment that make the world of politics an explicit object of their amusement, most obviously in the guise of 'satire'. Attention then turns to the portrayal of politics as a source of drama, especially within the genre of conspiracy movies, and after this the discussion moves on to consider the deliberate use of popular culture for political ends, whether for the promotion of political ideology or political identity. The argument is not that the politics of entertainment lies only with forms of popular culture that deal explicitly with the political, but that it is embedded in all forms of entertainment.

Political satire: politics as deluded and corrupt

Although politics and politicians come in for a great deal of criticism, from the sex scandals surrounding Silvio Berlusconi to the expenses scandal that bedevilled UK parliamentarians, they are still treated with a degree of respect, and with Barack Obama, almost reverence. Politicians are viewed, at least within the serious press and much broadcast media, as legitimate and influential political actors whose views are to be canvassed, cross-examined and recorded. Politicians may complain that they are given insufficient time, or that they are treated unfairly, but these complaints do not undermine the shared assumption that they *should* be accorded respect. This deference is not, however, evident in the treatment accorded to politics in the world of entertainment. There we find cynicism and disdain in roughly equal measure. Politicians are ridiculed for their vanity and pomposity, for their craven pursuit of self-advancement, for their lack of integrity and intelligence. Two obvious examples are Warren Beatty's cynical senator in the movie *Bulworth* (1998) and the slow-witted Jim Hacker of television's *Yes, Prime Minister*. Satire – the mockery of politics and politicians – is perhaps the most obvious way in which political life becomes part of entertainment. Or to put it another way: *The West Wing*, with its good-intentioned, if sometimes flawed, political actors, working together to realize the American Dream and to honour the US Constitution, appears as a notable exception to this general rule.

Satire is defined as the use of art – traditionally, prose and poetry – to make a moral point and 'to attack vice and folly'. Using 'wit and ridicule,' writes Dustin Griffin (1994: 1), satire 'seeks to persuade an audience that something or someone is reprehensible or ridiculous'. The classic period for satire is that occupied by Alexander Pope and Jonathan Swift, the era between 1660 and 1800. What was it that allowed satire to arise then, and what accounts for its subsequent appearance? Why, for example, did both the United States and the United Kingdom see a satire 'boom' in the late 1950s and early 1960s?

Satire, Griffin argues, can only work under certain specific conditions. These conditions are not simply produced by a rise in political corruption or venality; nor does satire take its cue from the state of public morality (whether that be one of conservatism or of confusion). In other words, there is no straightforward correlation between public behaviour and political satire. Indeed Griffin suggests that the rise of satire may have had more to do with movements in *literary* trends than in political or social ones. Satire supplies a genre in which literary power or authority can be usurped, a kind of revenge of the children on their parents. From this perspective, the origins and character of satire should be sought in the satirists and their social location as much as in the general features of their political times. Griffin (ibid.: 143) writes that 'the satirist was not a professional writer but a talented gentleman – usually without independent income'. It is notable that many latter-day satirists in the United Kingdom, though not their counterparts in the United States, came from a similar background (Carpenter, 2000).

An important related condition is the existence of an audience for satire. Griffin argues that the audience must display a familiarity with the genre, that it must understand the assumptions and tolerate the barbs that constitute satire (just as audiences must understand the generic conventions of news). Typically this means that it will be a 'fairly small, compact and homogenous reading audience ... located in the cultural and political capital' (Griffin, 1994: 137). Such an audience knows the protagonists and appreciates the in-jokes: without this knowledge and understanding there can be no satire. One final condition that helps explain the rise of satire in the seventeenth and eighteenth centuries is the persistent threat of censorship and the prospect of official disapproval. Looking at satire as the product of particular cultural trends, audience expectations and political contexts, it is possible to see parallel conditions foreshadowing the rise of satire in the 1960s, the period known as the 'satire boom'. In the United Kingdom, this era saw the birth of the magazine *Private Eye* and the television show *That Was the Week that Was* (*TW3*). In the United States, it saw the rise to prominence of performers like Mort Sahl, Tom Lehrer, Bob Newhart and Lenny Bruce.

In the post war decades in the United Kingdom, censorship was still a feature of both the theatre and the publishing business – famously, D.H. Lawrence's 1928 novel *Lady Chatterley's Lover* was not published legitimately until 1960; and the Lord Chamberlain's right to censor theatre, which was established in 1737, was not ended until 1968. The satirists themselves, people like Alan Bennett, John Bird, Peter Cook, John Fortune, Jonathan Miller, Dudley Moore and Richard Ingrams, were gifted gentleman amateurs with limited resources – products of public (that is, private) school and Oxford and Cambridge universities. Eleanor Bron and Millicent Martin were among the few women who featured in this generation of satirists. The satirists' targets were largely metropolitan, and depended upon inside knowledge of what were later to be called 'the chattering classes'. Modern mass media may have changed the reach and immediacy of satire, but they did not affect its metropolitan smugness.

Satire emerged slowly from cautious and constrained broad-casting institutions. Jokes about politics only gradually became acceptable (Wagg, 1992: 256). A parallel policy could be found among film censors, who were equally reluctant to pass films that dealt explicitly with politics (or indeed anything controversial) (Mathews, 1994). In the United Kingdom, the idea that politicians were funny, that they deserved mockery rather than deference, emerged in the 1950s with *The Goon Show* (whose main characters were played by Spike Milligan, Peter Sellers and Harry Secombe). The Goons' surreal humour was used to make fun of stuff-shirted aristocrats and bureaucrats. And, as Wagg suggests (1992: 257), *The Goon Show* was to inspire the more overtly political satire of the Cambridge Footlights revues, and of the Oxbridge humour of Cook, Bennett, Miller and Moore in their 1960 hit show, *Beyond the Fringe*. Politics featured prominently as the object of their mocking humour. It was not, however, inspired by any clear ideological position; it was a generalized attack on authority and those who styled themselves as leaders or would-be leaders. This spirit animated the television show that represents the highpoint of the 1960s 'satire boom', *That Was the Week that Was*. As one of the *TW3* team commented: 'We had no campaigning motives, no political beliefs' (quoted in Carpenter, 2000: 240). The idea for the show, according to Andrew Crissell (1991: 149–50), came from the then director general of the BBC, Sir Hugh Greene, but its genesis depended on the intimate links between the BBC and the elite universities who furnished the talent upon which broadcasting relied. Humphrey Carpenter (2000: 26) writes: 'Universities are natural breeding grounds for satire.' *TW3*'s success depended on this talent finding an audience, and, according to Crissell, this was supplied in part by the reforms instituted by the 1944 Education Act. By extending access to education, the Act produced an audience that was politically aware and critical of the old order.

In Robert Hewison's view (1988: 29), there was little in *TW3* that was 'threateningly subversive', but it did succeed in annoying Mary Whitehouse, who devoted her career to 'cleaning up' television. *TW3*, she said, 'was the epitome of what was wrong with the BBC – anti-authority, anti-religious, anti-patriotism, pro-dirt and poorly produced' (quoted in Hewison, ibid.: 29). She was not alone in being shocked by the programme. When *TW3* criticized the Conservative prime minister, Sir Alec Douglas Home, in October 1963, the BBC received 600 phone calls and 300 letters of complaint (Crissell, 1991: 145).

Satirical sneering at the establishment was to find published form in the magazine *Private Eye*. Once again the key players were products of elite institutions. Patrick Marnham (1982: 16) describes how '[t]he editors of *Private Eye* first met at Shrewsbury School', where they developed the skills by running the school magazine and taking part in the debating society. Public school not only provided the connections and opportunities that were to make *Private Eye* possible; it also supplied, as Hewison (1988: 34) notes, the sense of humour: the mockery of authority, the nicknames, the prejudices. These qualities were refined and developed at Oxford University, where the future editors were to reunite after their period of National Service. These individuals were not only responsible for *Private Eye*, they also wrote for, and performed in, *TW3*.

Private Eye's politics were not animated by any particular partisan allegiance; it attacked anyone who was in power. Indeed it did not just eschew party affiliation, it disdained all commitment. As Wagg comments (1992: 263), 'The *Eye* has seldom, if ever, explicitly endorsed a political cause.' The only exception to this general rule has been the campaign against corruption led by the socialist writer Paul Foot, and continued by the magazine after his death in 2004. But this campaigning was inspired by the general view that anyone who assumes authority or aspires to political office is somehow tainted or malign or vain, and as such is to be suspected.

Wagg (1992) traces a route from 1960s British satire to the internationally popular TV show, *Monty Python's Flying Circus*. Here the surreal humour of *The Goon Show* was combined with the iconoclasm of *TW3* and *Beyond The Fringe*. The Monty Python team were, once again, the product of Oxbridge (with the exception of their North American animator, Terry Gilliam). They delighted in mocking authority figures by extrapolating wildly the bizarre logic of bureaucracy and petty officialdom. Subsequently, the surreal satire of the 1950s and 1960s was to be incorporated into mainstream popular entertainment. Satire became a staple of situation comedies, most notably in *Yes, Minister* and *Yes, Prime Minister*. It was also used, albeit benignly, by mimics like Mike Yarwood and Rory Bremner. The sharper, more bitter satire of the earlier era surfaced occasionally in *Not the Nine O'Clock News*, in Rik Mayall's *New Statesman* and in the puppetry of *Spitting Image*. The current editor of *Private Eye* is a long-standing team captain in the satirical BBC quiz *Have I Got News For You?*, whose format is echoed in *Mock the Week*, which typically uses a gang of stand-up comedians to make fun of the week's news. Although the satirical form has diversified and has established itself in the mainstream, its central joke remained the same. The new shows continued to ridicule *all* politicians and the business of politics generally. Satire, as Wagg argues (ibid.: 261), 'represent[s] nothing so much as a fear of politics, of confronting social issues, of "taking things too seriously"'. Despite the apparent endorsement of personal liberty in the satire, there were strong elements of homophobia (in *Private Eye*) and misogyny (in *Monty Python*, and now in *Mock the Week*, which rarely includes a female comedian).

This brief review of satire in the United Kingdom since the

1950s highlights several important characteristics of the genre, all of which represent continuity with previous incarnations of the form. The satirists tend to be men, highly educated and middle-class (like their predecessors: 'talented gentlemen'). If anything, the satire of the 1960s was even more a product of privilege. For Wagg it emerged 'from *within* the culture of the dominant social classes' (ibid.: 255; original emphasis). Hewison makes a similar point:

> *Private Eye* shows how the satire movement was a means of ventilating ideas rather than challenging society with some new complete blueprint. The magazine's attacks were very much in Establishment terms …. The nicknames, the humour, the prejudices meant that this language was only understood within the Establishment, to which *Private Eye* became a parasitic attachment.
>
> (Hewison, 1988: 34)

The social origins of the satirists established their political perspective.

Because UK satire is marked by its disdain for politics, all politicians are seen as arrogant in their claim to know better, and hypocritical in their pretence to *be* better, than their fellow citizens. Compounding this view of politicians is a deep suspicion of the underlying assumptions of politics: the idea that there are ways of changing the course of events. For the satirist, there is no order, only chaos, a chaos that is bred in a world moved by individual greed and pride. Such a vision sees all attempts to improve society as deluded folly. This is a perspective that is necessarily antidemocratic and reactionary, and it takes sustenance from a moral perspective which treats all deviation from narrowly prescribed norms as ripe for mockery and condemnation. It is this which legitimizes the satirists' relish in reporting adultery and homosexuality, in their assumption that all actions, however worthy, are motivated by either stupidity or self-interest. This view of politics appears to occupy a territory between populism and elitism, and to issue from 'outside' (outside the elite, apart from the 'ordinary people'). This ideology of satire is, however, caught up in the apparent contradiction between the satirists' target and their social origins. Despite their vitriol and mockery, the satirists belong to the established order. But while a commentator like

Wagg sees this contradiction as invalidating the political force of the satirist's perspective, Griffin is more willing to recognize a positive political value in satire. Like Wagg, he acknowledges that satire is implicated in the system which it seeks to mock. This, though, does not necessarily destroy its political effect. 'Like all works of literature or art,' Griffin writes (1994: 159), 'satire is inescapably a product of and therefore implicated in the social, political and economic culture that produced it.' Despite this, satire can still exercise political influence by 'unsettling our convictions and occasionally shattering our illusions by asking questions and raising doubts but not providing answers' (ibid.: 160).

This discussion of satire has so far focused on the United Kingdom, but the points that it makes have a wider application. What the UK case study is intended to show is, first, that in thinking about the representation of politics in mass media, we need to look beyond the formally designated areas of news and current affairs and towards entertainment. Second, in looking at entertainment, we need to pay heed to the context that makes possible the satirical treatment of politics. Third, we need to note the processes and expressions that create the audiences and authors of the satire. And finally, we need to look closely at the values and attitudes contained within satire. These general points provide a framework for comparing and comprehending the satirical forms adopted in other times and places. So that it can be seen, for instance, how US television programmes, from *Rowan and Martin's Laugh-In* through to *Saturday Night Live* and *The Daily Show with Jon Stewart*, have shared with their British equivalents a mistrust of politicians, even if their view was that politicians are ineffectual rather than malign (Wagg, 1998: 258-63; Baym, 2005). What is worth noting, too, is that in the 1950s and 1960s US satire was not the product of the privileged WASP elite. Many of the key performers – Mort Sahl and Lenny Bruce, for example – were Jewish. Furthermore, US satire emerged, not against the benign torpor of the UK establishment, but against the fear and division created by the communist witch hunts (Carpenter, 2000: 99). The UK variant of satire can also be contrasted with the more politically radical (and sometimes more dangerous) satire that was circulated in the Soviet Union or Franco's Spain. Satirical writing has flourished in France (*Le canard enchaîné*) and in Germany (*Simplicissmus, Pardon,*

Titanic). But while there is evidence of variation, there is also evidence of homogeneity. Italian satire has followed the general pattern in its dominance by men and its mockery of all established forms of politics (Lumley, 2001). The format of *Have I Got News for You?* has been adopted by all the Scandinavian countries, as well as Germany and the Netherlands (Coleman et al, 2009a: 653).

One of the most obvious differences in the form taken by satire lies in the contrast between UK magazine and television satire and the satirical movies of Hollywood. The UK form of elite satire stands in stark contrast to the more populist form characteristic of the United States, as can be seen in such films as *Being There* (1979), *Mr Smith Goes to Washington* (1939), *Dave* (1993), *The American President* (1995) and *Head of State* (2003). Each of these films works by setting conventional political wisdom or practice against 'the ordinary person' or against 'common sense'. The immorality of politics is established in its contrast with the regular decencies of daily life. In comparison with elitist satire in the United Kingdom, these films mine a vein of populist satire and are the product of a very different political economy, not that of the BBC and Oxbridge, but Hollywood (Neve, 2000).

Where UK satire emanates from elite critiques directed at its own kind, a playing out of ruling-class rivalries, US satire (at least in its Hollywood guise) locates its politics in populist democracy. What Hollywood satire does (albeit in different styles and with different degrees of effectiveness) is to pit the intuitions and instincts of the commonplace against the presumptions and pretensions of the politicians and their aides. Everyday common sense is offered as a counterweight to the elite's being out-of-touch. The political ideals of the American Dream act as a counterpoint to the perceived reality. In a classic of the genre, *Mr Smith Goes to Washington* (directed by Frank Capra, 1939), Mr Smith (James Stewart) is given a tour of the Capitol, ending with a scene in which a child reads the Gettysburg Address to an old man. During the course of the film, Smith is educated in the wiles of congressional life and is given a harsh lesson in cynical politics. He rebels against this conventional wisdom and takes a stand against the bosses in the name of the ordinary people. One message of the film, according to Terry Christensen (1987: 47), is that 'good men, supported by the people, can fix things up'.

Forty years later, another Hollywood innocent delivered a similar message about political life in the United States. This time the messenger was Peter Sellers' Chance Gardiner in the film *Being There* (directed by Hal Ashby, 1979). Gardiner's banal homilies (taken from his knowledge of horticulture) are treated with veneration by the Washington establishment. It is another version of *The Emperor's New Clothes*, in which the audience is invited to laugh at the delusions and vanities of their leaders. To the extent that this theme dominates US satire, it represents politics as a kind of populist conservatism (as distinct from the elite conservatism of the UK variant). It insists on judging politicians in terms of their proximity to the ordinary citizen. *The American President* (directed by Rob Reiner, 1995) continues the tradition. The political integrity of the president (Michael Douglas) is measured by his willingness to act on the principles that govern private dealings. In *Primary Colors* (directed by Mike Nichols, 1998), based on the novel by the journalist Joe Klein and borrowing heavily from Bill Clinton's 1992 presidential campaign, the tension between the personal and political, between principle and pragmatism, is also explored. Despite its jaundiced view of the corrupting effects of politics, compared in the film to the fakery of professional wrestling, it nonetheless retains sympathy for the political idea of doing best by 'the folks'. *Head of State* (2003), directed by and starring Chris Rock, is another example of the innocent with the common touch who wins over the American people.

All these films, in their different ways, are defined by their evocation of populist solutions to American idealism, and by their opposition to the cynicism and deceit which are presented as the norm of politics. There is a tradition of films that deviates from this general line. It is to be found in the cynicism of a film like *Wag the Dog* (directed by Barry Levinson, 1997), which, according to Brian Neve (2000: 27), treats the White House as the source of 'total and untraceable' manipulation, or to Warren Beatty's *Bulworth* (1998), which expresses a profound disgust at an electoral system in hock to lobbyists and disdainful of the voters. This rival trend found its most wholehearted expression when the makers of the television cartoon *South Park* produced *Team America: World Police* (2004), which took aim at fundamentalist terrorists, politicians and Hollywood superstars, among many others. But even here, at its most cynical, the satire retains a grudging admiration for the wisdom and rectitude of the American people.

The populist tendency within US satire has, like its UK equivalent, distinct political implications. In satirizing political leadership, it forges a populist political identity for its audience. In the words of David Buxton:

> the ideology of populism, which was able to address social issues, distributes rights and wrongs while transcending class oppositions. ...The moral stigmatisation of the greed of individual members of the political and economic elite contained inherent melodrama, as well as integrating into the nation everyone who met elementary guidelines.
>
> (Buxton, 1990: 26–7)

Satire divides society into two: greedy, corrupt individuals and honourable, ordinary people.

So far, we have seen how the satirical representation of politics within popular entertainment bears upon the wider link between politics and mass media, extending beyond the narrow confines of news and current affairs. Our concern has been with the conditions under which satire emerges, the forms it takes and the interests it promotes. This involves thinking about not only the blurred boundary between politics and popular culture, but also the form of popular culture's politics. In looking at satire, we have been looking at the politics of comedy, at the ways in which jokes are expressions, not just of a sense of humour, but of a set of interests and values. Satire, though, is only one way of representing politics through entertainment. It is one example of a genre in which politics is, by definition, a central concern. It can be usefully compared with another such genre, the conspiracy film.

Politics as conspiracy

As Liesbet van Zoonen notes (2005: 113–14), while satire tends to portray politics as the product of incompetence and inadequacy, conspiracy films dwell upon deliberate scheming and deception. What conspiracy films suggest is that behind the appearance of democracy lies a reality in which everything is the result of the corrupt machinations of unaccountable and devious individuals or institutions. This is a worldview to be found, for example, in all the James Bond films, in Terry Gilliam's *Brazil* (1985), Michael Ritchie's *The Candidate* (1972) or in the Wachowski brothers' *The Matrix* (1999) and Michael Mann's *The Insider* (1999). In films like *Silkwood* (1983) and *The China Syndrome* (1979), the plot is built upon the idea of a conspiracy by the nuclear power industry to pervert the course of justice. In the 1960s, with Len Deighton's *The Ipcress File* or John Le Carre's *The Spy Who Came in from the Cold*, and the countless espionage movies that followed them, the conspiracy was organized by the Soviet bloc and their double agents in the Secret Service; in later years, domestic governments, and their agents (M15, CIA etc.) were the conspirators (as in films about Northern Ireland such as Ken Loach's *Hidden Agenda*, 1990, or about Latin America, such as *Salvador*, 1986, and most recently in the trilogy of *Bourne* movies with Matt Damon, in which the prime conspirator is the CIA itself). By contrast, in *Enemy of the State* (1998), starring Will Smith, or *Michael Clayton* (2007), starring George Clooney, the conspiracy emerges from secretive corporations.

The conspirators may vary, they may be power-crazed megalomaniacs or CIA chiefs, mafia bosses or Soviet spies, evil corporations or rogue governments, but the story is roughly the same. The plot is driven by the rivalry between subterranean forces and the representatives of liberal democratic integrity. Though an element of paranoia may inform such views of the world, and though this form of storytelling may be very traditional (the gods conspire in Greek myths), the idea of a conspiracy is not simply a myth. In the 1950s, C. Wright Mills' *The Power Elite* (1956) provided a powerful, if widely challenged, case for the reality of conspiracy. Mills portrayed a world in which all key decisions were taken by a hidden elite. Such a view continues to circulate in the popular imagination: malign forces (bureaucrats, the mafia, global conglomerates) dictate to ordinary citizens and their representatives (Aaronovitch, 2009).

In the 1950s and 1960s, during the cold war, the conspirators were often, either explicitly or by implication, the KGB and their allies. One of the most frequently cited (and arguably one of the best) conspiracy films was *The Manchurian Candidate* (1962), directed by John Frankenheimer, and starring Laurence Harvey and Frank Sinatra. During the Korean War, Harvey is captured and brainwashed by agents of communism. He is programmed to become an assassin, and to respond to commands issued by his mother (Angela Lansbury). The film is a bitter portrait of power and politics, equally withering in its views of communist and liberal democratic politics. Frankenheimer creates an atmosphere of brooding, paranoid fear. No one is to be trusted; everyone works for someone else. A similarly unnerving sense of mistrust inhabits Francis Ford Coppola's *The Conversation* (1974). In this film Harry Caul, a private detective, played by Gene Hackman, eavesdrops on a couple who, it transpires, murder a businessman (the same businessman who has hired Hackman). It is never quite clear what and who lies behind the events that Hackman witnesses, but the film foreshadows the emergence of a surveillance state in which 'we' are all being monitored by 'them' (a theme that receives a further update in *Enemy of the State* (1998) where multiple conspirators exploit a vast array of modern communications technologies).

The Conversation is unusual in its portrayal of an anonymous conspiracy. Hollywood prefers to identify the guilty people. In the 1970s, the US's own agents became the conspirators. In Alan J. Pakula's *The Parallax View* (1974), it was a shady business corporation; in *Three Days of the Condor* (directed by Sidney Pollack, 1975) it was the CIA; and in *All the President's Men* (directed by Alan J. Pakula, 1976) it was an alliance of the CIA and the White House. Coppola's *The Godfather* trilogy can also be read as a variant of the conspiracy movie. In Oliver's Stone's *JFK* (1991), the assassination of President Kennedy is attributed to the collective conspiratorial efforts of the White House, the CIA, the FBI, the KGB and several others. All these films suggest that the malign forces have to be challenged, but the only hope they offer for this challenge lies with the ingenuity, daring and integrity of the individual. Those formally responsible for fighting evil – the politicians – are in its pay or in some way morally compromised. Popular, collective action rarely appears as a solution. The people tend to be the dupes or victims of the conspiracy. In short, the conspiracy movie frames politics as the struggle between individual integrity, dark forces and popular indifference or impotence. Like satire, its view of politics is a cynical one, in which there is little hope for democracy. Or as Michael Rogin (1987: 245) says of the cold war films, 'They depoliticize politics by blaming subversion on personal influence.' In her detailed analysis of the politics of *The Manchurian Candidate*, Susan Carruthers (1998: 84) reaches a similar conclusion: the film 'refuses to accept the power of political ideas' and 'ultimately eschews politics'.

As with satire, the conspiracy film does not exhaust the ways in which politics is portrayed outside the realms occupied by news and current affairs. It is just another genre, whose conventions give rise to a particular view of politics. This is not to pre-empt the question of whether such portrayals make a difference to political attitudes and actions (see Chapter 4), except to say that, in talking about political influence, it cannot make sense to look only at news and current affairs as the possible sources of such effects. The key lies in how certain political ideologies are given space within entertainment, as within other areas of mass media. The conspiracy movie creates a world of hidden manipulators, just as satire creates a world of vain, stupid and corrupt politicians. What they have in common is a mistrust of politics itself.

Entertainment as propaganda

Satire and conspiracy films articulate a cynical account of the world, but entertainment can represent other perspectives. It can, for example, be used to promote political causes or to deliver state propaganda. Through its powers as cultural censor or sponsor, the state can try to create art that promotes its own interests and thwarts its enemy's ambitions. Before the collapse of the Soviet bloc, rock and jazz musicians were imprisoned or banned from playing music which the authorities feared would fuel criticism and dissent, while other, 'approved' forms of music were encouraged (Starr, 1983; Street, 1986). In contemporary China, popular culture is not only censored in the service of state ideology, it is also promoted to the same end. There are films, songs and television shows, all designed to deliver a particular message (Lynch, 1999; Tunstall, 2008). Such practices are not, however, the exclusive preserve of communist regimes. Recent research has revealed how the CIA deliberately created certain cultural forums (the magazine *Commentary*, for instance) to promote US interests (Stonor Saunders, 2000). The FBI maintained constant surveillance of John Lennon when, following the break-up of the Beatles, he lived in the States. FBI officers sat at his concerts laboriously (and ludicrously) transcribing the words of his songs and his banter at concerts (Wiener, 1984). The birth of rock'n'roll in the 1950s inspired a moral panic and attempts to suppress it, just as did punk music in the 1970s. State broadcasters across the globe have refused to play certain records for fear of the sentiments they represent. By no means all of this censorship is inspired by a fear of political dissent – much is occasioned by fear of sex and sexuality – but the point is that forms of entertainment are promoted or suppressed because of the kind of attitudes and habits they are deemed to represent or encourage (Cloonan, 1996).

The state's role in controlling and using entertainment has been matched by the desire of musicians and other entertainers to deploy their talents to make political points or to organize political campaigns. There is a long tradition of songwriters who have engaged directly with politics: Woody Guthrie, Bob Dylan, Phil Ochs, Tracy Chapman, Curtis Mayfield, John Lennon, Sting, Joan Baez, Bono, Bob Marley, Public Enemy, Asian Dub Foundation, Rage Against the Machine, Kanye West, Mos Def and Green Day. In doing so, they have drawn upon various genres: folk, blues, gospel, country, pop and hip hop. Pop musicians have also spearheaded political campaigns. Bruce Springsteen toured for Amnesty International; Sting campaigned to save the rainforests; Bob Geldof inspired the Band Aid/Live Aid fund-raising efforts for the victims of famine in Ethiopia; and, with Geldof, Bono has been in the forefront of campaigns to end third world debt. The point is not to offer, were it possible, an exhaustive list. Rather it is to highlight the fact that politics can be as explicit a part of entertainment as it is of news and current affairs. Furthermore, this phenomenon does not end just with those cases of entertainment that are deliberately used for political effect (whether by states or by artists).

The harnessing of popular culture to the political interests of performers and states is only one way in which it becomes a vehicle for propaganda. There is a tradition of thought, initiated in the early twentieth century by the Frankfurt School (Held, 1980), and represented in the writing of Theodor Adorno, Max Horkheimer and Herbert Marcuse, which sees all popular culture, or rather all the products of a culture industry, as propaganda for capitalism and for the attitudes of subservience and compliance required by it. From this perspective, shows like *American Idol* or *The X Factor* become not just means of producing commercially successful popular music, but platforms for reinforcing narrowly conceived notions of talent and ambition, and a culture that is conservative in every respect. The rise, too, of 'reality television', especially in its globally franchised form as *Big Brother*, fits within this same perspective. Reality television, and its attendant celebrity culture, becomes a device for policing popular ambitions and aspirations in such a way as to minimize the risk of dissent and resistance (Riegart, 2007; van Zoonen, 2005).

The politics of identity: from soap opera to sport

Soap operas, reality television, situation comedies and game shows – the staple diet of TV entertainment – are typically assigned to the category of 'escapism'. This sometimes leads to the presumption that they are devoid of political content, but such an assumption is mistaken: soaps, and indeed television entertainment more generally, are integral parts of a society's political culture. Hugh O'Donnell (1999: 226), for instance, argues that soap operas 'remain unique indexes of the societies in which they are produced', and that they actively embody the principles of social democracy, through their emphasis on solidarity, on concern for others, on defence of rights and on compromise and cooperation. Others writers have also invested soap operas with political significance, but drawn less benign conclusions about the character of their politics. Roger Silverstone wrote of soap opera's politics as:

> politics in and of the suburb is still, mostly, a domestic politics of self-interest, conformity and exclusion undertaken within political structures which are, mostly, barely recognised, let alone challenged. It is a politics of anxiety. It is a politics of defence.
>
> (Silverstone, 1994: 77)

It is noticeable, for instance, that the world created by a soap opera like *EastEnders* is served only by small, local industries; there is neither sight nor sound of multinational business or global franchises. And, for Paul Cantor (2001), the world of *The Simpsons* conforms almost exactly to that of the American Dream, for all the cartoon's apparent subversiveness.

These different accounts of the politics of soap operas or cartoons can themselves be contrasted with the politics of another TV genre, the game show. Gary Whannel (1992) treats the game show as a metaphor for the social order: both are based on a quasi-meritocratic competition between 'ordinary people' for success that is measurable in material terms. *Who Wants to be a Millionaire?* is a typical example of the game show's proto-capitalist ethos. Whannel (ibid.: 200) writes: 'Game shows carry no polemic for a particular form of education, but they do offer a set of messages about the relation between ordinary people, knowledge and material reward.' The film *Slumdog Millionaire* (2008) went some way in exploring the politics of such quiz shows. In the same way, we can read distinct social messages into the ruthless Social Darwinism of *The Weakest Link* or the indulgent superstitions of *Deal or No Deal*.

One of the key features of popular entertainment is the way it operates across the boundaries between the public and the private, thereby 'domesticating' politics, particularly through its emphasis on the family. For Tania Modleski, the essence of the soap opera, whether *Dallas* or *Neighbours*, lies with its propagation of ideas which assert the value of the family:

> It is important to recognize that soap operas serve to affirm the primacy of the family, not by representing an ideal family, but by portraying a family in constant turmoil and appealing to the spectator to be understanding and tolerant of the many evils that go on within that family.
>
> (Modleski, 1987: 268)

This domestic focus is what engages the audience and organizes their responses. Christine Geraghty (1992: 139) writes of the role of family life in soaps: 'The audience [is] invited to identify with these families and to see their struggles towards family unity as a realistic reflection of the difficulties which face families in the audience.' The identities constituted through soaps, argues Geraghty, emerge through the dynamics of family relationships. Issues of sexuality – especially of gay men and lesbians – are dramatized through the family rather than through social movements organized around sexual politics, as are issues of ethnic and racialized identity (Gray, 2005).

The negotiation of identity in soaps, and their domestic politics, can be contrasted with the politics of another TV genre, the situation comedy (Mills, 2005). Mick Bowes (1990: 129) argues that the genre embodies a different ideology from that found in soaps. Where the soap opera has a developing, progressive story line, the situation comedy always returns its characters to the position in which they found themselves at the beginning of the show. However, to see situation comedies as necessarily conservative is, argues Bowes, a mistake. He claims that situation comedies can and do deal with real sources of 'social unease', whether they be the constraints of class, of gender or of ethnicity, and that in dealing with these issues, they can treat them in a radical or conservative fashion (ibid.: 129–30). So, as he observes (ibid.: 133), situation comedies may revel in the triumph of the underdog, but set these achievements in 'small and badly run organizations'. Rarely do these power reversals take place in 'multinational corporations'. Humour is, by this account, highly politicized. This point provides schematic illustration in Trevor Griffiths' play *Comedians*, in which different kinds of joke are exposed as representing different points on the political spectrum, from jokes that reinforce negative stereotypes to jokes that try to undermine them. Just as music can be used as a weapon of the oppressed, so too can humour (see Littlewood and Pickering, 1998; Lockyer and Pickering, 2005; Wagg, 1998).

The politics of identity within situation comedy is explored in detail by Herman Gray (1995), who focuses upon the treatment of race within US mass entertainment. Gray is concerned with the ways in which 'blackness' is represented on television. He contends that, while these representations are necessarily contradictory and confused (there is rarely, if ever, a single unambiguous 'message'), they have typically been conservative. Situation comedies about African-American life have focused on individualist upward mobility and middle-class aspiration. 'Although blackness was explicitly marked in these shows [*The Jeffersons, Benson, Gimme a Break!*],' writes Gray (ibid.: 79), 'it was whiteness and its privileged status that remained unmarked and therefore hegemonic within television's discursive field of racial construction and representation.' In contrast, *The Cosby Show* signalled a new representation of black identity. This occurs because the Huxtable family is given an entirely different social location: 'The Huxtable family is universally appealing ... largely because it is a middle-class family that happens to be black' (ibid.: 80). With the Huxtables being made successful and rich, 'it was impossible simply to laugh at these characters and make their blackness an object of derision and fascination' (ibid.: 81). This strength was, though, matched by a weakness, a tendency to overlook the 'disparities and constraints' that faced many other African-Americans. What Gray says about the politics of *The Cosby Show* could also be applied to rap, where examples of ambiguous and contradictory political positions are plentiful, as they are in all cultural forms (George, 1999; Rose, 1994). This discussion parallels the earlier examination of the double-edged politics of satire, and while it cannot be resolved simply either, it serves to draw attention to the ways in which mass entertainment gives a forum to political questions of profound importance.

Just as soaps and other genres constitute identities of class, sexuality and race, so another identity and another politics is constituted through sport. Sport has immense cultural (and economic) importance, and as such it assumes considerable political significance. Sport plays a role in the creation of national identities and in marking out the boundaries that serve both to include and to exclude people. The way commentators construct a notion of 'us' and 'them' can reinforce jingoism. Mike Marqusee suggests that cricket, for example:

> proved the ideal vehicle for the national/imperial ideology which crystallized at the end of the nineteenth century .... Its transitional nature made it a peculiarly suitable vehicle for 'Englishness' in transition from the native heath to world dominance. As it spread through the empire, it provided the English with a global image of themselves.
>
> (Marqusee, 1994: 251)

In a similar vein, the Conservative politician Norman Tebbit devised a 'loyalty test' as part of his opposition to (a liberal) immigration policy. The test was to establish where you 'belonged', and this was revealed in the team you supported at international sporting occasions (ibid.: 137). The other side to this story tells how cricket is deeply implicated in the living out of post-colonial experience and in the assertion of new identities (Winder, 1999; Oborne, 2005).

Sport can also be used to reproduce a gendered division of labour. Sport is presented as 'masculine', as a space which women cannot occupy. Neil Blain and his colleagues write that:

> Sport is portrayed on television as a man's world where women's sport is treated as being of secondary importance. Women in sport are made sense of by continually attaching supposedly feminine connotations to their activity, or portraying them as crypto-men .... Both in production and content, football on television is a male dominated arena. The sexual division of labour is clearly articulated: men play, women watch.
>
> (Blain et al., 1993: 39)

Both sport itself and the rhetoric attached to it by the media serve to map out identities which in their turn fuel political thought and action.

In thinking about how sport, as with other forms of popular culture, is implicated in the constitution of political ideas and identities, we need always to bear in mind the process by which this culture is itself formed. Like popular music, sport is a major source of revenue and the object of a multimillion-pound empire. Indeed, in the last two decades major entertainment and media interests have transformed the availability and the character of sport across the globe. Media moguls from Kerry Packer to Rupert Murdoch have bought the rights to broadcast football, rugby union, cricket and so on (Cave and Crandall, 2001). This in turn has led to the transformation of the sports themselves, altering the access to them, control over them, and the meaning attributed to them. Sports teams have become part of the means by which media and other conglomerates wage economic war, and the teams' connections to their fan base and their locality are becoming ever more tenuous.

Conclusion

This chapter has looked at the way in which a view of politics is constituted through entertainment. How people see and experience politics is not confined to news and current affairs. It is part of almost all encounters with mass media. The form taken by politics in entertainment may be different in important ways from the form it assumes in news and current affairs, but this is no reason to ignore it. None of the foregoing discussion is intended to discount or deny the rewards which various forms of entertainment bring us. It is not meant to play down their capacity to give pleasure. Rather, it is to stress that this fun is not 'mindless'; it is not 'just a joke' or mere 'escapism'. It is to suggest that in thinking about the relationship between politics and mass media we need to look beyond the traditional corrals of news and current affairs, and to analyse the ways in which political values and the representation of politics are part of our daily pleasures. 'Politics' emerges in mass entertainment through the stories it tells, the jokes it makes and the motives it assumes. Margaret Thatcher once defended a comic who told a tasteless joke at a party rally: 'It is a pity if you cannot regard the remarks of a comedian as being exactly what they are: humour, and that is all' (*New Statesman*, 10 October 1997). This chapter has been an attempt to show that humour, and other forms of entertainment, cannot be dismissed so easily. Entertainment may be as important as traditional forms of political communication to the way we come to understand and react to our world. As Jeffrey Jones (2005: 27) has written: 'part of the process of making meaning of political and social realities will be located in the common sense narratives that television offers'. Such claims, and many of the others that we have so far encountered, rest upon the assumption that media influence us. It is to this issue that we now turn.

Chapter 4

Media Effects

So far our attention has been focused on media content and its politics. This has meant looking at the arguments about media bias, at the ways in which coverage of news frames a picture of 'politics', and at the political character of popular entertainment. These are clearly important topics in their own right, but for many commentators their significance derives from a more fundamental set of issues, which have to do with what the content does to us and to our world. Content matters, it is argued, only because it has an *effect*. 'Bias' is important precisely because of the further supposition that it blocks or distorts people's capacity to act as citizens, their ability to make political judgements and to act upon them. Bias serves relations of power which thwart democracy. In the same way, popular entertainment's engagement with politics matters because of how it shapes political values and images, which in turn influence perception and experience of the world.

It is, of course, widely assumed that mass media exercise influence. It is this thought that lies behind censorship of violent films or pornography, bans on cigarette advertising, complaints about unfair political coverage, and so on. It is this same assumption that underlies public outcries about, for example, the shootings of school students and staff at Columbine or Virginia Tech. Such incidents have prompted calls for more regulation of the violent films or computer games that are alleged to inspire the lone assassins. Accompanying these calls is often the testimony of 'experts' willing to argue that the killers learnt to shoot from playing video games. On a less dramatic scale, it is not uncommon to find other commentators who blame the media for undermining trust in government or for distorting the public's understanding of key political issues, whether the Iraq War or climate change or swine flu (Lloyd, 2004). In the United Kingdom, political leaders have blamed gangsta rap for the spread of gun crime, while one of the broadsheet papers reported

101

that 'Tabloid spleen blamed for attacks on traffic wardens' (*Guardian*, 7 June 2004). In the United States, there was the so-called '*Matrix* trial', where it was alleged that the killer had been influenced by the Hollywood film. In all these cases, the presiding idea is that media output influence media consumers. So, we might suppose, media reporting of the threat of climate change or other global threats leads automatically to a general fear of its consequences and a willingness to act to prevent it. But research by Travis Ridout and his colleagues (2008) suggest that, in the United States at least, the story of media impact is a great deal more complicated than this.

The first half of this chapter is concerned with research into the political effects of mass media, particularly as it relates to voting behaviour and to the behaviour of political elites. The second half broadens the discussion by suggesting that 'political effects' should not be analysed in isolation. The tendency to focus on particular media texts (news and current affairs) and particular political effects (voting and political agendas) provides too narrow a perspective. Instead, we need to look at other texts (at entertainment as well as at information) and at other forms of political expression (for example, political identities and emotions), setting both in the context of the mundane habits and practices that organize viewing and reading. This broader perspective is provided by insights generated by research from many fields, including psychology and cultural studies, and the thrust of this chapter is that political analysis of the media needs to draw upon these related disciplines.

To gain a sense of this broader perspective, consider a famous incident from US broadcasting history. In 1938, a US radio station transmitted a report that the Martians had landed. Some listeners panicked, and started to flee their homes. The report was, in fact, part of a dramatisation of H. G. Wells' *The War of the Worlds*. The programme's creator, Orson Welles, deliberately gave the broadcast the sound of a real event. What seemed to be a regular music show was interrupted suddenly by an announcer who took the audience straight to a terrified news reporter. The journalist told of an alien landing. Every effort was made to imitate a genuine news broadcast. The programme created a mood of panic and confusion, of momentous events happening – live, on air. *The War of the Worlds* evoked the same sense of news unfolding that accompanied the attack on the Twin Towers in

2001; only on this occasion the story was about an invasion from outer space.

That people believed that there had been an alien landing was taken by some observers to be proof of the power of mass media. For them, the panicking listeners were evidence that modern society was a 'mass society' in which new forms of communication could be used to manipulate and control whole populations. Mass society was characterized by the breaking-up of traditional ties of family and community. Small groups and traditional networks were being replaced by the amorphous crowd. Modern production techniques created a plethora of uniform goods for a mass market. The technologies of radio and cinema created vast audiences for the same product. Without the old connections and values in place, the mass could easily be herded like a flock of a sheep. In the 1940s, this argument was taken up by writers across the political spectrum, from the Marxists of the Frankfurt School (Adorno and Horkheimer, 1979) to Austrian economists like Joseph Schumpeter (1976). The reaction to *The War of the Worlds* was one illustration of the mass society thesis; the idolizing of Hollywood stars was another; and the power of modern tyrants like Stalin and Hitler was a further terrifying instance. Certainly, the idea that people could be persuaded to believe that Martians had landed does seem to confirm the persuasive power of mass media. Such power is not simply a thing of the past. In 1998, the New York art world was temporarily persuaded to believe in the existence of an artist who had, in fact, never lived. Critics and connoisseurs feigned knowledge of Nat Tate, an artist who inhabited only the imagination of the novelist William Boyd (BBC News Online, 7 April 1998). If people can be persuaded to believe in an alien invasion or a nonexistent artist, how much easier is it for them to be persuaded to vote for one party or another, or to adopt one ideology or another? Mass irrational behaviour is not a thing of the past. One of the most chilling features of modern society is the reported behaviour of people who, on seeing a potentially suicidal person standing on the roof of a tall building, will shout abuse and encourage them to jump (Surowiecki, 2004: 256–8). As individuals, it is unlikely that anyone would behave like this; but as part of crowd, some of them do.

It is, of course, not this simple. The appearance of media power and mass manipulation may not reflect reality. Even the example of *The War of the Worlds* is open to other interpretations. When it was broadcast, radio was in its infancy, but it had established itself as an authoritative source of information, and people had begun to rely upon it, to believe it. What they lacked was the sophistication needed to separate the parody from the real thing, to tell irony from authenticity. They trusted the radio, and this trust was encouraged by responsible news reporting and by the absence of spoof broadcasts. Their faith was exploited by Welles, who borrowed the rhetoric of the news to create his drama. To this extent, they had good reason to believe what they heard. Talk about life on Mars had also acquired a certain (temporary) scientific credibility, so the plot was not purely a case of science fiction. Added to this, there was also cause to fear invasion, albeit not from another planet. In 1938, the Nazis were mobilizing in Europe, giving cause to a very real fear, just as others were fuelling anxiety at alleged communist infiltration of the United States. There was a climate of anxiety that made US listeners very susceptible to the suggestions contained in *The War of the Worlds*. It is this focus on the context in which people engage with mass media that adds a further dimension to the way we think about 'influence'.

However we interpret the case of *The War of the Worlds*, it should make us wary of quick and easy judgements about the effects of mass media. It may *look* as if media representations of violence in films or video games inspire real-life murders, or that press coverage of health scares produces panic behaviour, or that biased political coverage produces election victories for particular parties, but any such correlation needs to be underpinned by a theory which connects the two, that pushes the correlation beyond coincidence into causality. The films and games and media coverage may, after all, *reflect* a set of actions and opinions rather than create them. For every confident claim that there is a clear and proven connection between screen and real violence, there are equally trenchant claims that 'there is no proved causal link between representations of violence on television and violent behaviour' (Cumberbatch, 1998: 272; see also Barker and Petley, 2001). And just as there is this debate about the effects of violence, so there is an equivalent debate about the effects of media on political behaviour. One famous example of this is the suggestion that US media coverage of the Vietnam War was responsible for the decline in popular support for US involvement. This widely held view is, though, equally widely disputed, by those who challenge both the assumed nature of the coverage (it was not totally negative) and the actual effect of television, when compared with other sources of influence, on audiences' perceptions (Carruthers, 2000: 146–53).

Here is one last example of media effects, which, as with the other cases, yields rather ambiguous conclusions. In 1960, John F. Kennedy and Richard Nixon were running for the US presidency and appeared together in a broadcast debate that was carried by both television and radio. Viewers who watched the debate on television felt that Kennedy had won. Listeners who heard the same debate on radio thought that Nixon had won. This apparent discrepancy has been explained by the fact that Kennedy made particular use of the opportunities offered by television. He wore a dark suit that stood out against the studio background; Nixon wore a pale one that blended with his surroundings. Kennedy wore make-up that disguised perspiration; Nixon did not, and sweat appeared on his upper lip. Kennedy stood at ease at the lectern; Nixon had a limp, and looked uncomfortable. The effect of all of this was to make Kennedy look better, and to win over the viewers as a result, irrespective of what he actually said. Certainly, it seems that the debate provided a test of the power of media, or at least the power of images, to affect people. James Druckman (2003), writing many years later, contends that the Kennedy–Nixon debate did indeed demonstrate the power of media images to affect citizens. Drawing on experimental tests, he concludes (ibid.: 569): 'television images matter – they prime people to rely more on personality perceptions when evaluating candidates, which, in turn, can affect overall evaluations'. Druckman may well be right, but we need to be careful of assuming that the results generated by experiments apply to behaviour outside the laboratory. It is time to look more closely at the ideas and evidence used in discussion of the mass media's political influence.

Seeing is believing?

If people do not believe what they see, hear and read, it is hard to understand how the contents of mass media can influence them. If we find something incredible or the source untrustworthy, we will tend to discount them – except even this intuition is not quite as robust as it might appear. When in *Goldeneye* (1995) James Bond performs some entirely impossible stunt (like freefalling to catch a pilotless plane, climbing inside and flying to safety), we do not automatically say 'This is ridiculous' and walk out of the movie. We are prepared to believe it: 'prepared' by the context (the habits of cinema-going), by our expectations (marketing hype and genre knowledge) and by the skills of the film-maker (who shapes the way we watch). 'Belief' is, in this sense, a product of a complex process, a process that does not, it should be emphasized, always succeed (Sanders, 2009: 236–7). Films fail when the impossible is 'unbelievable'. Credibility is not simply a matter of 'truth' but of the conventions of believability within a particular genre. The conditions for credibility, and the implications of it, differ according to genre. It is important to start, therefore, with the way credibility attaches to newspapers and news broadcasting. It is not just a fact of these forms of communication, as we saw in Chapter 2.

Across different time periods, different countries and different media the degree of credibility varies. Where in the United Kingdom, the broadcaster tends to outstrip the newspaper in the credibility stakes, in France and Germany it is neck-and-neck, the difference being that in France all sources are mistrusted, whereas in Germany they are all generally trusted (Kiousis, 2001; Kohring and Matthes, 2007). As regards the United States, Andrew Kohut and Robert Toth (1998) point to the variations in credibility between television and the press, and between different papers and channels. In doing so, they also note changes over time in the 'believability' of outlets like *USA Today* and *ABC News*. According to one UK survey, programmes about real-life crimes are given greater credence than news programmes, and party political broadcasts are treated with more respect than the *Sun* (Barnett, 1993). Over time, journalists have tended to lose people's trust, whereas judges have gained it. Journalists rank low in people's estimation, but not as low as politicians or senior EU officials (unless those journalists work for one of the red-top papers, in which case they are on a par with estate agents) (Sanders, 2009: 36–7). Credibility is a product of history, style and practice. It is also a product of prejudice. In the 1990s, Ralph Negrine (1994: 2–3) noted that people's belief in what they read or see varies according to the media they consume. Readers of broadsheet papers trust them, and rely less upon television, whereas readers of the tabloid press treat their papers with scepticism and depend upon television for their news. More recently, we have seen a general decline in trust in all media (Jones, 2004). For McQuail (1992: 209–10) such trends have less to do with the 'factuality' of the news, and more to do with the perception of 'impartiality' of the source. The implication of this is that evidence of bias or framing is not in itself proof of influence; other factors are in play.

Under the influence?

Evidence for the political effects of mass media does not refer to a single thing. Researchers distinguish, for example, between effects on voting and effects on perceptions; between priming effects and agenda effects (Davis, 2007; Norris, 1996). They distinguish between the effects of broadcasting and the effects of print media. And they distinguish between mass effects and elite effects. In other words, it is possible to claim that the media affect the way people think about politics or a politician, without necessarily determining how they vote. Equally, what we read may influence us more profoundly than what we see. Or it may be that elites are dramatically influenced by their media consumption, while the rest of us are largely unmoved. In a similar vein, there are different ways in which effects may be experienced. It may be that our views or our vote are reinforced by our media encounters; alternatively, the media may convert us from our previous disposition, or it may create a new set of preferences (Harrop, 1986). In short, we need to be wary of simple generalizations about 'influence'. It is important to establish what sort of influence we are talking about.

We should not expect straightforward answers. A moment's reflection will indicate how technically difficult it is to prove a political effect. The first and most obvious problem is that of separating cause and effect. While there may be a clear correlation between newspaper reading habits and voting behaviour (Social Democrat voters reading Social Democrat-supporting papers; Christian Democrat voters reading Christian Democrat-supporting papers), this might seem like proof of the influence of right and left-leaning papers on their respective readerships. But of course, it could equally represent the ways in which left and right-leaning people *choose* their papers. This is what Kenneth Newton and Malcolm Brynin (2001) term the 'chicken and egg' problem in media effects analysis. How do we know what people would have done if they had not read one paper rather than another, especially given the many factors that contribute to voting behaviour? How do we distinguish between the effects of the many different potential sources of influence?

John Curtice and Holli Semetko (1994: 45–6) provide a succinct account of the dilemma that faces any attempt to identify the political effect of the press. If people's votes are the product of their socio-economic condition, the paper they read makes no difference. Given a survey of people's voting record, reading habits and their socio-economic background, we can investigate the connection between voting and reading practices by controlling for the socio-economic factors. If there is a correlation, we may be tempted to conclude that the papers exercise an influence over votes. But if we think that votes are not determined by socio-economic factors alone, if we think people's attitudes to particular issues are important in determining how they vote, it will be necessary to control for these attitudes in investigating the connection between the press and voting. The trouble here, as Curtice and Semetko point out (ibid.: 46), is that, while socio-economic conditions may be independent of newspaper readership (reading a conservative paper does not make you middle-class), it is quite conceivable that attitudes are a product of the papers people read. If this is so, controlling for attitudes will be to misrepresent the effect of papers. These problems, though considerable, are not insurmountable. Consider first research into press influence.

Press and voting behaviour

Much of the early research into the press's effects on voting behaviour tended to voice scepticism about the extent of its impact. The most that media did was to reinforce pre-existing views and values, with some slight increase in impact on those who were politically uncommitted (e.g. Blumler and Katz, 1974; Harrop, 1986). This minimal effect thesis, as Aeron Davis (2007: 152) points out, found an ally in later work in cultural studies on the 'active audience' (Ang, 1996), and it continued to feature in later research on the press's influence. John Curtice and Holli Semetko (1994), for example, asked whether the Conservative-dominated UK press influenced the result of the 1992 general election. The idea that it had was widely touted in the aftermath of the election, not least by the *Sun* ('It's the *Sun* wot won it,' trumpeted its headline). John Major did indeed benefit from a late swing to the Conservative Party, but Curtice and Semetko argue that this was not a product of the *Sun*'s influence. They claim that, in fact, support for the Conservatives actually *fell* among readers of Conservative-supporting tabloids. Nonetheless, Curtice and Semetko do argue that there are some longer-term effects by which Labour papers strengthen Labour Party support, and Conservative papers do the same for the Conservative Party. The papers also, they suggest, play some part in influencing perceptions of the parties, but again this effect delivers no competitive advantage to either side.

These conclusions are reached by monitoring change in political allegiance over time. The assumption is that 'if newspapers do influence readers' voting behaviour, then we should find that, other things being equal, people who regularly read a paper come increasingly to share its politics' (ibid.: 46). The evidence does indeed seem to suggest influence over time, but it is also consistent with a hypothesis that today people take more notice of their papers than they did in previous eras. To eliminate this latter possibility, Curtice and Semetko examine the results of panel surveys which map the behaviour of the same people over time. This allows them to separate the consistent readers from those who switch papers. This does reveal some limited newspaper effects over the long term, echoing the results of earlier research (Harrop, 1986). Their overall conclusion chimes with the scepticism that dominates much of this research: 'many electors still appear to view newspaper reports (and watch television news) through a partisan filter that enables them to ignore politically uncongenial messages' (ibid.: 56). For the most part, the research seems to indicate that people read papers whose prejudices coincide with their own, or that people interpret the news through their own pre-existing value systems. They find little or no support for the conventional assumption of many on the political left that a right-wing press confers a huge advantage upon right-wing parties or policies. Research into media effects on the 1997 UK general election (Norris et al., 1999: 168) reached similar conclusions: 'newspapers have but a limited influence on the voting behaviour of their readers'.

But this general scepticism is not shared by everyone. Early dissenting voices were Patrick Dunleavy and Chris Husbands (1985) who argued that the press had a decisive influence on political behaviour. They attacked the complacency, as they saw it, of those who claimed that papers do no more than reinforce pre-existing opinions, or that readers select messages according to their prejudices. Instead, Dunleavy and Husbands claimed that a right-wing press helped to create a Conservative majority. Their research method entailed controlling for those factors which would otherwise, in their view, determine voting habits. By doing this, they were able to isolate the impact of reading habits on similar placed groups. So that in the case of manual workers, their evidence seemed to show that voting habits varied according to the papers their respondents read. Manual workers who read a right-wing press were much more likely to vote for the Conservatives than those who were not subject to the same kind of media exposure (ibid.: 117). In other words, the press to which people are exposed significantly influences their political behaviour.

Studying a subsequent election, William Miller (1991) reached similar conclusions, but his approach and evidence were rather more nuanced. Miller suggested that media effects must be linked to media use, and that use varies. It varies with the kind of purposes people have in using the media (whether, for example, they use the media for information or for excitement) and it varies with the conditions in which the media are used (the social background of users). He also separated two sites of influence: perceptions (how politics seems) and attitudes (what people think about what they see). In his study, Miller argued that press effects were discernible in attitudes and in voting behaviour (ibid.: 164, 176, 192–3). To this extent, he supported Dunleavy and Husbands, albeit qualified by his emphasis on media *partisanship* – rather than the press as such – as the key variable.

More recent research has continued to challenge the 'minimal effect' claim. Like those before them, Newton and Brynin (2001) have sought to move beyond correlation to causation. Their chosen method has been to examine the voting behaviour of three groups of readers: those whose vote coincides with their paper's political leanings; those who vote against their paper's leanings; and those who read no paper at all. The first group, they hypothesized, might be expected to have their voting intentions reinforced; whereas the second group were 'cross-pressured' and may therefore be less inclined to follow their political instincts. Controlling for all the other factors that correlate with voting behaviour – gender, class, union membership, age and so on – Newton and Brynin were able to isolate the impact of paper reading on voting (2001: 273). They concluded that: 'Conservative identifiers reading a Conservative paper are more likely to vote Conservative than Conservative identifiers reading a Labour paper' (ibid.: 276). 'Newspapers', they wrote, 'do matter'; parties gain or lose according to the partisanship of the press (ibid.: 280). They are wary of exaggerating the extent to which newspapers impact on voting, but they do contend that, where there is a close election, the partisanship of the press may be decisive. Or to put it another way: had the press partisanship taken a different character, a different government would have been elected. Such a conclusion challenges the sceptics' position, and suggests that there is evidence for the view that the press influence voting behaviour.

To summarize: research into the political influence of the press leads to two very different conclusions. On the one side, there are those who see newspapers as having a modest long-term effect of limited political consequence. On the other side, there are those who see them as making a decisive difference, albeit at the margin. These conclusions are partly a consequence of different attempts to solve a methodological problem; they are also the consequence of different theories of voting behaviour and larger questions about the relationship between structure and agency. Dunleavy and Husbands' 'radical' model of voting behaviour sees political preferences and interests as the product of the combined effects of social location and ideology. They argue that there is no intrinsic or necessary reason why certain practices are associated with one or other side of the political divide: why, for example, 'home ownership' is any more a right-wing or left-wing position. These questions are settled by the management of perceptions, by the creation of a political 'common sense'. A key device in this process is the media. From within this general framework, mass media inevitably assume a greater importance than they do in frameworks that explain voting behaviour in terms of issue preference or party identification. In other words, the argument about media influence involves larger questions of social and political theory as well as the specifics of elections and media coverage.

Television and voting behaviour

While there is disagreement about the impact of the press, there is an apparent consensus about television, at least in respect of voting. There is a general reluctance to attribute substantial influence to television. While television is 'informative', argues Miller (1991: 198–9), it is 'much less persuasive' than the press. It contributes little to the formation of political judgements. Pippa Norris (1996) cites evidence from the British Election Survey which demonstrates a very limited 'TV effect'. Those who watched a lot of television were marginally more likely to vote for Labour or Conservative parties than those who watched little television. One possible reason for the limited effect is the lack of concentrated attention given to the medium. Despite television's obsession with election campaigns and their saturation coverage of them, viewers appear to take little notice of what is being offered (Electoral Commission, 2005; Wober et al., 1986).

We need to be wary of presenting these claims as universal truths about television's impact. It may be that they apply to particular forms or systems of broadcasting. In particular, this limited impact result may be a product of the constraints under which public service broadcasting operates. The requirement to display 'due impartiality' in the coverage of political controversy may produce a form of television that – in contrast to the partial press – does not engage people in political argument and judgement. Either coverage is 'objective' and one step removed from the controversy, or it is committed to reproducing undigested the messages emanating from the parties. Such television coverage tends to reinforce ideas of party unity and popularity, and to address agendas that do not necessarily coincide with the concerns uppermost in the minds of the voters (Miller, 1991). In other words, it may be that television's apparent lack of influence is not a feature of the medium generally, but of particular ways of organizing it. Certainly, experimental research on television coverage (Norris et al., 1999) has shown that people can be influenced by what they see: differently skewed news reports can produce different questionnaire responses from audiences. We might, therefore, expect television that is not constrained by public service obligations – such as Fox News in the United States or Silvio Berlusconi's channels in Italy – to have more influence. And indeed, there is evidence (Morris, 2005) that Fox News viewers tend to share its agenda and prejudices, and that the channel does deliver some benefit to the Republican party (DellaVigna and Kaplan, 2007).

Influence beyond the ballot box

So far our discussion of media's political influence has focused on the electoral process and voting behaviour, and what we have found is a field in which there is a great deal of uncertainty and contradiction. In such circumstances the only reasonable response might be to treat all claims with scepticism. Indeed there is much to be said for taking such a position, but it should not be linked automatically with the assumption that the media have no influence over politics. After all, voting is only one element of the political process, and as we have already noted there are other potential sites of influence: attitudes, information, perceptions and agendas. More than three decades ago, Colin Seymour-Ure warned of the danger of concentrating on voting behaviour to the exclusion of all else. He wrote:

> 'Do the mass media change votes?' Many studies have sought to answer that question: indeed it must be the most studied question of all about the political role of the media. But ... such an interpretation is not just unnecessarily narrow but even dangerous. For it invites the easy and superficial conclusion that if media exposure by the electorate, studied over a few weeks or months, has changed few votes, 'the effect of media on the election' is insignificant.
>
> (Seymour-Ure, 1974: 43)

While researchers have responded to such warnings by looking for long-term changes in voting behaviour, their focus has remained largely on the ballot box. But this leaves a great deal of politics unexamined. At the level of the individual, it leaves untouched other aspects of their relationship to politics. It tends to elide perceptions and action when, in fact, perceptions of politics, while influenced by media coverage, may not translate directly into a decision to vote for a leader or party (Miller, 1991).

This is a point made by John Zaller (1992) in his pathbreaking study, *The Nature and Origins of Mass Opinion*. Zaller (1992: 6) argues that 'every opinion is a marriage of information and predisposition', and that citizens form opinions through the interplay of their values and their understanding of the political context. The media is a key intermediary in this process. Zaller's picture of opinion formation is refreshing in its wariness of the evidence supplied by survey questionnaires – 'most people really aren't sure what their opinions are on most political matters' (ibid.: 76). He does not, as a result, look for consistency in popular opinion, but rather he seeks out the factors that shape its construction. His model (ibid.: 210) combines such elements as the intensity of the political communications, the attention paid to politics, political disposition and the accidental factors that affect the salience of an issue. Zaller's perspective provides for a much more nuanced and multidimensional account of the formation of popular opinion and the media's role in it.

Neil Gavin and David Sanders (2003) echo Zaller in their assertion that what matters are 'people's attitudes towards politicians, parties or policy', and that we need to analyse media effects upon these; it is not enough to look at the media's general political line. Instead, it is necessary to concentrate on 'the *content* of press coverage and newspaper reports' (Gavin and Sanders, 2003: 575; their emphasis). They develop a model in which the focus is upon how press coverage 'affects voters' economic expectations', where these expectations are the key intermediaries in determining political preferences (ibid.: 580). Their evidence supports their general hypothesis that it is not the political line of paper that matters, but the character of its coverage and the character of the paper – red-top tabloid papers, they observe, have little impact, when compared with other papers in the market (ibid.: 587–9). This shift of focus, away from the vote and towards the coverage, is to be found in other writers. Roderick Hart (1999: 2) argues, for example, that television's key political influence comes in the way it shapes viewers' *feelings*, the way they respond emotionally to politics; in particular, the cynical disdain that colours their attitude 'in the voting booth'. This echoes Robert Entman's (1997: 78; see also Entman and Herbst, 2001) complaint that, insofar as journalists 'reduce policy argument to a clash of simple slogans', they produce only 'emotional responses' in their audience, and not 'rational thought'. The result, according to Entman, is almost always to discourage informed active citizenship. These intuitions find substance in the work of Shanto Iyengar and others. Like Gavin and Sanders, they explore how the content of media shapes dispositions to politics. For them, the answer lies in the way media 'frames' the world (for example, Capella and Jamieson, 1997; Gamson and Modigliani, 1989; Gilliam et al., 1996).

Iyengar (1991) shows how in establishing particular frames, news reports shape people's political judgements of responsibility and blame. In later work on public perceptions of crime, Gilliam and others (1996: 19) show how 'racial imagery in the news triggered fear of crime and a willingness to hold black people responsible for crime'. Such responses were the result of 'a mere three-second exposure'. In defiance of the general scepticism about television's power to influence, Iyengar asserts confidently (1991: 2): 'the only area of political life in which the impact of television has been empirically established is public opinion'. Gamson and Modigliani (1989: 2) offer a rather more hesitant version, suggesting that media discourse and public opinion 'interact'. Either way, news coverage is seen to shape public agendas and form political preferences. Iyengar builds upon this assumption by exploring television's capacity – by way of framing – to influence the perceptions of the allocation of responsibility: who is to be blamed or praised. This research rests upon the idea that 'the primary factor that determines opinions concerning political issues is the assignment of responsibility for the issue in question' (Iyengar, 1991: 8). Where people are ignorant of, or distant from, a topic, media representations are crucial to the assignment of responsibility.

In assessing effects, Iyengar argues that coverage can be divided between that which frames news in 'episodic' terms (a concern with individual cases and events) and that which frames it 'thematically' (background and trends). It is the former which is the dominant media mode (ibid.: 14–16). Iyengar's research involved subjecting groups of viewers to different types of coverage and then assessing their perceptions afterwards. These perceptions were measured first by reference to the 'causal' links made: how events were explained (why crime or terrorism occurred) and second by reference to 'treatment': how crime or terrorism was to be curbed. On the basis of a series of such experiments, Iyengar (ibid.: 67) concluded 'that network news stories can affect how people attribute responsibility for poverty and racial inequality'; and furthermore that episodic framing of poverty led people to see responsibility as lying with the individual, and thematic framing as attributing responsibility to society. For Iyengar, the results demonstrated how the media affected public opinion. More recent research by Kees Aarts and Holli Semetko (2003) has added a further twist. They point out that the type of political framing to which audiences are subject may vary according to the type of television channel they watch. Where commercial broadcasting may produce cynicism, public service broadcasting promotes engagement.

Robert Entman (2003) has coined the phrase 'cascading activation' to capture the interplay between media framing and the formation of political views. His focus is upon the means by which dominant perceptions and challenges to them can, under particular circumstances, lead to shifts in political opinion. Like Zaller and others, Entman's approach suggests that 'media effects' need to be understood within a broader political and media context. The political influence of media is not, therefore, to be measured in the willingness to vote one way or another, but rather in terms of political disposition more generally. This argument places media at the centre of a process of political transformation, in which the argument moves away from the conventional coverage of politics – news and current affairs – to the whole realm of media content – factual and fictional.

What this new agenda of media research represents, in one sense, is a concern with what media enables people to *do*. It takes us back to the narratives of media history that Curran (2002) outlines in which media are held to have transformed the power of citizens and the character of societies. From this perspective, media provide resources and opportunities. They do not just give people information; they give them power (or deprive them of it). Less benignly, control over information and knowledge becomes the site of political struggle, and management of media and media content is the embodiment of power in its various dimensions (Lukes, 2005). As Norris (1996) shows, there is a direct correlation between people's knowledge of politics and their media resources. Political power is not, however, just a matter of knowledge and information. It is also about dispositions and opportunities, about such entities as trust and engagement. And it is media's impact on these that has captured many researchers' attention.

Key to this has been the work of Robert Putnam (1995; 2000). In his book *Bowling Alone*, he argues, among other things, that television has been responsible for a catastrophic decline in 'social capital', by which he means the networks, norms and trust that allow people to act together. Television, he argues, has been an agent of 'social disengagement', where newspapers are agents of civic responsibility. Putnam writes, 'each hour spent viewing television is associated with less social trust and less group membership, while each hour reading a newspaper is associated with more' (1995: 678). Television represents for Putnam a form of privatized leisure, and within this private world mistrust flourishes, deadening people's capacity to operate as citizens. 'Just as television privatizes our leisure time,' he contends (2000: 229), 'it also privatizes our civic activity, dampening our interactions with one another even more than it dampens individual political activities.' Watching television not only takes time away from other activities (the time-displacement effect), it also isolates people and then feeds them messages about a 'mean world' to which fatalism is the only reasonable response. For Putnam (ibid.: 236–7), watching television causes civic disengagement.

Not surprisingly, Putnam's bleak conclusions have been challenged (for an excellent summary of the debate, see Stolle and Hooghe, 2005). Pippa Norris (2000) has questioned Putnam's interpretation of the US data, arguing that it reveals a much more positive story about media effects, while Peter Hall (1999) has argued that Putnam's analysis does not apply to other national contexts. Jack McLeod and his colleagues (1999) distinguish between the press (significant) and television (limited) in their capacity to influence political participation. Other research has focused on the time-displacement effect, producing evidence both that it does (Besley, 2006; Hooghe, 2002; Couldry et al, 2007) and does not (Moy et al, 1999) generate disengagement. Research on the 'entertainment effect' (see Scott et al, forthcoming, for a summary) has produced similarly mixed results.

Markus Prior (2005), for example, suggests that those who watch political programmes are more politically knowledgeable and more likely to vote, while those who opt for entertainment are less knowledgeable and less likely to vote. Marc Hooghe (2002) argues that the entertainment effect varies with genre of programme (crime vs soap), and John Besley (2006) that the key lies in the prior political leanings of the viewer.

Moving beyond Putnam's particular claims, Diana Mutz and Byron Reeves (2005) argue, on the basis of experimental evidence, that media expressions of 'incivility' in political discourse do erode trust. This concern stems from the rise of a US television genre in which politics is covered in a more confrontational, less deferential, less civil fashion. The examples they have in mind are *The O'Reilly Factor, Meet the Press* and *Crossfire*. Their hypothesis is that it is the manner of political discourse, rather than its specific content, that affects levels of political trust. 'Uncivil political discourse', they conclude (Mutz and Reeves, 2005: 13), 'has detrimental effects on political trust, directed not just at the politician but at the institutions of politics themselves.'

These more dramatic, system-wide effects provide a much broader agenda for those interested in media effects. They are more inclusive both in the range of political activities and in the range of media influences that they consider. They also have in common a concern to connect the specifics of the media text to the behaviour being affected. Crucially, they seek – following Zaller – to put media's impact into the larger political context. This approach is evident too in an area of media effects research which has opened up more recently, and which has shifted the focus from mass behaviour to that of individuals and elites. This research has been concerned with how policy-makers and other key actors are influenced by media (see Helms, 2008, for an excellent summary).

Elite effects

The most familiar example of media influencing policy-makers is the so-called 'CNN effect', named after the global media outlet Cable News Network. The CNN effect represents the idea that coverage of foreign news, especially where humanitarian issues are pre-eminent, can have a direct impact on public policy and government agendas. It is typically associated with famine or conflict in Africa, and the West's response to these, but according to Eytan Gilboa (2005: 327), the first use of the expression 'the CNN effect' in the United States was in relation to the Gulf War of 1991. Whenever the term originated, the phenomenon to which it is applied is recognizable, and it is intuitively plausible. We are acutely aware of how events like the Indian Ocean tsunami of 2004 or the Haitian earthquake of 2010 provoked immediate responses from governments, all of whom appeared to take their cue from media reporting of the events. But while the idea of a 'CNN effect' has a degree of plausibility, we need to be wary of what it says about media's power and influence.

The most sustained analysis of the CNN effect is by Piers Robinson (2002). As he points out (ibid.: 12), many of the claims about the CNN effect have been 'untested and unsubstantiated', a challenge which he takes up. He does so by identifying two key variables: elite policy certainty and media framing. The first refers to the thought that the media's impact varies with the policy certainty and elite consensus about a course of action; the second refers to how the media present the issue – as something for which action is or is not required. These are not easy variables to define or measure, but they provide the basis of Robinson's theoretical model (ibid.: 31) and the framework for his research. His hypothesis is that the CNN effect may be discerned a) where there is a lack of consensus among the elite, b) where this is combined with policy uncertainty, and c) when the media offers critical coverage of existing policy. He refines his model further by distinguishing between types of CNN effect, separating that which strongly effects policy from that which merely creates the conditions for such an effect. He then examines a number of humanitarian case studies (Serbia, Rwanda, Somalia, Bosnia and Iraq) in an attempt to isolate and analyse the CNN effect (or its absence). These require detailed exploration of media coverage and policy-making. He concludes that there is evidence of a CNN effect in some cases, in line with the predictions of his model (ibid.: 117–21). He is, however, wary of sweeping generalizations. Much depends on the type of intervention involved as well as the media coverage and other policy factors (ibid.: 126). Again following the example set by Zaller, Robinson's research stands as a model of its kind: a systematic and theoretically informed attempt to identify media's political influence at the elite level. There is now an emerging literature on elite effects, including that on the way media agendas shape political agendas in European states (van Noije et al, 2008). A particularly interesting example is to be found in Aeron Davis's (2003, 2007) research into the media influence on elite behaviour within central government and the financial sector. Rather than deploying Robinson's analytical modelling, Davis uses extensive interview data to map the stimuli to which, for example, city traders respond. His conclusion is similar to Robinson's. The impact of media is itself mediated by many other factors, but this should not lead us to discount its role altogether. It is interesting to note that similar conclusions are being reached by researchers in economics (eg Shen, 2009).

Even as research into media effects becomes more sophisticated and nuanced, providing as it does so ever more substantive support for media effects, there remain those who voice deep scepticism about the extent of these effects. One such example is Kenneth Newton's (2006) critique of media influence research. His contention is that, relative to the other forces (class, religion, education) affecting people's thoughts and actions, the media represent a 'weak force'. 'The powers of the media are weak,' he writes, 'because they are often diluted, deflected or even destroyed by more powerful influences that mediate the media by intervening between them and their effects on society' (2006: 225). Newton's conclusion, however, is not only at odds with that of others' research, but even with his own (e.g. Newton and Brynin, 2001). Rather than scepticism, a more fruitful path to follow might be one in which media effects are more fully integrated into the wider study of social and political change.

Media consumption in context

It is important to view media consumption, and its impact, in context. Neither large-scale surveys nor detailed experiments nor interviews replicate or reflect the actual experience of viewing and reading. There is, however, a considerable literature on routine audience practices, much of it deriving from cultural studies, that addresses exactly this issue. This final part of the chapter draws attention to the possible implications of this work (and the arguments it has provoked) for future study of media's political influence. What cultural studies offers is not only an extended notion of politics, one that applies to the pleasures of popular culture, but also a way of complementing our understanding of how culture is consumed and what skills and resources are applied to this consumption, and hence to its place in shaping political views and experiences.

The first and most obvious debt to cultural studies is the idea that the source of any potential political influence cannot be confined to news and current affairs. Within cultural studies, it is widely assumed, if not always argued, that popular culture is political (see Chapter 3). This insight is less often acknowledged within political science accounts of media influence. There are exceptions (Jones, 2005; van Zoonen, 2005; Wober et al., 1986) which argue for the need to recognize the full range of programmes to which people are subject. It makes no sense, they suggest, to isolate the political programmes. It is rare, though, to find this injunction being acted upon, although there is one notable exception in Richard Merelman's (1991) comparative study of the relationship between popular culture and political culture. But even Merelman does not reflect at length on the ways in which popular culture and political culture are connected.

One aspect of this connection emerges in the way that political texts (whether deriving from news or from entertainment) are interpreted. The literature on the political effects tends to treat political information as unambiguous (hence the tendency to label papers as left-wing or right-wing) and the readers or viewers as consumers of it. But if the messages are confused and contradictory, and if the audience's or readership's reception is complex, then the idea of 'influence' needs to be rethought (Barker and Petley, 2001). Certainly, the idea that the media produce a stimulus to which action and attitudes are a response is frequently called into question. The media do not simply produce 'messages' or 'information' which are received and appropriated; rather they circulate symbols and signs which require interpretation. Gamson and Modigliani (1989: 2), for example, talk of 'individuals making sense ... . Individuals bring their own life histories, social interactions, and psychological predispositions to the process of constructing meaning.' Entman describes the 'interaction of texts and receivers' (1993: 53). This move owes much to arguments advanced by Stuart Hall, who suggests that the emphasis on interpretation:

> promises to dispel the lingering behaviourism which has dogged mass-media research for so long, especially in its approach to content. Though we know the television programme is not a behavioural input, like a tap on the knee, it seems to have been almost impossible for traditional researchers to conceptualise the communicative process without lapsing into one or other variant of lowflying behaviourism.
>
> (Hall, 1980: 131)

Seeing texts as containing many different and contradictory meanings makes it impossible to think of them as operating in a stimuli-response mode. Media content has to be understood as part of a process where 'common sense' is constructed through the readings that can be made of the images and language of the text. Meaning is not to be read simply as neutral information supporting a particular worldview. It also engages feelings and passions, a desire to preserve or change the world, a judgement of the way others behave and think. What is being appealed to is the idea that culture 'structures feelings' (Hart, 1999; Williams, 1981). This is a very different idea from that of 'influencing a vote'. Recent writing on social movements, for example, draws on this dimension of culture's role to show that popular music organizes the sentiments that tie people to a cause (Eyerman and Jamison, 1998).

A further twist needs to be given to the story of media influence. Just as texts are rarely unambiguous, so interpretation of them is contingent. The conditions under which they are read or seen affect the way they are understood. Audiences do not simply 'exist', nor do they just act as media-devouring machines. They have to be created and organized, and in the process they assume a particular relationship to what they see, hear and read. Public service broadcasters construct the audience as a 'public', as citizens with a variety of tastes and interests but united by a common interest that is captured in the injunction that they be 'informed, educated and entertained'. Commercial television, by contrast, constructs its viewers as 'consumers'. Programmes are designed to deliver a particular market to a set of products. The construction of audiences takes place, as we saw in Chapter 2, through the use of scheduling, modes of address, camera angles and so on. The implication of this approach is that the potential for, and the character of, media influence will vary with the type of audience (Aarts and Semetko, 2003). The other dimension to reception that cultural studies has emphasized is *how* people watch, listen or read. Viewing is a social process marked by a number of factors, including material circumstances, social class and gender. Observers note, for example, that men tend to take possession of the remote control; they also record that not only do women and men watch different things, they watch differently. Men tend to adopt a silent individualism, while women talk during programmes, turning viewing into a social event (Ang, 1996; Morley, 1986). The evidence about reading practices is less substantial, but even here it is possible to cast doubts on the image of the reader as a solitary actor ingesting text, from page to brain (Hermes and Stello, 2000; Radway, 1991). Nicholas Garnham, however, warns that, whatever the value of ethnographic insights into reading and viewing habits, it is important to begin with material circumstances: 'patterns of media consumption remain closely tied to income levels' (Garnham, 2000: 116).

In drawing attention to the conditions under which audiences operate, and the role of the media in creating their audiences, we have reinforced the need to move away from any neat connection between what is seen and its effects. The detailed observations of audience behaviour and circumstance, which emphasize the socio-economic context of reception, distract attention from what is being watched to what is going on around the television set. This shift of focus makes it hard to talk of television or the press as manipulative, but it still allows for the possibility that they may influence attitudes. The text (and the 'biases' it contains) may become less important, only one factor in the business of reception, but not irrelevant.

There is no longer a mechanical chain that links the text (and its 'messages') to a group of attentive readers or viewers. Instead we have a set of contingent features, the particular configuration of which invests any given text with different meanings. This, however, is not the only conclusion that can be drawn. The simple models of media cause and effect may no longer work, but it does not follow that we should assume that the media make no difference to the way people think and act. It just means that understanding this process involves recognizing the complexity of people's relationship to the many texts they receive, the ambiguity of them, and the conditions under which they are interpreted. As Garnham writes: 'media messages do affect our understanding of the world, but how we interpret or act upon that understanding is related to social position and experience' (2000: 125). We need to acknowledge the ways in which other (equally ambiguous or contradictory) information and experience shape watching or reading. Writing of his own experience of research into television audiences, David Morley argues:

> Media communications have to fit into the fields of personal and institutional communications in which the people who constitute the audience also exist as voters, housewives, workers, shoppers, parents, roller-skaters or soldiers. All those institutions, all those roles within which people are situated, produce messages which intersect with those of the media.
>
> (Morley, 1992: 77)

This conclusion derives, as John Corner (1995: 135) points out, from the fact that 'any "transmission" of meaning [is] a good deal more complicated than a straight linear flow'. Meaning is not a transparent feature of a text, but the product of interpretation by readers and viewers. To this extent, influence is intimately linked, for Corner, to interpretation, and interpretation is itself a product of contingent features of the experience of encountering a text. The immediate implication of this is that meanings are neither stable nor consistent, and for this reason, as Corner notes, 'the very fact of *variation* works against the idea of any uniform influence' (ibid.: 137, his emphasis). This is not, though, to rule out the idea of influence. After all, television producers work with the very purpose of creating effects – shock, laughter, sympathy – and audiences respond to them. The point is to acknowledge the *interaction* between the two, between the text and the cues it contains, and the audience's reading of, and response to, them.

The move away from a crude account of media 'effects' means that there needs to be careful reading of media texts to reveal the way politics is framed or encoded. The media are viewed, not as having a distinct influence which allows particular texts to generate particular effects, but rather as putting a set of ideas into circulation, as normalizing a set of practices and attitudes, representing 'common sense'. This common sense is not without its contradictions and ambiguities. It does not contain a straightforward message; it is open to competing interpretations, but it sets limits: it does not admit of an infinite range of readings. The capacity to deduce other interpretations is, however, dependent upon the capacity of the audience to offer an alternative account. Newspapers and broadcasters supply a resource – ideas, responses – out of which people fashion their view of the world. These resources are not supplied by news and current affairs alone; they are contained in the story lines of soap operas, in chart hits and Hollywood movies. Indeed, they are not confined to mass media. How these resources are used depends on the experiences and conditions that are brought to their reception.

This approach will not yield the patterns of influence that some political scientists seek. It will not be possible to attribute responsibility for electoral outcomes to particular papers. Nonetheless, it will be possible to provide a more coherent picture of the way in which the mass media feature in the daily routine of political thought and action. The mass media may not be the direct cause of specific votes and attitudes, but they may be responsible for legitimating the operation of political agendas and ideologies.

The media (and especially television) exercise influence through the way in which they create a picture of the world that is 'realistic', and as such alters our perceptions and actions in relation to it. This influence may take many forms. As Corner argues (ibid.: 141), the situation is not one in which a choice exists between 'influence or no influence'. Rather it is a matter of assessing the type of influence. For Corner, the crucial determinant of political influence, given the interpretive–interactive construction of meaning, is the 'knowledge environment': the resources we bring to bear on interpretation. Corner's position represents, as does Hall's, a rejection of strictly behaviourist notions of cause and effect, and a rejection of dominant ideology versions (with their focus on the monolithic power of the text). Emphasis on interpretation argues for recognition that texts have to be made to produce meaning, and influence is, therefore, an altogether more complex idea. This does not mean that it cannot be researched, as Greg Philo shows in *Seeing and Believing* (1990). Philo illustrates how different groups responded to news about the British miners' strike of 1984–85. Depending on their own knowledge, political positions and personal experience, viewers sometimes accepted and sometimes rejected the picture being offered by the media. Such evidence encourages talk of 'media influence', but shifts the focus away from the texts to the conditions of their circulation and reception. It chimes too with Robert Entman's (2003) notion of 'cascading activation'.

This brings us to a final point: the idea that people bring skills and resources to the judging of political texts. Viewers and readers differ in their capacity to interpret and make judgements of political communication. This is part of Philo's argument, but it is also made explicit in the work of others (see, for example, Bourdieu, 1986; Garnham, 2000: 138–64) who locate value judgement in the social conditions of the judges. Taste is a product of a social process, and people's capacity to exercise judgement is a product of the distribution of cultural capital: the authority given to certain voices and interests. Mapping this power is crucial to understanding people's ability to use, and to be used by, media representations of politics. In short, talk of media influence needs to run in conjunction with thoughts of powers and capacities.

The most impressive example of work that brings together the many dimensions of the relationship between media and politics is that of Nick Couldry and his colleagues (2007). Any summary here will fail to do justice to their book *Media Consumption and Public Engagement*. What it represents, however, is a theoretically subtle and empirically detailed – using a variety of research tools – account of the manifold ways in which media use relates to forms of participation in the public realm. They write:

> media consumption, along with demographics, trust, efficacy and social capital measures, contributes to public connection and political participation. Different media contribute in different ways ... Particularly, those engaged by the news are more likely to vote and to be interested in politics. So news engagement feeds into a virtuous circle: the already-engaged become more interested, engaged and active; however, the opposite 'vicious circle' is also indicated, with the unengaged becoming, less interested, less engaged and more inactive.
>
> (Couldry et al., 2007: 170)

These conclusions, and the way they are reached, mark the future of research into the vitally important question of media's political impact.

Conclusion

The implication of an interdisciplinary approach to 'media effects' is that this very term becomes more complex. The emphasis shifts to the conditions under which readers read and viewers view, and the multiple factors affect all aspects of these conditions. This is not just an argument for more ethnographical study of audiences, and of the way they watch and interpret television. It requires recognition of the wider context of those interpretations and the production of the texts and the audiences. 'Political communication studies', writes Sally Young and her colleagues (2007: 55), 'need to take into account various contexts ... as well as closely interrelated aspects of media production, media messages and media audiences.' Or as Philo argued:

> Messages are situated within political and cultural assumptions about what is normal and acceptable within the society. In news production, these include beliefs about hierarchies of access, about who has the right to speak, what are the key political institutions, and what is 'acceptable' behaviour.
> (Philo, 1990: 5)

This translates into an argument for looking more closely at the interests that organize the conditions of consumption. It means examining the political economy of the press and television, to see what interests are shaping the access and opportunities available to audiences, to see who and what is creating those audiences in the first place. If, as McQuail (1994: 381) argues, it is evident that the media have power, then the key questions become who gets to use or benefit from it, and who has access to media power? Even if questions remain about the nature of media power, McQuail is surely right that any analysis of it must refer to the political economy of mass media. To assume that media have no effect would be, in Garnham's more trenchant formulation, to let 'media producers off the hook of any responsibility for what they do' (2000: 109).

Part II

The Political Economy of Mass Media

Chapter 5

State Control and State Propaganda

When the question of the state's involvement in mass media arises, there is a strong temptation to portray this in one of two ways. Either the state is represented as dominating and deploying the media for its own ends, or the media are seen as embodying a rival source of power, challenging rather than succumbing to state power. And typically this simple divide is mapped onto that between dictatorships and democracies, with the latter being defined as those societies that enjoy a 'free press' and the former where there is a subservient one (Siebert et al., 1956). So when it was announced that the Olympics were to be held in China in 2008, the Western media's immediate response was to ask whether they would be curbed in the same way that the Chinese media were. In this moment, two stereotypes of state–media relations were evoked.

Such neat divides are, however, more complex than they might first appear. Let us take the case of China. Certainly, as Jeremy Tunstall (2008: 199) reports, it has a history of running a state media: 'For most (but not quite all) of his 27 years as China's Supreme Leader, Mao was in the position of the only media mogul in a nation-state that had only one media conglomerate.' But as Tunstall (2008: 208) goes on to observe, there have been major changes since Mao, with Chinese media now enjoying many of the economic freedoms associated with the West, albeit while still being subject to ideological control. In other words, state control has taken a new, even ambiguous, form. On the other hand, while Western media are typically seen to embody press freedom, there are many critics (Edwards and Cromwell, 2006; Herman and Chomsky, 1988; Herman and McChesney, 1997; Pilger, 2003) who argue that the much-vaunted freedoms of their media are more imagined than real. Such debates tend to revolve around a rather a fairly crudely demarcated distinction

between the free and the unfree. In fact, there are many variations on, and forms of, the state's relationship with media. This
chapter is an attempt to map and explore them.

Why is this important? The answer lies in two thoughts. The
first is that media matter – in their capacity to shape the world
and our understanding of it. The second is that it therefore
matters who is responsible for the incentives and interests that
determine what media do. One key source of these drivers is the
state because it is responsible for the rules (or the lack of them)
governing media behaviour, and because media may or may not
hold accountable the vast political powers that necessarily reside
with any state.

The organization Reporters Sans Frontières (Reporters without Borders) presents the relationship between the state (and its
allies) and the media in an annual league table, their Press
Freedom Index (http://www.rsf.org/). In this, some 160 nations
are ranked according to the level of press freedom that they
afford. From the Scandinavian countries at the top of the poll to
China and North Korea and Eritrea near the bottom, the Index
paints a graduated picture of state interference in the media. It is
not simply a matter of capitalism versus communism, or of dictatorship versus democracy, but of other factors – or the role of
religion, of political structure, of economic development.
Nonetheless, the RSF approach is itself vulnerable. The Index is
compiled, not on the basis of systematic analysis, but on questionnaires to journalists and other (typically campaigning)
organizations in the respective countries. Furthermore, the questions which are asked – about levels of freedom and censorship –
are not standardized, so we are never quite sure what is being
measured and compared.

In some countries, a journalist's main anxiety is that their
expenses claim will be queried. But in other parts of the world,
journalists may have much more to fear. What freedom means in
each case will be very different. We need only to think of Anna
Politkovskaya, the Russian investigative journalist who was
murdered, it was widely believed, because of her critical reports on
life in Vladimir Putin's Russia, and especially the war in Chechnya
(*Washington Post*, 15 October 2006). Other journalists, in Russia
and in China, have been sacked for allowing criticisms of the
government to appear in their papers (*Guardian*, 8 June 2007
and 7 September 2004; Hutton, 2008: 134–6). In Algeria,

journalists have risked their freedom and their lives to report stories. 'Journalists are assassinated or face government censorship,' according to Omar Belhouchet, an Algerian reporter, 'that's why we can't live a normal life' (*Guardian*, 20 July 1998). The journal *Index on Censorship*, like RSF, relentlessly documents their trials and tribulations. Even in more liberal regimes, such as Canada, the state retains the right to take government officials and journalists to court for the unlawful disclosure of secrets or for refusing to reveal sources (*European Journalism Forum*, 10 May 2010).

Systems of control

It is often supposed that, in a global economy, the nation state occupies only a peripheral role. But though the state's role and relationships may have changed with globalization, it still remains a crucial player (Freedman, 2008; Hesmondhalgh, 2007). Through the imposition of regulations and the granting of liberties, through law and policy, governments and their agents shape the practice of journalism and the role of media. The threat of imprisonment is just one example of the measures available to the state in its attempt to dictate the politics of mass media. Every state exercises some control over what journalists write or broadcast. Sometimes this control is blatant, sometimes it operates in more subtle ways, but all forms of public communication are subject to an element of regulation. For a while it may have seemed that the internet was an exception to this rule (and indeed there are those who continue to subscribe to this view), but there is increasing evidence of regulation here too (Castells, 2009). The German government has, for instance, been putting pressure on internet service providers to ban anti-Semitic sites, just as the Chinese government brokered deals with Google to exclude certain sites from its search facility. The Burmese, Indonesian and Malaysian governments have also tried – with varying degrees of success – to control political use of the internet. Elsewhere, the libel law has been used to close defamatory sites; and incitement laws have been used against anti-abortion sites. With time, we can expect more, not less, regulation of the web, as it becomes inextricably linked to state and commercial functions (Hindman, 2009). After all, like every other form of public communication, the internet is a part product of government policy (Winston, 1998: 321ff; Loader, 1997; Naughton, 2000). The internet may offer more freedom, more open access than other media forms, but this is quite different from saying that it is unregulated.

In his account of the development of the media system in Russia in the aftermath of the Soviet regime, Jonathan Becker (2004) invites a more subtle reading of the processes involved, albeit around a familiar dichotomy. The main contrast he draws is between democratic and non-democratic developments. The former translate the central principles of liberal democracy into the media system. That is, the media are required to support citizens' capacity to participate politically. This requires popular access, diversity of view and content, and the absence of state control or monopolistic private control (Becker, 2004: 145–6). Becker contrasts this with neo-authoritarian media systems, which he distinguishes from totalitarianism (ibid.: 149). Authoritarian systems tolerate a limited degree of pluralism, a tolerance that does not extend to support for opponents of the state. Under neo-authoritarianism, there is some autonomy for the state-run media and some element of private ownership, but other mechanisms are used to ensure the same basic outcome: control over what is seen and read. Rather than the direct use of censorship, content is controlled by economic means (tax incentives, subsidies) and broadly defined libel laws and the like (ibid.: 149). Such mechanisms, in conjunction with a compliant judiciary, produce the conditions for self-censorship. Furthermore, says Becker, neo-authoritarian regimes typically focus their controlling instincts on television as, from their perspective, it is the most important form of media. By contrast, they allow relative freedom to the press (ibid.: 150).

Under Gorbachev and Yeltsin, Becker argues (ibid.: 147–8), there was evidence of press freedom in Russia. Under Putin, however, the media's autonomy was curbed, in line with the president's desire for central control. This control was most evident in the coverage of elections in Russia, where opponents were marginalized or ignored, despite the rejection by Russia's constitutional court of Putin's attempt to increase control over electoral coverage (*Guardian*, 31 October 2003). Putin weakened the key broadcasting empire (Media-Most) in Russia through 'selective application of tax and criminal law' (Becker, 2004: 151). Newspapers were not immune. Critics were 'harassed by tax inspectors and property officials' (ibid.: 151). In short, Russia represents a case where state control of media does not derive from one particular political ideology and does not take one form. It may involve many forms and operate at many levels

A similar lesson might be drawn from Des Freedman's (2008) comparison of the state's media involvement in two apparently similar systems – at least in terms of their general political sympathies: the United States and the United Kingdom. While working with the same media technologies and while loyal to similar political creeds, their form of media regulation differ in significant ways. The key lies, for Freedman, in the divergence in their political values. States articulate particular values, and these values inform media policy, having an impact not just on the way media operate, but also on how the larger society operates. Ownership or content rules have consequences for what can be said and who can say it. By drawing attention to the differences in US and UK policy, Freedman highlights both the importance of media policy but also the room for manoeuvre that exists for states. With this in mind, this chapter moves away from 'systems' of control, to focus on specific forms of control (censorship, secrecy, propaganda and regulation), before returning to the general matter of how states differ and how they might be compared in their relationship with media.

Censorship

Censorship is the most obvious form of state control. When the Taliban ruled Afghanistan, they banned all television, cinema and music (Griffin, 2001). In Algeria, the government owns many of the printing houses upon which the press relies, and it has used 'the non-payment of debts' by those publishers as a reason for refusing to print particular editions or papers (*Index on Censorship*, 4, 1999: 128). As a result, Algeria's military leadership have caused newspapers to be raided and banned, and for editors and journalists to be imprisoned. Elsewhere – in Iran, Syria, Morocco – journalists have been imprisoned, tortured and murdered by those who dislike what they write or say or draw (even cartoonists are not safe). In Zimbabwe, under Robert Mugabe, the law has provided for a maximum of seven years' imprisonment for the publication of 'false' stories that are likely to cause 'fear, alarm or despondency among the public' (*Index on Censorship*, 2, 1999: 21–3; Kwenda, 2009). In China, apart from the attempt to control access to certain websites, journalists and editors receive 'daily instructions on what may or may not be reported' (Hutton, 2008: 134). Typically, we think of censorship as involving this kind of direct intervention, and typically such controls are associated with non-liberal regimes. These expectations accord with Czechoslovakia's announcement of an end to its censorship laws in 1990, following the collapse of the Soviet bloc (Budge and Newton, 1998: 148), and with Kuwait's system of pre-publication censorship for its newspapers. In such instances, the state's role as censor is explicit and evident. But censorship can take a variety of forms, and it does not necessarily require direct intervention. A year after introducing its system of pre-publication censorship in 1981, Kuwait repealed it. This did not, however, result in a free press. State censorship was replaced by a system of self-censorship that required journalists to abide by a strict code of conduct which included the injunctions not to 'damage national unity' or 'spread rumours'. Breaking the code could lead to suspension of a paper (Reporters Sans Frontières, 1993: 177–8).

Self-censorship may indeed prove to be a much more common, pervasive and insidious form of state control, albeit without the appearance of such control. It has been reported, for instance, that, following the reversion of Hong Kong to China, a system of self-censorship emerged, without the direct involvement of the Chinese state. Chin-Chuan Lee describes:

> the press's tendency to dodge political controversy, the hiring of pro-China staff to assume responsible posts, the shift of editorial line to accord with Beijing's policies, the redesign of space to reduce the paper's political overtone, the firing of high-risk contributors, the dissemination of writing guidelines on 'sensitive' stories, and the placing of sensitive stories in obscure positions.
>
> (Lee, 1998: 57)

While the Chinese government amended the Hong Kong Basic Law to include rules that could become the basis of censorship, these rules have not been acted upon. Rather changes in press behaviour have been achieved through a culture of fear, and through a system of rewards (and implicit punishments) run by the Chinese authorities. By favouring certain media outlets and certain individuals with gifts, honours and prized information, the Chinese government has created an incentive structure that results in self-censorship rather than externally imposed censorship (ibid.: 58). Chinese censorship works through the routine practice of journalism: 'the orthodox theory of journalism overtly defines the role of the media as the mouthpiece, or the "throat and tongue", of the party and the people' (Bin, 1998: 45). While these same pressures have continued to operate, the increasing marketization of media in Hong Kong (and mainland China) has opened up some space for press freedom (Lee et al., 2004). China, it should be added, is not the only country to induce self-censorship. Recalling his experience of editing newspapers in the Middle East, Jihad Khazen (1999: 87) observed: 'The most prevalent form of censorship is self-censorship. Sitting at my desk, I feel at times that I'm not so much covering the news as covering it up.'

Furthermore, censorship is not confined to non-liberal states, even where the constitution appears to prohibit it. In Russia, President Yeltsin was known to sack directors of national television stations, despite laws protecting freedom of speech (Budge and Newton, 1998: 151). In France, during the Fourth Republic, the state broadcasting station (RTF) shared its premises with the secretary of state for information, and RTF journalists were obliged to follow the instructions issued by the ministry (Chalaby, 1998: 45). In Italy, Silvio Berlusconi interfered directly in the conduct of the state broadcasting system (Ginsbourg, 2005; Hardy, 2008: 109–11). In the United Kingdom, during 'the troubles', coverage of Northern Ireland was strictly regulated. Examples range from a ban on the voices of Sinn Fein representatives, to changes to drama and documentaries about the province, to the banning of pop songs (Curtis and Jempson, 1993). State security has also provided an excuse for censorship. In the mid-1980s, a BBC television programme on the Zircon satellite was banned by the government on grounds of national security, and the broadcaster's offices were raided by the Special Branch, who removed the offending tapes (http://www.bbc.co.uk/historyofthebbc/resources/pressure/zircon.shtml).

To say that 'all states censor' is not the same as saying that all states censor equally. They do not. There are systems in which censorship is institutionalized and extensive, others where it is more covert or ad hoc. There are, as we have seen, many ways to censor. Spain long maintained, even after the fall of Franco, the practice of running a two-minute delay on all live broadcasts, so that offending moments could be excised (Vilches, 1996: 180). One-party states tend to impose tighter restrictions than those in which there is political competition (Besley, 2007: 134ff). And some states, like the United States, formally deny the right to censorship in their constitution, but, as critics of the regime argue (Herman and Chomsky, 1988), this still leaves open the possibility of de facto censorship through the way in which commercial and other interests affect what counts as 'news' and what priorities are accorded it. Gerald Sussman (1997: 136) lists examples of what he sees as US censorship: the failure to cover the testing of biological weapons and the failure to report CIA involvement in Haiti. While such examples may challenge Western complacency, they do not, in themselves, constitute examples of state *censorship*. They may more accurately be seen as a system of corporate *information management*. It is not a question of the state preventing publication of facts and images, rather of organizing the publication of other facts and images.

Freedman (2008: 122) illustrates this rather more elaborate formulation in his comparison of 'content regulation' in the United States and United Kingdom, where he begins by drawing attention to the different forms of content regulation: subsidizing 'good' content, shaping lines of command to ensure that the 'right' people control content, and suppressing the 'bad'. He then goes on to contrast the systems operating on either side of the Atlantic. In the United States, the application of the First Amendment seems to dispose it to a tolerance that is not prescribed in the United Kingdom. But on the other hand, the UK system is less susceptible to the influence of lobby groups who want to restrict content, which in the United States, suggests Freedman (2008: 134), has led to a 'chilling of free speech that is just as likely to suppress imaginative and creative material as it is to remove crude and genuinely offensive material from the airwaves'. He also points to the impact of legislation introduced to combat the threat of terrorism – the so-called 'war on terror' – on news reporting and media content more generally (ibid.: 139–41). Such laws appeal in large part to ideas of national security in order to justify the restraints they impose, and this takes us to the second dimension of state involvement in media content: secrecy.

Secrecy

Rather than censor what threatens to become public, liberal states prefer to keep things secret, so that the issue of a ban never arises. If journalists know nothing, there is little need to censor them. As with censorship, countries vary in their policing of secrecy. The United States enshrines freedom of speech in its constitution and operates a practice of freedom of information. In theory at least, this means that journalists can have access to any official information, provided that it does not breach national security. Press freedom in France is also protected in French law, allowing infringement only in cases of defamation, bad taste and national security. The United Kingdom, by contrast, has traditionally operated a highly secretive system, and reforms have been very slow in coming. Its Freedom of Information Act was not implemented until 2005 (www.direct. gov.uk; Cockerell et al., 1985; Ponting, 1985, 1986). Where in the United States, the principle is that information be made available, unless there is a good reason for it not to be released, in the United Kingdom, the presumption has tended to favour secrecy. Even as the United Kingdom has changed its laws on secrecy, partly as a result of incorporating the European Convention on Human Rights, it has remained cautious. The new freedom of information legislation still grants considerable powers of veto to government and other public bodies who wish to deny public access to 'sensitive' information. And even while the Freedom of Information Act has opened a window on state information, other restrictions still operate. Ministers, for example, still swear an oath of office by which they are bound to 'keep secret all matters committed and revealed' to them (Hennessy, 1990: 344ff). The coverage of war remains highly restricted, with the reporting of more recent wars proving almost as difficult for independent-minded journalists as did previous ones (Morrison and Tumber, 1988; Thussu and Freedman, 2003).

Official secrets legislation, such as the UK's Official Secrets Acts (1911, 1920 and 1989), enables states to control coverage.

They provide a right to prosecute those who leak government documents. Sarah Tisdall, a UK civil servant, was prosecuted and imprisoned for leaking details of the movement of US Cruise missiles (Ponting, 1985; see also Leigh, 1979). An aura of secrecy is further induced by other conventions and restrictions, one example of which is the Osmotherly Rules. These are the rules that guide release of information by civil servants to Parliament. Such information, it might be supposed, is crucial to the operation of democratic accountability and to the ideal of parliamentary sovereignty. However, the purpose of the Osmotherly Rules is to 'avoid the risk of publication', a phrase redolent of the UK political establishment's attitude to the media and openness (Hennessy, 1990: 361–3).

The UK system may be peculiarly sensitive to breaches of secrecy, but all states, however liberal, have equivalent laws and other regulatory devices which are designed to restrict the flow of information. Australia, like the United Kingdom, operates a rule which prevents access to cabinet papers, the documentary evidence of government decisions and discussions, for 30 years (Schultz, 1998: 82). There is, though, a clear difference between states that operate on a principle of freedom of information and those that do not. In the absence of a freedom of information act, journalists have no right to government material; they also enjoy little legal protection if they wish to keep secret sources of such information. All bureaucratic structures manage information in pursuit of their institutional self-interest. In the struggle for power and influence, information is a key resource, and the value of information is inversely proportional to the extent of its dissemination. Insider trading in the stock market is an obvious example of the way exclusive information yields high rewards. What is true for financial information is also true for political information.

Propaganda

Censorship and secrecy are only two of the means used by states to manage media content. A third is to distribute information selectively. Susan Carruthers records how, in both world wars:

> British propagandists recognized that their task of courting American journalists would be easier if more lenient

arrangements for censorship were introduced, and if reporters were provided with easier access to the physical location of dramatic stories.

(Carruthers, 2000: 31)

The selective release of information is intended to protect and promote the interests of those in power. It is a relatively small step from this to the blatant promotion of the state and its leaders. Clearly, where the state owns and controls press and broadcasting institutions, it can use them for propaganda purposes, as was the case in Nazi Germany and the Soviet Union, and more recently in the former Yugoslavia under President Milosevic. All pretence at journalistic independence was essentially hollow. But even in liberal regimes it is possible to identify state attempts to use mass media for propaganda. Indeed, the argument of Edward Herman and Noam Chomsky's (1988) *Manufacturing Consent* is that all 'news' in the United States (and by implication, elsewhere) is primarily propaganda. More circumspectly, Daniel Hallin and Paolo Mancini (2004: 135–8) draw attention to the clientelist relationship which defines the link between media and government in some European states, and which leads to media acting as a mouthpiece for the dominant political interests.

Certainly, political parties and interest groups engage legitimately in propaganda exercises. Such practice, however, is conducted at their expense – by buying advertising space, for example. (Advertising also provides governments with a weapon against the media. In 1984, the New South Wales government switched its classified advertising, worth $1.5 million a year, from one newspaper group to another, in response to some unfavourable coverage: Schultz, 1998: 81–2). Equally, governments may seek to make the journalist's job as easy as possible by providing well-timed and well-structured press releases. It is, though, important to retain a distinction between public relations as propaganda and the direct political use of the press or television. In liberal regimes, it is assumed that parties do not buy or dictate a particular coverage. They are in the business of persuading or pressuring journalists to provide a certain type of copy; whether journalists deliver or not is a function of the relationship, but this relationship does not have the command structure of propaganda. There is a recognized (if negotiable) division of labour. It is when that division breaks down that the malign form of propaganda emerges – an accusation that has been levelled at past Spanish governments who have used their power over television to get favourable coverage (Rospir, 1996: 195), and, according to Hallin and Mancini (2004: 296ff), remains a characteristic of several other Western political and media regimes.

There are times when even direct propaganda is regarded as a legitimate part of the state's activities, and the media's compliance equally acceptable. The state is expected to issue propaganda for the public interest: to warn against the risk of AIDS or to prevent the spread of swine flu, or to notify its citizens of other risks to health and safety, just as it is expected to inform them of their rights and entitlements. This type of propaganda is legitimate in a way that promoting the party political interests of those who manage the state is not.

While these distinctions may appear to be relatively clear, they are inevitably the source of contradiction and confusion. Even in principle, it is hard to separate the public interest from the interest of the ruling party. This problem is compounded in practice by the difficulty in discerning what message any given advertisement conveys. When the Thatcher government was promoting the sale of shares in privatized utilities (a policy which had the formal backing of Parliament and the voters), the images it used – green fields, neat housing estates – were interpreted by some critics as advertising more than the new schemes; they were seen as selling the impression of a prosperous country ruled over by a dynamic government. Similarly, when the same government introduced its new policy for helping the unemployed, it was noted by critics that the television advertisements were shown during programmes that were not typically watched by their target audience (that is, the unemployed). Rather, they were being viewed by opinion shapers and by the government's natural political allies (Scammell, 1995: 221). When the 1992–97 Conservative government launched its Parent's Charter to outline the rights of children at school, it sent the document to 20 million homes at a cost of £3 million, despite the fact that fewer than 5 million homes had children of the relevant school age. And in the months prior to the 2001 election, the Blair government became the biggest spender on advertising in the United Kingdom (£30 million in March alone), a pattern that has been repeated subsequently (*Independent*, 26 April 2001; *Daily Telegraph*, 28 March 2009). Much of this money was spent on various forms of advertising that had as its message, or at least as its subtext, 'this is what New Labour has done for you'. In other words, the advertisements were seen as a form of political propaganda rather than political information. UK parties are not alone in using this means of propaganda. It has been an issue, for example, in both Australia and New Zealand (Young, 2007).

Advertising is but one way in which governments seek to represent themselves in a favourable light. Just as state systems can hide information so they can choose how to present it. Despite the increased access to data available through the internet, government still has a privileged control of key data, and it can use its comparative advantage to release data in ways that serve its interest. In the same way, it can use 'tame' journalists as the conduits through which it releases information. The relationship can work in reverse: journalists can supply the authorities with information. In the former East Germany, and elsewhere within the Soviet bloc, journalists acted as agents for the secret police, passing on information about dissidents (Garton Ash, 2009). Mostly though, the state selects its leaks in order to generate particular kinds of copy for particular constituencies.

Governments engage in 'tactical leaking'. Unfavourable or 'bad' news can be made to coincide with other, more distracting, events. The Thatcher government released details on the length of hospital waiting lists (the worst for four years) on Budget Day when the media's attention was elsewhere. The *Guardian* (26 February 1996) published a Ministry of Defence memo which discussed the best tactics for releasing news of the MoD's decision to maintain its ban on homosexuals serving in the armed forces. The memo read:

> An in-depth one-to-one briefing on a background basis for the selected journalist for a feature-type piece to appear on the day of publication. Despite (or because of) its generally hostile editorial stance, such a piece, emphasising the depth and breadth etc of the report would probably have most effect in *The Guardian*.

Ivor Gaber (2000) helpfully documents the manifold techniques that can be deployed to engineer the desired coverage. These techniques are not peculiar to the United Kingdom. Rodney Tiffen (1989: 97) describes very similar techniques being used in Australia; as he notes: 'Leaks and briefings are indispensable in contemporary politics.'

The coverage of war provides an especially intense example of the state's attempt to manage news, a fact brought dramatically to light in the United Kingdom by the Hutton report (2004), which while ostensibly delivering a verdict on events leading to the death of the government adviser David Kelly, revealed much more about the business of news management and news reporting. The US and UK government devoted considerable resources to media management during the Iraq War. This process extended from the seemingly frivolous – the setting used for the press briefings was designed by a Hollywood art director – to the more serious: every effort was made to squeeze out independent journalists, and to privilege those embedded with the troops (Stanyer, 2004: 426). In the United Kingdom, Alastair Campbell attempted to control coverage via Coalition Information Centres based in Washington, London and Islamabad. These were designed to provide information and rebut criticism (Brown, 2003). The previous Gulf War had seen the application of similar techniques (Bennett and Paletz, 1994; Carruthers, 2000: 39–43). In the United States, the government deliberately promoted the idea that Saddam Hussein was a tyrant ('the butcher of Baghdad') and that protecting Kuwait was a cause worth fighting for. Stories about Iraqi atrocities were actively circulated and reproduced. Gerald Sussman (1997: 156–7) claims that the US media were used to distort the truth, misleading the public over the destruction of Scud missiles and suggesting that the United States had bombed a biological weapons plant, when in fact it was an infant milk factory.

Whatever the techniques, it is clear that war pushes or leads states ever closer to using media for propaganda purposes. This is a long-standing practice. During the Falklands War in the early 1980s, the UK Ministry of Defence had almost total control over information and used it to feed false rumours and erroneous speculations. The MoD encouraged (or did not discourage) the spread of disinformation in order to disrupt Argentine intelligence, albeit at the cost of misleading the domestic audience (Morrison and Tumber, 1988: 205). The UK government also managed coverage through the access it granted to film crews.

The BBC journalist Brian Hanrahan complained that 'My particular team, which was one of two television cameras there, were
forbidden to leave ship for about ten days or so after the landings
[on the Falklands] had taken place' (Harris, 1983: 130).

   The distribution of information to journalists is, of course, not
typically conducted in an ad hoc manner. It is part of a system,
one aim of which is to maintain control. Carruthers (2000: 44)
argues that coverage of government is less a direct result of the
state publicity machine, and owes more to 'long-standing news
routines'. In a similar vein, Sussman (1997: 256) talks of the
network of institutions – 'embassies, CIA, the White House,
cabinet-level department, Congress' – all of which feed 'tips,
stories and contacts to the press on a regular basis'. One embodiment of this is the 'press release'. Research conducted in the
1990s suggested that about half the articles appearing in
Australian newspapers 'began as press releases' (Schultz, 1998:
56). Nothing much has changed, if anything it has got worse
(Davies, 2008). The impact of these public relations (PR) devices
is increased by dextrous use of timing: close to the deadline,
'which reduces the chances for gathering reactions and gaining
critical perspective' (Tiffen, 1989: 76; Gaber, 2000). Another
device for controlling content is the press conference. While they
serve the same purpose, press conferences (or their equivalent)
can be organized in different ways and under different rules. In
the United States, there is the open, public, televised presidential
press conference attended by the White House correspondents.
The UK version of this system has traditionally been represented
by the lobby, a club which allowed privileged access to government information to a select group of journalists, giving them
'exclusive' copy, and at the same time allowing the politically
powerful to give a particular spin to the coverage (Cockerell et
al., 1985; N. Jones, 1995). The closed lobby in the United
Kingdom is in direct contrast to the open system that operates in
the United States, where briefings are on record and on camera.
But even the UK system is not fixed and immutable. The lobby
has operated differently according to the practice of different
press officers, from the ruthless Bernard Ingham via the more
accommodating Gus O'Donnell to the abrasive Alastair
Campbell who, as Tony Blair's director of communications, put
lobby briefings on the record (Riddell, 1999). One thing that
emerges most clearly from Campbell's published diaries is the

constant desire to set the terms of media engagement (see, for example, Campbell, 2007: 34, 368, 41, 160, 179, 535).

The distribution and form of information is increasingly managed and institutionalized. Sophisticated machines exist to forge contact between politicians and journalists. These networks deliver political information (however (un)reliable or released for whatever motives) to an ever-wider range of outputs. They remain key aspects of government power (Cole, 2005). Governments, whether in the United States, the United Kingdom or Australia, bombard journalists with complaints about their copy, creating an atmosphere of anxious self-criticism (Campbell, 2007; Franklin, 1994; Gaber, 2000; Kurtz, 1998; Marr, 2004; Schultz, 1998). To some, there is in all this an eerie echo of the techniques used by the Chinese government to create the conditions for self-censorship in Hong Kong.

Regulation

So far attention has been upon what might be described as the obvious elements of state information management. Secrecy, censorship and propaganda represent the capacity of states to supply or suppress the flow of information available to the media. But underlying these capacities is the wider context of rules governing the use of information and the daily practices of media organizations themselves. As one commentator notes of how Putin's regime in Russia has handled the media: 'The Kremlin has pursued its unabashed intention of controlling the politically most influential federation-wide television stations by direct legal pressure and by use of the TV frequency licensing system' (Zasurskii, 2002: 19). The state is part of a *system* of news production; indeed, the state is a key part of the process by which the very idea of 'information' itself is constituted. The state establishes the forms of communication that operate within its territorial borders and regulates the content of those systems. At one level, any given state is responsible (albeit in conjunction with other states) for creating the market value of knowledge. Intellectual property rights form a regime around the use and transmission of certain forms of knowledge or expression. However laudable or worthy such laws are, they nonetheless act to constitute certain kinds of 'information' as a commodity to be traded, and to set limits to its use. To give one example of this, French law recognizes the right of individuals to claim copyright to their own image. This means that papers, in printing a picture of someone without their permission, may be in breach of copyright law. At a more mundane level, copyright law regulates the printing or reprinting of articles and documents, as well as designating the rights of control over those artefacts. Who owns the copyright to, say, private letters is not a trivial matter where the media wishes, for whatever reason, to publish that correspondence.

The laws of libel can be viewed in a similar way (Crook, 2009). US politicians, for example, are afforded much less protection from libel than are UK politicians (which has led, thanks to the global reach of the internet, to the phenomenon of 'libel tourism'). Another form of state regulation comes through privacy legislation. The ostensible purpose of such laws is to mark out areas that are protected from journalistic intrusion. The debate that such legislation engenders divides people between those who value the protection of privacy and those who see such protection as restricting excessively the possibility of investigative journalism. Also there are those who see privacy laws as working disproportionately to the advantage of the rich and powerful, rather than protecting the rights of those without access to, or resources for, legal redress.

These laws of copyright, libel and privacy, like many other such laws, help to construct the resources with which the mass media deal. The state, in this sense, constitutes the raw material which the mass media then process. But the state does more than produce the crude oil of publication, it also helps create the refinery. All forms of mass communication exist within a framework of law, regulation and rights. The opportunity to broadcast, to make money from the transmission of programmes, is a consequence of rules governing the use of the available electromagnetic spectrum, of cable networks and of geostationary orbits in space. Though the rules vary between countries, and though new digital technologies make issues of spectrum scarcity redundant, what is involved is a matter of degree, not of kind. The conditions and the context of communication are established by the state, and by subnational and supranational authorities; even the internet operates subject to the law, despite all the rhetoric to the contrary (Crook, 2009).

There are those, as we have seen, who argue that the state is an increasingly marginal political actor. For them, two general processes are held to support their contention. The first is the process of technological change, which, it is suggested, occurs independently of political control. States *adapt* to technical change; they do not lead it. Change is the result of an inexorable logic; one that takes us from the telegraph to the radio to the television to the satellite to digital broadcasting and beyond. The second, and related, process that appears to marginalize the state is globalization. The emergence of transnational conglomerates, empires built upon the exploitation of new technology, seems to create power bases which exist above the realm of any one nation state. As with technical change, it appears that states must adapt to the new sources of power, and in adapting they lose any claim to sovereignty and autonomy. But while these general trends are important, they do not account for the variations in the character and content of mass communication within their national borders (Cloonan, 2007; Hesmondhalgh, 2007). The rhetoric of globalization and of technological determinism leads to the false conclusion that all systems of broadcasting and publishing are the same. There are, in fact, considerable variations, and these are marked politically – not just by the difference between democracy and dictatorship, but by differences within these general types. How any mass media represent politics is itself a product of a regulatory regime, and these, argues Freedman (2008: 1), are products of political interests and political values.

Broadcasting took off in the United States and the United Kingdom at roughly the same time, using similar technologies, but developed into very different media systems. The explanation for this lies in the way the state, in conjunction with the commercial interests organized around broadcasting, reached an accommodation about the way the airwaves were to be managed (Freedman, 2008). The United Kingdom established a system of public broadcasting in which access to the airwaves was restricted, while the United States favoured a commercial system which allowed for the fuller use of the radio spectrum (Lewis and Booth, 1989). While there is an element of public broadcasting in the United States (*Sesame Street* being one of its most famous products), its role and profile are very different from those of its European equivalents (Ledbetter, 1997).

These divergent approaches in themselves created different

opportunities for state intervention and control. The relatively unregulated US system involved less direct government control. Freedman (2008: 68–71) points to how the notion of the 'public interest', as it applied to mass communications, was redefined by way of constitutional, ideological and commercial pressures that were specific to the United States. What emerged was a system in which diversity and pluralism were to be achieved through multiple media ownership, presided over by the Federal Communications Commission. The UK system, by contrast, emerged with a greater element of state regulation, or at least less reliance on the market. The BBC was expected to provide a formal independence from the state through a system of public service broadcasting. This was to be achieved through a funding and management structure that allowed for political accountability without direct political control. In the case of the BBC, funding was provided through a licence fee charged to all those who owned a wireless (and subsequently a television). Government set the fee, but the responsibility for spending it was left to the Board of Governors (now BBC Trust), formally appointed by the Queen on the advice of the government.

Both systems allow for direction from the centre, and the form of media that exists in each country can be attributed in large part to wider political interests and values, but this is different from saying that both systems allow for *equal* degrees of political control. The UK system is much more susceptible to direct political pressure. The UK government has, after all, a number of weapons in its hand. It can threaten to withhold the right to broadcast, although this is a threat which is more theoretical than actual: the political costs are likely to be too high. More modestly, the government has the power to affect the funding, by refusing to increase the licence fee. It can also make possible the appointment of fellow travellers and sympathizers to the BBC Trust. All of these weapons have been deployed, at least according to some commentators (Franklin, 2004). But it would be wrong to see the power as absolute. The weapons may not work; they are primarily negative and indirect. The power of the trustees is limited, and government appointees do not always deliver government policy. The threat to cut funding may not be credible, and it is notable that the Thatcher government, which waged a sustained campaign against the BBC, chose to remove uncertainty about the licence fee by linking it to inflation. There are, in any case, severe risks entailed in trying to interfere. It is not necessarily in the interests of government to be seen to be interfering in an institution that is thought of as independent and trustworthy. The government can gain more from the coverage of a respected institution than it can from one that is thought to be operating at its beck and call.

This system of public service broadcasting was also taken up by other European countries, and continued to operate into the 1970s, before giving way in a number of cases to the impact of deregulation and commercialization (Hardy, 2008). The principles supporting a public service system were roughly similar: a belief in the need to recognize the diversity of a nation while providing a forum for the creation of a 'public', relatively free from the dominance of the state or commercial interests. These shared principles, however, issued in different regulatory regimes and developed at different rates. Jonathan Hardy (2008: 52) nicely distinguishes between the relationships in which politics and media enjoy relative autonomy (the United Kingdom, Sweden, Iceland), those where there is 'politics in broadcasting' (Germany, Denmark, Belgium), and others where there is 'politics over broadcasting' (Greece, Italy).

When it was proposed to President de Gaulle in the 1960s that he might consider granting French state television greater autonomy, along the lines of the BBC, de Gaulle refused because he regarded television as his weapon against the press (Chalaby, 1998: 46). Only gradually and reluctantly did he relax his grasp. The French example was not untypical, but there has been considerable European variation in the degree of party political involvement and state financing (Budge and Newton, 1998: 143). In the case of Germany, political responsibility was devolved to the regions rather than being held by the federal government. And in countries where there are long-standing cleavages marked by political, religious or linguistic differences (as in Belgium), and these divisions may be acknowledged in the control of broadcasting. Just as the creation of public service broadcasting depends on government initiative, so too does its maintenance. Changes in state policy in Italy and Spain have made public service broadcasting vulnerable. These political shifts have also been accompanied by technological ones – satellite, cable, digital – which have limited the ability of states to determine what is transmitted within their territorial borders.

They have also been powered by a shift in ideology: neoliberal governments have made a virtue of deregulation and of creating new commercial opportunities around broadcasting, which have in turn created the conditions for the rise of the new media conglomerates run by men like Rupert Murdoch and Silvio Berlusconi.

Just as there is no automatic transition from public service theory to practice, there is no necessary relationship between the system of broadcasting regulation and that for the press. Each has its own history, each is the product of competing interests and ideologies. It is true, however, that single party systems, or systems that, for whatever reason, wish to limit the expression of dissent, will tend to regulate press and broadcasting (Sparks, 1998). Equally there are liberal–pluralist systems (ones in which the market plays a significant part) where both broadcasting and the press are subject to very light regulation. But there are versions of each of these general systems that combine regulation and non-regulation, so that a regulated broadcasting system may run in parallel with an unregulated press. This can be the case even where the same principle is being appealed to, whether it is freedom of speech or freedom of expression. Each can be used to justify regulation *and* its absence.

That a 'free press' means the right of individuals to own newspapers is the result of ideology and interest. Freedom of the press was defined *against* state ownership and regulation. It was the right to set up a paper. Freedom in broadcasting, by contrast, was defined through the idea that the radio spectrum was a scarce public good whose use had to be protected for the benefit of all. Broadcasting is generally more heavily regulated than the press. This seems to be true whatever the type of political system, although, of course, the degree of latitude allowed in each case varies considerably (McQuail, 1992: 107). Furthermore, it is not unknown for liberal democratic states to support and regulate the press as well as broadcasting. The Nordic countries, together with France, Italy and Portugal, have seen forms of direct state intervention in the newspaper market. The aim has been to bolster competition and counter market failure (Hardy, 2008: 77).

It is not a necessary condition of a liberal democracy, therefore, that the press is left to its own devices. This may be the case in the United Kingdom and the United States, but in Italy the state has, since the early 1980s, introduced major press legislation. Under the press laws of 1981 and 1987, the state has restricted the spread of monopoly press ownership, it has subsidized technological change and it has instituted a press regulator (Garante per l'editoria) (Sartori, 1996: 140). As Carlo Sartori notes (ibid.: 140–1), it is hard to establish the direct consequence of these laws and to make claims for their success, but they do serve to illustrate alternative models for press–state relations. Systems of media regulation appeal to principles which define the regimes that they inhabit. The most obvious contrast, but not the only one, is between liberal democratic states and state control systems. The latter are typified by the Soviet bloc and by Singapore.

The implication of these different structures of broadcasting and press regulation, and the techniques and devices deployed within them, is that changes in media policy will have a number of important consequences. These will be most obviously identified in the way politics is represented, and by the relationship between audiences/readers, journalists and political interests.

In the United Kingdom, the last two decades have been marked by two pieces of legislation that have altered significantly the politics of mass media. First, there the was Broadcasting Act 1990 which changed the basis on which commercial broadcasters operated within the UK's public service system. The right to broadcast to the country's different television regions was determined by competitive tendering. The highest bidder won, provided they met quality and financial thresholds. This system introduced a degree of transparency that its predecessor lacked, but it created immense economic pressure on companies to recoup their bids in advertising revenue, and this in turn meant that interest in current affairs and documentary programming has declined. This trend is not confined to the United Kingdom. It is also evident, for example in the United States and in other media systems where deregulation has led to greater reliance on advertising (Hardy, 2008: 123–7). But as Hardy (2008: 125) points out, this logic does not apply in all circumstances. If a media outlet wants to attract audiences with high disposable income, it may be in their interest to *increase* the coverage of politics to attract such a market. The second piece of UK legislation was the Communications Act of 2003 which created the Office of Communications (Ofcom) with responsibility for all forms of telecommunication in the United Kingdom

(Stanyer, 2003). This marked a further step towards market liberalization, albeit with the once diverse regional commercial sector now part of a single organization (ITV plc) in which four companies provide the UK's channel 3 television output. The new structure, it is argued, bears an ever-closer resemblance to that in the United States (Freedman, 2008: 116–20). And once again the effect has been felt on the coverage of politics. As in the United States, increasing market competition and dependence on advertising squeezes news and current affairs, limiting its time, resources and quality (Hallin, 2000). James Ledbetter (1997: 15) notes how public broadcasting in the United States 'relies more and more on corporate underwriting and an array of commercial gimmicks for its funding', and as a result 'its programming approach ... will look more and more like those of commercial networks'.

Despite formal requirements to serve the public interest, a feature of almost all forms of broadcasting, the effect of deregulation is felt on the coverage of politics. Rival broadcasters who schedule movies against your newscasts, or newscasts that gain audiences unattractive to your potential advertisers, put huge pressure on companies. In the United Kingdom, the commercial channels have, as a concession to their financial predicament, been relieved of the obligation to provide regional news. In the United States, Daniel Hallin (2000: 224) reports how, in the 1980s, 'networks were moving to eliminate the special status of news divisions, supervising them more closely and forcing them, like any other division of the corporation, to contribute to the bottom line'. Their ability to do this was partly a result of a relaxing of the Federal Communications Commission's interpretation of the 'public interest'. Insofar as news and political coverage matter to the operation of democratic societies, media policy can have profound consequences for those polities, and for the identities, interests and knowledge of those who inhabit them.

Comparing media systems

In reviewing the different ways in which the state engages with media and politicises it, the last section brought home a general truth. We are dealing with different regimes and systems, in which a crucial resource – media power – is being used and managed in various ways. In this last part of the chapter, we consider the categories into which these regimes and systems can be placed, to bring a degree of order to what might seem chaotic. We begin with general, even global, categories, before looking at the more subtle variations to be found within particular groupings.

Global variants

Eric Louw (2001: 40ff) argues that in the previous centuries there were only two contending media systems: those run by capitalists and those run by the state. But latterly this crude divide has given way to a wider range. These extend from the communist variant, in which media are run by or on behalf of the communist party, and in which no alternative media outlets are tolerated. This system is a close cousin of another government-run media system, that to be found in certain developing countries as the colonial powers departed. Moving further from direct state-run systems, Louw introduces the state-licensed media, in which the state allowed, under sufferance, outlets to publish. This system is associated with nineteenth century Europe and its colonies, to where the model was exported. A fourth variant is the now-familiar public service model, upon which much of the discussion above has focused. Versions of this model are associated with the United Kingdom, Canada, Australia and New Zealand. Louw is keen to distinguish the PSB form from a fifth variant, the state-subsidised media, which he associates with Northern Europe. Rather than establish a single public forum, the state supports the different voices in society, ensuring that each has its own outlet. As with PSB, the media is at one remove from direct state control. These systems, though, are to be distinguished from the system of private ownership associated with the press in the United Kingdom, and media more generally in the United States. The final category that Louw identifies is community media, a minority form, but one which has an increasing presence, in part as a consequence of the opportunities provided by new media. Here control is neither linked to the state nor to major corporate interests, but is based at the local level.

While there is much that might be said about the details of each of these variants, the key – at least for our purposes here –

is how they embody different political values and establish different answers to questions about the role of media and how it might be realised. We will return at the end of this book to these large questions. But to get a flavour here, we might consider the way each system constitutes an answer to the question of how citizens in any given country might best be informed about events in their world. For some, the US system of commercially driven, lightly regulated broadcasting diminishes, among other things, the quality of political discourse and news coverage generally. But for others, quite the opposite view is taken. Raymond Gallagher (1989), for example, argues that, in fact, not only do Americans get more choice of news, they also get more news. In particular, the quantity and quality of local news far outstrips that offered by the heavily regulated British broadcasting system (ibid.: 187–9). Certainly, local news attracts higher viewing figures than national, network news, but whether it still represents a *better* service is open to dispute. Hallin (2000: 224) contends, for instance, that the high ratings for local programmes dictate news values, with the result that politics is shunted into the wings, and sensation and human interest hold centre stage.

Beyond the answer to specific questions like this, the form of media system is also linked inevitably to the apparently radical and rapid changes wrought by the introduction of new technologies. Again, this is an issue to which we return, but it is worth noting here that, for some commentators, the internet makes redundant all forms of state sponsored and corporate controlled media. But stories of new media landscapes are counterposed by those of governments who use the internet to extend their existing powers of surveillance and manipulation, and who manage the internet with the same ruthlessness as they apply to traditional media technologies, just as commercial conglomerates re-establish their market power through their own colonisation of larger sectors of hyperspace.

Regional variants

There is a danger in contemplating these vast questions and emerging global scenarios that we miss out on the details that mark the variations within actually existing systems. This important truth is illustrated by Daniel Hallin and Paolo Mancini in

Comparing Media Systems (2004). Theirs is a very different typology to Louw's. Their attention is on variation within liberal democratic systems and their focus is not just on ownership and state regulation, but also on relationships between journalists and the political system, among other things.

They offer three distinct models, or ideal types: the Liberal Model, the Democratic Corporatist Model, and the Polarized Pluralist Model. These are distinguished both by the types of ownership that predominate, but also by the links between media and political and other interests in society. So the Liberal Model is defined in terms of 'the relative dominance of market mechanisms and of commercial media'; the Democratic Corporatist Model by a combination of 'commercial media and media tied to organized social and political groups, and by a relatively active but legally limited role of the state'; and the Polarized Pluralist Model 'by integration of the media into party politics', a less developed commercial media and 'a strong role of the state' (Hallin and Mancini, 2004: 11). The United States and the United Kingdom emerge as variants of the first model; Germany of the second and Italy and Spain of the third.

In generating the models and in comparing them, Hallin and Mancini (2004: 21) identify four dimensions along which comparison can be made. These are: a) 'the development of the media markets'; b) 'political parallelism' – the links between the media and political parties or political divisions; c) 'the development of journalistic professionalism'; d) 'the degree and nature of state intervention in the media system'. These dimensions are used to assign different national systems to particular models and to track their development. They note, for example, how the press in Southern Europe address an engaged political elite, while the press in Northern Europe tend to address an unengaged mass public (ibid.: 22). The type of press has implications for the media–politics relationship.

Another aspect of this relationship concerns the link with existing political parties. They represent this in the notion of 'political parallelism'. This is designed to measure the degree to which the media are 'captured' by the political system, and reflect only its divisions, or has some degree of autonomy from it. What Hallin and Mancini are keen to compare is the form and extent of political diversity that different systems embody. This, in turn, leads to contrasting forms of governance of broadcasting. The government model, in which there is direct control by the majority party/government, is contrasted with the professional model, where broadcasting is run by professionals independently of political control. These are to be compared with the parliamentary/ proportional representation model in which control is allocated to different parties, and the civic/corporatist model, where power lies with parties and other social groups (ibid.: 30–1).

The distribution of power within these different systems is also measured in terms of the extent of journalistic professionalism (ibid.: 34–7). Professionalism is a code for the autonomy, norms and public service orientation of journalists, and is contrasted with the 'instrumentalization' of journalists, by which they mean the extent to which journalists are deemed to serve particular interests. All these variants are themselves connected to the form and structure of the political system, where these differ between, for example, liberal and welfare state democracies, between consensus and majoritarian systems, between systems with liberal pluralist and corporatist forms, between clientelism and rational-legal authority, and between moderate and polarized pluralism (ibid.: 46–65). Their claim is that media systems are products of the political order in which they emerge, albeit not in a mechanistic or determinist way.

This brief summary does only scant justice to the arguments and evidence to be found in *Comparing Media Systems*, but it does serve to highlight the multidimensionality of the systems which organize the state's relationship with media. It also serves to highlight the fact that there are two other key actors to be considered: the media conglomerates and the institutions of journalism, the respective topics of the next two chapters.

Conclusion

This chapter began by looking at the techniques and devices that states use to manage the news and those who report it. It has ended by looking more broadly at the different systems through which states regulate the general practice of mass media. The system of regulation frames the context in which the state deploys its various techniques. The priorities that the state adopts and the form of regulation (or deregulation) it presides over will affect profoundly the character and content of mass media. In particular, it will shape political discourse and the constitution of the political realm. Changes in media system are also transformations of political communication. But as we have noted, the state is not the only important actor in establishing the mass media infrastructure. It is constantly engaged with the corporations and conglomerates that own the papers and networks and terrestrial stations that constitute the modern mass media. That is why we need to turn now to these particular pieces of the mass media's political jigsaw. Before we do so, it is important to note that our focus has been on nation states operating within territorial boundaries. This has been deliberate, in part to resist assumptions about the impact of globalization. The latter is, of course, important, but is the subject of a later chapter. The lesson of this chapter is, I think, that the death of the nation state has been exaggerated. Or rather, it is wrong to assume that it has been written out of the script before looking more closely at the routines and activities for which it remains responsible, and which vary between states despite globalization. It is clear that globalization is a vitally important dimension of the shifting dynamics of mass media politics, but the attention given to it should not lead us to overlook the part played by states and their agencies. Indeed, state intervention can be key to smaller states whose own media market is vulnerable to global media conglomerates – those very entities to which we now turn.

Chapter 6

Conglomerate Control: Media Moguls and Media Power

The evil villains in James Bond movies typically represent the anxieties of their era. During the Cold War, 007 battled against Soviet megalomaniacs and their fiendish plans for world domination. With the collapse of the Berlin Wall in 1989, the owners of the Bond franchise looked elsewhere for his nemesis. So it was that in the 1997 film *Tomorrow Never Dies*, Bond's rival was Eliot Carver (played by Jonathan Pryce), who – like all his predecessors – was hell-bent on global power. Carver was head of the Carver Media Group, a multimedia conglomerate, and he was using his company to ensnare governments with fake newscasts and other devious ploys. World peace once again hung in the balance, and it was a wicked media mogul who threatened the future of humankind. Who can the filmmakers have been thinking of?

Tomorrow Never Dies tapped into a widespread and persisting belief about the power that derives from media ownership and the malign ends to which it is (or can be) put. No one, as far as I am aware, has ever suggested that Rupert Murdoch of News Corporation, and people like him, actually seek global domination or the destruction of the planet, but nor do they think of them as entirely altruistic. Here is the economist Paul Krugman (2007) reflecting on the prospect of Rupert Murdoch adding to his portfolio: 'If Murdoch does acquire the *Wall Street Journal*, it will be a dark day for America's news media – and American democracy.' Murdoch is now the owner of the *Journal*. This chapter explores the issues prompted by Krugman's fears about the nature and effect of corporate of media power, a power most typically associated with the figure of Rupert Murdoch.

Alastair Campbell (2007: 71) reports a conversation with the former Australian prime minister, Paul Keating, who said of

Murdoch: 'he is a hard bastard and you need a strategy for dealing with him.' Andrew Marr, who was editor of the *Independent* until he fell out with his own corporate bosses, described Murdoch like this:

> He smashes unions. He squares politicians. He keeps in with national leaders, offering them news-space and book contracts (Thatcher and the Speaker of the House of Representatives Newt Gingrich, to name but two). Everywhere, he lobbies. He attacks regulations that threaten him, or tries to sidestep them .... The world stands gaping; national leaders feel a little smaller in his presence. His power is intense.
>
> (Marr, 1996: 200)

Murdoch's impact on the outside world, it seems, is matched by his power over those who work for him. One of his ex-editors, Andrew Neil wrote:

> When you work for Rupert Murdoch you do not work for a company chairman or chief executive: you work for a Sun King. You are not a director or manager or an editor: you are a courtier at the court of the Sun King.
>
> (Neil, 1997: 197)

What is involved here, in these awestruck accounts of Rupert Murdoch, is not just a portrait of corporate power. After all, he is not necessarily greatly different from any other CEO of a major conglomerate. What makes the difference is the power attributed to media and the ambitions associated with its exercise. The paradigm for this is Silvio Berlusconi, who combines both media and political power in the most explicit way. When Berlusconi first came to power, Paul Statham (1996: 88) wrote: 'Berlusconi's control of the media resources has transformed the basis for political communication in Italy.' His subsequent career has continued in a similar vein; it has been, comments Paul Ginsborg (2005: 10), 'the most ambitious attempt to date to combine media control and political power'. It has been achieved, it should be added, with more subtlety than is often acknowledged. Berlusconi employs his media power carefully, allowing dissident voices to sound occasionally:

His media regime is … one based not on the silencing of all dissenting voices, as under Fascism, but on the rule enunciated with acumen by the talk show compere, Maurizio Costanzo, in August 2001: 'Power does not belong to those who talk on television. It belongs to those who permit you to talk on television.'

(Ginsborg, 2005: 113–14)

This chapter explores the intermingling of corporate media power and political power. It begins by looking at the nature of the new media empires, and at their owners and their interests; we then turn to consider their ability to influence politics through these media outlets and the restraints acting upon such ambitions. This is not just a matter of identifying examples of influence. It has crucial implications for the debate about democracy and mass media. Put crudely, if particular individuals are seen to have power, or if certain partial interests predominate in the way that the media operate, and if these individuals and interests control political discourse to the detriment of other legitimate goals and values, then this may constitute the basis for restricting their rights to own such outlets or to have influence over them. In short, important policy decisions depend upon the conclusions we draw.

Media empires

Newspapers and broadcasting institutions sell products and services; newspapers and television programmes are commercially manufactured products, news itself is a product that has a tradable value in the market place. In Edwin Baker's (2002: 11) words, 'the media enterprise commonly sells media products to audiences and sells audiences to advertisers'. Public service media are an exception to this rule, but they too deal in the same market, and find themselves caught up in its incentives. For commercial media, the cost of production of the first product – the initial paper or the TV programme – is high, but subsequent copies cost very little. Because these products are protected by copyright – others cannot reproduce the original newspaper, media corporations are able to charge customers more than the marginal cost of each copy. As a result, they are capable of making very considerable profits (Baker, 2007: 32; Baker, 2002: 8ff). The economic facts of media production are key to understanding what corporations do and why their products (news or entertainment) take the form they do (Hamilton, 2004: 9ff).

The word 'empire' seems appropriate in describing the modern media conglomerate. Their reach is broad and seemingly comprehensive. Bertelsmann has multinational television interests, music and film businesses (Sony BMG, Universal), and a stake in the internet (NBC Universal Digital Media). CBS has television, radio, print and internet businesses, while Viacom concentrates upon television (MTV, Comedy Central and so on), film (Paramount, among others) and the internet. Disney combines television, print, radio and the internet. And so it goes on. At the turn of the century, Peter Golding and Graham Murdock described Time Warner as a textbook illustration of the emerging new order:

> it is now a major international player in book publishing, recorded music, feature film production and exhibition, satellite and cable television programming (through the CNN news channel, the Home Box Office and Cinemax movie channels, and the Cartoon Network), and animation, video games and children's toys.
>
> (Golding and Murdock, 2000: 78)

By 2010, these conglomerates boasted revenues of $11–40 billion, with Time Warner as the largest earner (Castells, 2009: 74–82).

But while media organizations are in receipt of vast sums and exist to make money, this is not necessarily their only motivation; not everything they do can be reduced to the cash nexus. They are complex institutions, and whatever economic rationality may dictate, institutional politics may cause other enterprises to defy the logic of the bottom line. Media conglomerates are not simply machines either for reporting events or for making profits; they are also bureaucracies with their own internal political orders. How they are organized, how power is distributed within the organization, will have profound repercussions for the kind of product they make. Structural reorganization of any media business, whether in the public or the private sector, involves more than the implementation of a new theory of organizational behaviour. It affects the programmes made by broadcasters and the coverage provided by the papers; and it determines the distribution of power within the business and whose decisions count. Both dimensions – the commercial interests and the organizational structure – are crucial to understanding the way that the media cover, and relate to, politics. The simplest way of revealing this connection between interests, organization and political coverage is to look at the changes that the media have undergone in recent years.

Once newspapers were simply the product of particular political fiefdoms or interests; they then became the commercial responsibility of the so-called 'press barons' (Curran and Seaton, 2010: 37ff). Subsequently, they became conglomerates, which, according to Graham Murdock (1982: 119), fell into one of two categories: the 'general conglomerate' or the 'communications conglomerate'. The first had a variety of interests, which had no necessary or direct relationship with their media interests. The communication conglomerate, by contrast, 'operate[d] mainly or solely within the media and leisure industries' (ibid.). Increasingly these distinctions have become harder to maintain as the new conglomerates have spread their commercial interests ever more widely.

These corporate histories are marked by increasing concentration of ownership, even while the number of media outlets has expanded over time. The apparent diversity of media alternatives is belied by the facts of ownership. Through its various outlets, Time Warner supplied in the late 1990s 120 million readers with books and comics and 23 million subscribers with its cable service (Sussman, 1997: 127). Now, it boasts 6.9 million subscribers to its internet service, 14.6 million to its cable network. Its television networks reach 98.9 million homes in the United States, and several of its broadcast services are delivered to 180 countries. Its television group has a presence in 200 territories and broadcasts in 45 different languages. Its Home Box Office channel has 40.9 million subscribers. It publishes 23 magazines in the United States (six of which appear in the list of top 25 magazines) and 90 outside of the United States. In 2008, it was directly responsible for producing 15 movies, including *The Dark Knight*, with its subsidiary New Line producing a further nine. It distributes these films to 125 territories (Time Warner, *Annual Report*, 2009).

News Corporation has a similar profile. In Australia between 1987 and 1993, according to Julianne Schultz (1998: 83), its subsidiary News Limited 'moved from being the smallest newspaper company to publishing more than 60 per cent of the nation's newspapers and holding a monopoly in four capital cities'. By 2009, it published 110 national, capital city and suburban papers in Australia. In the United Kingdom, it was responsible for six national newspapers, taking a major share of the overall market (the rest being dominated two other media groups). Then there are its US press and television interests (most notably Fox Television). It is also the owner of the global publishing house HarperCollins and the MySpace website. Its total assets were valued at $55 billion, with revenues of $30 billion, in 2009 (News Corporation website, http://www.newscorp.com/).

Other key players in this market for news, information and entertainment services are the global news agencies. By the end of the last century, Reuters dominated the global competition between news suppliers, leaving its rivals a poor second (Boyd-Barrett and Rantanen, 1998: 4). Ten years later, its presence continued to be felt, now as part of Thomson Reuters, another major media merger, with some 50,000 employees supplying a vast range of services, of which its news agency branch is but one – it alone provides news copy, graphics, images and video (http://thomsonreuters.com/).

There is a tendency, when surveying these media conglomerates, to see them as the products of some irresistible logic. But despite the commercial and market incentives for concentrating ownership, none of this is inevitable. Markets can be, and are, regulated. Governments can impose restrictions on the ownership of newspapers and can act against monopolies (as the US authorities did against Microsoft in 2000 and as the European authorities did in blocking the addition of EMI to the Time Warner-AOL merger). The same levels of media concentration are not necessarily to be expected in Australia as in the United States or in the United Kingdom. Media that were once concentrated in the hands of a Russian oligarch are now dispersed (European Journalism Centre, http://www.ejc. net/; BBC News online, http://news.bbc.co.uk/ 1/hi/world/ europe/4315129.stm).

The point is that concentration of ownership has consequences, not just for market competition (the capacity of other firms to enter the market and survive), but also for the range of ideas and values that can circulate. Media concentration threatens democracy (Baker, 2007). Regulation of media and the provision of public service media are both designed to counter the anti-democratic logic of unregulated, commercialized media. The public management of the economics of media concentration and the politics of public service media are a response to the particular characteristics of the media market and the value attributed to media. It is conceivable that the right to print papers could be distributed in the same way that broadcasters obtain a franchise to broadcast (Hardy, 2008). You could have public service papers just as you have public service television. Equally, there are those who argue the reverse: that conglomerate control is much more limited and much less worrying than state regulation (Beesley, 1996). Such a claim rests upon assumptions about how the media market behaves – whether it leads to cartels or productive competition, for instance. One example of this competition was the price war that divided the UK press in the late 1990s (Greenslade, 2004). The problem with such competition is that while it produced – for the reader – *cheaper* newspapers, it did not guarantee *better* ones, nor did it provide for greater media diversity (Baker, 2007). Such examples of naked competition are relatively rare. More common is the routine effect of market considerations upon media organizations; these shape the character and content of the information and entertainment they provide.

One example of how these interconnections can play out is provided by News Corporation. The publisher HarperCollins, a News Corporation company, had commissioned the autobiography of Chris Patten, an ex-Conservative Cabinet minister and latterly governor of Hong Kong, before it reverted to China. However, just before publication the book was cancelled, reportedly on the orders of Rupert Murdoch, who feared that it might affect adversely his media interests in China (*Guardian*, 26 February 1998; *Observer*, 1 March 1998; Page, 2003: 267ff). 'Kill the book,' Murdoch was said to have demanded (*Guardian*, 2 March 1998). But while this story, which Murdoch himself denies, received extensive coverage in rival papers, it attracted only belated attention in *The Times*. This was regarded as evidence that *The Times* was being used to improve relations with the Chinese authorities, as News Corporation sought to expand its business in the Far East. A sign of the success of this strategy, according to Francis Wheen (*Guardian*, 20 October 1999), was evident when President Jieng Zemin allowed 'the film *Titanic* into Chinese cinemas, to the delight of 20th Century Fox (prop. R. Murdoch)', an event which the *Sun* honoured with a review of the Chinese premiere. What this example illustrates is how commercial and political interests can become entwined within a multimedia conglomerate.

Silvio Berlusconi's rise to power has, in this sense, a logic to it, and serves as a further, albeit more explicit, example of the links between media and political power. Here was a media mogul who has become Italy's prime minister on three occasions, and who has made extensive use of his various media outlets in his campaigning and in his subsequent political career. His investment company owns three television channels, and from the beginning they have been used to advertise his party, and to marginalize his rivals (Hardy, 2008: 109–11; Statham, 1996: 94–6). One of the presenters from Fininvest was appointed to the Parliamentary Culture Committee (*Independent*, 9 June 1995). Meanwhile, his advertising company held a 65 per cent share of the television advertising market (Statham, 1996: 91). When in power he has been responsible for appointing those who run the state channels (Ginsborg, 2005; Hardy, 2008: 111). It might be supposed, though, that Berlusconi is the exception, not the rule, and that we cannot generalise from his example. Paul Ginsborg, however, argues that:

> his [Berlusconi's] rise to power in Italy is a highly significant expression of trends which have become ever more marked in modern democracies – new ways of marketing politics, the conditioning of the electoral process through blatant control of the media system, and the affirmation of personal, charismatic dominion at time when representative democracy is in crisis.
>
> (Ginsborg, 2005: 185)

Such claims suggest we need to look ever more closely at how media and political interests are connected.

Ownership and control

What is clear is that the commercial and political interests of media conglomerates are intertwined. As we have already seen, the opportunity to exist as conglomerates depends, in part, on government policy on monopolies. It is also apparent that commercial decisions have a political impact, through the effects, for instance, of closing a newspaper or amalgamating media interests. At the same time, commercial power – executive decisions about what to buy or sell, what product to manufacture – does have a bearing on the form of political coverage to be found in those outlets. But tracing connections is not the same as determining outcomes. The various actors in the media realm have – to different degrees – the capacity to affect its form and character.

The economic interests and incentives of the new media conglomerates are crucial to explaining elements of their behaviour, but there is no simple correlation between economic interest and the political content of papers or the way they behave in respect of the democratic process. The fact that we have seen the decline of press barons, whose interests were traditionally linked to politics and to exercising influence, does not mean that press ownership as a source of power died with lords Northcliffe and Rothermere. The activities of men like Murdoch are the constant object of political attention and of policy questions. Murdoch has been demonized by some, and lionized by others. He has been seen as the source of malign political influence, or the model of entrepreneurial genius or the author of political populism. Whatever the view, he has been regarded as more than a figurehead for his empire; he has been believed to wield power in pursuit of political goals. It is exactly this thought which inspires those who want to curb his influence through legislation designed to limit cross-media ownership or to protect editorial independence. But does it make sense to react like this to a figure such as Rupert Murdoch?

The power of Rupert Murdoch

Certainly, people think of Rupert Murdoch as powerful, not just because he has been the head of a major corporation, but also because he has not confined himself to making commercial decisions and to weighing up purely economic costs and benefits. Murdoch, it has been assumed, has wielded political power, using this power to influence what his papers say, what voters think and what governments do. As one biography says of him: 'His main titles have rarely strayed far from the right-wing fundamentalism in which he now so passionately believes' (Belfield et al., 1991: 4). To attribute this kind of power to Murdoch is also to attribute motive, to suggest that he has a reason for influencing his papers. More than this, it is to attribute a *political* motive to him, one that may either conflict or coincide with his commercial interests. It is, after all, conceivable that his commercial concerns overrode everything else. In other words, his only interest was in the bottom line, and although this may have profound political consequences, it was not those consequences that explained or motivated the decisions. The political line was of no particular interest to him, except insofar as it served his commercial interests. Alternatively, his political interests could be such that he was willing to sacrifice commercial gain. As a way of capturing the implications of these alternatives, consider the support given by Murdoch's papers to Margaret Thatcher's Conservative Party in the 1980s, to Tony Blair's Labour Party from 1997, and then more recently the reversion to the Conservatives under David Cameron in 2009. These switches of support could be seen either as a careful monitoring of the popular mood (or the readers' mood), or as a consequence of his own personal preference for the individual leaders, or a consequence of his expectations about who was most likely to win any given election and the need to ensure that his business interests would have government support.

It might be supposed that a simple test of the motives of owners is whether they run their enterprises at a profit or at a loss. If the latter, it might be assumed that their interests are political, not commercial. When Lord Thompson owned *The Times* the paper incurred considerable losses; similarly, in the early 1990s, News International reported a loss of £266 million. But such evidence does not provide incontrovertible proof of political motives. Losses can have commercial value: a loss-making enterprise can be set against tax or its losses may be a consequence of some larger commercial purpose. It is only if neither of these apply that we can talk of political interests taking precedence (assuming that neither incompetence nor other commercial explanations account for the losses). Where media organizations make a profit, as they commonly do, it does not follow that only commercial considerations matter. Even where they are profitable, it cannot be assumed that this represents the motivation behind every corporate decision. Different motives may coexist. The decision by HarperCollins to drop Chris Patten's book contract might be an example of this, if it was in fact done to protect another part of the News Corporation empire. In the same way, Murdoch's well-known opposition to the European Union, a view that his papers tend to reflect, may have as much to do with his commercial interests as with his anti-federalist political disposition (Hargreaves, 2003: 158). Nonetheless, because conglomerates are involved in so many different arenas, it is impossible to talk of a single motive extending over all decisions.

Beyond the immediate commercial interests, there lies a more diffuse set of interests. We could see Murdoch as operating to promote the interests of all media or of capitalism generally (even where the costs of this support may entail some short-term commercial loss). The problem with this line of thought is that, as rational choice theorists have pointed out (Downs, 1957; Olson, 1971), there is no way that a single actor can guarantee the success of the system, and thus it is rational to free-ride on the efforts of others. It would, therefore, be irrational for Murdoch to believe that his actions alone could preserve capitalism (however much he has to gain from its survival). Alternatively, insofar as owners wield power, this power may be exercised to promote certain side benefits (non-commercial ones). It is conceivable that media organizations provide gratification for the owners' vanity or grant them social status and access to certain social circles. The late Robert Maxwell was often assumed to be as interested in political influence as he was in commercial gain (Bower, 1988). It does seem, however, that such motives hold little attraction for Murdoch. One of his editors, Andrew Neil (1997: 199), claims that Murdoch was uninterested in 'the approval of the Establishment', and that he 'turned down a knighthood and a peerage'.

Whatever is the case, any analysis of the power of Rupert Murdoch must include an account of his interests and of the ends he has sought to realize. Even if we are able to rule out vanity and social climbing, we are still left with the problem of disentangling – or understanding – the link between the political and the commercial. Insofar as it is possible to do this, there remains a further task, which is to establish the means available to him to realize these interests. As a first step, it pays to look at the claims made about Rupert Murdoch's access to power and his use of it for political ends.

The appointment and removal of editors

Rupert Murdoch's media power has commonly been linked to his power to hire and fire editors. When Murdoch sacked an editor of *News of the World,* to whom he allowed only a three-minute interview, Roy Greenslade (2004: 214) explained: 'Murdoch was laying down the law: he was the boss and the editors marched to his tune.' He refused to renew the contract of the editor of *Village Voice,* the New York paper, when he took it over. His relationship with Harold Evans at *The Times* was marred by arguments over budgeting and politics. According to his biographer, Murdoch was concerned that Evans was 'spending freely but not always consistently', while Evans complained that he was kept in the dark about 'his formal editorial budget' (Shawcross, 1992: 246). They also differed over editorial policy (ibid.: 251–2). In the end, Evans resigned. His resignation has been seen as an indication of the fact that Murdoch wants editors who echo his politics (Greenslade, 2004: 382–3). Certainly, the appointment of Andrew Neil to edit the *Sunday Times* seemed to confirm this view. Neil appeared to share his proprietor's political instincts. They worked together for a long time and, when their partnership ended, the cause was less a matter of political ideology than one of corporate and journalistic interests. The *Sunday Times'* pursuit of the Pergau Dam affair, a story about the alleged misuse of funds by the Malaysian government, threatened Murdoch's business interests in that part of the world. Eventually, Neil moved to New York to work in one of Murdoch's television companies. Other editors and employees of his companies testify to Murdoch's power to hire and fire (Curran and Seaton, 2010: 68–70). But what is central to the argument is the extent to which these decisions are the result of political judgements, rather than business ones.

Involvement in editorial policy

In the debate about the war in Iraq, the *Observer* ran this headline: 'For a paper's view on Iraq, just ask the owner' (16 February 2003). There are many anecdotes that suggest that this is the case, that Rupert Murdoch has taken a keen interest in his papers' editorial line (Greenslade, 2004: 386). Here is a typical one: 'Murdoch could not stop interfering. In 1982 he said to Fred Emery, home editor of *The Times*: '"I give instructions to my editors all around the world, why shouldn't I in London?"'' (Belfield et al., 1991: 77). From the same source, it is claimed too that Murdoch told journalists on the *Chicago Sun-Times* that they could not criticize President Ronald Reagan. In the 1970s in Australia, Murdoch's support for the Labour Party took the form of writing a party press release, which subsequently became a news item in his papers (Tiffen, 1989: 148). At the *Sunday Times*, Neil (1997: 222) describes how, after the paper had been printed, Murdoch would 'lay the paper on the lectern then noisily turn each page, stabbing his finger at various stories or circling them with his pen. He had the uncanny knack of zooming in on the paper's weaknesses.' Another of Murdoch's former editors reports:

> The sight of Murdoch on the newsroom floor always seems to coincide with the most difficult news days. 'Is that really a story?' was all he needed to say to ensure a front page would be ripped up and an attempt made to start again .... Content, layout, display, he has a view on them all and doesn't hesitate to express them.
>
> (Dunn, 2007)

These were not one-off occasions. David Yelland, a former editor of the *Sun*, reports that 'when Rupert was in town we would regularly go through the *Sun* and the *Mirror*'(*Guardian*, 14 June 2004).

It is also assumed that the political line taken by the *Sun* and by his Fox News channel in the United States were the direct product of Murdoch's intervention. The decision that the *Sun* would support Tony Blair in 1997 was made, it seems, in the face of the opposition of the paper's political editor, Trevor Kavanagh. But not all his papers are subject to the same interference, at least according to the leading actors. For example, Peter Stothard recalls his experience as editor of *The Times*:

> He [Murdoch] has an influence in the sense that if you have known him for a long time you understand that he has good instincts about the way newspapers work. You are aware of that intelligence in the background and it does spur you on because he is a great encourager of risk .... He does ring up from time to time and asks what's going on. He listens a lot. There is a lot happening here in London that he wants to know about. He is interested in politics because he likes to know what's going on. But the idea that he is constantly on the phone is wrong.
>
> (*Guardian*, 28 June 1993)

As editor of the *Sunday Times*, Andrew Neil claims that only once in 11 years did he have to submit an editorial for approval before publication. This was when he wrote about News International's industrial dispute with the print unions, caused by the decision to move its papers from Fleet Street to Wapping. Neil (1997: 132) reports that the only change made was for 'legal reasons'. He says that 'he never barked orders to change what I was planning for the front page', and though Murdoch tried to get the paper to back Margaret Thatcher in the struggle for the Conservative Party leadership, he did not complain when the *Sunday Times* supported Michael Heseltine. At the same time, Neil (ibid.: 203, 222) notes that, despite his 'hands-off approach', 'Murdoch was always uppermost in the editor's mind ... sometimes he would leave you wondering if you had done anything right; ... other times, when he liked the paper, you felt you could walk on water.' Murdoch's influence, according to these accounts, has extended from direct instructions over what can and cannot be said, through to the creation of a culture in which a certain norm becomes part of the established 'common sense' of the paper, to the view that he had little or no impact.

Rupert Murdoch has offered his own version of his behaviour:

> I feel more restraint at the *Times* than I would at the [*New York*] *Post*. I walk around the *Sun* office a lot more than I walk around the *Times* office. And talk to the editor a lot more. I don't say do this and do that, but she [Rebekah Wade, the then

editor] will come into me and say Gordon Brown called me today about such and such and what do you think?

(*Guardian*, 11 June 2007)

In 1995 he provided a slightly different version. Asked if his papers would support the Labour Party, he replied:

> Look, what will happen exactly is this. *The Times* and *Sunday Times* will support whoever the editors wish to support. The *Sun*? I'm sure the editor will consult with me and I will have some input into that.

(*Guardian*, 22 May 1995)

Commercial policy

But involvement in the details of editorial policy, however extensive, remains marginal when compared with the larger commercial issues that face newspapers, and in which Murdoch has been closely involved. The decision to move his publications to Wapping and to create new working arrangements were, by all accounts, driven by him (Page, 2003: 384; Greenslade, 2004). It is inconceivable that the price war of the late 1990s would have been launched without his agreement, just as *The Times'* revamping of its layout in 2000 required prior approval (if only because of the costs incurred). When the *Sunday Times* wanted to introduce a books section, it was opposed by the advertising department, but with Murdoch's backing it went ahead (Neil, 1997: 215). Murdoch himself has admitted that he paid close attention to the budgets of his papers and acted to cross-subsidize the losses. News Corporation has invested heavily in digital broadcasting and has bought into sports teams in the United States, and paid a reported $580 million for MySpace (*Observer*, 24 July 2005). It has become a major player in sport across the world, not just through its investment in teams, but also through its broadcasting interests (Cave and Crandall, 2001). Not only do all these decisions have profound implications for the company's policy, they also affect its bargaining power and the relations it has with, among other things, the political economy of the countries with which it does business. It is hard to imagine that these allocative decisions have been taken without Murdoch's direct involvement.

So, in summary, it is evident that Murdoch has access to many of the levers that direct the course and content of his media outlets. But there is one question that always has to be asked. Does he use these powers to pursue a particular political line? Certainly, one of the claims made about Murdoch's media power is that he wields it on behalf of conservative causes. This was why he supported Margaret Thatcher and attacked Bill Clinton. His biographer William Shawcross (1992: 154), however, casts some doubt on such claims. He recalls how in its early Murdoch days, the *Sun* opposed 'capital punishment, apartheid, racism and the Vietnam war'. In 1970, the Murdoch press backed Labour (in the United Kingdom and in Australia) and, in 1972, it supported striking UK miners. But whatever the party political sympathies his papers displayed, it is argued that Murdoch's own politics were less a matter of partisanship, and more a general mistrust of 'the establishment' coloured by republican sympathies (Greenslade, 2004: 212; Marr, 2004: 242). It was this disposition that led him to appoint Andrew Neil to edit the *Sunday Times*. Neil was an anti-establishment figure himself, a young outsider, someone who represented the modern meritocracy and opposition to traditional power. This general political position was not, of course, inconsistent with his support for Margaret Thatcher, nor was it entirely inconsistent with support for Tony Blair (as a challenge to the Tory establishment).

While Murdoch has been involved in editorial policy, argues Shawcross (ibid.: 184), he has not done this at all times and in all places. When he replaced the editor at the *Village Voice*, he did not replace her with a more conservative editor and he did not influence coverage (even tolerating – albeit grudgingly – criticism of himself). Shawcross also contends that the pressure to remove Evans from *The Times* had less to do with Murdoch, who initially was supportive of his editor, and more to do with the journalists' dislike of Evans' style (ibid.: 245–54). With Andrew Neil, Murdoch agreed contractual terms that gave the editor considerable protection. If he were to be fired, he would be paid two years' salary (rising to three years after two years in the job); besides, as an unconventional appointment, Neil was more difficult to remove without Murdoch losing face. Similarly, when asked about his dealings with the Chinese authorities and the decision to drop Chris Patten's book, Murdoch refutes the story told about his involvement: 'No. I was never asked to back out of the Patten deal. As far as I know, they [the Chinese] didn't know he was writing a book. It was done very clumsily by HarperCollins' (*Guardian*, 29 November 1999). One of those involved in the decision gives qualified support to this view, suggesting that HarperCollins acted out of a spirit of 'anticipated compliance', rather than in response to a direct order (Dover, 2008: 133). This does not demonstrate that Murdoch had no involvement in the decision to drop Patten's book, but it does raise doubts about the motives and responsibility for that decision. Certainly, there is a danger in making too much of the anecdotal evidence (witnesses, after all, may have a vested interest in conveying a particular impression), or of assuming that the anecdotes all point to one conclusion. The ambiguity stems, in part, from an approach to power which seeks out such examples. It runs the risk of focusing exclusively on the individual actor and too little on the context in which they act. One way to counter this slant is to look at other, rival sources of power.

Readers and viewers

Readers and viewers certainly matter to the rhetoric of mass media. They help to legitimize the activities of journalists: sales and ratings are taken as indications of popularity and of public interest. The underlying assumption is that mass media reflect the tastes of those who buy their papers or watch their programmes. It follows that, for sound commercial and political reasons, owners and editors cannot afford to ignore their customers. So, for example, the reason for News International outlets in the United Kingdom taking the line they do may have more to do with the shifts in the opinion of readers and viewers than with the whims and prejudices of the corporate executives. To ignore public opinion is to risk commercial punishment. When the *Sunday Mirror* published pictures of Princess Diana working out in an exclusive gym, the paper's readership fell by 250,000; just as readers of the *Sun* boycotted their paper in protest at the way it covered the death of Liverpool football fans in the crush at the Hillsborough stadium in 1989 (Snoddy, 1992).

Individual incidents do not, though, represent a complete picture. Such power is exercised only belatedly and occasionally;

it is a protest after publication, not a means of controlling what gets published in the first place. To claim that consumers are a significant force means establishing a mechanism by which their preferences can be registered on a regular basis. Such arrangements do exist; there is the letters page, the feedback show, the publication of public opinion, the phone-in and other forms of audience participation, and increasingly the use of websites and interactive technologies to engage audiences. In the United States, there has been an attempt to systematize this form of public participation under the guise of 'civic journalism', where journalists take their agenda directly from the revealed preferences of the public (Clark, 1997), and more recently, with the arrival of blogging, there is talk of 'citizen journalism' (Wright, 2009). There is also evidence, produced by economists (for example, Gentzkow and Shapiro, 2006), which suggest – in the United States at least – that papers respond to the political affiliations of their readers.

There are, however, limits to the impact that these forms of popular involvement can have. Reader boycotts have had very little sustained effect, and depend upon the coordination of some other agency. Equally, the regular forms of participation (the letters page, the phone-in) are carefully mediated by media professionals. Civic journalism has been much criticized for actually limiting, rather than extending, the critical function of journalism (Grimes, 1997; Jackson, 1997), and it is still too early to assess the full impact of blogging and citizen journalism. Certainly, individual consumers can achieve very little, especially as the decision not to buy a paper may be taken on any number of grounds (of which politics may be the least). Nonetheless, it is important not to see this state of affairs as a fixed and inevitable condition of relations between audience/readers and their media. Rather it is a result of the way that the relationship is organized and structured. Put simply: readers could exercise more power if there were established systems of accountability, or if – as happens in some community radio stations (see Lewis and Booth, 1989) – listeners are subscribers or contributors. It is only where such systems of audience or reader participation do not exist that the media remain largely impervious to popular demand and more susceptible to the expectations of their advertisers (their paymasters in default of some other form of financial support).

Advertisers

All papers depend upon advertisers, but not all papers depend equally. Crudely, the red tops depend more upon income from their readers, while upmarket papers depend more upon advertisers. Commercial television depends overwhelmingly upon its advertisers, as do the free papers. The local press has depended upon local advertisers. Traditionally, according to Bob Franklin (1994: 42), the local press in the United Kingdom derived 25–35 per cent of its income from advertising, the tabloids derived 30 per cent; and the broadsheets 70 per cent. But does this dependence, however large, actually influence the politics of the paper? In particular, do the interests of advertisers conflict with those of readers and viewers?

Such links are hard to prove, but the evidence is growing (Baker, 2002 and 2007; Curran, 1986; Hardy, 2008). The suggestion is that the criteria used to select media content are distorted by the need to attract advertising (Baker, 2002: 24). The challenge faced by such claims is obvious. There are, after all, an infinite number of stories that are not covered, and to show that a particular one is not covered because of a fear of offending an advertiser would require evidence of pressure. The journalist Blake Fleetwood claims that a piece he wrote for the *New York Times* about Tiffany's jewellery store was subtly changed, and was accompanied by a much blander editorial than the story warranted, because Tiffany's was a major advertiser (*Washington Monthly*, September, 1999). In a similar way, the *New York Daily* found itself in conflict with one of its advertisers, Bell Atlantic, after the paper had run a piece critical of the company. These instances do not demonstrate a systematic pattern of influence, although there have been reports of advertisers exercising direct editorial control, either by demanding to read copy before placing advertisements, or by the merger of news and advertising departments (Medium Wave, BBC Radio 4, 4 January 1998). In October 1999, the *Los Angeles Times* published a 164-page supplement about the Staples sports arena. The supplement raised $2 million in advertising, which, it turned out, was split between the sports arena and the paper (*Guardian*, 3 January 2000). The effect of this episode was to call into question the editorial independence of the *LA Times*. Such examples, however, remain relatively rare, and in any case they do not exhaust the ways in which the connection between the advertiser and political coverage may operate.

The political influence of advertisers may be identified, not in the specific content of any given magazine or paper or programme, but rather in the *kinds* of stories that appear. The sections into which papers are divided will often owe much to the kind of advertising they want to attract. Car, homes and garden, and travel sections all provide hooks with which to tempt advertisers. Attracting advertisers also depends on being able to deliver the audience/readership they seek. This may be detected in various ways. It may result in a general shift away from 'hard' news to human-interest stories. The media outlet has to create an environment that disposes its readers/ viewers to consume. More precisely, it has to create a bridge between consumers and advertisers. As the chief executive of a UK television news service explained the conditions under which he worked:

> The dynamic is really news attracting the kind of audiences that advertisers want to buy, and the channel controllers sitting there saying 'I want those kinds of advertisers, I need this kind of content. I need the news to deliver this kind of audience.'
>
> (*The Times*, 12 March 1999)

The logic of this does not automatically work against the coverage of politics. As Colin Sparks (2000: 275–6) points out, insofar as the affluent reader or viewer has a taste for, or interest in, detailed coverage of politics, 'it makes very good business sense' for media outlets to provide such coverage. But, according to Michael Schudson (2000: 178), this logic works only where there is a concentrated, elite audience. Where the audience is of a different kind, the logic results in a quite different conclusion. When in the United Kingdom, the main evening newscast on ITV was moved from 10 pm to 11 pm, the channel earned a reported £70 million more in advertising revenue (while losing 2 million news viewers), because the programmes now running at 10 pm were more attractive to advertisers (*The Times*, 3 March 2000). The media outlet has to be attractive to advertisers, and a measure of this attractiveness is the ability to reach a particular market. If the paper can show that it has a readership from a certain social category, advertisers who want that market will use such an outlet. This type of relationship will dispose the paper or programme maker to address some topics and not others. And, to this extent, advertisers set an agenda for the media, which is political insofar as it recognizes certain interests and excludes others.

From this it is possible to derive an argument for the conservatism of the broadsheet press. The advertisers that they want to attract will be, in turn, after an affluent readership. Such people are likely to have an interest in maintaining the status quo. Hence it is possible to trace a line from advertising to political disposition, but in doing so it is important to bear in mind other pressures and constraints. The tabloid press also takes a conservative line without having the same dependence upon advertisers. Besides, there are instances when papers have chosen to ignore their advertisers. When one advertising client complained to Rupert Murdoch about a *Sunday Times* story, Murdoch simply banned the client from advertising in his paper. In an ensuing conversation with his editor, Murdoch asked how much the lost account was worth. 'About £3 million,' he was told. 'Fuck him, if he thinks we can be bought for £3 million,' came the reply (Neil, 1997: 201).

Sponsorship of programming adds another dimension to this issue. While rules govern sponsorship (what can be sponsored and how), the need to attract sponsors undoubtedly has an impact on the kind of programmes that are made. This, though, constitutes a system that is relatively transparent. Audiences are notified of the sponsor and might be expected to connect content and the product. Nonetheless, the need for sponsorship can have an impact on the type of programmes made (it is easier to get sponsorship for drama than for documentaries). The same applies to product placement, both in terms of its regulation and its potential impact.

The combined effect of economic recession, hitting the pockets of consumers and corporate marketing budgets, and of the impact of new media, creating new sites for advertising, has had dramatic effects upon traditional media income streams. This has, in turn, had consequences for news coverage, if only in reducing staff. Insofar as advertisers and sponsors are important to the revenue of media outlets, they will have an indirect effect upon coverage of politics. The measure of this will not simply (if at all) be the political line so much as the presence of politics itself. The need to attract advertising revenue leads to a tendency to marginalize politics, and to adopt a populist approach to scheduling and news coverage, in which 'hard news' makes way for 'human interest' stories. These trends can be identified and mapped (Curran and Seaton, 2010: 88ff) and can be used to indicate the possible – if not irrefutable – influence of advertising on the content of media. To this extent, advertisers and sponsors, like readers and viewers, represent a counterweight to the influence of owners.

Reconsidering media power

In shifting the discussion of media power away from the actions of an individual and towards the practices of collective entities like audiences and advertisers, we are inviting a different perspective on the relationship of media and political power, one in which the role of the individual is less important than that of the corporate actor and the incentives to which they respond. Certainly, we need to be careful of confusing the perception of power with its reality, while noting that the *belief* that an individual is powerful may provoke behaviour that seems to confirm the original presupposition. It is clear, for example, that the Labour Party came to *believe* that the *Sun* had lost them the 1992 General Election and that to win in future they needed it (and its owner's) support. It may be that the party was wrong in this belief (Curtice and Semetko, 1994; Norris et al.,1999), but they behaved as if Rupert Murdoch, and the media more generally, mattered greatly. Alastair Campbell records on a number of occasions in his diaries how he worried about losing the *Sun*'s support (by which he meant Murdoch's support), how delighted he was when they secured it (Campbell, 2007: 156, 161, 477), and how frustrated he felt when he failed, as happened at a dinner at which Blair despaired of changing Murdoch's mind on Europe because it was 'so fixed and OTT' (Campbell, 2007: 363). Tony Blair too acted in ways that seemed to confirm Murdoch's power, meeting the tycoon frequently, including three times in the nine days before the Iraq War began (*Guardian*, 19 July 2007). Piers Morgan (2005) records in his diaries that when he was editor of the *Mirror* and the *News of the World*, he was constantly surprised at the ease of access he had to the prime minister.

But beyond the idea of power as operating as much through reputation and impression, there is the larger matter of its structural character. To see power as emanating from individuals or small groups can mean losing sight of its systemic character. Graham Murdock (1982: 122) introduces this thought by identifying two distinct forms of power: allocative and operational control. The first applies to the general strategy of the conglomerate – its merger and acquisition decisions, its financial plan and the use of its profits. Operational control is exercised at a lower level (that is, within the general strategy set through allocative controls). Allocative power is typically held by the company's board (which is, in theory, responsible to the shareholders). Insofar as these distinctions apply to the operation of a media conglomerate, it matters for our notion of media power what types of decision falls to whom. More importantly, suggests Murdock, is whether 'decisions' are taken by responsible individuals, or whether they are the product of processes over which individuals have relatively little control (ibid.: 123–4). These two positions return us to the familiar debate within the social sciences between structure and agency. Is change to be understood as the product of individual decisions and actions or as the consequence of structural forces which are indifferent to the individuals who are caught up in these forces? Murdock is unhappy with this dichotomy, and argues that a proper understanding of control in mass media needs to recognize both dimensions (ibid.: 125).

Rather than making the distinction between structure and agency disappear, as Anthony Giddens (1979) is accused of doing with his notion of 'structuration' (Hollis and Smith, 1991b), the point is to acknowledge both. This is to adopt a version of Karl Marx's powerful idea that people make their own history, but not in circumstances of their own choosing. What this suggests is that we need to combine an understanding of individual rationality (agency) – what it makes sense for someone to do – with an appreciation of the context and institutional forms (structure) in which they act (Hollis and Smith, 1991a; Dowding, 1994). Colin Hay (1997) captures something similar is his notion of 'context-shaping' power, as does Bent Flyvberg (1998) when he describes power's capacity to define the 'reality' on which rationality works. Power is seen as setting rules and constraints within which actors, with different resources and

capacities, act to realize their goals. Both individuals and structures are relevant. The general features of the media economy –
the market, the state regulatory structure, the corporate structure
– organize and prioritize a range of alternatives and possibilities,
but within this context individual and collective actors operate
more or less effectively to realize their interests. Writers like Des
Freedman (2008) and Gillian Doyle (2002) highlight this aspect
of power when they compare the rules of the media game as they
are set out in the United States and the United Kingdom.

The implication of this approach to power is that we need to
focus on the incentive structure under which control is exercised.
Murdock (1982: 125–9) again detects two competing perspectives. The first locates power within capitalism: power is exercised in pursuit of the interests of the capitalist class. The second
locates power within industrial society, and the incentives are
generated not by the larger economic context, but by the particular features of the industry's organization. Common to these
perspectives is the view that managers (editors, advertising executives and so on) rather than owners are the decisive actors, and
that managers are motivated by the benefits the organization
provides, and not by the need to realize profits on capital investment. A crude distinction between the perspectives can be drawn
by asking whose interests predominate in corporate decision-
making. In the first, profit is central, and hence considerable
power is attributed to the source of those profits (advertisers, for
instance); in the second, the emphasis is on other measures of
success (sales and ratings), pushing readers or viewers to the fore
in policy decisions. Murdock's purpose in introducing these
differences and distinctions is not to establish a final, definitive
view of the distribution of power in the mass media, but to
produce a framework or set of questions that enable us to reflect
on the character and form of that power. Where the market
predominates, argues Colin Leys (2001), we have 'market-driven
politics' and market-driven media, which in turn legitimate the
politics. The recent history of modern media is, for Leys, the
history of a process of commodification in which the public role
of media to provide for a national conversation is being marginalized by the drive to find new ways to sell and exploit media
technologies and products. This may mean that media change,
but not their power, which merely shifts to a new location. It is a
thought that has occurred to Mr Murdoch himself. The

Guardian (14 March 2006) quotes him as saying: 'Power is moving away from the old elite in our industry – the editors, the chief executives and let's face it, the proprietors'. While Murdoch may muse upon his own demise, the larger point is that the operation of the media market – and the degree to which it is regulated or not – has important consequences for the character of the political system; in particular, for the ideas that circulate and for the interests that find expression. This is an issue to which we return in Chapter 12.

Conclusion

In this chapter, our main concern has been power *within* media organizations, but our interest in this has been motivated by the thought that this power has a wider social and political significance. By way of illustration, we have concentrated on a particular example of (alleged) media power, that of Rupert Murdoch. This is not to suggest that Murdoch is unique; the record of other conglomerate leaders tells similar stories (see Tunstall and Palmer, 1991). Rather, examining one example provides a richer picture of the nuances of power and influence, and Murdoch stands out as the figure whose power has become an international obsession. As has been apparent, there is only so much that can, in fact, be said about Murdoch's power, and such analyses need to be supplemented by a focus on organizational processes and market incentives, rather than on individual authority (more structure and less agency, as it were). Attributing power to individuals like Murdoch risks missing the larger context which shapes and makes possible their actions. At the same time, while structural factors may shape the roles which individuals fulfil, and hence constrain their thoughts and actions, they are still required to interpret these roles; no two people do this in identical ways. To this extent, power is an attribute of individuals, as well as structures.

Ideally, the two approaches should be combined in detailed examinations of particular processes and decisions. The form and extent of control over media outlets cannot be the subject of sweeping generalizations. As our discussion of Rupert Murdoch makes clear, the exercise of power is complex and open to competing interpretations. Central to any account of power in the mass media must be an acknowledgement of the way in which this control is mediated. Both the internal structure of the media outlet and the wider political structure within which those outlets are situated act to channel the flow of political influence. The degree to which the editor is beholden to those above him or her can be affected by the constitution of the paper. Ownership of media outlets is also subject to political regulation that can determine the interests and opportunities of owners. These can be influenced by government restrictions on cross-media ownership and by judgements on unfair competition and antitrust legislation. Markets are politically constituted systems; they do not exist as autonomous entities. Media power is a product of political decisions, values and processes. So in thinking about the political consequences of media ownership we need to examine the commercial interests of media conglomerates, the practices of owners and the policies of government. We need to be constantly sensitive to the conception of power that underlies the discussion. This same injunction applies as we turn to another source of potential power: journalists and editors.

Chapter 7

Watchdogs or Lapdogs? The Politics of Journalism

There are those who view journalism, not as a guarantor of democratic accountability and representation, but in wholly cynical terms. As one ex-BBC news executive told Nick Davies (2008: 135): 'News is a way of making money, just as selling bread is a way of making money. No one believes that news and journalism are simply a service to democracy.' Such attitudes are not confined to those who have left the profession. The news presenter Jon Snow is quoted as saying that 'Journalists are lazy, they live in a goldfish bowl, they're not interested in breaking out and breaking this stuff [controversial stories] themselves' (Edwards and Cromwell, 2006: 184). Pierre Bourdieu shared some of this disenchantment, seeing journalism as being driven by the obsessive need to avoid what is boring and to provide amusement wherever possible, which leads to a 'tendency to shunt aside serious commentators and investigative reporters in favor of the talk show host' (1998: 3). For Bourdieu, it was less a matter of seeing journalism cynically, but of seeing the cynicism in journalism: 'The journalistic field represents the world in terms of a philosophy that sees history as an absurd series of disasters which can be neither understood nor influenced' (ibid.: 8).

These unflattering portraits of journalism are painted in liberal democratic regimes that, rhetorically at least, place great store by their journalists. These are the people – the professionals – who provide the information upon which citizens rely; it is they who act out the rituals of accountability when cross-examining politicians. They are expected to represent their readers and audiences, or more broadly the 'public', and to speak and act on their behalf. The question raised by the cynical critics is whether this trust is warranted. Do journalists practise their profession on behalf of democracy? Are they independent,

185

servants of political truth and the public interest? Or are they the hired guns of particular political and commercial interests?

Although practices vary across the world, it is rare to find systems in which journalists are licensed to practice or required to meet particular professional standards, maintained by a professional body of some kind. There is professional training, and there are regulatory bodies, but nothing that compares to the regimes that license and regulate lawyers or doctors. And while journalists do not – at least not typically – have direct responsibility for the health and freedom of citizens, they remain vital to the well-being of democratic systems. In a recent report, Stephen Coleman and his colleagues explain the importance of trust in the media and journalism in particular:

> trust in the media amounts to more than confidence in journalistic accuracy. It involves feelings of a kind that accord the media a legitimate place in the ordering of the world. Those who provide news do more than tell daily stories; they frame and shape a common sense of the world, both distant and local.
>
> (Coleman et al., 2009b: 7)

If we share this view, it matters greatly if we discover that journalists are beholden to the political or commercial interests of their proprietors, or if we find that their copy is regularly reworked by, or on behalf of, their employer. We might be equally concerned if these journalists are at the beck and call of parties and other political interests. There have been reports, for instance, of UK government ministers trying to influence appointments made to editorial positions in the national press (*Sunday Telegraph*, 10 May 1998). But even if the interference is more modest, if they are the willing victims of the skilful manipulation practised by political spin doctors and public relations professionals (Kurtz, 1998), our concern remains. We worry that journalists, instead of being the knights in shining armour of *All the President's Men*, where the journalists Carl Bernstein and Bob Woodward exposed the corruption of President Nixon's administration, might turn out to be the dupes of the cynical manipulators of *Wag the Dog*, who lead gullible journalists to accept half-truths and bare-faced lies.

Much is at stake here. If the fears prove to be genuine, and, because of the machinations of owners, governments and spin doctors, journalists turn out to be the lapdogs of partial interests, and not, therefore, the watchdogs of the public interest, then the well-being of the political system is compromised. This chapter is an attempt to assess the political role played by journalism, by looking at the influences operating on it and at the interests which organize its practice. We begin by examining claims made for the power of the spin doctors over journalists. From here, we go on to consider more important trends in journalism – in particular, the alleged demise of investigative journalism and its replacement by 'real life programming' (docusoaps and shows like *Big Brother*) and 'dumbed down' news. At heart, we are concerned with how journalism operates: is it the product of individual adherence to a professional code or is it the result of a process, led by market forces and commercial pressure, in which individual initiative and skill have relatively little impact? These competing models of journalism have important consequences for the way we understand the links between media and politics, and the power and interests at work within the relationship.

The power of the spin doctor?

The journalist Nick Davies (2008) paints a bleak portrait of the current state of his profession. It has, he suggests, become prey to the PR industry, forced to regurgitate press releases rather than offer critical, independent reporting. This fear has been present for some time. Ten years earlier, a spin doctor was reported as saying, 'People would be horrified by the degree to which journalists prostitute themselves.' It was he, not the journalist, who 'had final clearance of the picture, headline and all copy of a supposedly "un-PR-able" newspaper' (*The Times*, 10 April 1998). In recent years, many books, television documentaries and acres of newsprint have been devoted to the spin doctor and to their powers. The main accusation is that it is these people, not the reporters or owners or the advertisers or the readers, who control what the media say (or do not say) about politics. The evidence is there, it is suggested, in the generally positive coverage accorded to political parties at elections, in the appearance of the same phrases or frames in the same stories in different papers

(Billig et al., 1993; Deacon et al., 2001; Miller, 1991). The conclusion drawn is that the news which appears in papers or on broadcasts is not the product of independent journalistic endeavour, but is instead the carefully crafted product of the public relations industry, and in politics, of the spin doctor.

'Spin doctoring' refers to a number of activities and individuals (Gaber, 2000). Alastair Campbell (2007), as Tony Blair's director of communications and strategy, might not have adopted the title of spin doctor, but his diaries are an invaluable insight into the work that such people do. The role includes the 'gatekeeping' of journalistic access, granting or denying interviews, as well as briefing of interviewees on what to say and what not to say. It also includes the glossing of stories or speeches to journalists, pushing particular lines or interpretations. For some, it stretches the boundaries of what might be considered ethical behaviour: 'You have to be economical with the truth sometimes,' as a spin doctor once explained (*Guardian*, 6 October 1997). It means creating good photo-opportunities, or making sure that journalists and photographers are in the right place at the right time. It involves the writing of the speeches, and of the accompanying press releases, and it extends to pressuring or persuading journalists, through threats and flattery, to represent your employer or client favourably. Spin doctors do not only work within the confines of traditional party politics; almost every organization, from the most upright of businesses to the most radical of social movements, employs people to sell their 'brand' to the media. They may not be called 'spin doctors', they may work in 'public relations' or count themselves as a 'spokesperson', but their job is roughly the same: to make sure that the coverage their organization or client receives is the coverage they want.

In *Spin Cycle*, Howard Kurtz (1998: 78–82) tells a story which neatly illustrates the art and the guile of spin doctors. In 1996, President Clinton and his wife Hillary had been on a world tour. Mrs Clinton had been reluctant to give interviews, and kept journalists off her plane. Having maintained her distance, she eventually relented and granted a brief interview to two journalists, who were invited to join her in the cramped confines of her car. Unprepared and awkwardly perched, the journalists listened to Hillary Clinton outline her views about welfare reform. One of them picked up on Mrs Clinton's use of the phrase 'formal role' when talking about her responsibilities, and interpreted this as meaning that the First Lady was to take a prominent place in the Clinton administration (she had taken a back seat after the failure of her attempts to reform health care). When the story hit the street with the headline, 'Reinventing Hillary', the White House reacted immediately, denying that Mrs Clinton had ever said what she was quoted as saying. The piece was 'trashed' by the spin doctors. Even when the journalist proved the report was accurate by playing the tape of the interview, the White House spokespeople kept challenging the story. A day later, when the pilloried journalist met Hillary again, the First Lady is reported by Kurtz as remarking: 'Don't worry .... Your story's fine.' Political news is rarely a simple product of politician and reporter, but is actually an artifice crafted by many intermediaries.

Some spin doctors remain anonymous, lurking in the background, others assume star status. In the United States, the names of Mike McCurry, Don Baer, Marlin Fitzwater and Tom Snow became regular features of news broadcasts and press stories; just as did Jamie Shea, NATO's press secretary, during the Kosovo War; and just as did Bernard Ingham, Charlie Whelan and Alastair Campbell in the United Kingdom. Whatever their public profile, the assumption is that these people are not just aiding the production of political news; they are making the news. When Whelan resigned as press secretary to the then chancellor of the exchequer, Gordon Brown, his memoirs secured banner headlines in the *Mirror:* 'I SPUN IT MY WAY'. Critics of spin doctoring see such claims as proving that people like Whelan distort and manipulate the political process, making impossible the mechanisms of accountability that are central to the democratic process. This was one of the central themes of the film *Wag the Dog*, in which wars and weapons were invented simply to distract attention from the president's misdemeanours. In the United Kingdom, the suspicion was that Alastair Campbell was more influential than his political master, or that Whelan was more important than his ('Chancellor Whelan' was one paper headline) or that Mrs Thatcher played up to the image of her created by Bernard Ingham (Franklin, 2004; Harris, 1990; N. Jones, 1995). There is no little irony, therefore, in reading these comments from Ingham, who was himself once the object of such criticism:

Campbell and Whelan are more concerned by a story than its veracity. They bully journalists, they reward and punish. Whelan, I think, is a very dangerous man. ... They are getting a free ride from a press that seems transfixed. But it's short term. The chickens will come home to roost, or this is no democracy.

(*New Statesman*, 24 October 1997, p.13)

But are such fears justified? Writers like Brian McNair (2000) warn us of the danger of leaping to conclusions, conclusions that often appeal to some mythical media golden age before spin doctoring. Politicians and others have always sought to get favourable coverage, and all that is different now is the method rather than the practice itself. Todd Gitlin (1991: 129–32) argues that many of the targets of current anger about political coverage and media manipulation have a history that can be traced back to the mid-nineteenth century (and arguably the strategy, if not the means, originated earlier, in the writings of Machiavelli). Spin doctors themselves argue that they are merely expediting the process of disseminating news and information, and some journalists, far from seeing spin doctors as intrusive bullies, acknowledge that 'it is part of the job of reporters to have their ears bent by them' (*Independent*, 3 October 1997). Whether or not spin doctoring is a new phenomenon, and whether or not it is a cause for alarm, it might be argued that to focus upon it is to distract attention from the larger picture.

The argument about the power of the spin doctor tends to focus on the relationship between these individuals and the journalist. It does not say much about the context in which this relationship takes place; that is, the political economy of the media. The increasing need to generate advertising revenue has caused an expansion in the space to be filled. The more space there is, the more copy is needed to fill it. When space was limited, the opportunity for discrimination was greater, and the balance of power favoured the editorial staff; but as the space has expanded, so power has moved in the other direction (Hamilton, 2004: 121ff). The same effect occurs with the expansion of media outlets and with the emergence of 24-hour news services. There is also a pressure to provide copy that is attractive and accessible. One journalist complained that competition between newspapers was leading to a:

shift downmarket on at least the news and features pages ....
The emphasis is on attracting marginal and younger readers
who are believed to be less interested in reading about 'heavy'
politics – that is policy rather than personality.

(Guardian, 20 September 2000)

The fifth and final episode of the US television series *The Wire*
dramatised the relationship between journalism and the changing political economy of media. Neatly crafted sound bites and
photo-opportunities fit with this new order. Popular attention
cannot be assumed amidst the noise of competing outlets; journalists have to grab attention. Together, these factors conspire to
create work for the spin doctor.

Spin doctoring, therefore, can be seen as the product of a larger
set of changes, and the arguments about its effects have to acknowledge these factors. Fighting the influence of spin doctoring, if it is
agreed that this needs to be done, cannot simply be a matter of stiff-
ening the sinew of journalists so that they can 'stand up' to their
would-be manipulators. Rather it is a matter of considering the
wider trends affecting changes in the media generally.

The rise of churnalism

In his book *Flat Earth News*, Nick Davies (2008: 59) characterizes these wider trends by the term 'churnalism'. By this he means
that journalists are forced, because of pressures on their time and
other resources, to reproduce as 'news' the material provided by
press and PR agencies. According to Davies, and the research
commissioned for his book, journalists are responsible for origi-
nating only a very small proportion of the copy and having to fill
more space at faster speed with fewer staff (ibid.: 52 and 62ff).
One of the consequences of this is that not only are there fewer
hard news stories for citizens, but also that Parliament and other
elements of the political process are systematically neglected
(ibid.: 80 and 93–4).

Journalists now work in what he calls a 'news factory' (ibid.),
and as a result journalism has become a 'corrupted profession'
(ibid.: 3). This is not a product of the inadequacies of individual
journalists, but of the circumstances in which they find themselves. Despite their best intentions, they fail to get at the truth

and fail 'to perform the simple basic functions of their profession' (ibid.: 59; see also, 13). Nor is this state of affairs the result of specific owners:

> In an imaginary world we might remove Rupert Murdoch and all his influence on all his outlets; we could replace him with Rupert Bear: the Murdoch newspapers and television stations would continue to pump out falsehood, distortion and propaganda.
>
> (Davies, 2008: 22)

Davies lays the blame on the 'internal mechanics of an industry that has been deeply damaged' (ibid.: 23), by which he means that there is a 'tendency for the media to recycle ignorance ... [which] flows directly from the behaviour of the new corporate owners of the media who have cut editorial staffing while increasing editorial output' (ibid.: 73).

Davies's views on the fate of journalism, which he sees as a general problem and not specific to any one country, are couched in strong language and have attracted considerable attention. He is not alone. Other journalists, like John Lloyd (2004) and Andrew Marr (2004), have voiced similar concerns. The decline of traditional journalism is allied not just to a failure to cover the important news, or to the dominance of pre-packaged news, but to the rise of celebrity news to fill the gap. Furthermore, these views are not confined to practitioners; academic commentators too have come to express concern over the capacity of journalism to fulfil its democratic duty (Baker, 2007; Barnett, 2002; Franklin, 2004; Hamilton, 2004; Schlesinger, 2006). While these various writers may not all share Davies's stark and very bleak perspective, they do have in common an anxiety about the fate of investigative journalism.

Investigative journalism and the 'dumbing down' of news

Discussion of the fate of investigative journalism is intimately linked to the ideas of 'churnalism' and celebrity news. The former evokes a time when journalists devoted themselves to uncovering serious cases of corruption. Allegations of rendition and torture, local government and police corruption, corporate bribery of national governments, the cavalier disregard for health and safety by Western firms in developing countries – these are the proper topics of a responsible investigative journalism. 'Doorstepping' celebrities and politicians caught up in adulterous affairs, revelations about the life of their children, or claims about their sexuality: these may emerge as a result of investigation, but they are at best exercises in trivial sensationalism and at worst gross abuses of privacy. They represent a devaluing of journalism, which is compounded by a set of news values that place the world of show business and human interest stories above those about corruption and poverty.

In many ways, the notion of the investigative journalist epitomizes the popular ideal of the profession. It is enshrined in the image propagated by films like *All the President's Men*, *The Insider* and *State of Play*. The ability of journalists to investigate, rather than merely to report information given out at press conferences or in press releases, is often presented as a key defining feature of mass media in a democracy. It addresses the 'watchdog' function, the role of journalism as scrutineer of officialdom and elected representatives. The job of the journalist is to expose wrongdoing and deceit in public office, to act as a key mechanism of public accountability in a democracy. For journalists to operate like this, they have to be able to extract information from people who do not want it revealed. For this, journalists need resources and they need to be free of direct commercial and political pressure. Investigative journalism does not just happen; it is not just a matter of journalists following their 'natural instincts'. Investigative journalism has to be organized, resourced and protected. It depends on trained journalists, supportive editors and a substantial budget. The history of investigative journalism in Australia, culminating in programmes like *Four Corners* and *60 Minutes*, tells of the particular coincidence of circumstances, opportunities and resources (Schultz, 1998: 166ff). It is not the tale of heroic loners.

More recently, writers have argued that we are now witnessing the decline, and even the death of investigative journalism (Barnett, 2002; Doig, 1997; Hamilton, 2004). The heyday of the 1960s and 1970s, when newspapers and television programmes exposed the Thalidomide and Watergate scandals, when miscarriages of justice were pursued and resulted in the release of the innocent, is now past. Newspapers rarely commit resources to exposing these stories. Broadcasters that once scheduled current affairs programmes at peak viewing times now move them later and later, or scrap them entirely. Those that remain concentrate less on politics and more on consumer issues, and what once were revealing documentaries are now docusoaps. 'Bad TV is driving out good, as the satellite and digital wastelands encroach,' remarked David Leigh, himself once an investigative journalist for the axed *World in Action* (*Guardian*, 9 December 1998). In the United States, there has been talk of a 'crisis in journalism' and particularly a 'crisis of tabloidism'. Journalism, it is claimed, is being dominated by 'marketing' and 'demographics'; it is these interests that determine what is covered and how. Journalists are now perceived, not as watchdogs, but as lapdogs (*Columbia Journalism Review*, April 1998). Gitlin (1991: 123) writes of election campaign coverage as a case of 'reporters dancing attendance at the campaign ball while insisting that they were actually following their own beat'. Edwin Baker (2007: 38–9), argues that the death of critical reporting has been hastened by the emergence of the media conglomerate and its multiple interests.

While this narrative of decline is widely accepted and assumed, we need to be wary of embracing it uncritically and without qualification. It is context specific. Writing about media–politics relations in China, Haiyan Wang (2010) argues that, while the label 'investigative journalism' is used, it does not mean the same as in the West. Because of the degree of political control exercised over the media, there is a clientelist relationship between politician and journalist, and as a result investigative journalism, as with other forms of journalism in China, remains subservient to its political masters. Another dimension of the context of the narrative of decline may be that it is specific to a particular form of media. The emergence of bloggers and of websites like Wikileaks (http://wikileaks.org/), which has posted classified and secret documents without apparent reprisals, has led some to ask whether a new era of investigative journalism is emerging (Matheson, 2004). Others are more sceptical (Baker, 2007). Perhaps it is too early to tell, but it is not too early to reflect upon the framework which we might use to make sense of the changes in journalism and its capacity to fulfil its manifold roles.

If there has been a decline in investigative journalism, it is highly unlikely that the explanation for it lies in the fact politicians are now less corrupt than they used to be. An explanation for the decline in investigative journalism has to be sought elsewhere. We need to look to the impact of changing social attitudes, increasing competition and so on. In particular, we need to look at the conditions that establish and promote particular types of journalism. Putting the problem like this is to assume that the changes in journalism have less to do with the individual practitioners and more to do with the structures that shape their working conditions. To explore the implications of, and the assumptions behind, this account of journalism, it helps to look more closely at competing accounts of journalistic practice.

Models of journalism

There are many ways of conceptualizing 'journalism', each of which makes different assumption about the sources of power that shape political coverage. Some versions of journalism make it susceptible to influence, others make it impervious. Three models are set out here, not to offer a comprehensive picture, but rather to identify distinct and different perspectives.

Journalism as observation

The novelist Christopher Isherwood once compared the art of writing to photography: 'I am a camera,' he wrote in *The Berlin Stories*. A similar metaphor is evoked by the rhetoric of journalism. The job of the journalist, it is suggested, is to observe events and to report the experiences of others. The journalist is a mere cypher. The training manuals and the codes of conduct, which the professional journalist is expected to observe, do much to propagate this idea, as does the strict demarcation that is maintained between opinions and facts, between editorial and news pages. In its *Guide for Journalists*, Eastern Counties Newspapers (ECN, n.d.: 7) proclaims: 'Our papers are independent of all political parties and must be seen to be impartial and unbiased.' When accused of bias, media outlets are quick to respond. The BBC's editor of the *Nine O'Clock News* dismissed a complaint of racism in his programme's treatment of a story by saying: 'Our coverage was balanced, accurate and of the usual high standards of integrity expected by our viewers' (*Observer*, 20 February 2000). The style of reporting is intended to reinforce such claims. It must be impersonal, dry, and matter-of-fact. It is not personalized, richly embroidered or highly emotive: 'Stories can be written in a lively and interesting way without using adjectives .... A good story does not need to be dressed up or overwritten. The facts will speak for themselves' (ECN, n.d.: 13). It was Reuters who evolved the convention that an absence of adjectives ensured 'unemotional' coverage and suggested objectivity (Read, 1992: 371). A similar rhetoric is embodied in the saying that 'the camera does not lie'.

No one who holds to this view of journalism would claim that reporters record *everything* they see and hear. They have to make judgements about priorities (what is the important detail) and about news values (which stories matter). These judgements are, however, established by the professional codes and training which define journalism. In March 2000, Independent Television News (ITN) successfully sued the magazine *Living Marxism*, which had suggested that two ITN journalists had fabricated a news report. There was some criticism of the fact that a major news organization had taken on such a small outlet (which subsequently was forced to close), but the justification was that the integrity and credibility of ITN's reports was at stake. In their coverage of the 2000 presidential election, the US news media rushed to 'call' the result, to be the first with the news. They got it wrong, and their credibility was seriously dented. Papers appeared with the banner headline 'BUSH WINS', when, at the time, he had not won. Journalism depends on the belief that it tells the truth, which is why sanctions are taken against those whose lies are publicly exposed: one US newspaper columnist was sacked because she made up the fact that she had a terminal illness (*New York Times*, 12 May 1999); another was fired for falsifying quotations (CBS News online, 17 August 2003); and a UK editor was forced out after publishing faked photographs (BBC News online, 14 May 2004).

The professionalization of journalism enables it to resist the blandishments and bullying of interventionist owners. If newspapers did not cover the news, or if they skewed it to favour their proprietor, they would lose credibility. If one paper consistently operated a different set of (partial) news values, it would look odd on the newsstands. In short, news content is a product of the combined effect of events in the world and professional practice; it is not the product of the will or whim of the individual journalists (or, for that matter, the owner).

Subjective journalism

Against this objectivist view is the claim that journalism is subjective, that it is the product of the prejudices of the individual writer. This argument depends, in part, upon the claim that objectivity is an incoherent idea or an impossible stance. Every story is written from a 'point of view', which inevitably favours one set of interests or actors over another. Journalists are individuals both in the sense that they have different views and in the sense that they have different skills (Henningham, 1998) This means that any two journalists may interpret the same event differently, and some may do it better than others, by being more resourceful or eloquent than their peers. A classic representative of this model of journalism is the late Hunter S. Thompson, once feted along with Tom Wolfe as an exponent of the 'new journalism' (Thompson himself preferred the expression 'gonzo journalism'). In a typical passage from *Fear and Loathing on the Campaign Trail '72*, Thompson demonstrated his own distinctive approach to political journalism:

> For a variety of tangled reasons – primarily because my wife was one of the guests in the house that weekend – I was there when McGovern [at this stage running for the Democratic nomination] arrived. So we talked for a while ... and it occurred to me afterward that it was the first time he'd ever seen me without a beer can in my hand or babbling like a loon about freak power, election bets, or some other twisted subject ... but he was kind enough not to mention this.
>
> (Thompson, 1973: 236)

The radical spirit of this kind of journalism is discussed in detail by Chris Atton (2002), who labels it 'activist-journalism' or 'native reporting'. He (ibid.: 496) traces its origins further back than Thompson, to Jack London and George Orwell, but what he values in it is the same: the attempt to capture how situations and circumstances are *experienced* by those involved.

This version of journalism derives its sense of integrity from the 'honesty' and 'authenticity' with which it chronicles the subjective responses and experiences of the reporter. There is no pretence at Olympian objectivity. The wider assumption is that, while every news report contains a bias of some kind, these biases are randomly distributed across and between media outlets. If subjectivity rules, it is at least plausible that the owner can affect what gets written, to the extent that they are responsible for selecting journalists who share their prejudices. But equally, if the value of journalism lies in the distinctive voices it supplies, skill rather than political values may count for more in the selection process. In any case, owners tend to be involved only in the selection of editors, and it is unclear whether they, or the editors they appoint, would select journalists only for their prejudices, rather than for their journalistic skills. Where the first model of journalism puts the emphasis on professional values and suggests that, like the ideal of the scientific experiment, the results are indifferent to the party doing the job, this second approach stresses the individual's contribution to the outcome. Both, in their different ways, propose that ownership is largely irrelevant to the political character of coverage.

There may well be an element of truth contained in these models, both of which share a notion of journalistic autonomy. But what is missing is an explanation of why journalists come to write about one thing rather than another. Instead, the attention is upon *how* they write about a given event, not *why* that event is selected over any other. It might be countered that they simply report 'events' out there in the world, but of course what counts as 'an event' is not self-evident. An event, or at least one worthy of news coverage, has to be defined as such, and any definition is necessarily contingent and fluid. What is an 'event' to the London *Times* is not necessarily one for the *New York Times*. On the same day, different papers and programmes report different stories. The explanation for this cannot lie with the events themselves, or with the journalists reporting them; it must lie with the process that identifies and prioritizes the stories to be covered. This is the argument of the third model of journalism.

Journalism as structured activity

In this final model, 'news' is not the product of some unanticipated event to which news reporters respond. It is pre-planned and anticipated. News is the product of the availability and distribution of material resources and interests. The ex-journalist Martin Bell once remarked, 'People tend to suppose journalists are where the news is. This is not so. The news is where journalists are' (quoted in Marr, 2004: 292). And for Edward Herman and Robert McChesney, the reporters are where the money is; they (1999: 198) note that in 1996 NBC news made the Olympics its most covered story of the year, while for the other network news programmes it was not in the top ten. 'Perhaps it was a coincidence,' they remark caustically, 'but NBC had the US television rights to the Olympics.' For Herman and McChesney, news, and what journalists cover, is a product of the distribution of corporate interests. This has become, according to McQuail (1992: 106), a much-quoted 'law' of journalism. But commercial interests are not the only factor at play. Changes in media technology also shape the character of news coverage. The development of electronic newsgathering technology (ENG) reduced the cost of, and increased access to, pictures of events. When this was combined with portable satellite systems, news editors could get stories from the so-called front line 'as they happen'. Peter Selb describes the change that new technology made to war reporting:

> One of the most striking improvements in real-time technology was the ability to report live while on the move. CNN used a videophone connected to an enclosed antenna with a gyroscope-controlled platform that kept the antenna pointed toward the satellite regardless of the journalist's land vehicle or ship at sea.
>
> (Selb, 2004: 49)

What this does to television news values is to change the criteria of newsworthiness and to put the emphasis even more upon the visual.

Often, if there are no pictures, it is not news. Susan Carruthers (2000: 211) gives the example of two events in Iraq in the early 1990s, both involving death and persecution. One was the Shia rebellion, the other was the plight of Kurdish refugees. As it happens, the first cost more lives, but it was the second that appeared on the nightly news, because there were cameras to record it. There were no cameras for the Shia rebellion, and so it was not news. Earthquakes on the other side of the world do not happen (in the sense that they do not appear on the news) without film footage; events in East Timor during the 1990s went largely unreported in the West because, it was suggested, film crews and journalists could not operate safely there (Pilger, 2006). There are limits to this argument. The availability of images matters for some stories (especially foreign news), but not for all. Other stories, about the economy, for example, are 'news' even without an accompanying illustration. A recession is news, even if the only picture is a library photo of a bank or of a deserted factory. What all this suggests is that journalism is the product of a process in which technology and other elements determine what journalists report as 'news'.

According to this perspective, to explain the character of journalism, we need to look at structural rather than individual factors. We need to think of news as a product delivered by rival producers to a market. 'Exclusives' and 'scoops' are about gaining a competitive advantage; news organizations attempt to brand themselves as trustworthy and accurate. To understand journalistic practice, we need to look at the pressures on the editorial budget brought about by competition with rivals and for scarce advertising revenue. Advertisers may want lifestyle features, rather than investigations (especially of their clients) (Baker, 2002: 24–6). Equally important may be the political pressure from parties and politicians who through their techniques of media management seek to shape the news.

The implication of this perspective on journalism is that the fate of investigative journalism lies with managerial decisions (and the material interests behind these decisions) about how to allocate resources. Schultz describes the economics of Australian investigative journalism in the 1980s:

> At the same time as editors at the *Sydney Morning Herald* were saying they could not afford a team of three investigative reporters, *60 Minutes* was prepared to let producers and researchers work on major items for several months.
>
> (Schultz, 1998: 192)

Andrew Neil (1997: 56–7) tells of his decision to axe the *Sunday Times* Insight team (often thought of as the embodiment of the investigative journalism tradition (Doig, 1997)). This executive decision had nothing, says Neil, to do with the 'far left politics' of the team's leader, but was made because they were only working on 'second rate investigations'. Nick Davies's (2008) account of the decline of investigative journalism suggests that, rather than being caused by a fall in quality, it was the result of a corporate strategy that saw such journalism as an expensive luxury. This corporate strategy is itself a product of more than the interests of a single paper, but of the interests that derive from ownership (Baker, 2007). The explanation is not to be found in 'events' in the world – there is always something to investigate – but rather in terms of the political economy of the media.

This third perspective on journalism rejects the main premises of the other two. Journalism is necessarily selective and partial, but the selectivity and partiality are not the product of individual values and skills or professional codes. Instead this structuralist model sees coverage as the product of a news-generating process. Understanding the content of news, therefore, means studying the structures that organize it: the division of labour and distribution of resources, the technology and the hierarchy within newsrooms. 'News' is, by this account, what the organization determines it is. Rather than news events creating news stories, we have a situation in which newsrooms create news stories. Take, for example, the distribution of foreign correspondents.

All news organizations make decisions about the allocation of these reporters – about the number of staff, about whether they are on a permanent contract or stringers, and about which countries they are allocated to. The effect of these allocations is to shape the news from which the outlet selects. As far as readers and viewers are concerned, nothing happens in countries without foreign correspondents. The character and quantity of foreign coverage is shaped by the general size of the budget and then by its allocation. Jeremy Tunstall (1996: 339–40) shows how the 'upmarket' daily papers in the United Kingdom increased their foreign staff, from around 70 in the 1980s, to more than 100 in the 1990s. The 'downmarket' tabloids, by contrast, employ no foreign correspondents at all, while they used to 20 years ago. Also important is how these correspondents were distributed; Tunstall (ibid.: 347) reveals that they are concentrated in Europe and North America. Africa gets much less attention, and what it does get is heavily skewed towards

South Africa. These structural factors are key to the character of the resultant journalism, especially when humanitarian crises strike (Scott, 2008; Smith et al., 2006). This is an example of a general phenomenon, one that we encountered in discussing the representation of politics: news is a product of its sources. William Gamson and Andre Modigliani (1989) talk of the 'sponsors' of news – official sources, interest groups and so on – to explain the form taken by the coverage.

If one factor shaping the practice of journalism is the deployment of journalists and their sources, another is the allocation of resources. Stories cost money, and with a limited budget news organizations have to determine what they can *afford* to cover (or put another way, what they cannot afford to ignore, because of the ratings and advertising income they need to generate). Al-Jazeera English (AJE) has a budget of $20,000–$30,000 for a 20 minute film (Padania, et al., 2006: 17). A disillusioned ex-member of the BBC's *Newsnight* current affairs team wrote:

> I know how budget cuts and management fads have neutered Newsnight: I've lived through the process. I have seen the most well-resourced, creatively gifted and filmically talented programme-makers turned, through sheer force of cost-cutting, into an understaffed, overworked team whose first thought must now always be the bottom line.
>
> (*Guardian*, 16 February 1998)

Budgetary factors are not the only ones shaping the news; organizational changes have an impact as well. The managerial structure is important in determining which priorities and interests dominate the scope and character of news coverage. This may be evident in the organizational distribution of power: how editorial decisions are taken and who is involved – the way the 'total newsroom' of US papers combines both marketing and editorial interests. As director general of the BBC, John Birt reorganized the structure of the corporation, creating, among other things, a new management structure for news and current affairs. This, argued Philip Schlesinger (1987), had the effect of altering the news priorities with which the BBC operated. Jay Blumler and Michael Gurevitch note how internal organizational changes can affect the coverage of elections (2002: 216–17). The impact of organizational factors may also be apparent in the more mundane relations of reporter and sub-editor. In the United Kingdom, sub-editors, a dying breed, typically have had the autonomy to rewrite stories; in the United States, reporters are expected to approve the changes. Such arrangements affect 'the news'.

In the structuralist view of journalism, it is possible to see a place for proprietorial intervention, not (as in the second view) through the selection of journalists, but through the organization of the news machine. Insofar as owners (or their interests) play a crucial role in setting budgets, allocating space and so on, their actions frame the way journalists operate. These factors may not affect the particular character of any one story, but they can set the framework within which all stories exist. One example of how this might be done is provided by AJE which is working to create a network of locally based film-makers to supply news and documentary films, thereby reducing the costs of foreign news, delivered by the traditional system of foreign correspondents (Pandania et al., 2006). At a more general level, the commercial interests of the media conglomerate play directly into the resourcing and practice of journalism.

Even changes in the political regime itself can affect the practice of journalism. Liu Hong reports that, before the process of economic liberalization:

> all newspapers in China had the status of the emperor's daughters. They did not have to worry about their dowries or marriages. Most papers received their subscription from the public purse .... It made no difference whether people wanted to buy the paper or not.
>
> (Liu Hong, 1998: 32)

Journalists were answerable only to the communist authorities. However, when economic reforms were introduced in the 1990s, the incentives changed to make journalists more responsive to their readers (or the perception of their readers). Again the suggestion is that journalism is shaped by wider structural factors.

The full implication of this, argues Michael Schudson (2000), is that we need to view the organization of journalism from a variety of perspectives, not just the political economy one offered here, but also one deriving from the sociology of organizations –

the daily routines and habits of news production – and one deriving from a cultural account of the values and worldviews that construct 'news' itself. These perspectives give added weight to the general sense of journalism as part of an embedded process.

But because journalism is constantly being constructed and reconstructed, we have to be conscious of its changeability, and of the possibility that journalism itself may be eliminated in the same way that it was formed. Journalism as a career has already been overtaken by public relations. Added to this, politicians are increasingly interested in finding ways of reaching audiences that do not involve journalists: by appearing on chat shows or by using the internet. At the same time, there has been growing awareness of the possibility that new media create for new forms of journalism, and threaten the old: 'new political media are precipitating an awareness, at least among some mainstream political journalists, that their jurisdiction over political news reporting is in jeopardy' (Dooley and Grosswiler, 1997: 43–4). Certainly, new media (which we discuss in detail in Chapter 10) have been changing the journalistic landscape, not just through the proliferation of commentators in the blogosphere, but through the phenomenon of 'user-generated content'. Stuart Allan (2003; 31) anticipates 'a re-configuration of what counts as journalism in the global network society'. It may still be too early yet to determine the full impact of new media, but there is little doubt the emerging technologies constitute a further element in the restructuring of journalism, and hence of the way in which politics is covered.

In the United Kingdom in the 1990s, political coverage was primarily a matter of reporting directly the proceedings of parliamentary life. Now the emphasis, as we saw in Chapter 3, has shifted to the commentator and the columnist (Tunstall, 1996: 282). It is the commentators in the traditional (and increasingly in new) media who command the space and the kudos. Their stock-in-trade is to pass judgement on the political story (with its own heroes and villains), telling us how it began and where it will end. The political commentator is, therefore, instrumental in establishing a picture of politics in which personality is as important as principle. This development in political coverage is a product not simply of the changing agenda and interests of the writers, but of the pressures and interests that caused them to be appointed and to be allocated space. These include the shifting commercial incentives and interests of the newspaper industry which squeeze out direct political reporting, because it is costly and cannot rival broadcasting coverage. Besides, attracting advertisers pushes the agenda away from political stories to 'human interest' ones, a trend that is itself compounded by the way in which the flow of political information is increasingly managed and controlled. In short, it is possible to see the rise of the political columnist and political commentary as the product of shifts in the political economy of the media. James Hamilton (2004: 215ff) talks of 'journalists as goods' and 'as entertainers', whose journalistic language is shaped by the market incentives under which their employers operate – to secure advertisers and the brand loyalty of their readers/audiences.

In this spirit, Steven Barnett (2002: 403–6) chronicles what he describes as the four ages of political journalism, drawing on and developing categories originally devised by Larry Sabato. The first phase is that of deferential ('lapdog') journalism, where the reporter simply reproduces the words of the politician; the second is that of 'equal engagement', when exchanges between journalists and politicians were more robust, and when each challenged the other to defend their corner. This period, says Barnett, has been followed by the era of journalistic 'disdain', in which the journalist adopts an attitude of deep suspicion of the motives and reliability of politicians. This leads to an era, the present one, of 'contempt'. For Barnett, this final phase contributes to the general cynicism that affects popular attitudes towards politics. In keeping with this model of journalism as structured activity, Barnett (ibid.: 400–2) locates the emergence of types of journalism in the larger political economy of the media. The key factors are the decline in the press market, the relaxation of media regulation, and the pressure on budgets.

Because the third model of journalism places the emphasis on the effect of the political economy within which journalists operate, there is a useful parallel to be drawn between the organization of journalism in the media industry and the organization of other industries. This is to reinforce a theme that runs throughout this book: the need to see the coverage of politics as a commercially mediated cultural activity. At the beginning of Chapter 6, we noted that media industries are producing products and services, and that their practices have to be understood in the same way that other businesses are understood. But these conglomerates are also producing culture, products that have meaning for the way people identify themselves and others. Our understanding of the behaviour of these organizations needs to reflect this fact. One implication of this might be that we need to take account of research into cognate cultural industries, whether Hollywood or the record industry. Work by Keith Negus (1999), for example, has pointed to the ways in which record companies organize themselves to support particular musical genres (and to marginalize others). 'News' can be understood as a genre in the same sense, and we can see how changing corporate strategy can affect the conditions for different types of journalists (artists). The columnist is, as Hamilton (2004) suggests, a performer or entertainer. The idea that journalists be seen as sober-suited versions of the pop star may seem faintly ridiculous, but then to look at the salaries paid to newscasters is to remind ourselves that they are celebrities at the very least, and more often than not 'stars', no different in the way they are made and marketed by corporate strategy from Julia Roberts or Kanye West. The marketing of the performers is intimately linked to the marketing of the content, and just as Hollywood plot lines are shaped by corporate strategy, so are the stories told in the news. In his analysis of *The Daily Show with Jon Stewart,* Geoffrey Baym (2005) gives an interesting twist to this perspective. For Baym, *The Daily Show* has created a new form of critical journalism through its mixture of satire, talk and news. It is not just offering 'infotainment' (ie making news more 'palatable'); it is developing a new discourse for comprehending and responding to the world at large, in which politics and media culture coexist.

Conclusion

It might be supposed that, if journalism is structured in the way that the third model suggests, the prospects for reform are limited, that attempts to counter 'dumbing down' are bound to fail. This conclusion is not warranted. Rather, what the third model does indicate is that the answer to the problem does not lie in eliminating spin doctors or in the good intentions of journalists. Reform has to focus on the conditions of journalism. The arguments for regulating journalism are discussed in Chapter 12, what needs to be noted here is that legislation can make a difference, insofar as it shapes the conditions under which journalism is done. But it is equally important to address the market conditions under which media operate and the regulatory regimes that apply to them. As Alan Doig (1997: 206) writes: 'Any revival of investigatory journalism ... must work within a very different environment than that which promoted investigative journalism in earlier decades.' By this he means that the revival must address the commercial pressures that make 'ratings and profit' of greater importance than 'performance and the public interest'. Others suggest that the key lies in the opportunities created by new technology, in the guise of sites like Wikileaks making investigation an online activity, and making all of us citizen journalists (Gillmoor, 2006).

Certainly, the third model does not absolve journalists (citizen or otherwise) of responsibility for what they report and how they report it. There is still a place for journalistic ethics. The structuring of journalism shapes the *role* which its occupant has to fulfil, but the role is not so tightly defined as to straitjacket its inhabitant. Roles are *performed*, and individuals have the scope to interpret the rules and conventions that define their activity. To this extent, journalists are in a position to make judgements about what it is legitimate to say or do in the pursuit of a story. In return, society is entitled to pass judgement on how that role is fulfilled and to require different standards. What those standards should be are discussed later. For now, we end by recalling the experiments in 'civic journalism' which were mentioned in Chapter 6.

Civic journalism was an attempt to improve the quality of election coverage, and to counter the political management of news. The coalition of media organizations in North Carolina created a common agenda, based upon the priorities of their readers and viewers. Politicians were required in interviews to address this agenda, rather than their preferred one (Clark, 1997). The results were not always viewed as successful, with critics complaining that civic journalism was essentially conservative and uncritical (Jackson, 1997), but the point is that the North Carolina experiment represents an instance of the way in which the organization of news gathering directly shapes the output. Civic journalism underlines the argument that the capacity of journalists to play a democratic role is not simply a matter of individual integrity or of the willingness of reporters to resist the pressures applied by spin doctors. What was true for civic journalism may also be true for its new incarnation as citizen journalism or public journalism (Rosen et al., 2000). Journalism's ability to serve democracy still depends on the allocation of resources and the organization of its practices. It maybe that the new citizen journalism lacks the formal deliberate intent of civic journalism, but its potential is being assessed in similar terms (Allan, 2003; Gillmoor, 2006; Matheson, 2004). And the stakes may be very high. As Matt Carlson writes of the use of blogging in the United States on Election Day in 2004:

> Journalists are now faced with a competing form of political discourse, but one that challenges journalism's normative foundations. It is more than a competition for eyeballs; it is a different way of producing and consuming political communication.
>
> (Carlson, 2007: 275)

Not everyone agrees (Baker, 2007), but the possibility of radical change is one that has to be taken seriously. We return to this later, but first I want direct attention to another major issue: the impact of globalization on media's relationship to politics.

Chapter 8

Dream Worlds: Globalization and the Webs of Power

In July 2005, huge pop concerts were staged in eight countries around the world under the banner of Live8. They all had one aim, to persuade the leaders of the G8 nations to reduce the debts of the developing countries. The two prime movers, Bono and Bob Geldof, claimed that they had a mandate from the people of the world for their cause. Twenty years earlier, again at the instigation of Geldof, rock stars had also assembled for a good cause. This time it was to help the victims of famine in Ethiopia. The event was Live Aid. Once again the stars claimed a global mandate, this time in song: 'We are the world'. Although the impact of these events is much debated, few would deny that they both represent examples of the presence and potential of a global media, a media that straddles the world, creating new communities and creating new political possibilities. Without such a media, neither Live8 nor Live Aid could have happened.

Other, equally dramatic claims have been made for global media. This was what Rupert Murdoch argued in a speech in London in 1993:

> Advances in the technology of communication have proved an unambiguous threat to totalitarian regimes: fax machines enable dissidents to bypass state-controlled print media; direct-dial television make it difficult for a state to control interpersonal voice communication; and satellite broadcasting makes it possible for information-hungry residents in many closed societies to bypass state-controlled channels.
>
> (quoted in Page, 2003: 467)

In a similar spirit, Ithiel de Sola Pool (1990: 65) wrote, 'With a satellite, the communications distance between all points within its beam has become essentially equal .... Boundaries partition

209

nothing.' Such pronouncements, made many years ago, might seem now like statements of the blindingly obvious. We have global media that have transformed our world. They have alerted viewing publics to wars and famines; audiences have become party to international negotiations and virtual partici-pants in acts of diplomacy and peace keeping (Carruthers, 2000: 197–205; Curran, 2000: 136–7). Governments, the UN, relief agencies and others have all used the global presence of television crews and reporters to shape political agendas and policies.

But as with anything that seems obvious, the reality is much more complex and much more ambiguous. We need only to listen to the critics of global media, those who draw attention to the media empires that are delivering a space without borders, and who see not a world united in a common goal, but McWorld (Barber, 1997), a global US shopping mall. So, for Edward Herman and Robert McChesney (1997: 136), though the effects of media globalization may, in the short term, be 'benign or positive', in the longer term it threatens 'democratic politics'.

This chapter explores these competing perspectives on the political impact of global media. In doing so, we look at the actual content and character of the new global media industries, and cast a wary eye on the rhetoric of globalization from whichever camp it emerges. What looks like a global industry may in fact, as David Hesmondhalgh (2007: 212ff) suggests, be more a case of 'inter-nationalization', of the extension of media markets rather than of their total transformation; of power being located within specific nations, rather than being transposed to the global realm. Or to qualify the rhetoric in another way, Jeremy Tunstall argues that the much vaunted 'global audience' is – in reality – rather more parochial, devoting 80 per cent of its time to viewing domestic, national media, and only 20 per cent of its time to media content from outside its own borders (2008: 449).

What we are trying to establish, then, is the extent to which the media that operate across and beyond national borders represents an important source of political power, and who or what benefits and loses from this. There are three elements to this power. The first is associated with the influence and reach of the new media conglomerates. The second is their power relative to that wielded by national governments and nation states. And finally, there is the matter of whether these new media conglom-erates change the way citizens think and act; do they give us new cosmopolitan identities and new global ethics? If, as the cliché has it, knowledge is power: who controls and shapes the flows of information that now envelope the globe?

Global players

Signs of the global media economy are already familiar ones (as we saw in Chapter 6). They can be seen in the worldwide presence of corporations like Disney and Sony, News Corporation and Reuters, organizations that appear to have a stake everywhere. This is not a new phenomenon; arguably, it is the continuation of the legacy of earlier empires when shipping routes represented a form of global communication and trade. Nonetheless, recent changes have been rapid and far ranging. In the early 1990s, CNN transmitted its rolling news to 137 countries (*Economist*, 2 May 1992: 26); in 2010 it claimed to be available to audiences in 212 territories (http://www.timewarner.com/corp/). Back in 1994, the cable company Viacom paid $10 billion for the Hollywood studio Paramount, adding to its ownership of MTV (Music Television), the publishers Simon & Schuster, *Beavis and Butt-head* cartoons, the Blockbuster video chain, and Virgin Interactive Entertainment (Herman and McChesney, 1997: 77–81). At the time, the chairman of Viacom described his company as a 'global media powerhouse of unparalleled proportions' (*Independent on Sunday*, 6 April 1994). Since then Viacom has continued to expand. As its website boasts:

> Our family of prominent and respected brands includes the multiplatform properties of MTV Networks, BET Networks, Paramount Pictures and Paramount Home Entertainment. MTV Networks includes favourites like MTV, VH1, Nickelodeon, Nick at Nite, COMEDY CENTRAL, CMT: Country Music Television, Spike TV, TV Land, Logo and approximately 155 networks around the world. In addition, digital assets such as Neopets, Xfire, Atom, Harmonix and Quizilla offer compelling and interactive content, providing an even deeper connection with our devoted and focused demographics.
> (http://www.viacom.com/, visited on 1 February 2010)

And here is Time Warner reporting on one of its more recent global ventures:

> In September 2007, Warner Bros. Entertainment partnered with ALDAR, Abu Dhabi's leading real estate developer, and the newly established Abu Dhabi Media Company to form an unprecedented, long-term, multi-faceted strategic alliance calling for the creation of a theme park and hotel, jointly owned multiplex cinemas, a co-finance agreement covering feature films and videogames, and the build-out of the infra-structure for Abu Dhabi's digital transformation.
> (http://www.timewarner.com/, visited on 9 July 2008)

The history of the media conglomerates is littered with such alliances, but what is new is the addition to the mix of other global players, like the mobile phone companies that increasingly focus on providing a range of media services, led by Apple and now increasingly dominated by Google (Hindman, 2009: 38ff).

Before Google's ascendancy, it was the Microsoft empire (estimated value in 2007: $260 billion, with 90,000 employees in 105 countries) that acted as the gatekeeper for almost all forms of computer-based communication, colonizing the internal software of computers and their capacity to communicate with each other. One of the other major players in the global market has been the BBC, particularly via its commercial wing, BBC World, which was available in 2003 to some 241 million homes in 200 countries (Thussu, 2003: 119). In 2007, the BBC's commercial arm paid £89 million for a controlling stake in the Lonely Planet travel guides, and used its vast archive of travel and natural history footage to create a new website to promote the Lonely Planet brand (BBC News online, 1 October 2007).

Looming above both Microsoft and the BBC is Google, with the many services that have emerged on the back of its search engine – from emails to phones and beyond. One of the most interesting examples of Google's recent ascendancy has been the fate of its accommodation with the Chinese authorities, which meant that certain sites (especially those that relate to Tiananmen Square and Tibet) were not accessible to Chinese users. But more important is Google's position – together with Microsoft and Yahoo! – as the occupier of a pivotal position in the distribution of all information. Manuel Castells (see also Hindman, 2009) refers to the emergence of 'Googlearchy' in which:

> their actions are increasingly setting the agenda for other multimedia giants .... Now that Google owns YouTube, Yahoo! owns Xanga, and Microsoft has a stake in Facebook, they control critical nodes between the media sphere and the online sphere.
>
> (Castells, 2009: 96–7)

All these ventures reflect an ambition to provide a complete media package. Indeed, what these organizations represent is an ability to control cultural production – whether news or entertainment – whenever and wherever it takes place. They are the warlords of commercial and cultural global domination; they are the new emperors. Or at least this is how they seem. Importantly, the politics involved apply not only to corporations and governments, but also to the cultural politics of identity, space and place. To assess their impact, we need first to look at the conditions and processes that have been bracketed together in the idea of globalization. Globalization did not just appear, driven by some law of nature; it had to be made to happen.

A history of the future

Mass communication has existed for little more than the average person's lifespan, and yet in that short time we have moved from what now seems the most basic of radio communication (the crystal set) to the apparent sophistication of digital broadcasting, interactivity and time-shifting, and thence to 3-D and beyond. We have yet to experience the full consequences of these latest developments, but we can be sure that, 80 years from now, people will look at our system of communication and think of it as being as primitive as we now regard a valve radio. Of course, it will not just be the technologies that change. It will be the way in which people relate to these new forms of communications, and how these relations order human identities and communities. You can, after all, change the amount people talk, and who they talk to, just by rearranging the furniture in a room.

It is impossible to separate the notion of globalization from the possibilities created by technological change. Indeed, the story of mass communication is inextricably bound up with the story of technical innovation, and this is as true for global media as for anything else. What is important, though, is how the tale is told. It is relatively easy to get agreement about the innovations that have mattered and what they involved. First there was radio, the capacity to transmit sound over distance, without the need for any physical connection, and with the signal available to anyone with a receiver; and then there was television, which added pictures to the sound. Both were developments of the technologies of the telegraph and the telephone, themselves the inheritors of work in electromagnetism and electricity.

These technical changes were marked by more mundane, but no less important developments in component technology: the replacement of the valve by the transistor, opening up the possibility of portability and reliability, as well as cost reduction. From here the path led to integrated circuitry and the microchip, crucial to the creation of the computer and satellite technology, which were themselves dependent on theoretical work in mathematics, philosophical logic, astronomy and so on. And later still, this knowledge and technology were harnessed to create, with innovations in computer language, the world wide web and the so-called 'digital revolution'. The latter has delivered a one-stop media platform, in which news, music, television, films, books, social networking and much else besides is available through a single device. Together and individually, these facilities have the potential not just to change what we know, but how we act and think, how we relate to each other, indeed with whom we relate.

But while it is relatively easy to get agreement about the key technologies and what they make possible, there is much less of a consensus about why it is happening and therefore what interests and processes are implicated in the changes. Sometimes it is made to seem that we are in the grip of a process of (natural) evolution, and that we need only to adapt to this changing order, reluctantly at first perhaps (worried by what it is doing to the world we know), but soon embracing it (and then wondering how we ever managed without it). This kind of interpretation of events is associated with writers like Ithiel de Sola Pool (1990) who see each wave of technological invention as building progressively upon its predecessor. It makes no sense to resist. We have to accept the political, social and cultural changes that new technologies bring in their wake. For de Sola Pool, this means the acceptance that, if new forms of communication technology destroy or make redundant national borders, we need to give up our quaint affection for a world of sovereign nation states.

This way of thinking about the development of communications can be labelled technological determinism. It assumes that technology is driven by an inner scientific logic, a logic of progress in which each stage adds to its predecessor, enabling people to do more than they could before. To defy this logic is to act irrationally: it is to refuse the opportunity to improve the quality of life; it is to deny the inevitable. The only reasonable response is to adapt. This is a view that has a strong intuitive appeal. There does indeed seem to be a logic to technical change, one that takes us from the transmission of sound to the transmission of pictures. It is hard to mount arguments against technologies that appear to give us more of what we already have, especially if it is cheaper, faster, and more reliable. Who would swap their digital receiver for a valve radio, their car for a horse? It is easy to succumb to the pressure to adopt, and adapt to, each new development. To be without television and radio in developed countries is to be cut off, to be marginalized. Groups like White Dot (http://www.whitedot.org/issue/iss_front.asp), who campaign for the abolition of television, seem from this perspective to be anachronisms, no more in touch with social or scientific reality than flat earthers or creationists.

But however attractive the idea of technological determinism, we need to be wary of its charms. Brian Winston (1998), for example, offers a quite different perspective on these changes: they are not the product of some persistent logic; they are instead the consequence of interests and intentions. The route taken by technical development is not mapped by the logic of 'progress' but by the allocation of resources, itself the consequence of political and economic priorities.

Radio was the product of military needs, a way of coordinating the movement of vast armies. In the same way, the transistor was designed to meet the needs of submarine technology; and the integrated circuit (the microchip) was needed for space exploration and the security interests allied with it. The internet too is the product of corporate and state interests. Initially created as a failsafe system of communication to enable the US military to continue to function in the aftermath of a nuclear attack, the internet was developed by scientists who wanted to use the computer networks to communicate with each other. Only with the appearance of user-friendly computer languages has the current form of the web become possible. Similar processes have transformed the net's anarchic chaos of information into a highly lucrative commercial market. We need only to think of Google's purchase of YouTube for $1.65 billion in 2006.

Domestic access to news, entertainment and sport is not simply the consequence of technological innovation. It is the product of, among other things, commercial initiatives. In 1993, the Bell Atlantic telephone company merged with Tele-Communications (TCI). The deal was worth $33 billion and created a giant communications conglomerate that could reach 42 per cent of US homes. Murdoch's News Corporation made a similar deal with the second biggest telecommunications company in the United States. The tie-up allowed Murdoch to supply films, news and much more to its newly acquired subscribers. Moves like this created the material reality that allowed modern forms of communication to exist. So it goes on: technology is the product of priorities established within the corporate and political system. Not all such mergers bring success and untold riches. The Time Warner–America Online merger, agreed in 2000, was described ten years later as a disaster on a par with the Vietnam and the Iraq wars (*New York Times*, 10 January 2010). But even the failures form part of strategy to locate new markets and to have a controlling stake in new forms of media. Furthermore, they all depend on the cooperation of government. 'Globalization' is, after all, as much a political as an economic phenomenon, a product of neoliberalism as well as of the 'logic' of the market. The globalized media economy depended crucially on the 1997 decision of the World Trade Organization to deregulate telecommunications. Without a liberalization of trade and other barriers, the global networks could not operate (Hardy, 2008: 161ff).

But this version of technical change, in which intent and interest are decisive, is itself open to criticism. It may exaggerate the extent to which the key players themselves command the outcome of research and development (think of the failure of the Time Warner merger with AOL, or the decline of

MySpace and Bebo). Neither the technologies nor their consequences can be anticipated fully. Organizations are as often coping with the effects of old technologies as they are calling new ones into being. Technologies do indeed develop some degree of independent momentum; and while the various actors may be instrumental in instigating and regulating these technologies, they are never fully in command (Hughes, 1983). One factor in the equation, for example, is governments, which, for a variety of different reasons and in a variety of different ways, also regulate systems of communication. The extent to which they succeed may be debated, but they cannot be ignored. Similarly, the use made of the new technologies is not controlled absolutely by the corporations. The music industry, for instance, has struggled to develop a business model to cope with the potential that digitization and the internet have created for the distribution of high-quality copies of songs (Knopper, 2009).

The degree to which the use of technology can be controlled and predicted varies from case to case. Marshall McLuhan (1994/1964) represented this difference in terms of 'hot' and 'cool' technologies, Ivan Illich (1975) in terms of 'hard' and 'soft'. What both were trying to capture was the extent to which some forms of communications technology (the telephone, for example) allowed for considerable control by the user, while other forms (television) allowed for very little. We decide what is said on the phone; broadcasters decide what we see (or used to, before time-shifting and catch-up sites). In other words, the technology itself is one element in the way the story of technical and social change is told. In contemplating the future of mass communications, therefore, we should not think in terms either of technology automatically dictating the shape of the world, or of that world being determined by political will and/or commercial interest. Rather, the future is a product of complex interactions between the technical, the commercial and political realms. It is this third approach to technical change that is used here in exploring the political consequences of a globalized media. Technological change is made possible by the new conglomerates, but it is these conglomerates that give impetus to the technology, and both are dependent upon the mediating effects of political regimes and other participants in the process.

Globalization or internationalization?

As we move from looking at the key players and the forces that drive change in the political economy of mass communications, we come to focus ever more closely upon their collective impact. Here we begin to confront two sets of arguments. The first is that between conceptualizing change as 'internationalization' or as 'globalization', with the different distribution of power each implies. The second, which accepts the existence of globalization, begs the question as to whether its impact is beneficial or malign; whether it provides the conditions for liberty and creative hybridity, or for cultural imperialism. David Hesmondhalgh takes on both arguments, contending that the changes we are witnessing constitute, more often than not, internationalization, rather than globalization, and that the case for cultural imperialism has not been made (2007: 214–19). For him the weakness of much of the current debate about globalization lies in its lack of empirical detail. He is therefore wary of announcing the arrival of the entirely new order that the term 'globalization' tends to herald.

Globalization has many different meanings, but one of the most straightforward definitions is that offered by John Tomlinson, who writes:

> Globalization ... refers to the rapidly developing process of complex interconnections between societies, cultures, institutions and individuals world-wide. It is a social process which involves a compression of time and space, shrinking distances through a dramatic reduction in the time taken – either physically or representationally – to cross them, so making the world seem smaller and in a certain sense bringing human beings 'closer' to one another.
>
> (Tomlinson, 1999: 165)

Globalization represents the idea that traditional borders are being superseded by a system which operates at a supranational level.

The expression of this new order may be found in the *content* of communication: the same images and icons wherever you go. This is most typically illustrated by the ubiquity of Coca-Cola or of film and pop stars (Brad Pitt, Angelina Jolie, George Clooney,

Madonna, Beyoncé), but it can be represented also in the same photos of the same event appearing everywhere: the attacks on the Twin Towers; Princess Diana's funeral cortege; Cathy Freeman or Usain Bolt winning Olympic gold medals. Or globalization may be identified in the system of *distribution*, with everyone inhabiting the same networks of communication: the same corporations supplying television programmes and news to everyone. Finally, globalization may refer to a system of *production* by which the control of the means of communication lies with organizations that exist above and beyond individual nation states.

To draw attention to these three dimensions of globalization is not to be committed to the view that they all accurately describe changes in the world or that they necessarily run harmoniously with each other. While the same transnational corporations may distribute the same music across the world, those corporations are also involved in marketing particular performers to distinct markets, with the global acts being packaged differently for different contexts. Cultural content is not standardized, rather it is customized. This is one aspect of what Roland Robertson (1995) calls 'glocalization'. Globalization is not necessarily about creating homogeneity and uniformity, although it may indeed do this; it is about the redistribution of power and about the technologies and interests that are linked to the new order.

The point of drawing attention to the three dimensions of globalization is not to suggest that they represent the complete picture, but to enable us to separate the different ways in which globalization may tie media and politics. The driving dynamic of globalization may stem from the same set of technological developments and the commercial interests that organize them, but the political consequences cannot simply be read off these facts. To assess the implications of globalization for the link between media and politics, we need to focus on two issues. The first is the effect of globalized media on the powers of national governments, the formal sites of legitimate political power, to regulate media in the name of whatever political interests those governments claim to represent. The second, and related, effect is on the cultural politics of identity, on the way in which the 'people' are constituted and reconstituted in global networks.

These two aspects of globalization are nicely captured in two stories about Rupert Murdoch's attempt to bring India within his media empire. The first is an account of a trip he paid to India in the mid-1990s. Alan Rusbridger wrote:

> He [Murdoch] kept all his appointments, attended all his lunches, gave numerous interviews and made a big impression all round. 'He had India eating out of his hand,' said Tavleen Singh, a leading columnist with the Indian Express. 'It was like the visit of a head of state.'
>
> (*Guardian Weekend*, 9 April 1994)

This story tells both of the way in which Murdoch's global power commanded respect, and of how he needed to win people over to his ambitions. The other story takes place four years later, when it was announced that a New Delhi lawyer had convinced an Indian court to issue a warrant for Murdoch's arrest, on the grounds that the movies transmitted on his Star channel (*Dance of the Damned, The Jigsaw Murders*), 'were vulgar, obscene and unfit for Indian audiences' (*Guardian*, 9 August 1998). In this case, cultural content, rather than cultural control, was the issue. But both stories tell of the complex politics of a globalized media.

Conglomerates, governments and identities

Rupert Murdoch's trip to India is typical of the way he has sought to build up a global media business. He has deliberately courted those in power. Commercial success is not just a product of commercial resources; it depends on constant negotiations with governments who both need his corporations and have the capacity to set the terms under which they operate. Murdoch's Star channel is a classic example of this. Star TV was delivered via the AsiaSat-1 satellite and had a potential reach of 45 million viewers. It gave access to seven out of the ten fastest growing economies and to markets that were worth a fortune in advertising revenue. Star's existence depended on government support, or at least acquiescence. Murdoch had been assiduous in his cultivation of political leaders, without whose cooperation he could not succeed. He dropped the BBC's world service from AsiaSat-1, out of deference to the political sensitivities of the Chinese authorities, just as one of News Corporation's subsidiaries, the publisher HarperCollins, dropped its book contract with Chris Patten, and just as Andrew Neil's tenure at the *Sunday Times* ended in the aftermath of his paper's claims about corruption in Malaysia (Dover, 2008: 133–8; Page, 2003: 464–79). These instances are taken by critics as examples of Murdoch's reluctance to antagonize political leaderships with whom he needs to do business.

The journalist John Pilger, one of Rupert Murdoch's most persistent critics, argues that the media entrepreneur goes to considerable lengths to secure the support of the Chinese regime:

> his Star TV broadcast a documentary series made by the Beijing regime, eulogising the life and times of Deng Xianoping .... [A] hagiography of Deng written by his daughter was published by Basic Books, a division of Harper Collins; ... Mrs Deng was flown to Murdoch's US ranch and feted with lavish parties.
>
> (*Guardian*, 16 March 1998)

Similar claims are made for the ways in which Murdoch cultivated his links with Margaret Thatcher and then Tony Blair (inviting the latter, when he was still in opposition, to address a meeting of News Corporation executives in Australia) (Page, 2003: 431).

But while Murdoch has cultivated alliances in pursuit of his empire, states have continued to react against the trend towards a globalized media. One source of concern is that global products are in some way 'harmful', economically or culturally. So it is that governments opt for regulation in order to protect the interests of local companies (and the economic benefits – and votes – they represent) or to protect the integrity of the national culture. While there may be a general trend towards economic deregulation, all nations continue to operate immigration, trade and cultural polices which restrict or manage the access their citizens have to external sources of media and culture (Cloonan, 1999; Freedman, 2008; Tunstall, 2008).

To get an idea of the fears that lie behind such policies, take the case of the Reuters news agency, supplier of news to commercial companies, financial markets, broadcasters and newspapers. In 1991, Tunstall and Palmer noted, 'Reuters has become the biggest distributor of computer-based information services, with offices in 81 countries and fixed revenue earnings from some

200,000 terminals in 35 countries' (1991: 46). In 1998, the Reuters business had expanded so that it distributed news 'to over 260 client broadcasters in 85 countries' (Paterson, 1998: 79). By 2003, Reuters' own television service was operating in 150 countries (Thussu, 2003: 120). In 2007, Reuters merged with the Canadian publisher Thompsons, to become 'the world's biggest financial news and data company' (*Guardian*, 9 May 2007). The issue is not just the ubiquity and size of Reuters, it is also about what its clients get. As Tunstall and Palmer explain:

> For the world's leading electronic publisher, products, technology, markets and systems are interdependent: Reuters deals in real-time information services, transaction products, trading-room systems, historical information and last (as a revenue earner) but not least, media products.
>
> (Tunstall and Palmer, 1991: 46)

Reuters' aim is to provide 'complete information packages', but in serving all their customers, there is a danger that they satisfy none of them. Only stories with a universal resonance are carried, and those specific to particular settings are ignored (ibid.: 58). Global news, it might be suggested, creates a monolithic view of the world, one in which regional and national differences are lost to view, and everybody is subsumed within a specific dominant news agenda. Paterson observes another trend in the global supply of news: the concentration of control over the selection of news as the market is dominated by a few powerful players (1998: 80).

This process of standardization and concentration seems to threaten culture as well as news, exacerbating fears about the ways in which globalization distorts cultural identity and difference. In its place, says Benjamin Barber, stands 'McWorld':

> With or without resistance, nations with proud traditions of film-making independence like France, England, Sweden, India, Indonesia and Japan are in fact gradually succumbing to the irresistible lure of product that is not only predominantly American but, even when still indigenous, is rooted in the glamour of the seductive trinity sex, violence and money, set to a harmonizing score of American rock and roll.
>
> (Barber, 1997: 90)

Globalization, it is argued, produces homogeneity: the same ideas and values, the same films and songs, carried to all parts of the world. This process squeezes out local culture. In villages in India, in rooms lit by 20 watt bulbs and warmed by open fires, people watch satellite TV:

> We began with MTV .... A touch on the zapper brought us *The Bold And The Beautiful*, a sub-*Dynasty* American soap .... Zap, and suddenly the features of famed British telly-chef Keith Floyd .... Zap, and we have skiing on Prime Sports.
> (*Guardian Weekend*, 9 April 1994)

Don Ayteo of MTV boasts: 'We've revolutionised the way Indian kids devote themselves to leisure .... We've created a youth culture where there was simply none before' (quoted in *Guardian Weekend*, 9 April 1994). Howard Stringer, then at CBS, told the Royal Television Society:

> The new media giants that win control of UK broadcast properties may view them as cash cows whose resources are to be wrung dry – and invested elsewhere in their global empire. Or they may prefer to replicate for Great Britain shows that they have already produced elsewhere – and thereby reap enormous cost advantages over native competitors. Your country could become a backend market for companies that can produce bland, generic, all-purpose, trans-cultural programming more cheaply than you can produce your own distinctive programming.
> (quoted in *Independent on Sunday*, 21 February 1993)

These visions, and their account of the technological and commercial logic behind them, are not, however, grounded in hard data and rigorous analysis. Writers like Jeremy Tunstall (2008) and David Hesmondhalgh (2007) counsel caution, both in terms of the reality being projected (ie a homogenized product) and in terms of the direction of travel (in other words, globalization versus internationalization).

Nonetheless, because they have become worried by such developments, governments in Canada, France and Scandinavia have erected tariff barriers and imposed quotas. Their intention has been to protect local economies and cultures. So it is that rules have been established to limit the number of foreign imports to be shown on a channel or about the provision for, and supply of, news coverage. The French persuaded the European Union to introduce a Directive that required that 51 per cent of TV output came from Europe and that the World Trade Organization deregulation of telecommunications left untouched domestic support for national cinema. Canadian governments have introduced quotas to guarantee space for Canadian music and have blocked US investment in Canada's media and culture industries (Cloonan and Frith, 2008). This approach is not confined to the West. Governments in Singapore, Malaysia, Saudi Arabia and Iran have banned satellite dishes (Sreberny, 2000: 113). Not that such injunctions always work: piracy and illegal technology always threaten to subvert state power (Held et al., 1999: 371). Despite this, governments continue to try to control what their citizens can see or hear (or should be prevented from seeing or hearing).

Where broadcasting systems are based within the borders of a nation state, governments have been able to regulate the content of broadcasts, although this depends on the constitution of the country concerned. The US Constitution's First Amendment protects in principle content in the name of a free press, but its practice is, of course, more complicated (Freedman, 2008: 122ff). But where states still retain the right to control, their power to do so is nullified if the transmitter is based elsewhere or if the corporation providing the service has, by virtue of its commercial power, the capacity to rebuff government intervention. This is not a new problem. During the cold war, both the East and West sought to win over their rival population by taking advantage of the difficulty of controlling external broadcasts (the United States, with the help of the CIA, set up Voice of America, Radio Liberty and Radio Free Europe (Stonor Saunders, 2000)). Such regulation not only has a past, it has a future too. Although new media might seem to enable users to circumvent state regulation, Google's relationship with China's authorities once again suggests a more complicated picture.

Attempts at regulation are partly about economic control, partly about politics and partly about cultural character. The latter, for example, explains France's concern over the integrity of its language and concern about 'imported' words. (This is one aspect of a more general worry about the fact that English has become the dominant language of the global village.) Concern over economic control is expressed in the subsidies for French cinema. Both aspects represent efforts to protect a particular notion of national sovereignty and to assert the capacity of nation states to operate with relative autonomy. Insofar as governments, for whatever reason, cannot impose regulations on new forms of communication or on their corporate backers, a degree of national sovereignty, and by implication national identity, may be lost. But note this points to a contingent outcome, not a determined conclusion.

Not only does globalization threaten to alter the capacity of states to control communications within their borders, it also affects the relationship between states. In particular, there is a trend towards information inequalities. Less developed countries (LDCs) struggle to participate in the new global system. In 1990, sub-Saharan Africa had 3 per cent of the 2.1 billion radios in the world; Latin America had 8 per cent, Asia 30 per cent, Europe 27 per cent; and North America 29 per cent (*Economist*, 2 May 1992). In 2002–03, there were 62 television sets for every 1,000 people in sub-Saharan Africa, compared with 600 per 1,000 in Europe (Earth Trends, http://earthtrends.wri.org/). And to the extent that these LDCs do participate in the world media market, they do so within delivery systems created and maintained by the global corporations (Malm and Wallis, 1993). The limited space available to geostationary satellites has been monopolized by the powerful players. If information and communications represent a capacity to participate in the making of the new world order, inequalities in the distribution of media resources constitute a form of disenfranchisement. An interesting insight into this world was provided by the announcement that GTV was about to launch a satellite service for audiences in sub-Saharan Africa. GTV, it turns out, is a UK-based enterprise whose parent company, Gateway Communications, 'provides the networks for many of Africa's mobile phone providers' (*Guardian*, 23 May 2007). The key product offered by GTV is football from the English Premier League; access has been priced to undercut the more expensive rivals that have limited market penetration in Africa. Such an example plays easily into the criticisms of the anti-globalists: a UK company selling an English product to a market in which it already manages a key part of the telecommunications system.

But again we have to ask whether these fears of globalization are warranted. There is a real danger of getting caught up in the rhetoric and the hype, and in overlooking the more mundane features of mass communications. India is a vast and disparate country, with nearly 20 different languages, and with many religious and social divides. Is it realistic to see mass media corporations, however large, imposing a single culture? It is certainly important to resist the idea that there is inevitability about the process. Michael Tracey has argued that it is:

> simply untrue to say that imported television programmes, from the U.S. or other metropolitan countries, always have a dominant presence within an indigenous culture. Certainly, they do not always attract larger audiences than homemade programs, nor do they always threaten national production.
>
> (Tracey, 1985: 34)

And while Tracey wrote this some time ago, more recent evidence from China and Japan (De Launey, 1995; Zhao and Murdock, 1996) accords with his general point that Western culture does not automatically find an audience. Indeed, as Jeremy Tunstall stresses (2008: 10, 56), most of the television watched around the world is local, and most of the revenue generated by major conglomerates like News Corporation derives from within the United States.

What is more, governments find ways of countering or mitigating the effects of global culture. Just as different states organized the same broadcasting technology into different regulatory frameworks, so they have developed strategies for deflecting globalizing tendencies. Governments have imposed limitations on cross-media ownership. They have imposed quotas and introduced subsidies to ensure that local and national cultures are represented and encouraged. Even where populations are exposed to the most global of cultural icons or images, there is no guarantee that they will be transformed into a uniform mass, blessed with a single set of tastes. The way the culture is used and interpreted is not determined by producers and distributors alone, but is the consequence of local contexts and conditions (Scott, 1997). Despite Rupert Murdoch's concerted efforts to establish News Corporation in China, he was thwarted by the Chinese authorities (Dover, 2008).

Global cultural networks have, it might be argued, made possible a cultural politics of empowerment. This has enabled the coordination of protest of the kind that was seen at the World Trade Organization meeting in Seattle in 1999 and in the 18 June Carnival Against Capital earlier that same year. It has facilitated the creation of alternative sources of news and information, the new technologies making possible independent reporting of events that challenge the official version. It has also led to greater cultural hybridization. Some of the responses to globalization have been informed by the idea that each country or nation state is marked by a single, monolithic culture that has to be protected like a rare endangered species. But if it is assumed that all cultures are hybrids, made up of components taken from each other, then the need for regulation is felt less strongly and the prospects of globalization are less fearsome. But these other aspects to the globalization process are not purely self-sustaining; they too – like the major conglomerates – depend on the mediating role of the political authorities. In this instance, they depend on the existence of some form of public sphere, a forum within which views can be exchange and debated.

Typically, it is public service broadcasting that has provided this public sphere. Public service broadcasting is supposed to regulate access (what programmes, which views), not in terms of commercial or political power, but in terms of some principle of pluralism and diversity. There is much disagreement as to whether public service broadcasting can and should serve democracy in this way, but our immediate concern is with whether, whatever its costs and benefits, the public service form can survive the globalized order. The Canadian Broadcasting Corporation cut more than 3,000 jobs between 1995 and 2000, and cut a mainstay of its schedules, *Midday*. Similar pressures were felt in Australia and Europe, leading Tracey to conclude that 'public service broadcasting now seems to be a corpse on leave' (*New Statesman*, 24 July 2000). But a decade later public service broadcasting continued to exist and to enjoy continued popular support (Hardy, 2008; Ofcom, 2008).

Certainly, the new mass media make it much harder for public service television to continue in its current mode. With the proliferation of channels, the notion of the 'public' itself is being reconstituted into a mass of special interest audiences. Digital television creates the possibility of multiple channels for each home; not only that, it also allows users to customize the schedule to accord with their particular preferences. This makes it very much more difficult to talk about 'the viewing public', since there is no guarantee that people are watching the same thing at the same time. In 1998, the TV executive Barry Cox argued that digital television 'will intensify the fragmentation of audiences .... Broadcasting becomes narrowcasting – the distribution of content to small, niche audiences' (*Prospect*, November 1998: 16). This fear of balkanization also accompanied the emergence of the internet (Sunstein, 2001). In its original incarnation, public service broadcasting was an attempt to address the differences between people and their commonality. Different tastes were catered for within a single schedule on a single channel, or a small number of channels. With the proliferation of channels, audiences become increasingly segmented as the channels also seek to find niches to fill. The net effect is to erode the central pillar of public service broadcasting, the 'public' itself. This is overlaid by the threatened erosion of the nation state which also served to frame or bound the public (although it is not necessary for publics to be tied to nation states).

A second tenet of public service broadcasting is its independence from commerce, or the preservation of a distance between commerce and content. But through the combination of channel proliferation and deregulation, the broadcasting environment has been changed so that, even if public service broadcasting is sheltered from commerce, it still has to compete with it. In the face of commercial competition, public corporations like the BBC undoubtedly struggle to identify their role within the new political economy. This can be measured by the battle over the right to cover certain major events. Public service broadcasters have to compete with the commercial sector in their bid to hold on to major sporting events, which are crucial not only to ratings and the legitimacy of the public sector, but also to the notion of a 'common culture' and the identity that grounds it. The effect of competition can also be witnessed in the type of programming, in the pressure to move news programming out of peak viewing hours or to introduce tabloid news values (Franklin, 1998; Hallin, 2000; Hamilton, 2004). Despite these gloomy projections and critical judgements, it is too early to pronounce the death of public service broadcasting. While it remains under constant review (see, for example, Ofcom, 2008), it remains a major player in many different media systems (Freedman, 2008: 147ff; Hallin and Mancini, 2004: 165–70; 106–9). It seems possible, nonetheless, that in years to come, public service broadcasting will be reinvented as a minority service or organized along different principles. But this remains a matter of speculation, not a fact of a globalized world.

If public service media do become marginal features of the new communications order, what replaces them? For some, the future is imagined as one in which media service a monolithic cultural and economic order in which choice has replaced diversity (Baker, 2007). Such a vision derives from a focus on the economic power of the new multimedia conglomerates, and the idea that their commercial strength is deployed to standardize the content of their cultural product: that news and entertainment are processed and packaged like McDonald's hamburgers across the globe – except, as anyone who has seen *Pulp Fiction* knows, even McDonald's varies according to location. There is another vision to be evoked of the impact of globalization on mass media: a world marked by chaos and diversity. For Danilo Zolo (1992), the new communication technologies have the effect of speeding up the pace and increasing the complexity of the modern world. Citizens' experience of politics and of society is derived directly from mass media, and is no longer mediated by church, school and trade union or professional association. At the same time, this encounter with the world is marked by a proliferation of information, but little explanation. This experience creates a sense of chaos and complexity, which generates in people a feeling of fatalism and despair (Putnam, 2000).

In the face of this diversity of media forms and this chaos of cultural signs, the temptation might be to conclude that power has devolved to the consumers, to the operators of the remote controls, video players and set-top boxes. Manuel Castells has argued forcefully against such conclusions. While 'decentralization, diversification and customization' may be the new media order, this does not, Castells contends, 'imply loss of control by major corporations and governments over television. Indeed, it is the opposite trend that has been observed during the last decade' (1996: 340). His later work (Castells, 2009) continues this same theme, as he casts the world communications order in the form of overlapping networks. This combination of choice and control is central to understanding the character of globalization and its implications for the connection between politics and mass media. Globalization can describe centralized control and resources, which stand in defiance of the powers of national governments, but the global corporations deploy their resources to particular audiences. In Castells' phrase, we live, not in a global village, but in 'customized cottages globally produced and locally distributed' (1996: 341). This does not mean, however, that as customers we 'demand' the goods that the conglomerates produce.

Perhaps most importantly of all in getting globalization into perspective, we need to remember that the 'world' that we have been examining only covers a small part of the earth's surface. At the end of the last century, as Sussman observed (1997: 231–2), for the third world, the 'digital revolution' was as remote as the nearest phone: Manhattan had more telephone lines than there were in all of sub-Saharan Africa; the 80 per cent of the world's population who lived in less developed countries had only 30 per cent of the world's newspapers. The picture has changed, but the inequality remains (Norris, 2001b; http://www.internetworld-stats.com/stats.htm). Unequal access to the means of communication gets reflected in slanted representation. Writing in the late 1990s, Chris Paterson (1998: 96) concluded in his study of the global news agencies: 'Television coverage of the developing world is already deplorably infrequent and misleading. The developing world appears now to be more excluded from contribution to the global flow of television news than it has ever been.' A decade later the same problems remained; the developing world was still marginalized and misrepresented (Padania et al., 2006; Scott, 2008 and 2009).

Conclusion

This chapter has tried to pin down some of the so-called globalizing trends and currents that are seen to be shaping the form of modern mass communications and to be affecting the politics of mass media. We began by looking at the emerging players and the changing technologies that are integral to, but not determinant of, these trends. We then moved on to consider the twin effects of globalization, first on national governments, and then on culture, before ending with some reflections on future developments. Throughout, I have tried to suggest first that the term 'globalization' may misrepresent the processes involved, and that Hesmondhalgh's preferred characterization, 'internationalization', may better describe the process. Whatever the best description, it is clear that what is happening across the world is much more complex and ambiguous than some would have us believe. Nonetheless, we need to be aware of the new forms of media power brokers and new forms of media technology, which together pose fundamental problems for the regulation of mass media by nation states, at the same as the need for regulation is felt more acutely with the impact of globalization. Globalization does, though, also represent possibilities that may challenge the existing order, but such outcomes cannot be viewed as somehow 'inevitable' features of the changes being wrought. They depend on the way the opportunities offered by new media are taken.

At the turn of the century, Tore Slaata wrote, in a challenge to much of the conventional wisdom:

> New media will not make old media disappear .... But they will probably have an impact on their production technology, their distribution and potential markets and thereby also their contents, but these impacts need to be analysed empirically. The impact of new media on collective identity formation will in the foreseeable future remain modest, and will probably first of all make existing organizations and institutions, like national media, parties and civil society groups, become more efficiently able to network within existing boundaries of the nation-states.
>
> (Tore Slaata, 1998: 338)

Ten years later, it was not clear that Slaatta was wrong. What we have seen is a shift in the centres of media power. In 2008, PriceWaterhouseCoopers predicted, for instance, that the balance of media power was shifting dramatically towards China, as it overtook the United States as the largest broadband market (Entertainment and Media Outlook, June 2008, http://www.pwc.com/). But changes in the location of national economic power does not constitute evidence for globalization, particularly when, as Jeremy Tunstall points out at the end of his survey of world media:

The national level of media is dominant in the countries where 90 percent of the world's people reside. Audiences today prefer their own news, weather, sports, comedy, soaps, games, reality, and other cheap factual programming.

(Tunstall, 2008: 450)

We need to remain vigilant as we observe shifts in the political economy of new and traditional media, but we need also to remain wary of exaggerating the changes and their political impact. There are others (Castells, 2009), as we shall see later (Chapter 11), who take a rather different view of how we and our world are being transformed by modern media.

Part III

Mass Media and Democracy

Transforming Political Communication? The Rise of Political Marketing and Celebrity Politics

In the last part of this book, the focus is upon the relationship between mass media and democracy. This is an issue that has been present throughout. After all, why else are people interested in media bias or corporate ownership, if not because of the worry that systematic distortion or media concentration harm the capacity of citizens to judge and respond to the exercise of power? The next four chapters confront directly the question of how, in a democracy, the relationship between the political process and the mass media should operate. Each chapter considers a different dimension of this relationship. We begin with the business of political communication itself, how ideals and values are conveyed by parties, politicians and political movements. In particular, the focus is on the changes in political communication that have occurred over the last few decades, and the extent to which they have enhanced or damaged the quality of democratic discourse.

This question has a long history, and has taken many incarnations. It has been linked to general discussion of the 'dumbing down' of culture (for example, Postman, 1987) and to the more specific 'packaging' or marketing of politics (Franklin, 2004; Savigny, 2009). The key idea is that public representations of politics are increasingly being managed and controlled by parties and politicians, through such people as spin doctors. The effect of this, it is claimed, is to diminish the quality of democratic political discourse. Political arguments are trivialized; appearances take precedence over reality, personalities count for more than policies, the superficial matters more than the substantive. The blame for this state of affairs is typically directed at the politicians and at their professional cohorts, and at a media world which compounds the damage by representing politics as a cynical exercise in image management (Lloyd, 2004).

More recently, these trends, and the debates they provoke, have found a target in the rise of 'celebrity politics'. This is seen by some as the logical extension of the marketing or packaging process. Politics becomes a branch of show business, in which politicians mimic the style of pop stars and film stars, in an attempt to make themselves more attractive to increasingly disillusioned voters and media. Meanwhile, rock artists and actors start to represent themselves as politicians. In 2003, readers of UK newspapers were treated to these two front-page stories: the first pictured the prime minister strumming an electric guitar (the home secretary was on drums) (*Daily Mail*, 14 February 2003); the second, a week later, announced that UK pop stars had 'blitzed' Tony Blair over his policy towards Iraq (*Daily Mirror*, 21 February 2003). In the same year in the United States, Arnold Schwarzenegger, hero of Hollywood blockbusters like *The Terminator*, was elected governor of California. Once again, as with the debate about marketing and packaging, these developments have prompted a debate about their consequences for the health and well being of democracy (West and Orman, 2003).

Why do such things matter? Why is the content and character of political discourse important? The simple answer is that these are central concerns for democracy. If it is assumed that democracy is a viable and desirable political form, there are certain conditions that have to be met for it to be realized. 'Rule by the people', the most basic of definitions of democracy, depends upon the capacity of 'the people' to form judgements about what policies or representatives they want, and about whether those policies or representatives have delivered what they promised. Formulating such judgements requires, first, information (about politicians and their actions) and, second, the opportunity and skill to convert this information into a coherent assessment. Those who complain about the 'packaging' of politics or about 'celebrity politics' are arguing that political information is being presented in ways that seriously hamper the capacity of citizens to reach well-informed judgements about what is being done in their name, or that those acting as their representatives are incapable of fulfilling the role expected of them. Either way, the costs to democracy are deemed to be high. This chapter is an attempt to assess these claims, to explore the arguments and evidence that are used to either praise or condemn these new modes of political communication.

Packaging politics

The idea that politics is 'packaged' derives from a wider mistrust of modern techniques of commercial marketing, in which goods are designed to present a particular image rather than to serve a specific function, and that the key players are those in the advertising department. Packaging also suggests that nothing is left to chance; everything is controlled (Jamieson, 1984). The critics of modern political communication see the same techniques being applied to politics. They point to the explosive rise in the number and the influence of media consultants and image-makers, people who are seen to have changed the style and techniques of political communication. Evidence is plentiful: the ever-larger advertising budgets of parties and governments; the ubiquity of advertising personnel and skills in the promotion of politicians; the pre-eminence of photo opportunities and sound bites in election campaigns. The two leading contenders in the US presidential race of 2008 spent over $1 billion. Some 40 years on from Joe McGinniss' *The Selling of a President* (1969), which was one of the first insights into the emerging techniques of political marketing, we are now witness to an elaborate machine served by an increasingly large army of professionals (speechwriters, pollsters, advertising executives, film-makers, and so on). This transformation is explained in terms such as 'modernization' or 'Americanization' or 'mediatization' (Swanson and Mancini, 1996; Meyer, 2002), and it is seen to herald a world of 'packaged politics' (Franklin, 2004) or 'designer politics' (Scammell, 1995). While some of the language verges on the apocalyptic, others, while noting the changes taking place, are more wary of the hyperbole. Ralph Negrine, for example, counsels caution, seeing the changes as those of adaptation and professionalization (2008: 195).

Just as there is not complete consensus about the nature of the change, so there is divergence over the judgements to be attached to it. For some, the new order is to be greeted positively, as a rational adaptation to contemporary realities (Temple, 2006).

For example, Liesbet van Zoonen writes that the popularising of political communication 'should be seen as an attempt to restore the relation between politicians and voters, between the people and their representatives, to regain the necessary sense of community between public officials and their publics' (1998b: 196–7). This welcome for new techniques is often accompanied by the claim that media management techniques have, in any case, always been part of politics (Abramson et al., 1988; Kavanagh, 1995; Rosenbaum, 1997; Scammell, 1995). The new political techniques of the electronic era are merely an extension of a well-established tradition of politics, which is to adopt and adapt to the prevailing forms of communication.

Against these generally positive views, there are others who, though recognizing the continuities, view these developments more warily. One of the earliest warnings was sounded in the early 1970s with the publication of Jacques Ellul's (1972) *The Political Illusion*. Thomas Meyer (2002) continues the tradition with his argument that politics has been 'colonised' by media logic, to its detriment. Media logic places emphasis on the immediate, whereas politics needs to adopt a longer-term perspective. In a similar vein, Todd Gitlin (1991: 129, 133) has expressed concern at the fate of an American politics which has always been 'raucous, deceptive, giddy, shallow, sloganeering and demagogic for most of its history', but which is now covered by a media that is obsessed 'with speed, quick cuts, ten-second bites, one-second "scenes" and out of context images', and is therefore intolerant 'of the rigors of serious arguments and the tedium of organized political life'. Certainly, commentators on recent UK general elections have observed that images dominate the word, and that the electoral contest is fought over competing appearances (Deacon et al., 1998). In a similarly worried tone, Danilo Zolo (1992: 162) remarks on 'the penetration of advertising techniques deep into the political system' and the creation of a world in which 'telegenicity' becomes a key political criterion. For Colin Crouch (2004), these various elements constitute features of a 'post-democratic world' in which the practice of democracy has been emptied of substance, and all that remains is the spectacle. To advance this debate, it is necessary, first, to review briefly the ideas behind the marketing or packaging of politics. Only then can we assess the issues that divide observers.

Packaging techniques

The idea that politics is being 'packaged', or less pejoratively 'marketed', trades on the thought that parties, individual politicians and governments are developing ever more effective ways of using the media. There are many examples of this, and what follows is just a selection.

Interviews

The political interview is a staple part of politics and political coverage. For the media, it is a cheap method of filling space, while also providing some prospect of excitement through its gladiatorial structure and some version of accountability through its conventions of cross-examination. For the politician, it represents an opportunity to articulate a view or to promote a policy initiative. Ostensibly, the interview is built around a dramatic tension in which both sides have reputations at stake. But 'the interview' does not represent a fixed and permanent phenomenon. Over time it has changed greatly, as politicians have become less wary and aloof, and interviewers have become more assertive and less deferential (Barnett, 2002; Cockerell, 1988; Day, 1991; McNair, 2000). And as formats have changed, with one-to-one exchanges being joined by phone-ins, chat shows and their ilk, so we have seen the emergence of new conventions and rules for the interview.

These have been designed to control the conduct of interviews. Their efforts have focused on such things as interview technique (not breathing in at the end of sentences to avoid interruption), staying 'on message' (saying what you want to say, not what the interviewer wants you to say), how to sit and dress (the semiotics of posture and fashion). They have also become more determined to set the ground rules. This begins with who is to be interviewed and under what terms: whether live or pre-recorded (the first giving the control to the interviewee, the second to the editor), whether alone or with others. All of these issues touch upon the balance of power between interviewer and politicians, and are deployed in order to tip this balance towards the latter, to enable them to say what they want (Harris, 1991). The intention is to make the interview a platform for the politicians who, according to the critics of packaging, are intent upon delivering propaganda rather than being made accountable, or at least to reduce political communication to a form of PR, in which journalists become mere ciphers. The many rules that apply to televised political debates are further examples of this.

One symptom of this trend is the 'sound bite', a single phrase or idea which is intended to be the sole message of any exchange between interviewer and interviewee. As the BBC journalist Nicholas Jones has written:

> In their pursuit of publicity even the humblest and most obscure MPs have had to become slaves to the sound bite, capable of encapsulating their arguments in a few short, sharp sentences suitable for inclusion in a broadcast news bulletin.
>
> (Jones, 1995: 12)

Another strategy has been to opt for a different style of interview; to move away from hard news to the chat show or other less challenging sites. Bill Clinton appeared on MTV, Tony Blair on the *Des O'Connor Show*, David Cameron on *Friday Night With Jonathan Ross* and Barack Obama on *The Ellen DeGeneres Show*, on which he hit a punch ball and danced with the host.

These new forms of political interview have a number of purposes: to convey sides of the candidate's personality that might otherwise go unnoticed, to 'humanize' them by revealing their 'private' side, to reach a wider (or less political engaged) audience, and to avoid politically difficult topics. They become key parts of the performance in which any politician is engaged (Corner, 2003).

Images and appearances

The performing politician does not just deal in words. As Margaret Scammell argues, parties and candidates '*must* attend to political image if they want to be serious players in the political market' (1999: 729). Parties work at 'branding' themselves to create a distinct image that provides a simple key to the party's general stance or values. The advertising executive Winston Fletcher (*Guardian*, 23 October 1997) said of Tony Blair's New Labour: 'it is clear that the establishment of New Labour as a trustworthy brand name was a textbook marketing operation'.

A brand is a way of capturing the essence of a product or a

party in a single memorable image or phrase. Over time, politicians and parties have increasingly devoted their attention to generating images (rather than detailed policy proposals). This process begins with personal appearance and dress, and continues into the way party conventions and conferences are designed. It is evident in political advertisements that increasingly mimic the language of commercial advertising; it is blatantly demonstrated in the crafting of sound bites and photo-opportunities. In many ways, the latter two are the most important because they are intended to appear in regular news broadcasts, and as such acquire the legitimacy and veracity of *news* as distinct from propaganda (although, as Kathleen Hall Jamieson (1992) points out, party advertisements can themselves (by design or default) become part of the news because they provoke a particular political controversy). Whatever the format or forum, the intention is to create images and slogans that are easily recognized or digested, and which spark a series of associations that crystallize a political response. It is important to note that these practices are not confined to political parties. Interest groups and social movements also deploy them; indeed, they are among the most skilled practitioners of 'branding', as they are of the exploitation of celebrities to promote political causes (supermodels against fur, pop stars for relieving third world debt, film stars for an independent Tibet). Governments too increasingly depend on celebrities to market their policies. In the United Kingdom, the winner of a TV talent show was photographed in a bath of condoms to promote sexual health among the young (*Observer*, 4 January 2009). Celebrities bequeath their glamour, popularity or coolness to the politician or party or government with which they are associated (Pringle, 2004). Barack Obama's presidential campaign was a classic example of this phenomenon, as film, music and sports stars flocked to endorse him. New Labour's harnessing of the Britpop of Blur, Oasis and their like enabled the party to acquire the 'Cool Britannia' brand (Harris, 2003).

Spin doctors, media consultants and advertisers

The adoption of celebrities to acquire glamour, credibility and popularity is no more inevitable than it is risk-free. It is an approach that has depended on the advice and ingenuity of a new breed of political advisers and consultants. This is why

Hollywood directors have been hired to make political propaganda – for example, Hugh Hudson (*Chariots of Fire*) and Stephen Frears (*High Fidelity*) for the British Labour Party; Spike Jonze (*Being John Malkovich*) for Al Gore. It is why a comedy writer like John O'Farrell (*Spitting Image*) is hired to supply jokes for political speeches. Such initiatives stem from a new stratum of media managers within the political process, people with expertise in polling, advertising, marketing and public relations. Their task has been to revamp party images and to secure for politicians the coverage they crave, and their brief extends to negotiating the terms of interviews, providing press releases (and discreet leaks), devising sound bites and arranging photo-opportunities. Their aim is to manage the media in such a way as to enhance the image and message of the parties they serve.

This is how insiders in the White House described their job to the journalist Michael Kelley:

> the day is composed not of hours or minutes, but of *news cycles*. In each cycle, *senior White House officials* speaking on *background* define *the line of the day*. The line is echoed and amplified *outside the Beltway* to *real people*, who live *out there*, by the President's *surrogates*, whose appearances create *actualities* (on radio) and *talking heads* (on TV). During the *roll-out* of a new policy, the President coached by his *handlers* ... may permit his own head to talk. There are various ways he might do this, ranging from the simplest *photo-op* to a *one-on-one* with a media *big foot*.
>
> (*Guardian Weekend*, 20 November 1993, original emphasis)

The importance attached to this work has made its practitioners key actors in their party's power structure. Party organization and strategy have been reshaped – have been professionalized – to accommodate their authority and to respond to their advice (Bartle and Griffiths, 2001; Kavanagh, 1995; Negrine, 2008; Wring, 2005).

Arguing about marketing

The application of these techniques has provoked considerable debate. For writers like Nicholas Garnham (1986) the change is symptomatic of a wider transformation, in which mass communications are now organized around advertising. The 'public' is now the 'market', and media now address and constitute citizens as consumers. When this logic is applied to politics, P. David Marshall argues, it invites irrationality: 'The product advertising campaign provides the underlying model for the political election campaign. Both instantiate the prominence of irrational appeal within a general legitimating discourse of rationality' (1997: 205). Paul Statham describes Berlusconi's party as operating 'along the lines of a commercial company, extending the logic of product marketing to the political sphere' (1996: 91). Danilo Zolo, generalizing from the Italian experience, bemoans the ways in which advertisers are employed to apply 'the criteria of commercial propaganda to political communication', and that the result is 'the penetration of advertising techniques deep into the political system' (1992: 162). Writing of the United States, Dan Nimmo has complained of the prevalence of 'the ahistorical and nonhistorical packaging of campaign information', in which 'factoids' have replaced facts (1996: 40). Factoids are 'pithy assertions of facts widely treated as true even though supporting evidence is not available'. The net effect is a 'virtual politics' made up of a 'media-created, politician-manipulated reality' (Swanson and Mancini, 1996: 270).

By contrast, other writers see the introduction of marketing as democratising. Joseph Schumpeter (1976/1943) made this point many years ago when, reflecting on citizens' limited capacity for complex political judgement, he noted their sophistication in making judgements on matters of direct concern to them. Schumpeter constructed a model of democracy out of these skills by modelling it on the market, and making parties entrepreneurs who depend for their survival on the quality of their product. As Margaret Scammell has subsequently observed, 'the marketing concept may possess intrinsic virtue precisely because, in principle, it makes politics more democratic' (1995: 18). And there are those who contend that the focus on appearance and the use of sound bites does indeed pay electoral dividends (Landstsheer et al., 2008)

While this debate cannot be settled one way or another, it is important to recognize that the presence of marketed or packaged politics is not simply a consequence of the political will of spin doctors and others. It also needs a compliant media, and there is evidence that media systems differ in their susceptibility to the worst excesses of marketing. Susceptibility to pressure from spin doctors varies across countries. German media are less vulnerable than that in the United Kingdom because of the different news values in place – German coverage is traditionally less obsessed with 'balance' and more with 'objectivity' (Esser et al., 2000; Semetko, 1996). Some systems guarantee airtime for politics (for example, the United Kingdom and France), but others do not (for example, the United States). In France there are also strict restrictions on the images that can be used in representing candidates (Negrine, 1996). Another factor affecting susceptibility to new techniques of political communication is the commercial environment. Packaged politics fits into the agenda of media who are acutely conscious of the chill winds of the market. Competition for readers and viewers, like the competition for advertisers that underlies the need to boost sales and ratings, reduces the resources available for investigative journalism and increases the incentives for accepting pre-packaged material (Curran and Seaton, 2010: 88ff; Hamilton, 2004). It also fuels the demand for 'human interest' and celebrity stories. Neither the resources nor the interest exists for serious analysis. Packaging, by this argument, fills the gap left by the shifting priorities of the media (Franklin, 2004: 119ff). On the other hand, it is argued that market-based broadcasting is less inclined to succumb to politicians' blandishments, and that it is state-regulated systems that are most easily exploited by parties (Semetko, 1996; Semetko et al., 1991). Market competition does not allow the media to indulge the parties in the desire for bland coverage. Either way, the extent to which 'packaging' is a characteristic of media–politics relations is dependent not just upon political actors, but also on the willingness of media outlets to play the same game. Rather than pursuing the debate about marketing and packaging further, I want to turn to a specific development in the transformation of political communication: the rise of the celebrity politician.

The rise of the celebrity politician

The word 'celebrity' typically refers to those people who, via mass media, enjoy 'a greater presence and wider scope of activity

and agency than are those who make up the rest of the population. They are allowed to move on the public stage while the rest
of us watch' (Marshall, 1997: ix). This general definition covers
a wide variety of public figures, but Darrel West and John
Orman identify five variants that apply specifically to politics
(2003: 2–6). There are those who acquire celebrity status by
birth (the Kennedys), those embroiled in political scandal, and
those who, like Jesse Jackson, become celebrities through their
charismatic public performances. They also include those 'famed
nonpoliticos' who move from careers in show business into politics. Their fifth variant is 'event celebrities', people who attain
celebrityhood by their involvement in crime or scandals. While
West and Orman offer a comprehensive overview of the political
celebrity, my concern here is with those who make a deliberate
attempt to create a political persona using the resources provided
by popular culture. By this I mean either those 'famed nonpoliticos' – Clint Eastwood or Arnold Schwarzenegger or Gilberto Gil
– who move from careers in popular culture to politics, and those
with careers in politics ('politicos') who make use of the artefacts, icons and expertise of popular culture. These two categories of celebrity politician are, first, the traditional politician –
the legitimately elected representative (or the one who aspires to
be so) – who engages with the world of popular culture in order
to enhance or advance their pre-established political functions
and goals. This is the *celebrity politician*. They can be captured
in the following ways:

- An elected politician (or a nominated candidate) whose
  background is in entertainment, show business or sport, and
  who trades on this background (by virtue of the skills
  acquired, the popularity achieved, or the images associated)
  in the attempt to get elected.
- An elected politician or candidate who uses the forms and
  associations of the celebrity to enhance their image and
  communicate their message, most typically in the form of a
  photo-opportunity, So, in the past we have seen the UK prime
  minister posing with the England football team; the German
  chancellor appearing on stage with the Scorpions rock band;
  or the Japanese prime minister singing Elvis Presley songs
  with Tom Cruise. We have even seen Nelson Mandela
  pictured with the Spice Girls.

- The use of what might be called 'celebrity formats' to promote the politician. These involve examples of the kind already mentioned of appearance on chat shows (Baum, 2005), or on quiz shows like *Have I Got News for You?* (Coleman et al., 2009a). One of the more unusual examples was Tony Blair's 'appearance' in *The Simpsons* (Campbell, 2007: 690).
- The adoption of the techniques and expertise of those who market celebrities. A *Le Monde* journalist complained that during the 2002 French presidential campaign, the left-wing party Lutte Ouvriere borrowed its 'tactics from movie stars' agents. Accreditations have to be applied for; there are waiting lists and you only get three timed questions with the star. It's as though you were interviewing Julia Roberts or Andie MacDowell' (quoted in *Guardian*, 14 April 2002).

While this first type of celebrity politician has received much recent attention, the phenomenon is not new. Over 20 years ago, Neil Postman wrote:

> Political figures may show up anywhere, at any time, doing anything, without being thought odd, presumptuous, or in any way out of place. Which is to say, they have become assimilated into general television culture as celebrities.
>
> (Postman, 1987: 135)

There is a second kind of celebrity politician, the *political celebrity*, who was perhaps less visible at the time Postman was writing. This is the entertainer who pronounces on politics and claims the right to represent peoples and causes, but who does so without seeking, or acquiring, elected office. Their engagement tends to take the form of public gestures or statements aimed at changing specific public policy decisions. This version of the celebrity politician uses their status and the medium within which they work to speak out on specific causes and for particular interests with a view to influencing political outcomes. One example is the many stars of show business who signed the published petitions against the war in Iraq and who used whatever other opportunities they had to draw attention to their political views. Those involved included Hollywood stars like Tim Robbins, Susan Sarandon, Robert Redford, Bruce Willis and Cher, and musicians like Madonna, Damon Albarn (Blur), Chris Martin (Coldplay) and Ms Dynamite, among many others. The most prominent of all these has been Bono, who has had audiences with President George W. Bush, President Chirac and Pope John Paul, among many others, in his campaign to reduce third world debt. Media play a key role in this kind of celebrity politics. They provide the political platform, whether in the guise of interviews or, more substantially, in the televising of events like Live8.

Before we go on to consider the causes and impact of these new forms of political communication, it is worth making a couple of points. The first is that not all attempts to court celebrities are successful. When he was Tony Blair's deputy, John Prescott attended the Brits 1998 music industry awards, where he was the unhappy recipient of a bucket of water, thrown over him by Danbert Nobacon of the rock band Chumbawamba. A picture of a soaked and angry Prescott was in all the next day's papers. The second point is that the political celebrity is not new. Hollywood has a long association – as has the music industry – with political power (Blanning, 2008; Wheeler, 2006).

These points, however, do not detract from the general trend towards celebrity politics and to the perception of politics as a form of show business. Reporting on the Philippine National Elections, James McEnteer observed:

Many political rallies resembled talent shows. At one such event, a senatorial candidate danced a cha-cha, another sang ditties in dialect, and a third offered a baritone rendition of 'More than the Greatest Love I've Ever Known'. Instead of discussing social or economic issues, candidates literally gave the voters a song and dance.

(McEnteer, 1996: 114)

In the New York Senate race in 2000, one of the candidates, Rudolph Giuliani, appeared at a rally dressed as John Travolta in *Saturday Night Fever*. (Giuliani later retired from the race, but not because of this particular offence against good taste.) Not unnaturally, such examples provoke considerable debate about the character of political communications. At the heart of this debate is the question of whether these new forms of political communication enhance or harm democracy.

The critique of celebrity politics

Both types of celebrity politics have prompted all manner of criticism. For the moment, I want to concentrate on those criticisms that relate to the issue of representation, a key term in liberal democracy. Can the celebrity politician or political celebrity be said to represent effectively or well those on whose behalf they speak? For the critic, the complaint is that celebrity politics undermines any claim to 'representativeness'. This is either because the elected politician impoverishes the relationship between representative and represented by marginalizing issues of political substance in favour of irrelevant gestures and superficial appearances (Franklin, 2004; Postman, 1987; West and Orman, 2003), or it is because the political celebrity boasts irrelevant qualities and superficial knowledge that do not justify their claim to 'represent' (Hyde, 2009; West and Orman, 2003). As the website, 'Citizens against Celebrity "Pundits"', declared:

> We the undersigned American Citizens stand against Wealthy Hollywood Celebrities abusing their status to speak for us. We do not believe that they have a clear understanding of how we live, what we fear, and what we support.
>   (ipetitions.com/campaigns/hollywoodceleb/)

This is not a new complaint. It builds upon familiar distinctions between the trivial (entertainment) and the serious (politics), and a concern about the infection of the latter by the former. This was Postman's worry: 'Our politics, religion, news, athletics, education and commerce have been transformed into congenial adjuncts of show business' (1987: 4). Appearances and images, according to Postman, have come to dominate politics, so that 'we may have reached a point where cosmetics have replaced ideology as the field of expertise over which a politician must have competent control ' (ibid.: 4; also 129). In such a world, he continued, politics is diminished: 'You cannot do political philosophy on television' (ibid.: 7). It is not, therefore, arguments that decide whether voters will support one candidate rather than another, but 'style'; that is, 'how they [the politicians] looked, fixed their gaze, smiled, and deliver one-liners' (ibid.: 100). In such circumstances, complained Postman, it becomes impossible to determine 'who is better than whom, if we mean by "better" such as more capable in negotiation, more imaginative in executive skill' (ibid.: 137).

Postman's concerns can also be detected in Joshua Meyrowitz's (1985) elegy for traditional forms of political leadership. He claimed that the increasing reliance on television as a medium of communication had shifted the criteria by which politicians were judged and by which they operate. Television's intimacy, its use of close-ups and one-to-one conversations, focus attention on politicians' 'human' qualities. The result is that populist empathy rather than elite leadership becomes more valued. In such a world, either politicians learn the skills of the medium or those already skilled in it (the celebrity) come to dominate it. This anxiety is still present. Thomas Meyer, for example, has written:

> If democracy is nothing but legitimation by the most successful form of communication, then the communication artist is the best democrat, with no effort whatsoever. And if the authentic play of body politics is the most efficacious form of entertaining communication, then 'briefcase politics' with its institutionalised procedures and long-winded arguments might as well bow out now.
>
> (Meyer, 2002: 79)

For such critics, 'telegencity' has become the measure of 'representativeness' (see Zolo, 1992: 162) and 'mob rule' replaces deliberation (Crick, 2002: 85–90).

The themes of these critiques continue to echo through the current debate. While critics acknowledge that celebrity politics may 'reinvigorate a political process that often stagnates' (West and Orman, 2003: 112), these potential benefits tend to be outweighed by the costs. In their assessment of celebrity politics, West and Orman argue that the rise of celebrity politics has seen the displacement of traditional political skills (bargaining, compromise) and their replacement by those of media management and fund-raising (ibid.: 112). The qualities of the celebrity politician are ill suited to the duties of statecraft which representatives owe their constituents. These inadequacies are compounded by ignorance. Celebrities lack knowledge of, or expertise in, public policy: 'Serious political issues become trivialized in the attempt to elevate celebrities to philosopher-celebrities' (ibid.: 118; see also Hyde, 2009). Furthermore, according to West and Orman, the elevation of the celebrity politician leads to a distortion in the political agenda in favour of those issues that interest the rich (who are the source of the politician's campaign funds), and marginalize more pressing social problems. In summary, the argument is that celebrity politics risks 'short-circuiting' representative democracy and endangering the system of accountability (ibid.: 113).

These criticisms of celebrity politics are premised on a set of assumptions about, *inter alia*, the proper nature and character of political representation. Their particular claim is that representatives owe citizens a duty of informed political judgement. Both types of celebrity politician threaten the principles of representative democracy, either because they privilege style and appearance over substance, or because they marginalize relevant expertise.

In defence of celebrity politics

One line of defence is to note that what is being discussed is not as novel, or as atypical, as is sometimes implied by critics, and that the criticisms are misplaced, at least insofar as things are seen as changing for the worse. With respect to the political celebrity, there is a long and respected tradition of celebrated non-politicians engaging with politics (John Milton, John Dryden and Andrew Marvell all contributed to the political debate during the English Civil War). And with respect to the celebrity politician, Leo Braudy (1997) points out that the eighteenth century saw the proliferation of public representations of political figures in the form of busts and portraits. The subsequent development of photography – used in particular by Abraham Lincoln – gave further impetus to the drive towards visual representations in politics, placing emphasis on appearance and style. Film compounded the trend. As Leo Braudy explains, movie stars like Douglas Fairbanks Jr., Mary Pickford and Charlie Chaplin helped to:

> 'sell' the [1914-18] war to a strongly isolationist American public uninterested in European problems .... War was a commodity that had to be advertised, and the alliance of

performers and politicians is as emblematic as Lincoln's frequent trips to Mathew Brady's photographic gallery in the dark days of the Civil War.

(Braudy, 1997: 556–7)

A defence of contemporary celebrity politics in terms of its historical precedents draws upon the idea that the phenomenon is a necessary or inevitable product of social and political change. In particular, celebrity politics, and the cult of the personality that it embodies, can be seen as a product of the transformation of political communication. According to Paolo Mancini and David Swanson (1996), the breakdown of traditional social structures under the strains of modernization have created the need for a form of political communication in which new 'symbolic realities' have to be created, containing 'symbolic templates of heroes and villains, honored values and aspirations, histories, mythologies, and self-definition' (1996: 9). In such a world, the focus shifts onto individual politicians, and politics is 'personalized'. In Sweden, for example, Kent Asp and Peter Esaiasson have noted that the increasing attention devoted to 'party leaders as private persons' (1996: 84). Similar trends are found in Germany, Poland and the United Kingdom (Schoenbach,1996: 104; Jakubovicz, 1996: 145; Billig et al., 1993; Deacon et al., 1998; Langer, forthcoming). This trend is accentuated by a mass media whose generic conventions favour this form of personalized politics (Mancini and Swanson, 1996: 13) and whose stereotypes – especially around gender – give the personalization a particular twist (Muir, 2005). The new styles of political communication are logical extensions of this reality. The advertisement (and the conventions of advertising) comes to define political communication. Politicians become stars, politics becomes a series of spectacles, and the citizens become spectators (Crouch, 2004). Such a world also chimes with those who have argued that parties are engaged in creating brands rather than ideologies (Downs, 1957) and voters increasingly think and act as consumers (Clark and Inglehart, 1998; Crewe and Sarlvik, 1983; Deacon and Wring, 2002).

The logic of this is explored in the wider discussion of the relationship of politics to marketing (Lees-Marshment, 2001; Savigny, 2009; Scammell, 1999). The suggestion is not that politics just makes use of the practices and techniques of marketing, but that, for good or ill, *politics is marketing*. As the logic of marketing takes hold, it necessarily shapes the conception of 'representation'. Representatives sell themselves to their market; successful parties are like successful entrepreneurs. To the extent that celebrity politics is a form of marketing, then the celebrity politician is simply making use of the relevant techniques, either by selling themselves, or by endorsing a product (a policy or a politician).

In short, it is possible to counter the claims of critics of celebrity politics by offering a different account of the emergence of the phenomenon, an account which sees it both as having historical precedents, and insofar as it is new, as being part of a process of modernization and the enhancement of political communication. But offering an alternative account of the emergence of celebrity politics does not go to the heart of the various criticisms. The critics' main objection, as we have noted, is based on two elements. The first has to do with the excess attention given to image and appearance, and the second has to do with the irrelevance of the expertise that political celebrities possess. The fact there are precedents or contributing social trends for celebrity politics does not invalidate these criticisms. That we can explain the rise of the celebrity politician in terms of media trends does not provide a validation for them. Those media trends may be the product of the commercial and political interests of the press, which leads to the 'tabloidization' of the news agenda (Franklin, 1998). The celebrity politician is then simply the result of a celebrity-obsessed media, acting counter to some notional public good. In these circumstances, the question remains as to whether the use of images or the involvement of stars undermines representative government. To address the core criticisms, it is important to ask whether forms of celebrity politics can actually enhance, in principle, representative government.

To defend celebrity politics on these lines means paying attention to the character of the link between the represented and the representative. Can the involvement of popular culture strengthen the representative relationship? Stephen Coleman, for example, argues that forms of popular culture can resonate with people in ways that traditional forms of political communication cannot (2002: 254). The popularity of *Big Brother*, he suggests, owes much to the fact that the contestants were seen as 'representative', as 'people like us. They spoke and behaved in ways that appealed to sections of the public who traditionally feel intimidated by the language and discourse of politics.' It may be, as Coleman acknowledges, that the *Big Brother* housemates are no more typical of the population than are MPs, but what is important to the perception of them as 'representative' is 'the ordinariness of their preoccupations: what to eat; when to sleep; wanting to be liked' (2003: 31). These constitute the realities of daily life which condition the legitimation of representation. The *Big Brother* contestants are scrutinized by their audience in respect of their authenticity, itself a measure of integrity and trustworthiness, and in doing so they establish criteria of representativeness that could be applied to politics (Coleman, 2003: 32).

In a similar vein, John Keane has argued that the success of maverick political figures (like Ross Perot, Ralph Nader, Pauline Hanson, Martin Bell and Pim Fortuyn) owes something to the fact that they can 'claim to champion the interests of the unrepresented, all those who don't identify with politicians' (2002: 13). The 'popularity' of these politicians is a measure of their ability to establish claims to represent the people. It is a claim that derives from a world, which, says Keane (2002: 13–15), is marked by 'communicative abundance', and in which popular identities derive from the role models provided by the celebrities who inhabit this world. Insofar as people's sense of self and others is mediated in this way, it becomes plausible to claim that political celebrities 'represent' the people, and for celebrity politicians to base their claim to 'representativeness' on the icons and techniques of the celebrity.

What is involved here are a number of different and competing notions of representation. There is the representation we get through a system of voting; there is the representation that we have through people acting on our behalf; and there is the representation we experience in those who resemble us or share our experiences (Birch, 1964; Pitkin, 1967). Crudely, the contrast is between representation as a product of procedures, and representation as reflection or resemblance (Coleman, 2003: 30). And the latter appeals to the idea that representation has to be understood in symbolic or aesthetic terms (Daloz, 2003; Saward, 2006). Representation necessarily entails 'appearance' and cultural performance.

Judging by appearance

One of the assumptions of the critics of celebrity politics is that judging by appearance is an inappropriate basis for the evaluation of representatives. Rather, they claim that representatives should be judged in terms of the quality of their policy proposals, the ideological coherence of their manifesto, the sophistication of their political skills, or the legitimacy of their selection procedures. But while such issues are indeed important to the representative–represented relationship, they do not exhaust its character and content. Geoffrey Brennan and Alan Hamlin (2000) argue that 'appearance' has a legitimate place in democracy. For them, voting is an 'expressive act'; it is not just about achieving certain ends – a reduced tax rate, more public spending, or whatever. As an expressive act, the vote is understood as allowing the voter to identify with politicians and to seek out what they [the voters] find 'politically attractive'. Although 'attractiveness' can be measured along many axes, included amongst them is 'appearance'. Brennan and Hamlin write that 'it would be perfectly rational (in the strict sense) to vote on the basis of a candidate's appearance or speaking voice if those are the characteristics the voter identifies with' (2000: 178). The more typical basis for assessment, according to Brennan and Hamlin, is 'character and competencies'. But whatever the focus of the assessment, the suggestion is that rational actors faced with the decision of whom to select as their representative will do so on the basis of factors other than policy coherence or ideological consistency. 'Appearance' may stand as a proxy for such things, but it is the appearance of competence or political empathy, not the fact of it, that is being discerned. In this context, the repertoire of gestures associated with celebrity politics assumes a greater importance for celebrity politicians, who use them to demonstrate their political character, and political celebrities, who use them to establish their authenticity or integrity.

One implication of this argument is that political analysis must develop methods of 'reading' appearance, as well as taking cognisance of the traditional aspects of political communication and action. In the words of John Corner and Dick Pels, this means 'straddling the "higher" dimension of political rationality and political speech and the "baser" one that admits affect, body language, "looks", dress code, and other stage props of political performance' (2003: 16). By this account, new dimensions of political communications are opened up: the images in political advertisements, the sound of campaign anthems, and the dress sense of political leaders. Political representation, and the political communication upon which it is based, become a matter of aesthetics. This argument is most forcefully made by F. R. Ankersmit (2002).

Ankersmit argues that representation is literally that: re-presenting political reality to voters in an attempt to capture their imagination. He writes that 'the politician must possess the essentially *aesthetic* talent of being able to represent political reality in new and original ways' (2002: 116–17, his emphasis). This is a matter of 'political style' (Ankersmit, 2002: 132ff). Style is the way in which politicians and parties communicate their relationship to the electorate and their future public goals. As Dick Pels puts it, 'Political style ... enables citizens to regain their grip on a complex political reality by restoring mundane political experience to the centre of democratic practice' (2003: 50). Frank Ankersmit writes:

> When asking him or herself how best to represent the represented, the representative should ask what political style would best suit the electorate. And this question really requires an essentially creative answer on the part of the representative, in the sense that there exists no style in the electorate that is quietly waiting to be copied.
>
> (Ankersmit, 1996: 54)

In summary, the suggestion is that political representation in modern democracies is constituted and experienced aesthetically. From this perspective, the phenomenon of the celebrity politician takes on a different aspect. It is not to be dismissed as a betrayal of the proper principles of democratic representation, but to be seen as an extension of them. Celebrity politics is a code for the performance of representations through the gestures and media available to those who wish to claim 'representativeness'. It does not follow from this that all forms of celebrity politics are to be welcomed (any more than all forms of art or political ideology are to be welcomed). What it does suggest is that we need to approach differently the analysis and understanding of political representation, to see it as part of a media performance.

Politics as media performance

For John Corner, this performance is centred on the creation of a political persona. A politician is engaged in the business of establishing him or herself as 'a *person of qualities*' within the public space of '*demonstrable* representativeness' (2000: 396, his emphasis). Rather than siding with those who bemoan the 'personalisation' of politics, Corner argues that the individual political figure serves to 'condense the "political"' for those they represent (ibid.: 401). Through their mediated public performance, politicians try to demonstrate certain political qualities and to connect them to political values. For Corner, the analysis of a political persona depends on an understanding of both the intentions of the politician and the interaction between him or her and the available media systems. The analysis is of a performance that involves demeanour and posture, voice and appearance (ibid.: 391).

Seeing political representation in these terms takes it much closer to the realm of show business and the world of the celebrity. 'In politics,', writes P. David Marshall, 'a leader must somehow embody the sentiments of the party, the people, and the state. In the realm of entertainment, a celebrity must somehow embody the sentiments of an audience' (1997: 203). Marshall argues that the existence of politicians as *celebrities* has to be understood as part of a process of filling out political rationality to include the affective relationships as well as the instrumental ones. If they are to be the objects of affection, to be 'attractive', then this intent informs the way in which they seek to communicate. It suggests that spin doctors are indeed the equivalent of PR people in film and record companies, managing the image and appearance of their clients. It is about deciding what interviews, with whom, when; it is about rationing the supply of images and information to coincide with the release of the latest record release/policy initiative. Explaining the political success of Governor Jesse Ventura, his media adviser said, 'Jesse's worked in movies, he's been a pro-wrestler, and he understands pop culture. He gets it. He knows what's going to play in public, and he's not afraid to take chances' (quoted in West and Orman, 2003: 11). Or as President Ronald Reagan once reportedly said, 'Politics is just like show business' (quoted in Postman, 1987: 128).

Political representation is an art that draws on the skills and resources which define mass-mediated popular culture. Thomas Meyer uses a theatrical metaphor to discuss the mediation of political representation. Politicians are to be seen as:

> embodying qualities, forces, tendencies, virtues, programs or powers that carry powerful resonance in a country's political culture and mythology. Thus Tony Blair and Gerhard Schroder were cast as men of will, virtue, innovativeness and the 'can-do' spirit, regardless of the actual content of the programs they stood for.
>
> (Meyer, 2002: 32)

These characters occupy 'dramas' and 'narratives' that draw from myth and popular heroes, sliding between life and art. Meyer talks of the 'artistry of entertainment in politics' (2002: 33), referring to the way in which politicians use the formats of entertainment 'to prove that they have the common touch and know how to relax.' Meyer sees politics as being 'revisualised' (made visible) by the technologies of mass communication, drawing on the rhetoric and devices of popular culture.

What Corner, Marshall and Meyer all suggest is that we need to understand the representative relationship as one that is not just analogous with other forms of popular performance, but is derived from it. Adoption of the trappings of popular celebrity is not a trivial gesture towards fashion or a minor detail of political communication, but instead lies at the heart of the notion of political representation itself. All politicians, in a sense, are celebrity politicians whose performances are judged as a success or a failure. All political communication entails elements of the wider media and cultural landscape.

And what is true for traditional politicians is also true for the stars of popular culture that choose to engage with politics. They too perform political representativeness; they too are part of a political and cultural process. But they do so in different ways from their political counterparts. Their claim to represent derives from the phenomenon of fandom. Liesbet van Zoonen (2005) argues that the idea of fandom applies equally to the political and cultural realm, and John Thompson (1995: 220–5) has suggested that being a 'fan' is an important, even defining, characteristic of modernity. Fandom entails the formation of relations of 'intimacy with distant others' (Thompson, 1995: 220), and this can be seen to be the basis of a form of (political) representation. This sense of being represented in the experience of fandom is captured by Nick Hornby in *Fever Pitch*, his account of his life as a fan of Arsenal football club. Writing of a championship victory, he says:

> The joy we feel on occasions like this is not a celebration of others' good fortune, but our own .... *The players are merely our representatives*, chosen by the manager rather than elected by us, but our representatives nonetheless, and sometimes if you look hard you can see the little poles that join them together, and the handles at the side that enable us to move them.
>
> (Hornby, 2000: 179; emphasis added)

This representational relationship is established by the 'affective' capacity of the cultural performance. Indeed, Lawrence Grossberg suggests that this very capacity is intrinsically political in that it can generate a sense of 'empowerment' that makes possible 'the optimism, invigoration and passion which are necessary for any struggle to change the world' (1992: 86).

Not all stars have this power; not all of them can turn fans into movements. When Geri Halliwell of the Spice Girls was a UN goodwill ambassador, she was mocked, while Bono is taken seriously (Drezner, 2007; Hyde, 2009). Why? Sexism probably plays a part, but it may also be a matter of the genre in which the celebrity works or with which they are associated. It is apparent that certain genres establish conventions and opportunities for political engagement (for example, folk, rock, hip-hop, country music), in ways that others do not (teenpop, easy listening). And even genre-based accounts of the representative claim have to take account of the ways in which these genres are themselves constituted by media representations and business strategies as 'political'. Folk music is not 'intrinsically' political; its politics are the product of the ways in which certain political movements (for example, the Popular Front or CND) 'captured' the music for their purposes (Cantwell, 1996; Denning, 1997). Ron Eyerman and Andrew Jamison (1998) argue that, during the 1960s, the capacity of folk and rock stars to assume a political role was a product of the context created by the social movements active at the time, which required of them the role of 'truth bearers'. What this suggests is that the claim by celebrities to speak for others is conditional upon a number of factors, which include generic conventions, but extend to the larger social and political context in which they operate.

Furthermore, the capacity to 'represent' is not simply a product of the artist and their genre's conventions. Bob Geldof and Bono's ability to represent the conscience of those concerned about developing country debt was dependent on the willingness of broadcasters to make airtime available for the Live8 concerts (Street et al., 2008). Without the mediated public sphere provided by the broadcaster, Geldof's claims would have been silenced. In a similar way, the oppressive actions of states can, unintentionally, create platforms and opportunities for performers to become political representatives. Where the state monopolizes the conventional forms of political communication and seeks to regulate all forms of artistic expression, it becomes possible for musicians and other performers to assume a leadership role, legitimized by their success as artists. The state, in its regulatory role, politicizes artistic expression, and the aesthetics of the art in turn makes possible an alternative form of political expression. Peter Wicke (1992), for instance, argues that East German rock musicians were instrumental in uniting the opposition to the Honecker regime and in bringing about the collapse of the Berlin Wall. Meanwhile, Peter Sheeran claims that 'it was the dissident content of coded Soviet lyrics that caused most damage to the longevity of the Soviet system' (2001: 8).

Before ending this discussion of new forms of political communication, there is one final issue to address. Do celebrity politicians make a difference? Research into the mass effects of celebrity politics is at a formative stage. There is, however, evidence that people's attachment to particular causes can be affected by the association of a celebrity with them, and that celebrities vary in their capacity to inspire allegiance (Jackson and Darrow, 2005; Jackson, 2007). There is also research that suggests that campaign endorsements by a celebrity – for example, Oprah Winfrey's support for Barack Obama – can benefit a candidate (Austin et al., 2008; Garthwaite and Moore, 2008; Pease and Brewer, 2008). But there are those who claim that the 'celebrity effect' is minimal (Couldry and Markham, 2007), and a team of researchers at the University of Michigan-Dearborn have reported that the power of celebrities to push a cause or issue to the top of the news agenda is limited (Thrall et al., 2008). While there may be uncertainty about the discernible impact of celebrity politics, it is clear that it remains a key component of contemporary political communication, and a site of many different arguments about its value.

Conclusion

Our concern in this chapter, and in the ones that follow, is about media's role in a democracy. Here we have considered the ways in which political communication – a vital dimension of media's democratic role – has been changing, and the arguments provoked by this. In reviewing these arguments, we have seen the deep divisions that emerge between those who condemn the marketing of politics or the rise of the celebrity politician, and those who welcome them. Their disagreements are rarely, if ever, about the facts of the case, although they do play a part, but more often about competing values and interpretations. We cannot conclude that democracy is (or is not) being harmed by these new forms of communication. What we can do is see what is at stake in the disputes, and to see the complexity they contain. We need to discriminate between forms of packaging and marketing, between styles of celebrity politics. Just as there are good and bad popular culture, and good and bad political arguments, so there are good and bad forms of political communication. The issue is how these judgements are made, about what is being conveyed and what should be conveyed in democratic political communication. Some forms of marketing may engage citizens more than others, just as some celebrity politicians may be more or less successful in winning support for causes, which may or may not deserve support. What is needed is a careful examination of political communication in all its forms in order to understand both how they work as communication and how they might be used in the routines of democratic life.

Chapter 10

New Media, New Politics?

The growth of the internet has been extraordinary by any standards: from a local secret among scientists at the beginning of the 1990s to the topic of everyday conversation at the end of the decade, from an anarchic information network for the bizarre and the banal, to a chaotic economy of self-made (paper) millionaires and inflated share prices, to a world of Twitter, Wikipedia, social networking sites and a media political economy which is fast becoming the domain of Google and its like. The figures for internet use – not an exact science – suggest that, in the first decade of the twenty-first century, numbers have grown by over 380 per cent. There were some 360 million users in 2000; at the end of the decade there were 1.7 billion – one in four of the world's population (http://www.internetworldstats. com/stats.htm). The accompanying rhetoric has been similarly dramatic, with talk of every aspect of human life, including politics, being transformed by this new form of communication.

This chapter is about the present and future political consequences of the net. If the last chapter was about the way in which political communication is being transformed by new uses of traditional media, this chapter is about the political impact of a new system of communication. In particular, it considers how the web may be reconfiguring democratic participation. Traditionally, citizens have been passive recipients of political information from their papers, radio stations and television channels. They have enjoyed a modest degree of participation through letters columns, phone-ins and the like, but for the most part they have been communications' consumers. The internet appears to change all this, by enabling people not just to become more involved in traditional media coverage of politics (via email, texting, phone-voting and so on), but also to create their own coverage and to use new media to enact forms of political activism and leadership. Such changes have profound implications for democracy – or at least this is what much recent political rhetoric would have us believe.

Transforming politics? A five-step programme

There are many ways in which, it is claimed, new media are changing the political landscape, but here I shall mention just five. The first, and perhaps most obvious political impact, has been on the operation of government. In the early 1990s, the Clinton administration set itself the goal of creating 'a seamless web of communication networks, computers, databases and consumer electronics' that would protect and preserve democracy (quoted in Glencross, 1993: 3). In 1995, the G7 nations met to discuss the emerging 'information society' and the White House boasted that it could be reached by the click of a keyboard, as could endless other political information resources (see Harrison, 1994). Even the UK civil service tentatively opened itself to the gaze of travellers on the superhighway. By 1998, the UK government had issued a discussion document that proposed a future in which electronic communications would distribute information, collect taxes, administer regulations and compile statistics (www.democracy.org.uk/groups/gov-direct/). Subsequently, we have seen governments across the world deploying the internet to deliver services, inform and consult citizens, and implement policy (Chadwick, 2006; Coleman and Gotze, 2001). Sites such as Data.gov in the United States and data.gov.uk in the United Kingdom (initiated by Tim Berners-Lee, the creator of the world wide web) have offered new opportunities for citizens to access government information. These developments, argues Catherine Needham (2004: 43), have the potential 'to radically reconfigure the state–citizen relationship'.

The second area of impact has been in the conduct of elections (Coleman, 1998). During the 1994 congressional mid-term elections, an online political activist from California was quoted as saying, 'I think that by 1996, we will begin to see some number of campaigns either won or lost because campaign operations either use or fail to use network communications and organization' (*International Herald Tribune*, 9 November 1994). A year later one of the presidential hopefuls, Lamar Alexander, began his campaign on the internet (*Guardian,* 1 March 1995). By 2000, the chairman of the Republican National Committee was reporting that 'the internet is introducing a fundamental shift in terms of communications and organizations' (Nicholson, 2000: 80). The sentiment was echoed by the Democratic National

Committee: 'Democratic candidates will have more opportunities to speak directly and personally to the American people, through venues like Internet chat rooms' (Romer, 2000: 83). Within a very few years, these assessments have come to look almost quaint. Barack Obama's 2008 campaign for president was portrayed as the culmination of all the promises of what the internet might deliver. Nick Anstead and Will Straw (2009: 2) describe it 'as the most technically sophisticated campaign of all time', while Jennifer Stromer-Galley dubs it the 'Web 2.0 election'. She (2009: 50) recounts how prospective voters were engaged 'though viral videos, social networking sites, blogging and microblogging, and text messaging'.

We can add to the new media's impact on campaigning, its increasing impact on the business of voting too. In the last years of the twentieth century, the UK government was reported to be bringing 'push button voting a step nearer', following its pre-election promise to use the internet to allow people to 'participate in decision-making' (*Guardian*, 18 August 1998; Labour Party, 1995). Increasingly, the internet has emerged as a formal part of the electoral process, particularly in the United States (Solop, 2001). It has also been seen as integral to the development of deliberative democracy, itself seen as a step up from liberal representative democracy (Coleman and Blumler, 2009).

A third area in which the internet's impact has been felt is that of political and social movements (Norris, 2002: 188ff). The net has become an increasingly important device for marketing and recruitment by established and formally legitimate organizations, such as NGOs like Oxfam or Amnesty (Webster, 2001). Friends of the Earth were quick to use new media to create innovative organizational forms – 'networks of networks' – that gave substance to the familiar green slogan 'think globally, act locally' (Pickerill, 2000, 2004; Washbourne, 1999, 2010). But new media have assumed even greater prominence through claims for their use in organizing spontaneous, 'smart mob' demonstrations across the world (Hermanns, 2008) – such events as anti-capitalist protests in London or dissent in Tehran at the result of the Iranian elections in 2009.

The internet is seen, in this guise, to be enabling new forms of political activism (Kahn and Kellner, 2004). On 18 June 1999, a spate of public demonstrations erupted across the world. In London, marchers, chanting to the accompaniment of a samba band, occupied a mainline railway station, before moving on to trash a McDonald's restaurant. Similar scenes were witnessed elsewhere in Europe, the United States and Latin America. Five months later, in Seattle, another group of demonstrators disrupted the meeting of the World Trade Organization. These, and many similar spontaneous demonstrations, were coordinated through the internet and mobile phone technologies. Websites and e-mail discussion groups provided the infrastructure for political activities which, it seemed to the frustrated authorities, had no leaders and were not dependent on hierarchical political structures. They were virtual and very real. Such examples have formed part of what some commentators see as a 'civic networking movement'. This is represented by 'a new anarchic political community in which traditional political identities linked to territorial and sectional interests are undermined, and new forms of politics emerge free of state coercion' (Bryan et al., 1998: 6–7). Sometimes, this activism takes the form of terrorism, as terrorists too take advantage of the possibilities created by new media (Louw, 2005: 241ff)

A fourth area where the impact of new media has been felt is journalism. There are two elements to this. On the one hand, the contours of political commentary have been changed by the rise of the blog and the so-called blogosphere. We have seen the proliferation of blogs run by politicians and political activists, as well as by those who see themselves as independent political commentators, unconstrained by the ideological and regulatory conventions that hamper the commentator in traditional media (Matt Drudge, Guido Fawkes). The latter have been responsible for breaking stories about both personal indiscretion and political scandal. Measuring their impact is harder, but research is emerging that suggests that the blog may be altering the form and content of the public sphere (Coleman, 2005; Stanyer, 2006; Wright, 2009). The other way in which journalism is being affected is through the growth of 'user-generated content', which, according to John Kelly (2009: 5), 'makes every citizen a publisher'. Here the internet is seen to enable 'ordinary people' to act as journalists, uploading news reports and mobile phone footage to traditional and non-traditional news sites. Much of the reporting of the terrorist attacks in Mumbai in 2008 and the Haiti earthquake in 2010 used the contributions of citizen journalists.

The possibilities for information gathering have led commentators to identify a fifth, and rather different arena in which the new media impact on politics. Rather than opening up government and politics, the suggestion is that the internet and associated technologies enable the state to ever more effectively act as an Orwellian 'Big Brother' (Lyon, 2001, 2003). In direct critique of those who celebrate the internet's liberatory potential, Evgeny Morozov (2009) writes of how, in Belarus, the authorities have used it to monitor and arrest dissidents. What happens in Belarus also happens in China, Egypt, Saudi Arabia and Russia. 'Despite what digital enthusiasts tell you,' Morozov writes (2009: 36), 'the emergence of new digital spaces for dissent also led to new ways of tracking it.'

These five aspects of new media's impact on politics – and further ones emerge almost daily – have inevitably prompted grand talk of the dawning of a new political order – not always, though, the same political order. There are competing visions, as the last of the five above suggests. Eric Louw (2005: 122) describes three different attitudes to the likely impact of new media on politics. There are the *optimists* who see new media as essentially progressive and improving the quality of political life. There are the *sceptics* who regard the claims made for new media as overblown and unrealistic. And then there are the *pessimists* (or Luddites) who fear the impact of new media, seeing it as a turn for the worse. In order to negotiate these competing evaluations, and the multiple effects that new media are thought to engender, the rest of this chapter is dedicated to exploring the particular relationship between new media and democracy. My aim is not to produce a definitive picture – were either I capable or it possible – of what is happening, but rather to try and highlight the issues and arguments that emerge in discussion of so-called 'e-democracy'.

E-democracy: practice and promises

The idea that democracy can be enhanced and developed through the use of technology has been around for several decades. Even before the internet established itself in popular consciousness, there were debates about how the use of computers could advance democratic processes (Barber, 1984;

McLean, 1986, 1989). By the mid-1990s, political leaders were talking of a 'virtual Congress' (Newt Gingrich) or of 'electronic town meetings' (Al Gore), and the claim was being made that 'The Net is the world's only functioning political anarchy but it could soon become a major tool for democracy' (Fenchurch, 1994: 11). Since then the concepts of 'electronic democracy' or 'democracy online' have become ever more familiar (see http://dowire.org/).

Many visions inspired this talk, but one predominates: the belief that the world wide web has created the conditions for a more advanced or a more effective form of democracy. With the networks in place and interactive technology to hand, people will be able to vote on issues, inform themselves on government policy and interrogate their representatives. They can become the active, effective citizens of the democratic dream. This is to move beyond using the web as just another device for packaging politics or for parties to address voters; it is to enable those voters to take charge, to talk with each other as well with politicians. So it is that we have witnessed the rise of consultative and deliberative forums at all levels of government, from the local to the supranational (Oates et al., 2005; Wright, 2005), with this evolving into a network society in which traditional hierarchies and divisions of labour have been eroded (Castells, 1996, 2009).

In short, the web appears to have created the possibility of a citizenry actively engaged in politics. But this is to beg two questions: is this really what is happening, and if it is, is it desirable? Does the internet enable democracy to function, as one enthusiast suggests, as a jukebox which, because its tunes are chosen by the people, is listened to more intently:

> while some of us may dread the prospective democratization of democracy via the Internet ... make no mistake: The full interactive potential of the Internet offers a real chance to restore some purpose to our politics by restoring some power to our people.
>
> (Bailey, 1999)

And if it does work like this, should we welcome it? Is this what we mean by 'democracy'?

The practice of e-democracy

Let us deal first with the issue of current reality. It is, of course, impossible to generalize about the many schemes that are out there. We can, though, make the claim that there are more opportunities for citizens to register their views, that elected political representatives and public officials can be more easily reached, and that accessing information about politics and public policy is less costly. The result, it is suggested, is that we are seeing the development of a less hierarchical social order, one in which the network rather than the pyramid is the defining image. Such general claims have to be tempered. The first and most obvious qualification is that while the technology has formally increased the potential for political engagement, it does not follow automatically that this potential is being realized. There are two reasons for this. The first is that the technology is not itself universally available, whether we look within or between countries – in 2009, while more than 70 per cent of those living in the United States were online, less than 7 per cent of those living in the continent of Africa were (http://www.internetworldstats.com/stats.htm). This is what Gerald Sussman (1997: 174) calls 'the political and economic realities': 'the ventures of opportunity-seeking commercial interests and the concerns of those who would restrict public communication in the cause of security, moral guardianship, or property protection'. No adequate account of new media's impact can be given without acknowledging its political economy (Mansell, 2004).

The second reason is that access to the technology is not itself a guarantee of the ability to use it; or rather the technology does not create equality. New media may actually serve to promote the interests of the powerful. This may be a result of a lack of training or education, but it may also stem from a sense of alienation from the technology. Such estrangement is not a failure of particular individuals, but of the way a technology is made inaccessible. Feminist critics of technology point to the way it comes to be designed and organized for the benefit of men and to the exclusion of women (Wajcman, 1991). Access to technology, including new media, is socially stratified: between classes, generations and nations. Manuel Castells (1996: 371) talks of the division of the world into those who are 'interacting' and those who are 'interacted'. The latter remain on the receiving end of pre-packaged communications opportunities. Thus, those who dominate the offline world may also dominate the online one, by virtue of the resources, skills, and cultural capital that they possess (Norris, 2001b). Mathew Hindman (2009) provides further evidence for this conclusion. He argues that new media may change the names and faces of the political elite, but not the fact of that elite's existence and power.

Beyond the practical question of who is online, and who has capacity to use its potential, there is then the matter of what they are able or choose to do. Several writers have argued that, while the rhetoric is of popular empowerment, the reality is rather different. Systems of consultation tend to become less about listening than informing; that what seems to be dialogue is in fact a monologue (Wright, 2002). This is, in part, because online engagement is not a simple product of technology, but is the result of the design and operation of the technology. This means that any claims made for what the net contributes to political life needs to be accompanied by careful scrutiny of the systems of moderation and of design (Wright, 2006; Wright and Street, 2007). Hindman sees the architecture of the web and the behaviour of search engines as reinforcing existing inequalities. As he writes, 'There is ... good reason to believe that communities on the web function as winner-take-all networks' (2009: 51). The implication of this is that because of the way search engines operate, discussion of any given topic tends to be dominated by a narrow range of perspectives (ibid.: 56). Added to all this is the question of what people use the internet for. Apart from the vast miscellany of non-political uses to which the internet is put, and the proliferation of political views and comments now available, there is evidence to suggest that, rather than using the virtual world to explore new ideas and possibilities, we remain creatures of habit and convention. Users tend to employ the internet to pursue those interests they already have, and not to develop new ones (Feynoe, 2010). Such behaviour leads writers like Cass Sunstein (2001) to fear that our brave new world is an increasingly balkanized one, in which we all pursue our interests, indifferent to the concerns of our neighbours.

For these same sceptics, the net effect is that the problems of access that beset previous forms of democracy are reproduced in the new electronic order. The same imbalances and inequality of resources continue to distort participation. Hindman (ibid.: 128) contends that for all the wealth of bloggers competing for our attention, those 'who come out on top' are the 'well educated white male professionals'. Despite the rhetoric of participation and equality in a new electronic democracy, the reality is a system in which corporate power acts to depoliticize politics, transforming the citizen into the consumer (Weizenbaum, 1984; Zolo, 1992). Pushed to its extreme, this corporatism imagines a future electronic democracy in which the elite already knows how the citizen is going to vote because it has complete information on everyone and everything. Voting itself becomes entirely redundant because it is entirely predictable. The system of electronic participation is in fact a system of surveillance, monitoring citizens rather than responding to them (Lyon, 2003). This bleak scenario chimes with Andrew Calabrese and Mark Borchert's observation (1996: 264–5) that, while 'the discourse on electronic democracy is aesthetically pleasing', it has to be treated cautiously: 'visions of empowerment are illusory or manipulative if they do not rest on the foundation of a clearly articulated vision of government'.

These criticisms of the practice of new media serve only to sensitize us to the possibility that the rhetoric of e-democracy and its technology may not be reflected in the reality of its use. There is, though, the second question. Even if the technology worked perfectly, was distributed evenly, and created networks not hierarchies, would we want the results that it produced? Would it deliver democracy?

The promise of e-democracy

Among advocates of the idea of 'electronic democracy', two different agendas can be detected. For some, the technology represents a way of improving the existing form of (liberal) democracy. For others, it constitutes an opportunity to create a new form of democracy – or rather, the revival of an old one: the direct democracy of ancient Athens. Electronic polling offers the chance to get 'Back to Greece' (Adonis and Mulgan, 1994). The distinction is not trivial, nor is it new. It defines, it might be said, the history of democratic thought. Two very different models of democracy are being offered: on the one hand, representative democracy; on the other, deliberative democracy. These two competing models have been evident in the very earliest discussion – in the late 1970s and early 1980s – of the potential of information technology. The political scientists who have explored the possibility of an electronic democracy or cyberdemocracy have themselves fallen into one of the two camps (Abramson et al., 1988; Arterton, 1987; Barber, 1984; Budge, 1996; McLean, 1989; Tsagarousianou et al., 1998; Van de Donk et al., 1995). But despite the differences in political values between those who assess the promise of e-democracy, they continue to share some basic assumptions about what is on offer. For this reason, it pays to look briefly at the general arguments that emerge around the promise of technologically enhanced democracy.

The argument for e-democracy

Although advocates differ over their preferred model of democracy, they are linked by a shared belief in the ability of new media to create the conditions for political participation. As one enthusiast wrote early in the debate:

> Modern communications technology can provide the means to broadly educate and enlighten citizens, to engage them in discussions of the public good and the means to achieve it, and to empower citizens in their quest for self-determination.
>
> (Staton, 1994: 31–2)

For others the net provides a forum for a truly free exchange of ideas and views, unconstrained by imbalances of power and resources (Ess, 1996). Underlying such claims is the thought that attempts to guarantee full participation in modern democracies have been wrecked by four previously insurmountable problems: time, size, knowledge and access. In earlier eras, democratic participation was limited because of the problems of assembling large numbers of people at one time and in one place, because of the limits to political knowledge of ordinary citizens, and because of the inequalities in the distribution of resources which hamper people's access to power and their capacity to participate (see Held, 2006, for an overview). Taken together, these difficulties made direct participation and popular deliberation both impractical and undesirable (Mill, 1992).

New media seem to offer a solution to all these problems, thereby opening up the possibility of full participation. For example, online voting has been proposed as one solution to the problem of declining electoral turnout. A wired-up world would eliminate the constraints of time because communication and participation become instantaneous. Citizens can participate at the click of a mouse or by sending a text message. They do not need to meet in cold halls or travel to polling booths. Similarly, problems of size are solved because physical space becomes irrelevant. It is no longer necessary to gather people in a single place. Social networking software has created an infinite array of virtual public forums. So it is, too, with problems in the distribution of knowledge. Not only is information on any subject now widely available, access to it is relatively easy. Wikipedia and online archives provide citizens with almost instant access to a vast array of information and data. Furthermore, individuals can search this data, or those individuals can avail themselves of the cornucopia of commentators and experts in the blogosphere. The costs of information and access are dramatically reduced, and in turn organizational costs are cut. Demonstrations and protests can be organized at little or no cost. The net seems to provide a way around the practical problems posed by democracy, whatever its form; citizens can exercise their vote, deliberate on public policy or participate directly. But it is precisely this sort of reasoning that appals critics of e-democracy.

The argument against e-democracy

There are three main lines of criticism directed at e-democracy, or at least at the arguments above. The first concentrates upon the inherent theoretical difficulties within the idea of democracy. As Iain McLean (1989) points out, there are some 'problems of democracy' that cannot be solved by the application of technology, however ingenious the software. Democratic decisions are not just the product of citizen choices. It depends on how you register those choices. You need only consider the arguments mounted for changing electoral systems. They all share one assumption: the character of the electoral system can crucially affect the result. You get different majorities and different winners depending on whether you use first-past-the-post or a list system, whether you use an electoral college or a simple majority. What counts as 'the best' will depend upon judgements about how democracy *ought* to work, what interests *ought* to feature and what results *ought* to be produced. Science and technology do not produce answers to such questions. This is because, as Robert Dahl (1956) and others have pointed out, there may not be a majority among any given population. There are instead 'cycling majorities', in which any given winner is the product of agenda setting and voting rules. Where there are three policy options, and supporters for each, none of whom can command a majority on their own, then any option can be defeated by a coalition formed by the others. There is no majority choice and, where one appears, this is the result of the way the agenda is set and the voting conducted (it has very little to do with the actual distribution of popular opinion). Once again, the problem cannot be solved by the expedient of new media. Technology does nothing to solve the conceptual and constitutional problems that democracy generates (McLean, 1989).

A second line of criticism derives from the assumption that, by increasing access to (and the availability of) data, new media technologies improve the quality of democracy. While there are powerful reasons for seeing freedom of information as a central tenet of democracy, it does not follow that all information in itself enhances democracy. Democratic decisions are not equivalent to mathematical calculations; they also involve judgements. Just because capital punishment might be the popularly preferred option, it does not follow that it is right. Nor are decisions necessarily improved by the simple expedient of acquiring more data. Just because we know the content of the human genome, it is not immediately obvious how this knowledge should be used. All decisions require a judgement, and the art of judgement may, in fact, be hampered by an excess of information or 'communications abundance' (Dennett, 1986; Keane, 2009; Vickers, 1965); or rather, that information has to be examined and explored in a dialogue, not simply computed.

These first two lines of criticism lead to a third: that the kind of democracy being proposed is a debased, impoverished version. This criticism does not apply automatically to all advocates of electronic democracy. It applies to those who treat the democratic process as a mere device for registering preferences and politics as a version of the market in which we exercise our choices as individual consumers. Critics see this as a gross misrepresentation of the democratic ideal. Michael Walzer says:

Modern technology makes possible something like this ... we might organize push-button referenda on crucial issues, the citizens alone in their living rooms, watching television, arguing only with their spouses, hands hovering over their private voting machines .... But is this the exercise of power? I am inclined to say, instead, that is only another example of the erosion of value – a false and ultimately degrading way of sharing in the making of decisions.

(Walzer, 1985: 306–7)

Like Walzer, Jean Elshtain has argued that electronic political participation is equivalent to making consumer choices on the shopping channel. The key element of democracy – deliberative, public policy choices – is replaced by privatized, instrumental decisions: 'advocates of interactive television display a misapprehension of the nature of real democracy, which they confuse with the plebiscite system' (1982: 108).

New media and politics

The arguments about e-democracy would seem to represent entirely incompatible positions, divided by fundamentally different views about the nature of democracy. This is perhaps true if democracy is viewed only as a tool for solving particular political problems, and hence new technology as offering a technical fix to those problems. If, however, we see the relationship between technology and politics in a different way, the differences become less stark. In her attack on e-democracy, Elshtain wrote that:

A true democratic polity involves a deliberative process, participation with other citizens, a sense of moral responsibility for one's society and the enhancement of individual possibilities through action in, and for, the *res publica*.

(Elshtain, 1982: 109)

The assumption here would seem to be that deliberation of this kind was incompatible with the technology. It is not clear that it is, and indeed there are those who argue that this is precisely what new media offers (Bruns, 2008). They make possible the kind of deliberation, through the creation of a virtual public sphere, that classical notions of democracy evoke. However, leaving aside questions raised by Hindman and Castells about the actual political character of that virtual public sphere, we should not overlook the claims of those who regard deliberative democracy with scepticism and who are unpersuaded of the values attributed to it (Bellamy, 2007). The point is that there are two distinct issues involved. The first is a debate about what values democracy can and should represent, in which there are legitimate questions to be asked about both the virtue of both representative and deliberative democracy (Weale, 1999). The second issue involves the relationship of technology to politics.

To illustrate this latter relationship, consider arguments around free speech. It makes little sense to talk of 'free speech' without reference to the methods by which people communicate – that is, what practices are entailed in 'speaking'. The ability to speak freely depends on access to the means of communication, and this is not a necessary or natural state of affairs. It has to be created and organized. A coherent political theory of free speech must be attached to an account of (a) the processes by which the technology of communication itself is developed and directed, and (b) the way this technology gives form to the ideas, values and opportunities that may be imagined. Arguments about the virtue of electronic democracy, or about the relative merits of competing versions of it, must incorporate some assumption about the technologies necessary to realizing it and society's ability to control technical change, to help achieve particular ends. Only with this control is it possible to advance or delay certain forms of electronic democracy. If no such control is feasible, if technical change is autonomous, arguments about the *kind* of democracy become largely irrelevant.

This, though, cannot be the end of the story. Supplementing arguments about electronic democracy with discussion of theories of technical change creates an artificial divide between theory and practice. Technical systems and political values are not discrete entities; rather they are extensions of one another. We live through our technology; our values and our identities both shape and are shaped by it. Think of the way that technologies of mobility (the car, the plane) have changed our views of the world and our place within it. In this sense, technology is cultural; and so is political theory: it is embedded in our forms of life in the same way that technology is (Winner, 1986). Arguments about e-democracy must go beyond questions of theory and technique, to look at the ways in which the technology constructs the kind of people and places that will form this new democracy; it must ask, what kind of citizen, what kind of public will inhabit hyperspace?

Developments in delivery systems (satellite, cable and so on), the proliferation of channels, and the tendency towards narrowcasting, are seen, by some commentators, as creating a political order in which politics is being 'domesticated' and citizenship is being privatized (Garnham, 2000; Habermas, 1989; Keane, 1991; Silverstone, 1994). This process is reinforced, it is argued (S. Jones, 1995: 28–9), by the way in which new forms of communication are dissolving traditional communities and the bonds and obligations that connect them. The result is a political life marked by instrumental, individualistic self-interest, in which the 'common interest' has no place (Sandel, 1998). These pessimistic prognostications are rebutted by those who argue that this same technology is in fact creating ideal conditions for a new democratic order, one in which citizens are forging new transnational interests and in which participatory democracy becomes a reality (Rheingold, 1992).

What lies behind these competing claims is an argument, not simply about what constitutes a just or free society, but what kinds of forces drive and shape current society. One of the elements in this argument is the part attributed to technology – it matters whether we understand technology as the neutral product of disinterested scientific enquiry, or as the result of the political interests which drive technical change, or as the autonomous result of its own internal logic. Proponents of electronic democracy tend to adopt the first of these perspectives – the idea that the technology is neutral. For them, information technology provides a 'technical fix', as we mentioned above. The 'problems' of democracy are seen as merely practical, and solvable by the application of technology.

But technical fixes are only 'fixes' because of the way the problem is defined. They do not constitute 'the' answer, but 'an' answer. Technical fixes do not solve a problem, rather they *impose a particular definition* on what the 'problem' is, a definition that invites the preselected solution (Habermas, 1971). If democracy's problems are practical, then technology may solve them, but if they are not, then technology merely reproduces them in a different form – in the same way that building motorways may simply relocate congestion and pollution rather than eliminate them.

Criticisms of the 'technical fix' approach lead to the second account of technology, one that focuses upon the interests behind the technology. Technology exists for a reason: to serve the interests of those with power. Seeing technology this way automatically raises suspicions about electronic democracy. Rather than being a way of empowering citizens, electronic democracy may as easily be a device that deskills and depoliticizes citizens, reducing their capacity to threaten the existing system (Campbell and Connor, 1986; Castells, 2009; Lyon, 1994, 2003). If this is the assumption, then the rhetoric of electronic town halls and virtual participation disguises a reality in which the corporate commercial and political interests invested in the technology are using the new possibilities for their advantage: to sustain the status quo rather than change it. But this version of technical change, as the product of corporate political interest, overlooks the question of how the technology itself is brought into being. The internet was not created by sheer act of will. Drawing attention to the commercial, political and military interests linked to it (see, for example, Calabrese and Borchert, 1996; Herman and McChesney, 1997), while important, does not in itself establish them as the intentional authors of the technology. They are as often forced to cope with the many unanticipated consequences of technical change as they are able to plan that change.

This gives rise to the third of the three accounts of technical change; this is the idea that technology is autonomous, that it is directed by a technical rationality which is not only independent of centres of political power, but actually dictates to them. Such a view can inspire technological dystopianism (Ellul, 1964) or utopianism (de Sola Pool, 1990), both of which suggest that we can do little more than accept the inevitable technological (and subsequent social) revolution. So it is that e-democracy is seen as the necessary outcome of general patterns of change, led by technologies which apply themselves to all aspects of human life: we do our shopping, we choose our life partner, we participate in politics, all on the web, and each of these activities is subsumed within the rhetoric and relations of consumerism (Sartori, 1989). People's connections to each other become purely instrumental and politics is affected by the same logic. Voting is treated like any other instrumental, consumer activity, having no more significance than the choice made between cereal brands in the supermarket. More than this, the infrastructure for 'e-democracy' creates the same kind of manipulative devices that mark consumption generally: marketing, advertising and so on. This account of technology rests on a strong notion of determinism, which assumes that the same technology follows the same course and has the same effects wherever it operates. But the same technology can have a different meaning and different effects according to its place in space and time. The culture in which it is embedded also constitutes it.

In short, the three views of technology – as neutral, politically chosen or autonomous – are flawed to the extent that they overlook the combination of political, scientific and cultural processes that construct the technology. The debate about e-democracy has to recognize the mutual dependence of political argument and technology. The core ideas within the political argument are themselves the product of our relationship with technology. At one level, the technology is the embodiment of certain interests and possibilities, but at another it is the bearer of effects: it changes what we can imagine and what we can want; it shapes our politics. Though we can identify the interests and choices around a given technology, these interests and choices do not design that technology and dictate its effects. Technology is not something that exists as a simple object for our use. It acts to structure our choices and preferences, but not in a wholly determinist way. The relationship is in constant flux: political processes shape technology; and it then shapes politics (see Street, 1992; Wright and Street, 2007, for fuller versions of this argument).

The internet is a product of military and scientific interests, but its development and use have not been controlled by those interests. It has created possibilities and problems that no one could have anticipated. What possibilities and alternatives exist at any one time is a matter of empirical investigation, an investigation that does not end with either the technology or the political interests promoting it. This is the value of work by Manuel Castells, Mathew Hindman and others who call attention to the impact of 'Googlearchy' on the distribution of information. Debate about e-democracy has to avoid political idealism and technological determinism; it has to acknowledge the complex interplay of political ideas and technical practices.

Debates about democracy are debates about information and power, about how they are distributed and how they are used (see, for example, Arblaster, 1987; Lively, 1975). Any attempt to think about e-democracy must therefore consider how information technologies do (and should) structure access to, and use of, political knowledge. As we saw earlier, there are those who argue that the current forms of mass communication threaten democracy by 'distorting' political knowledge, adversely affecting people's ability to perform the role of the democratic citizen and to exercise political judgement. Elshtain's talk of the citizen being transformed into a consumer is based on the thought, to misquote Oscar Wilde, that the consumer knows the price of everything and the value of nothing. In the process, politics becomes a form of market exchange; it is 'privatized', and hence what is called 'public opinion' is merely a summation of private desires (Sartori, 1989). The citizen ceases to exist as a self-conscious actor, and as such is incapable of deliberative political participation.

These gloomy prognostications recall the familiar story that accompanies almost all new technologies of culture and communication. Television destroys the art of conversation, just as the phone makes letter writing redundant, and e-mail eliminates the need for human contact. Equally familiar are the rebuttals which stress the possibilities in the technology: that technology fuels our imagination and broadens our perspective, that we can use technology and not be used by it. This argument maps a dichotomy between choice and determinism, between citizens as freely choosing agents or as consumers whose choices are pre-packaged. But instead of being forced to accept these extremes, we can see people's relationship to new media and the meaning attached to its contents as being created in the material and social context of their lives. The way technology is used, and the significance of the messages it delivers, are contingent (Ang, 1996; Corner, 1995; Wright, 2005).

The implication of this is that we need to see how systems of communication construct different opportunities for political engagement. As Eric Schickler (1994) observes, variations in format can produce variations in types of participation. The phone-in, for example, 'seems conducive to prejudiced, sloppy thinking, and to extremely simple views of the social and political process' (Schickler, 1994: 194). Other settings may produce more coherent thought. Similarly, Langdon Winner (1994) argues that the tendency to present information in restless 'bite size' chunks (along the lines pioneered by MTV) fragments political understanding, just as notions of community – who 'we' are – can be organized differently according to the character of the communications network (who is linked to whom, in what relationship) (Friedland, 1996). The implication of these claims, whether or not we accept their particular formulation, is that the way information is presented and organized is correlated with forms of political discourse. In other words, the citizen's capacity to make political judgements is dependent upon the way in which political information is delivered and received.

Thinking about electronic democracy has to be sensitive to these issues, but it also has to be linked to the larger setting in which that democracy might operate. As Blumler and Gurevitch argue:

> the media can pursue democratic values only in ways that are compatible with the socio-political and economic environment in which they operate. Political communication arrangements follow the contours of and derive their resources from the society of which they are a part.
>
> (Blumer and Gurevitch, 1995: 98)

Compatibility cannot be guaranteed. Kee Brants et al. point to one potential cause of tension in their study of communication networks in the Netherlands:

> Network technology has the potential to create a new public sphere which fits the social structure better .... However, politics does not yet fit the new technology. Politicians feel uncomfortable with the different role they play in such a challenging direct democracy.
>
> (Brants et al., 1996: 246)

In their study of the use of the internet in Australian elections, Rachel Gibson and Stephen Ward (2002) conclude that most parties tended to use it as an extension of existing practices, rather than as an opportunity to introduce new ones. The debate about e-democracy has to be sensitive both to the technical forms that are on offer and to the way in which representation and legitimation operate within the wider political system.

It is not enough, however, just to draw attention to how the new technologies of communication may affect participation, or to the tensions between different interests within the political system, or to the organization and distribution of access. All of these are crucial components of an adequate response to the spread of new technology, but there is yet another dimension. These matters are overlaid by the question as to what kind of democracy is being sought. As we have seen from the current debate about electronic democracy, the protagonists appeal to competing notions of democracy. There are those who favour a direct form of democracy and those who advocate a representative one. This division has consequences for the organization of the technology as well as for political practice. So in arguing about electronic democracy and the potential represented by the internet, we have to think not only about technology in its wider political context, but also about the competing notions of democracy, between those, for example, that seek to aggregate preferences and those that aim to create a forum for deliberative decision making.

If new media are to furnish individuals with more information about issues that relate to their personal interests, then the danger is that politics becomes a form of market exchange and the citizen becomes a privatized consumer (Lewis et al., 2005). Although this objection is presented as a general critique of e-democracy, it does not have this force. It is, in fact, just an objection to one way of organizing e-democracy and one kind of democracy. Or, to put it another way, if electronic democracy is organized differently or a different model of democracy is defended, these objections collapse.

There is no insurmountable reason why e-democracy should not take another form. It could, for instance, be used to support a system of deliberative democracy. There are powerful reasons for supposing that democracies in which citizens are required to deliberate on the choices that face a society, rather than simply register their preferences, produce better decisions (Fishkin, 1991; Miller, 1992). The point of the deliberative process is to allow people to form opinions, not just express them (Miller, 1992: 67). If this is the purpose allotted to democracy, then the forms of communication must accord with it. Citizens must not only be able to interrogate databases and acquire an expertise of their own, they must be able to reflect upon this knowledge in dialogue with their fellow citizens. This means that the hierarchies that tend to protect forms of expertise have to be broken down. At the same time, it is not just a matter of increasing access to information and allowing for discussion. There has also to be the opportunity for deliberation, which requires networks that enable an open dialogue about the public good. People have to make decisions, not just exchange thoughts or register interests.

If we are persuaded by this version of democracy, a further set of issues is raised. What type of collectivity is to do the deliberating? Who are the 'public'? The terms that define the community depend again, as with the choice between types of democracy, on political judgement. Do we want, for instance, to enshrine the notion of 'community' as the exclusive, rule-bound 'club' or as the more inclusive 'commonwealth' (Bellamy and Hollis, 1995)? These questions have to be settled both in terms of their political desirability and in terms of the conditions that make them possible. This thought lies behind Peter Levine's suggestion (2002: 8) that 'the Internet now needs a voluntary, democratic organisation that can demand something of its members and take collective action on their behalf'. Offering a technological parallel to ideas of commonwealths or communities, he proposes the idea of 'associational commons' to create conditions for a fully realised democracy (see also, Blumler and Coleman, 2001; Bua, 2009).

These matters require political debate and judgement, but they are not confined to the realm of political theory. They also engage with the ways in which forms of communication are organized. Political relationships depend upon the structures of communication that enable them to occur. These questions cannot, therefore, be answered by political theorists alone. We have to see arguments about 'democracy', not as abstract ideas, but as contingent upon, and bound up with, the political economy that helps to constitute those ideas. It is not enough simply to identify a form of democracy as desirable, and to sketch out the role that the technology has to play in fulfilling it. The technology is itself the product and expression of competing and contradictory political interests.

Conclusion

If the debate about e-democracy is to move beyond the crude dichotomy established by those who advocate it and those who decry it, and if we are to reflect cogently upon the experiments in such democracy which are emerging, we need to be explicit about what kind of democracy is being advocated. If deliberative democracy is the preferred option, it is important to state and defend this, but the argument cannot end there. It is not just a matter of applying new media to this particular ideal. Rather we have to think through the implications of deliberative democracy for both the forms of address and the political economy of the means of communication. At the same time, the possibility of such a democracy cannot be attributed simply to acts of political will. That kind of control over the technology is not possible because technological change is not simply the product of political choice. So the idea of democracy to which we aspire must be understood as partly a product of the political economy that surrounds it. Political ideas cannot be separated from the medium in which they are thought, and hence it makes little sense to talk of returning to ancient Greek democracy via new technology, or of simply 'improving' an existing democratic form. Technical change brings with it new ideas and possibilities, and new notions of democracy; at the same time, these possibilities have themselves to be subject to critical political analysis, informed by a particular notion of democracy. The politics of e-democracy are also the politics of technology, and both are tied intimately to the fact that forms of communications are also systems of power.

Chapter 11

Power and Mass Media

Reflecting on George W. Bush's presidency, William Connolly (2005a) argues that it entailed a particular alliance of 'cowboy capitalism' and 'evangelical Christianity'. But crucial to Connolly's story is the role of the media – without it, the alliance would not have been forged. The three elements formed what he describes as 'a resonance machine', amplifying and echoing each other's concerns to create the power base and ideological support upon which Bush depended, not as a coherent doctrine, but as 'affinities of sensibility' (Connolly, 2005a: 871). Media, according to Connolly, constituted and circulated the sentiments and sensitivities that gelled as popular support for the Republican programme. Whether Connolly is right to characterize US politics in this way or to attribute this specific role to media is open to debate. The key, though, is the thought that any account of the circulation of power in modern society, and hence any attempt to assess its claims to being democratic, inevitably leads to claims about the role of media. And for some writers, media is the key to power. 'Communication power', writes Manuel Castells (2009: 3), 'is at the heart of the structure and dynamics of society.' This chapter looks at this general claim and at the various perspectives on media power. In particular, it explores a central theme of this book: the extent to which media are transforming politics.

To the casual observer, it seems obvious that media have power. They determine the fate of politicians and political causes; they influence governments and their electorates. They might, therefore, be numbered with other political institutions – parliaments, executives, administrations and parties. This is the view of Paolo Mancini and David Swanson, who write, 'No longer merely a means by which other subsystems, such as political parties, can spread their own messages, mass media emerge in modern polyarchies as an autonomous power center in reciprocal competition with other power centers' (1996: 11). Such views are now almost commonplace. Mass media are taken as seriously as parties and parliaments, sometimes more so. They receive this attention because, it is implicitly or explicitly assumed, television, radio, the press and the new media are 'powerful'.

The same assumption runs throughout this book. Media bias, the ownership and control of the media industry, the political uses of the media, all matter because they have some effect upon the way the political process works. And the interests that drive media, it is also assumed, shape the political outcomes – who gets what, when and how. But while the assumptions are widely shared, there is considerable disagreement as to what exactly is meant: where and how does this power manifest itself? Such a question is central to mass media's relationship to democracy. To claim that some set of arrangements is 'democratic' is to make a claim about the distribution of power. Put simply, in a dictatorship power is held by an unaccountable elite who use their power to exploit the powerless; in a democracy power is 'legitimate' because those who exercise it are deemed representative and accountable. This crude dichotomy reappears in accounts of the way the media operate. In a dictatorship, there is monopoly control of media, which are used to disseminate propaganda; in a democracy, control is dispersed and content is pluralistic. Of course, there is much to debate about the key terms, but the point is that 'media power' – who controls the media and their content, about what effects they have – is crucial.

The study of power is driven by the desire to know who is responsible for the things that affect our lives: who is to blame for the current state of affairs, how can it be changed for the better (Morriss, 1987)? Such questions focus attention on the different ways in which media may be implicated in the distribution and exercise of power. Media power does not, after all, take a single monolithic form. It appears in different guises and operates in different ways. We begin by looking at three forms of power: discursive power, access power and resource power. Each of these captures aspects of the ways in which media power is typically discussed, and each of them is linked to the debate about media and democracy. They raise questions about how media content shapes political ideas and arguments, and about how forms of media affect political access and participation.

Discursive power

The familiar claim that 'knowledge is power' captures the most commonly cited connection between mass media and power. The idea that 'knowledge' is a source of power, and that mass media are central to this power, rests on some fairly straight-forward, if not uncontroversial, claims. Power is taken here to refer to the capacity that A has to get B to do something they would not otherwise have done, and the suggestion is that the distribution of knowledge is a key to achieving this. Control of the flow of information about what the authorities are doing, keeping the people in ignorance, provides a way of preventing political protest. If people knew their government was system-atically torturing dissidents, or if they knew that their rivers were being polluted or their food contaminated, there might be widespread public disruption and challenges to the legitimacy of the regime.

It is this sort of thinking that lies behind political censorship and repression. It helps to explain why the Chinese authorities have been so determined to regulate access to the internet and why they blocked access to sites that refer to events in Tiananmen Square in 1989. The corollary of this type of repres-sion is the use of media to propagate false or distorted informa-tion – this is what fuels Edward Herman and Noam Chomsky's critique of US news reporting. The media are seen to operate as part of a propaganda machine. Insofar as knowledge is power, then the media's role in providing or suppressing information implicates them in the exercise of power. Although it might be contended that the important source of the power is not so much the medium itself as those who have access to it. This is a point to which we return.

Thinking of media power in terms of knowledge and informa-tion, though important, is rather limited and crude. It presumes a notion of truth and falsity, what is *really* happening versus what 'they' *pretend* is the case, which is hard to sustain. What if reality is itself an artifice? What if 'reality' is constructed not reflected or revealed? What if our world is the product of the discourses we use to claim knowledge of it? Media become important, not in relation to truth or falsity, but in their part in constituting – in Michel Foucault's (1984) terms – our discourses of knowledge. As Kate Nash explains:

> Knowledge as discourse is not knowledge of the 'real' world as it exists prior to that knowledge. Although it presents itself as *representing* objective reality, in fact, discourses *construct* and make 'real' the objects of knowledge they represent.
>
> (Nash, 2000: 21; original emphasis)

From this perspective, media power operates through the way it privileges particular discourses and constructs particular forms of reality.

This is to see the media as exercising *discursive* power. It is, I would suggest, what Connolly has in mind when he talks of media's role in the resonance machine. The assumption is that the way people act is conditioned by what they think and feel, and that what is thought and felt is affected by the picture of the world conveyed by the mass media. This is what Manuel Castells describes as his 'working hypothesis': 'the most fundamental form of power lies in the ability to shape the human mind. The way we feel and think determines the way we act, both individually and collectively' (2009: 3). This power may not be translated directly into particular behaviours. We do not have to assume that because newspapers support one party or ideology this will directly influence the way people vote, any more that we should assume that violent films will increase the level of violence in society. Some connection is supposed, but it is not a simple matter of cause and effect. Nonetheless, insofar as mass media are responsible for the circulation of particular ideas and images, and insofar as these shape thoughts and actions, the mass media are understood to wield discursive or ideological power. A further assumption is that the media operate on behalf of a distinct set of interests which benefit from the ideology being propagated. The implication of this approach to media power is that we need to analyse in detail the content of mass media texts, to reveal the particular account of the world encoded within them and the sensibilities they engender.

This emphasis on how media may operate ideologically extends the notion of their power beyond 'information'. Media power is not confined to news and current affairs, the formal sources of 'information'; it includes soap operas and films which also create a 'common sense' for individual and collective action. Media also help to construct people's identities, sensibilities and interests, and hence their relationship to 'reality'. People do not pick and choose freely these identities and interests with the apparent casualness of supermarket shoppers. Just as the design of supermarkets, the organization of the shelves and aisles, is intended to increase the amount of money spent, and just as people's use of the stores is constrained by their resources, so encounters with the media are organized and affected by those supplying the images and by the resources (and skills) people have available in consuming them. But however the process is organized, what is at stake is people's sense of themselves. These identities have political consequences because they underpin the interests which animate people's demands on, and expectations for, the political system.

Access power

Implicit in the idea of the media's discursive role is a process that produces these discourses. One way to think of this is to ask whose voices, identities and interests populate our screens and newspapers. Insofar as the media provide a valuable resource for those who wish to promote or maintain their interests, there is the possibility that power may operate in decisions about who has access to this resource. This power of access is revealed in control over the range of voices or interests able to use the various formats, either as viewers/readers or as contributors. At one level, this can take the form of media market concentration which narrows the variety of sources to which access is being gained. At another, it can refer to the range of interests or identities that find expression within the choice of media. The satirical magazine *Private Eye*, for example, delights in discovering gratuitous puffs for the various other News Corporation products and services – its televisions channels, its Hollywood movies – in the pages of its newspapers. But these perhaps trivial synergies underlie the more fundamental integration of interests within media conglomerates (Baker, 2007). Either of these forms of exclusion and inclusion have an impact on the status accorded to particular ways of life and interests: think of how women are represented in the media: as victims of, or appendages to, men; think too of the way in which 'telegenicity' (or the idea of 'telegenicity') arbitrates the fate of political careers. Those who do not meet the criteria of telegenicity, or those who are not deemed worthy of attention in their own right, are denied access to social and political power. Even if the decisions are being made by others (parties decide who is to be their leader), the criteria used in the selection derive from media logic (Meyer, 2002). The media are directly implicated in decisions about who to interview or what topic to address from what angle, thereby setting agendas that, at the very least, may only be tangentially (if at all) linked to the concerns of viewers and readers.

These barriers to access can be shaped by a variety of factors. They can lie in the routine practices of journalists, whose news values identify certain incidents and witnesses as more or less important or relevant than others. They can exist in the ways in which commercial interests determine what kinds of programmes are made or what coverage a newspaper provides. They can be found in the mechanisms for collecting and disseminating news, in the privileging of certain news sources over other ones. They can also be found in the divisions of labour that operate within media institutions: how the conflict between the interests of editorial staff and marketing staff is resolved (a battle over the allocation of space in the paper or the schedule), or the conflict within editorial offices between foreign and domestic news, between sport and arts, and so on. The outcome of these turf wars finds expression in who and what is covered. The routines and cultures of media, their commercial and structural interests, all operate to determine the opportunities for access to the airwaves and newspaper columns. The power over who gets to speak and whose voice is heard clearly overlaps with discursive power, in that it shapes how the world is represented. These dimensions of power, in turn, overlap with a third dimension: resource power.

Resource power

If discursive power refers to the way in which a popular common sense is created, and if access power refers to the way in which particular interests or identities are acknowledged or excluded, resource power refers, primarily, to the way in which media conglomerates can affect the actions of governments and states, but also to the distribution of resources *within* media conglomerates and hence who it is that dictates – albeit indirectly – the voices to be heard and discourses to be propagated.

The external form of discourse power identifies the bargaining power that media conglomerates have in their dealings with national governments and other agencies. Governments need media conglomerates for the delivery of infrastructural services (the provision and circulation of information) and for the income and employment they generate. The need for such things makes governments vulnerable, limiting their capacity to regulate these valued media actors. Imposing barriers on cross-media ownership or enforcing particular regulations on media content can be costly for governments, either because of the antipathy they generate from the media conglomerates (expressed through their media outlets) or because these conglomerates may move elsewhere, to more 'liberal' regimes. The power relationship here is between the media industry and governments.

The internal form of resource power has to do with chains of command and influence within the organization. It does not necessarily refer to identifiable individuals, but rather to the incentive structure operating within the corporation. Claims, for example, about the 'tabloidization' of news or about the rise of 'churnalism' are typically grounded in accounts of how commercial decisions to attract particular advertisers or cut specific costs impact upon routine editorial and journalistic practices. These decisions attribute power to certain actors and departments (and not to others).

Theories of media power

These three aspects of media power help us to think abut the way in which power circulates within media. They do not, however, tell us about the specific effects the power has over the conduct and character of politics. For this, we need to think more about theories of media power, because these connect the different dimensions of power into a narrative which links media and political practice. The theories do not just map the connection between the dimensions of media power, but identify the cumulative effect that they have. To illustrate this, I want to compare four different theories of how media are transforming politics. The four approaches are pluralist, constructivist, structuralist, and network power. What I want to show is that, in taking different views of media power, they also conceptualize differently the notion of 'communication', the field that is 'politics', and finally how the balance between 'structure' and 'agency' is struck. The latter refers to the attribution of responsibility for any given outcome – whether outcomes, crudely speaking, are determined by structural or systemic factors or by the choices and actions of relatively autonomous individuals.

The pluralist perspective

A dominant theme of much contemporary literature on the relationship between media and politics in liberal democracies has been that of 'crisis'. The fear has been that the democratic process is threatened by the erosion of the public sphere and by the failure of media to fulfil their role as the fourth estate (Davies, 2008; Franklin, 2004; Lloyd, 2004). One of the earliest, and most detailed, statements of this concern is to be found in Jay Blumler and Michael Gurevitch's (1995) *The Crisis of Public Communication*. They argued that public communication in the United States and the United Kingdom was getting into 'ever deeper trouble', and was 'impoverishing' the way in which citizens were addressed politically (1995: 203). A similar concern emerges in Robert Putnam's *Bowling Alone* (2000: 283–4), in which responsibility for civic disengagement is attributed to the mass media, or more particularly entertainment television. Putnam's thesis fits within a phenomenon observed in the 1970s, and dubbed 'video or media malaise' by Michael Robinson (1976). As we saw in Chapter 4, Putnam's thesis has been challenged, most notably by Pippa Norris and others. Norris argues that 'contrary to theories of video malaise, the cumulative effects of watching television news and reading the press are largely positive' (1999: 182).

While Norris and Putnam reach different conclusions about media's impact on politics, they work from a very similar model of the relationship between the two. The focus of their attention is the political system, characterized in liberal democratic terms. This system should, if operating properly, deliver rule by the people, albeit mediated and articulated by the interaction of political leaders, parties and interest groups. The role of the media is to serve this process. Where Norris and Putnam and others disagree is over the extent to which the media help or hinder the realization of the political norms enshrined in liberal democracy. The system itself is not in question, at least not in any radical or fundamental sense; the issue is its current operation and the part played by media in it.

From within this perspective, media are themselves understood in a particular way. They are primarily deliverers of political information. Furthermore, this information is conveyed in a relatively straightforward manner: 'who (the source) says what (the content) through which channel (the media) to whom (the audience) with what effect' (Norris et al., 1999: 9). In short, it is seen as 'a sequential process' that starts with a message and ends in 'the casting of a ballot paper' (ibid.: 19). The assumption is that the individual voter processes information in accordance with their interests and dispositions, and engages in rational computation, within the limits of their available resources and skills. Norris examines the operation of this model of communication in a number of different settings. She argues that, while media have changed over time and differ between countries, there has not been a decline in the quality or quantity of political information. For Norris, mass media generally contribute positively to political knowledge, by which she means the 'practical knowledge' that helps people 'to connect their political and social preferences to the available options' (2000: 213). Her evidence makes her sceptical of talk about 'video malaise'; hence her disagreement with Putnam. But while she and Putnam reach different conclusions about the effects of media on political engagement, they still have much in common.

They both, for instance, ally themselves to the conventional distinction to be drawn between political and non-political content. This is explicit in Putnam's critique of the deleterious effect of television entertainment, and Norris's concern only with 'serious political coverage' (ibid.: 28). What constitutes or defines 'trivial' political coverage is assumed, rather than argued. Such value distinctions reflect a wider assumption, which is that media content is to be viewed, at least in its relationship to politics, as 'information' – which is either right or wrong, trivial or serious (ibid.: 212). Media coverage is not viewed as part of some larger ideological system in which 'common sense' is imposed on an unsuspecting mass. Instead, Norris operates with a different view. The 'mass' is in fact constituted by relatively autonomous individuals engaged in a 'two-way interactive process' with media messages (ibid.: 18). This is the way in which practical political knowledge helps connect preferences to options.

These effects, though, are of a limited kind. They relate only to the ways in which 'information' changes decisions about how to relate preferences and options. It does not relate to the *constitution* of those preferences or options. Norris's account, in this sense, sits squarely within a pluralist paradigm in which agents' preferences are given, and the media act only as instrumental intermediaries between those agents and the options offered by the political system (for a critical discussion of Norris's approach, see Coleman and Blumler, 2009). While Putnam's version of events generates much larger concerns for the health of the system, and attributes greater blame to the media, he relies on a similar model of the general relationship between media and politics, in which the former are instrumental in determining the proper (or inadequate) functioning of the latter, via the information they provide to voters. Contrast this account with the one that follows, in which media are understood not as instruments in the running of the political system, but as the architects of its construction.

The constructivist turn

The pluralist account stands in stark contrast to one in which the media 'construct' that political system and the relations between the agents within it. Where in the pluralist account the media is one actor among many, in the 'constructivist' account they are the playwrights, summoning politics into existence. A popular classic of this view is Neil Postman's *Amusing Ourselves to Death* (1987). Postman, as we saw in Chapter 9, despaired at what was later called the 'dumbing down' of political communication, a process which he saw as part of the logic of the medium of television. It was this logic that turned political communication into a variant of show business, in which superficial appearance replaces subterranean substance. From this perspective, the political world is reconstituted according to the conventions of the medium in which it comes to exist; it is constructed as 'reality' by media that present and report it, a reality in which politics is a trivial game of surfaces.

With his concern for the 'packaging of politics', Bob Franklin (2004) can be seen as preparing the ground for this view. Franklin has eloquently documented what he sees as the decline of political communication, and the damage to democracy that it has engendered. The new forms of political communication, according to Franklin, privilege presentation over substance, appearance over policy. The new architects of this era – the spin doctors and advertising executives recruited by governments and parties – serve to disempower citizens and to diminish politics. But while Franklin has been concerned with the large questions of the effect of political communications on democracy, he has not sought, for the most part, to provide a systematic or theorized overview of the connections being made. He has not sought to re-inscribe Postman's picture of an all-encompassing transformation. He has, instead, remained focused on the fairly narrow field of political communication and campaigning, tracking the detailed changes in the ways in which parties in particular now operate, and the specific impact of media on their behaviour. To this extent, he is a 'constructivist' of a relatively modest kind. Certainly, he is not to be allied with writers like Roderick Hart (1999), who have argued that television has rewritten the relationship between voters and politics, shaping the way that people see, and *feel* about, politics. This claim is not just about the instrumental changes to political communication; rather it is about the transformation of politics as a realm of activity. Such a thought is captured in expressions such as 'new politics' or 'mediated politics'.

These see politics as constituted by its media representations. The media thereby play a determining role in constituting what we mean by 'politics'. In this vein, Michael Delli Carpini and Bruce Williams (2001: 161) argue that the association of 'politics' with a discrete social realm, which can is contained by news and current affairs, is a fiction: 'politics is largely a mediated experience'. In direct contrast to Norris's identification of political communication with 'serious political coverage', they draw attention to the 'political significance of popular culture in the construction and interpretation of the news' (Carpini and Williams, 2001: 161). An example of this is to be found in the way works of fiction are used by journalists and others to report and explain the real world, as has happened with the real-time US drama series, *24*, and its hero Jack Bauer (Kiefer Sutherland). *24* has served as a perspective on the forces at work in contemporary international politics (Teneboim-Weinblatt, 2009).

For the constructivist, the political realm is being transformed by 'new and old communication technologies' (Bennett and

Entman, 2001: 3). So, for example, Peter Dahlgren suggests that 'politics no longer exists as a reality taking place outside the media, to be "covered" by journalists. Rather, politics is increasingly organized as a media phenomenon, planned and executed for and with the co-operation of the media' (2001: 85). Politics is constituted and transformed by the media that formally report it.

There are three moves that are implicit in this constructivist argument and the story it tells of media power. The first is to call into question the focus on 'communication', and the models of it adopted by Norris and others. John Corner and Dick Pels write:

> Political communication is both too limiting in its suggested scope (centred, sometimes exclusively, upon political publicity and political journalism and with a bias towards electoral campaigns) and too functionalist in its implications of a defined role self-consciously performed.
>
> (Corner and Pels, 2003: 5)

The second move is to shift the focus onto the aesthetics of politics, onto the idea of politics as an exercise in symbolic interaction – hence, the focus on the presentational and performative aspects of politics. The third move is away from the sharp dichotomy established by the media malaise debate, and instead to represent it as a more ambiguous and contradictory state of affairs.

Corner himself is a good example of these new tendencies. He notes how the 'figure of the politician' looms very large in political culture (2000: 401). It is there in endless journalistic profiles and narratives of politics, and in the popularity of the political biography. This prominence, Corner notes, is not reflected in political analysis (for notable exceptions, see Langer, forthcoming; Stanyer and Wring, 2004). Corner argues that this oversight causes political analysts to miss the way in which individuals in politics serve to 'condense the political' by acting as a focus for 'political values and ideas in a way that goes beyond the limits of their sphere of practice' (2000: 401).

Drawing on Machiavelli's advice that princes do not have to have good qualities, but do have to *appear* to have them, Corner focuses attention upon how particular appearances are necessary to the conduct of modern democratic politics. Such appearances are constructed via the performances given, and the styles adopted, by politicians. These are performances and styles that exist within and depend upon the mass media. In other words, the study of politics requires study of the way in which performances are constructed and styles articulated, because these constitute the transactions between represented and representatives in democracies. Political relationships are constructed through media performance, and the connection between politics and mass media has to be understood in these terms.

Although Corner is drawing attention to one neglected aspect of politics, his approach has important implications for the way in which 'politics' more generally is theorized. It invites the thought that the realm of politics is to be understood as the product of cultural construction in which mass media play a decisive part. Mass media do not function simply as means of communication, as instruments of politics, but instead constitute the very relations of politics. This perspective rejects the account of communication and of agency that characterizes the pluralist paradigm, replacing them with the interpretative processes of encoding and decoding and the social construction of reality and of identity.

Constructivism qualified: politics colonized

Few would argue that politics is only that which is constructed by media representations. 'Constructivism', Thomas Meyer (2002) argues, must assume a world outside that which is being constructed. It is only acknowledging the existence of this realm outside the process of constitution that allows judgement of the adequacy or value of the construction (Meyer, 2002: 49–50). Otherwise, asks Meyer, what is the construction *of*? He insists on the need to separate the two realms, that of media and that of politics, and on identifying two different 'logics'. Political events have a logic which is independent of any media account of them: 'whatever construction the media code may try to impose on the political events to be represented, however much it may attempt to transform them, in the end the logic of the events themselves has to shine through in the media's finished product' (ibid.: 10). This distinction is crucial to his argument that media logic 'colonizes' politics. The idea of colonization preserves the thought that there is something that pre-exists the imperial intervention, but that is then taken over by it. This is what separates his position from wholesale constructivism.

Media's logic, according to Meyer, is contained in two filters. The first involves the selection of 'news': what counts as 'newsworthy'. The second involves presentation, the means by which the audience's attention is grabbed – typically, by the telling of dramatic stories. In pursuit of this logic, politics is increasingly seen and assessed in theatrical and aesthetic terms (a process driven by the commercial incentives that apply to all communication conglomerates and their public service competitors) (Hamilton, 2004). This is how politics is colonized; it is forced to acquire the values of the media that reports it. As a consequence of this colonization of political logic by media logic, media time-horizons usurp political time-horizons. The latter are necessarily longer, to allow for deliberation and consensus building; the former work towards the instantaneous and immediate. News is not news if your rivals have already reported it; the development of new media technology is directed towards the ability to transmit sound and images live, as they happen, from wherever they happen. 'Media communications', writes Meyer (2002: 44), 'are forced into an uncompromising presentism.' This tension between political and media notions of time is resolved in the process of colonization, in which the latter takes over the former.

For Meyer, the outcome of the struggle between media and political logic is that politics is stage-managed. Legitimacy is established via media-generated perceptions. Political communications recognize media logic and 'becomes increasingly *politainment*' (ibid.: 53, his emphasis). In other words, media set the rules by which politics is conducted, and increasingly actual political processes get lost to view. As Meyer puts it: 'Once the sphere of politics falls under the influence of the media system, it changes considerably: it becomes dependent on the latter's rules, but without completely losing its separate identity' (ibid.: 57).

For many popular representations of this process, the cause is the spin doctor (for example, N. Jones, 1995), but Meyer's account reverses this causal claim. Spin doctors are not responsible for the transformation; rather, they are called into being by the need to manage the process of colonization:

The more crudely the mass media present politics, guided by the superficial criteria they are accustomed to apply, the more politics has to call on its own cast of spin-doctors so that it does not lose control over the way it is portrayed.

(Meyer, 2002: 61)

As the terms of politics are increasingly redefined or reinter-preted in the logic of media, politics increasingly takes on the appearance of a 'vivid, scintillating show' (ibid.: 65). Parties and other intermediaries are marginalized by this media coloniza-tion; their time-horizons are incompatible with the 'relentless presentism' of media logic (ibid.: 107).

Meyer's own logic does not lead him to conclusions about the impact on citizens of media representations of politics. He appears to share the general conclusions of the media malaise thesis: that some citizens become disengaged by virtue of their viewing habits and social location. But importantly, he sees this as a corollary of larger political changes. His argument is that the media's most significant impact is upon the political system: 'By marginalising parties and the intermediary system,' argues Meyer, 'the media diminish the opportunities that civil society might have to exert influence on political inputs' (ibid.: 108).

Meyer's case is persuasively made, but it does beg questions, some of which we return to in the next chapter. These have to do with the process of decolonization, and the need for what he calls 'a culture of democratic responsibility in editorial offices' (ibid.: 133). It is not entirely clear what this entails and how it might be realized. The more immediate concern is Meyer's organizing ideas of media and political 'logics'. These imply an essence which is hard to identify – what exactly is the logic of politics? The two 'logics' might be the products of an overarching power rather than of some innate characteristics of the realms themselves. The emphasis on external power informs a third theoretical narrative that attempts to make sense of the relationship between politics and mass media.

The structuralist's story

Nicholas Garnham stands as exemplification of this third, struc-turalist perspective. Where the pluralist deals in 'information' and 'knowledge', Garnham deals in 'power'. In almost direct reversal of Norris's pluralist communicative model, Garnham writes, 'Who can say what, in what form, to whom for what purposes, and with what effect will in part be determined by and in part determine the structure of economic, political, and cultural power in society?' (2000: 4). Political communication is not, by this account, that which may or may not benefit the political process, but rather is a product of it. Garnham also stands against constructivism, in that, rather than media constructing politics, politics constructs media. Media practice is a product of the distribution of material resources and of economically determined power relations.

For Garnham, studying the media is part of a larger project of social theory, which has to do with the perennial issues of structure and agency, the constitution of communities, and the nature of the subject (2000: 10–12). From such a perspective, issues such as the 'dumbing down' of political communication, or media malaise more generally, are assigned exaggerated or misplaced importance. The development of mass media has, according to Garnham, to be understood as part of a larger process of state formation and capitalist development. Their role and character, therefore, are to be analysed in terms of the particular political and commercial demands and interests operating at the time. 'Dumbing down' appeals to some (idealized) prior situation of 'intelligent' communication, when in fact the process being described is better understood as the commodification of communications (ibid.: 30–1). 'Media systems,' Garnham writes (ibid.: 59–60), 'are at their core, just like supermarkets. They are systems for packaging symbolic products and distributing them as rapidly and cheaply as possible.' Garnham's claim is that 'all theories of the media rest upon historical theories as to the process of the historical development of media institutions and practices and their relationship to the development of modernity and its characteristic social structures and practices' (2000: 38). For Garnham, this history is a product of the logic of the *commodification* of media, rather than of media *per se*.

Garnham's focus is upon the structural power that allocates resources and constrains behaviour. These forms of power account for the regulations that operate in the media realm and determine the fate of the public sphere. This means that the core concern of those interested in the relationship between media and politics is not the capacities and behaviour of individuals or the practices of parties and journalists, but rather the systems of political regulation that organize media systems.

One way of illustrating this is to contrast Norris's focus on political knowledge with Garnham's on education. Education is, Garnham suggests (2000: 4), the major form of communication, one which serves to accredit and train people to fit within a larger process of social stratification. Hence Garnham argues against a focus on the products of media systems – newspapers, programmes – and instead for a focus on the producers of these products. The corporate management of journalism becomes the key to understanding the representation of the political world. This contrasts again with Norris's theoretical model, in which messages are conveyed rather than created.

Garnham claims to be offering an alternative to the 'methodological individualism' and 'simplified behaviourist linear cause–effect model' that tends to characterize the literature on media effects within the pluralist tradition (ibid.: 109). But he also has little time for ethnographic research into the 'active' audiences, decoding and interpreting media messages that might be associated with the constructivist approach. Instead, he argues for the need to begin research 'with family expenditure surveys and the studies of demographics and consumption patterns used by advertising agencies and marketing departments' (ibid.: 116). Such information provides evidence of the opportunities (or the lack of them) that audiences have to control the flow of information: the 'fields of action that are opened up or closed down' (ibid.: 118). It is 'social position and experience' that determines people's capacity to act on what the media offers (ibid.: 125). In short, Garnham represents an account of the politics–mass media relationship that locates it within the structures of the political economy that organize both.

Garnham's account of media's place within a wider social and political theory fits with Timothy Besley and Andrea Prat's (2006; also Besley, 2007) modelling the capture of media by government. The captured media suppress (or fail to report) information about corporate and political corruption. Besley and Prat show how the ability to capture media is dependent on, *inter alia*, systems of media ownership. Using international comparative data of media regimes, indexes of corruption, and political longevity, Besley and Prat point towards systematic, if not unequivocal, evidence for the structuralist account of media power relations. They portray the linkage between media and politics not as a product of the direct and intentional intervention of particular groups of media or political actors, but rather as the operation of systemic features.

Network power

The more complex picture of cause and effect that emerges from the structuralist approach leads to a fourth and final one. This is characterized as 'network power', in that it sees power circulating through a system of intersecting networks, which lack the (metaphorical) fixity of structures. This perspective owes a great deal to the work of Manuel Castells, and especially to his book *Communication Power* (2009). Castells' approach shares much in common with the previous three, but argues that the emergence of new forms of communication and their attendant institutional forms are creating a new, global society. This claim is premised on the thought that communicative action holds the key to power and that networks represent the means of its circulation (Castells, 2009: 13–22). He paints a picture of 'A network society ... whose social structure is made around networks activated by microelectronics-based, digitally processed information and communication technologies' (ibid.: 24).

In this network society, power takes two forms. It may either constitute a form of domination, or of resistance to this domination (ibid.: 47). The exercise of power by either side in this struggle takes the form of control over the connection between, and access to, the networks. The key actors are identified by Castells as 'the switchers' or programmers; those who have the capacity to shape the operation of networks. Such actors extend from media corporations to the Federal Communications Commission to the activists who forged the Jubilee campaign to reduce developing country debt. This chimes with Mathew Hindman's (2009) account of the operation of search engines.

Whereas, for Castells, the fundamental sources of power have not changed; 'the terrain where power relationships operate has changed' (2009: 50). It is now organized around networks. The study of power, and the role of media in it, requires detailed analysis of the organization and form of new means of communication. And because of the nature of modern digital communication, which allows, in Castells' phrase, 'mass self-communication', our world is being organized as networks of the mind as well of the community or state. Modern forms of communication are, argues Castells, radically different from those that preceded them. People 'do not "watch" the Internet as we watch television' (ibid.: 64). Now we engage in a form of communication that is 'self-generated in content, self-directed in emission, and self-selected in reception by many who communicate with many' (ibid.: 70). The result is a 'framing of the mind' (ibid.: 155), echoing Connolly's 'affinities of sensibility' with which this chapter began. This is how Castells summarizes his long and complex argument: 'Power is primarily exercised by the construction of meaning in the human mind through processes of communication enacted in global/local multimedia networks of mass communication, including mass self-communication' (2009: 416).

Castells' thesis, as with the others discussed here, is more nuanced and subtle than my account would suggest (see Fuchs, 2009, for a more detailed discussion). However, together these theories serve to highlight – albeit schematically – the contrasting approaches that can be taken to the suggestion that media power is transforming political practice, and the consequences for the distribution of power.

Conclusion

In setting out the different perspectives – pluralist, constructivist, structuralist and network – I have tried to capture the main ways in which the relationship between media and politics has been analysed. Others will (and do) disagree. They highlight other trends and features of an ever-expanding field. John Corner and Piers Robinson (2006), for instance, argue that what divides the various perspectives is not the different theoretical paradigms adopted, but rather the perspective on power, and whether we adopt a pluralist or an elite view of power – simply, is it dispersed or concentrated? It is this, they contend, that really determines how we think media and politics are connected. Certainly, the discussion above makes no pretence to being comprehensive or complete. Rather, it serves to draw attention to the profoundly important issue of media's role in the circulation of power and the conduct of politics. In doing so, the competing perspectives raise important questions about how we understand the process of communication, how politics is to be conceived and what scope is available for individual or collective attempts to alter the flow of power and its consequences.

These perspectives help to organize our thoughts about the specifics of media power and its multidimensional form (as discourse, access and resource power). They also help in analysing larger debates about media content and effects, political control over media, and the character of modern political communication that occupied us in the earlier chapters of this book. The competing perspectives help in analysing the rival ideological and party political positions adopted in relation to the media, where the focus is upon the appropriate mechanisms for regulating the media. Underlying all such arguments are claims about what power media do (or do not) wield and what power media *should* have, the topic to which we now turn.

Chapter 12

A Free Press: Democracy and Mass Media

In *Democracy in America*, Alexis de Tocqueville (1988: 517–18) wrote: 'I am far from denying that newspapers in democratic countries lead citizens to do very ill-considered things in common; but without newspapers there would be hardly any common action at all. So they mend more ills than they cause.' Though these thoughts were published in the first half of the nineteenth century, de Tocqueville's cautious acknowledgement of media's contribution to democracy might resonate with many modern commentators who feel a similar ambivalence.

The constitutions of almost all modern states include some reference to the role of the media. They do not agree, however, what exactly that role should be. So it is that the US Constitution's First Amendment insists that 'Congress shall make no law ... abridging the freedom of speech, or of the press' while, by contrast, Saudi Arabia's Fundamental Law (Article 39) requires that:

> Mass media, publication facilities and other means of expression shall function in a manner that is courteous and fair and shall abide by State laws. They shall play their part in educating the masses and boosting national unity. All that may give rise to mischief and discord, or may compromise the security of the State and its public image, or may offend against man's dignity and rights shall be banned.
>
> (http://www.saudinf.com/main/c541f.htm)

Even where there is no such statement, as in Australia or the United Kingdom, the courts may act as if there were one (Ward, 2006). In each case, the assumption is that, in establishing the political order, the place and function of mass media has to be demarcated clearly. For one state, this means protecting press freedom; for another, it means restricting it.

303

Of course, it is not nearly this simple. No state, whatever its constitution, tolerates complete freedom of expression. All states operate codes that provide for restrictions on the content of news reports, documentaries, advertisements and on all forms of entertainment. What freedom means, and what limits should apply to it, form part of an endlessly evolving political debate. It is a debate that has echoed throughout this book, and especially the last chapters, where we have looked at the ways in which new forms of political communication and new technologies of communication are raising questions about the relationship between democracy and mass media (and about much else besides). In this chapter, we focus on the issues that underlie this relationship. What principles are supposed to apply to the organization and character of mass media in a democracy? The need to answer such a question stems, first, from the fact that democracy places considerable weight upon communication (for accountability, for deliberation, for representation), and the system of communication, therefore, must meet these requirements. The second reason for addressing this topic is that democratic theorists have paid relatively little attention to the question of what principles and practices should guide the operation of mass media in a democracy (for notable exceptions, see Curran, 2000; Keane, 1991, 1992; Lichtenberg, 1990).

It might be objected, of course, that there is no real need to reflect upon the role of mass media in a democracy because, by design or default, a satisfactory solution has emerged. Think of the way elections are covered across the globe. Election coverage tends to be very earnest, almost obsessive. Every nuance of style and speech is pored over; every fluctuation in the opinion polls recorded; every advertisement and broadcast subjected to semiotic scrutiny. Candidates are trailed everywhere they go, photographed in a variety of guises and predicaments. And all of this is done in the name of democracy. The media treat elections as the lifeblood of the democratic process, and their coverage of them provides citizens with a wealth of information upon which to base their vote. There does not seem to be any need for further philosophical reflection.

In any case, most states go further, establishing rules and regulations that enshrine the requirements for responsible election coverage. In the United States, there are rules about political advertising; in France, rules about the use of particular images.

In Italy, these rules apply to the relationship between media outlets and political partisanship; in Britain, the law stipulates how public service broadcasters (if not their newspaper colleagues) should represent the election. In other words, a combination of rules and common practices has created a working relationship between mass media and democracy.

But while states have evolved systems for regulating mass media in a democracy, they have all produced *different* systems. The fact that the relationship does not take one single form suggests that there are important questions of value and judgement entailed. We can see what is involved by imagining what might happen if the regulations were changed. What if, as some have suggested, the rules governing reporting of elections were relaxed? Would the democratic roof fall in? What if the media were to ignore the election campaigns, or to treat them as a joke (or at least as light entertainment)? Some might say that they do so already. What exactly is the proper role of mass media in a democracy, and what is the best means of ensuring that this role is fulfilled? Answers to such questions usually begin with a qualification: 'It depends what you mean by "democracy."'

There are, of course, as many definitions of democracy as there are democratic theorists. They include liberal, direct and deliberative democracy. Each generates very different positions on the question of the media's role in a democracy (Schudson, 2008). Liberal democracy argues for some notion of a free, but responsible, press; direct democracy for more tightly regulated media, in which there is some form of popular control; and deliberative democracy requires, according to John Thompson (1995), 'regulated pluralism' to enable citizens to reach informed, collective views of the public good. This chapter looks at all these versions of democracy, and at the role of media within them, but it concentrates mostly upon the liberal democratic version, the model that fits most closely with actually existing systems in the West.

Liberal democracy and the free press

The liberal democratic model goes under a variety of guises. Variants extend from those, like the democratic elitists (Joseph Schumpeter, for example), who place the emphasis on the election of relatively autonomous representatives, to those, like the pluralist Robert Dahl (at least in his earlier writings), who model democracy on the interaction of interest groups. What they have in common is a view of democracy in which individual preferences take precedence and in which the state's role is constrained out of respect for individual freedom. Indeed, priority is given to freedom, characterized negatively, in Isaiah Berlin's (1969) famous distinction, as the absence of impediment.

The rationale for this is, among other things, the thought that there is no single answer to the question of how we ought to live. There are many alternative versions of the 'good life', and there is no way of determining a priori which is the better (Dworkin, 1978; Rawls, 1971). It is a matter of choice. So it is that the important political questions should be settled by voting (the formal equality of one person, one vote) and that the government be enjoined to respect the aggregate choices made by its citizens. It is not intended that citizens vote on all public issues; matters of detailed policy are left to their representatives. One of the reasons for this system being favoured is that it allows citizens to be spared the business of directly running their political affairs. This is deemed to be both practical and desirable – practical because of the constraints of time and competence, desirable because of the dangers of populism (Dahl, 1956; Schumpeter, 1976/1943). The task of government is best left to those with the skills and aptitude for such pursuits.

Within such a democratic order, the media perform a range of political functions. Michael Schudson (2008: 11–26) identifies seven of them. I shall highlight fewer here. First, they are not bound to provide an endless diet of politics. The liberal assumption is that people are not political animals, and that politics is to be viewed instrumentally, as a means to an end. Where the media are to provide a political forum, their aim should be, first, to enable citizens to choose between those who wish to stand for office and to judge those who currently are in office, and second, to provide a platform for interest groups to publicize their concerns and claims. This means informing citizens about their (prospective) representatives' plans and achievements; it also means reflecting the range of ideas and views that circulate within society, subjecting those who act in the name of the people to scrutiny, to make them accountable. These conditions allow citizens to make informed choices. The realization of this ideal is captured in the notion of a 'free press', an idea that embraces all forms of media. The free press is defined as that system of communication that allows for a diversity of ideas and opinion and that is not an agent of a single view or of state propaganda.

This, though, constitutes only a partial definition. It leaves untouched, first, the issue of what restrictions (if any) might be placed on the range of views or images that might then be made available. And second it begs the question of how this free press might be organized. For some libertarians (Beesley, 1996; North, 2007; Veljanovski, 1989), the answer to both is simple. A free press is one in which there are no restrictions on what might be said or seen, and that this state of affairs is generated by the operation of a free market in media outlets. But is such position possible or coherent or desirable? Certainly, there are those who will argue that no society can function without some restriction on freedom of expression. For them, censorship is a fact of life. Simon Lee, for example, notes that 'In our everyday lives, censors are all around us. We censor one another through withering looks, subtle threats of sticks or promises of carrots' (1990: 11). Jim McGuigan makes a similar point in relation to the distinction between regulative and constitutive censorship (1996: 155–61). The former is composed of the formal institutional mechanisms for controlling the content of mass media; the latter refers to the internalized constraints – often contained in social convention and habits of thought – that regulate discourse in order to enable society – any society – to function. Censorship can be both a necessary component of social cohesion and a restraint on free political thought. For these reasons, we might argue that absolute freedom of speech is inconceivable. At the same time, it does not follow that all restrictions are equally valid. We shall return to this.

The other libertarian suggestion is that the media become 'free' when they are not subject to centralized control. James Curran (2000: 121) summarizes this view: 'Only by anchoring the media to the free market, in this view, is it possible to ensure the media's complete independence from government.' Two moves are being made here. First, 'freedom' is being defined as the absence of interference; second, the achievement of this ideal is dependent on market competition between media outlets. The problem with this position is that it assumes that all freedoms are compatible. They are not. We cannot all speak at once if any of us wants to be heard. Furthermore, media markets may fail, or may develop monopolies that distort free competition (Baker, 2002). It may well be that liberal democracies require free speech; it does not follow that this means media markets and an absence of censorship.

The value of free speech

To move the argument forward, we need to begin by asking a simple question. What is the value of free expression? Why should we wish to defend or protect such a thing? Many arguments have been advanced for the value of free speech. John Keane (1991: 10–20) identifies several of these, tracing them back over many centuries. They first emerged in the seventeenth and eighteenth centuries. The argument for a free press, according to Keane, gains momentum with the poet John Milton's *Areopagitica*, written in 1644: 'Where there is much desire to learn, there of necessity will be much arguing, much writing, many opinions; for opinion in good men is but knowledge in the making.' Milton argued for religious tolerance in the face of the tyranny of religious orthodoxy. People had to be free to follow their conscience and able to test their convictions against rival claims, thereby strengthening their faith. Any attempt to impose a particular view would be counterproductive. Milton's seventeenth-century rationale for non-interference was echoed in the nineteenth century by John Stuart Mill. For Mill, knowledge of the world depended upon constant cross-examination of conventional wisdom. Dogmas could not be allowed to stand unexplored; they had to be subject to rigorous scrutiny. Only with the public demonstration of diversity and difference could ideas flourish and people cultivate their individual character. Mill writes in *On Liberty* of the way people live 'under the eye of a hostile and dreaded censorship' (1972: 119). He is here referring to the controlling powers of conformity, the pressure to do what is expected of one. The consequence of this is that 'the mind itself is bowed to the yoke' (ibid.). To break this yoke, it is important that different ideas be circulated and subjected to public scrutiny. Eccentricity or heresy are to be welcomed, not suppressed. A free press is a necessary corollary of this.

Running parallel to the arguments for a free press based on

freedom of conscience and thought, there are those based on individual rights. Deriving from the claims of writers like John Locke, Thomas Paine and Mary Wollstonecraft, the liberal asserts that individuals have rights which have to be respected by a legitimate government. Rule has to be by consent, and this entails the right to dissent: the opportunity to hold and express dissident views. A state press or state censorship would be an infringement of these rights. These justifications for the free press continue to circulate and to serve as the rationale for a free press today. They echo through arguments about censorship or through celebrations of the apparent freedom afforded by the internet. Stephen Holmes (1990), for example, cites Milton, among others, in his defence of the notion of a free press and the means it provides for limiting, and rendering accountable, political power.

The limits to free speech

The value to be placed upon a free press is therefore consider-able. It is evident why we might wish to defend such an idea and why it assumes a place in founding documents like the US Constitution or the European Convention on Human Rights. But placing a value on free speech is not the same as placing an absolute value on it. As we have already seen, this is not coherent. The question is rather what sorts of restrictions are acceptable? Is it appropriate to protect privacy, for example, when it clashes with freedom of expression? Should hate speech be denied the freedom allowed to other forms of expression, and if so what counts as hate speech? Does it include burning a cross? Was it legitimate for the Danish newspaper *Jyllands-Posten* to publish cartoons in 2006 that satirized Islam?

Onora O'Neill (1990) argues that the right to speak freely has to compete with other rights. The problem with freedom of expression, suggests O'Neill, is that it protects an individual's right to say whatever they like, but it pays no heed to those on the receiving end. If mass media are in the business of *communication* rather than expression, the rights of receivers have to be protected too, and this means curbing freedom of expression. Communication involves the interaction of two or more people. Expression requires only one person. Different conditions apply in each case. For O'Neill, communication requires protection of the rights of both parties. She writes, 'Toleration of *expression* may need only noninterference; toleration of *communication* must also sustain conditions of communication' (ibid.: 167, original emphasis). Democracy requires communication and hence requires regulation of free expression.

Michael Sandel (1998) makes a similar case, arguing that democracies have to set limits to free speech in order to realize other values. He criticizes those who place too high a value on free speech, and who fail to see the harm that can be done in its name. According to Sandel, the dominant liberal tradition regards individuals as free agents, making relatively autonomous choices. Given this perspective on the individual, the responsibility of government then becomes that of respecting the differences between those individuals. Its processes and actions must be judged in terms of their 'fairness', the even-handed way they deal with differences. When applied to free speech and the regulation of the media, the logic of this position, at least as it is interpreted by the US courts, means that the fact that views are abhorrent is not in itself a reason for banning them (see Irons, 1997, for examples of such cases). To do so would be to fail to honour the First Amendment and the need to respect individual rights to free expression. The content is 'bracketed' by the judges, and treated as irrelevant. In 'bracketing' the content and the competing claims made for it, the courts deal only with the question of whether there is any other legitimate basis (threats to public order, for instance) for banning the source of offence (for example, pornography or neo-Nazi propaganda). The rationale for this bracketing of the images and ideas themselves stems from liberal wariness about pronouncing on the competing conceptions of the good life that are assumed to find expression in media content, but the effect can be to disempower.

Sandel argues against the version of liberalism that underpins such court rulings. People must be understood as 'situated selves', as having identities that are constituted by the groups and cultures to which they belong and the self-understandings that derive from dialogue with others. This version of the self makes speech an integral part of the constitution of identity. The views we hold and the images we encounter are co-extensive with our identity; they are not things we choose to see or utter, they are us. Kathleen Sullivan (2005) makes this case in criticism of First

Amendment rulings in respect of women and the actual relations of power that shape their experiences. Thus insofar as speech is more than 'opinion', more than mere utterances, it has the potential to embody or damage identities (Sandel: 1998: 89). The liberal demand for respect for persons, argues Sandel, cannot allow the 'bracketing' of morally repugnant expressions. Certain speech acts should, though, be condemned because of the way they compromise the integrity of an individual's or a group's identity. Democracy, by this account, requires censorship in order to empower and recognize those who might otherwise be ignored. What O'Neill and Sandel represent is a liberal democratic argument for the regulation of media content, based on a different account of the liberal ideal. Their position derives from a particular set of assumptions about the nature of the self and the place of speech in the constitution of that self. Other accounts of both will, of course, produce different conclusions.

Free press/free market?

Rather than resolve these profound moral questions about what constitutes free speech, it might be argued that we should instead establish a process by which practice, rather than principle, determines the boundaries of acceptability. One such process is the market. Acceptability is determined by what it is that people will pay for. Media outlets should therefore be left to compete without external interference. This is what is meant by a free press. In his James McTaggart Lecture in Edinburgh 2009, James Murdoch, chairman and chief executive of News Corporation (Europe and Asia), provided a vehement defence of a market-based free press, in which the regulator and the public service broadcaster played no part. This is what he argued:

> Yes, the free press is fairly near the knuckle on occasion – it is noisy, disrespectful, raucous and quite capable of affronting people – it is frequently the despair of judges and it gets up the noses of politicians on a regular basis. But it is driven by the daily demand and choices of millions of people. It has had the profits to enable it to be fearless and independent. Great journalism does not get enough credit in our society, but it holds the powerful to account and plays a vital part in a functioning

democracy. ... People are very good at making choices: choices about what media to consume; whether to pay for it and how much; what they think is acceptable to watch, read and hear; and the result of their billions of choices is that good companies survive, prosper, and proliferate. That is a great story and it has been powerfully positive for our society.
(28 August 2009, found at http://www.broadcastnow.co.uk/, last accessed 16 July 2010)

For Murdoch, the operations of the market provide the conditions of a free press, bypassing the need for reflection upon what is or is not acceptable, save by individual customers.

James Murdoch's views may be crudely stated, but they resonate with a widely held interpretation of the history of mass media's development and context. Commercial and economic change can be seen to have promoted the idea of the 'free press' that Murdoch expounds. In the late nineteenth and early twentieth centuries, newspaper publishing ceased to be a matter of personal political indulgence, and became instead a viable commercial venture. The key to this was the emergence of advertising as a major source of revenue (Curran and Seaton, 2010: 23ff). The notion of a free press was, in this context, an extension of the idea of a free market, one in which the press responded to the commercial incentives and opportunities created by advertising. Globalization through the liberalization of tariffs and border controls is a modern equivalent of these earlier industrial pressures for a free press. Furthermore, the commercial pressure that helped establish the case for a free press was itself dependent on the technology that made mass production possible. The move from the hand-operated press to the production-line system allowed for a greatly increased circulation, and with this the possibility of a mass-readership 'popular' press, responsive to the interests and tastes of its readers (Winston, 1998).

It is true that broadcasting has been treated differently. Initially, the technologies of transmission and reception were associated with the need to restrict and regulate access to the airwaves, partly because their use was linked to military and security interests, but partly because the resource on which they depended was limited. There were only so many radio frequencies available; broadcasters using the same or adjacent frequencies would interfere with each other. Systems of regulation and licensing were needed to distribute and control this access. Freedom, in this context, was defined through the principles that organized this access and the conditions imposed on licence holders. But the new possibilities of digital broadcasting have essentially ended the problems of scarcity, and hence have changed the terms in which broadcasting freedom is conceived. Regulation is no longer required to manage scarcity. This shift is paralleled by the trend towards globalization in communications. The modern technologies make state borders ever more permeable, and therefore make regulation increasingly difficult. The image of a global, largely unregulated internet has become a symbol of the modern ideal of the 'free press'. From these historical and technological perspectives, therefore, James Murdoch's arguments might be seen as a product of their time, and to coincide with it.

However, Murdoch's critics – and there were many – do not share his confidence in market forces. One of their concerns is whether commercial incentives and freedom always coincide. In the film *The Insider* (directed by Michael Mann, 1999), the story is told of a whistleblower, Jeffrey Wigand, who wants to expose tobacco industry malpractice. His claims are about to be aired on CBS's *60 Minutes* when the plug is pulled. The television executives fear that the tobacco company would engage in expensive litigation, and that this in turn would jeopardize an imminent bid to take over CBS. Corporate interests clash with news values, and appear to win, until a last-minute initiative by the show's producer. Such an incident, and the film is based on a true story, illustrates what critics of the 'free press' see as an irreconcilable tension between a free press and a free market. Indeed, Edwin Baker (2007: 38–9) uses this example in his critique of the claim that the market is a guarantor of free speech.

James Curran (2000) is similarly mistrustful of the market. He notes that, though much is made of the media's function as a scrutineer of power, remarkably little time and space are given over to this function. The media are much less vigilant than might be expected, given the rhetoric. The reason for this, Curran suggests, is that commercial interests work against such vigilance (ibid.: 123–4). First, the media are themselves big businesses with close links to other state and corporate interests, and as such wary of investigating their own kind. Second, the market does not 'incentivize' investigative journalism, because of its costs and its relative weakness in attracting advertising revenue.

Equally, the media's ability to provide a range of different views is compromised by the cost of gaining access to media space and by the effect of media concentration (Baker, 2007). The free market, argues Curran (2000: 128), restricts 'the freedom to publish', 'the circulation of public information' and 'participation in public debate'. Readers and audiences do not have the ability, via the market, to influence media content. The concentration of ownership and the high entry costs marginalize consumers (ibid.: 131).

If the free market fails to provide for a free press, what is the alternative? Some argue that governments need to introduce much stricter anti-trust/anti-competitive regulations. These would require that all mergers be scrutinized carefully and subjected to scrutiny by journalists, and that editorial freedom be protected. Torbjorn Tannsjo (1985) argues that, for liberal democrats to realize their ambitions for a democratic mass media, the issues of ownership and control are central. If a democratic order is one that seeks to enhance the growth of knowledge, cultural pluralism and access, it cannot afford to allow an unfettered right to private ownership of media. The threat to democracy, by this account, comes not from the state but from the mass media industries themselves. Private ownership necessarily limits access, and in pursuit of its interests it will seek to control and limit the supply of knowledge and information; it will create an undemocratic media. Tannsjo's argument is that there is a tension between the ideal of 'free expression', which entitles people to say what they like, and 'sound mass communications', which is about guaranteeing a plurality of views, growth of knowledge and equality of access (ibid.: 553). 'Freedom of expression', he argues, 'is neither necessary nor sufficient for sound mass communications' (ibid.: 554). The reason for this is that 'freedom of expression', the right to say what you want, justifies the private ownership of media outlets.

This has two consequences which work against sound mass communications. The first is that private ownership leads to the creation of media monopolies; the second is that these monopolies come to treat news as a commodity, whose value is determined by the operation of the market. These two consequences work directly against the growth of knowledge (news is not valued for its contribution to knowledge and understanding, but for its commercial value: its ability to deliver audiences to advertisers). They also work against the principles of pluralism and open access because monopoly control by its nature restricts access.

Tannsjo is not alone in drawing these conclusions about the problems for democracy of private ownership. John Keane, for example, argues that 'information' needs to remain a public, not a private, commodity in a democracy. He writes:

> friends of the 'liberty of the press' must recognise that *commu-nications markets restrict freedom of communication* by generating barriers to entry, monopoly and restrictions upon choice, and by shifting the prevailing definition of information from that of a public good to that of a privately appropriable commodity. In short, it must be concluded that there is a struc-tural contradiction between freedom of communication and unlimited freedom of the market.
>
> (Keane, 1991: 89; original emphasis)

The effects of the market are felt not just on news and current affairs, but on entertainment too. Philip Green ends his lament for the decline of American popular culture with this claim: 'the free market can never produce anything but unfree culture' (1998: 57). The quality of culture, it is assumed, is as important to democracy as the quality and accuracy of news. Keane, Tannsjo and Green all conclude that regulation of ownership is necessary for media to fulfil their democratic role. This is not a matter of state ownership and control, but rather a matter, according to Tannsjo (1985: 553, 558), of putting all media 'under political, democratic control'.

Democratic regulation?

The thought that a democratic media should be democratically regulated itself begs further questions – most obviously, what should be regulated and how should it be regulated? Rather than attempting to give a comprehensive answer, what follows is a brief survey of some of the issues prompted by such questions.

Regulating for bias, impartiality and representativeness

It is often assumed that an impartial media are a condition of democracy. Citizens need to be reassured that their media provide them with a non-partisan, comprehensive and balanced picture of the issue and behaviour over which they expected to form views and pass judgement. Put another way, bias can have two adverse effects upon democracy: it can misrepresent the people or it can misinform them. Just as an elected assembly should represent the nation, so media should represent the views, values and tastes of their audiences. More than this, 'representation' is not just taken to mean giving space to the range of formally articulated political and moral views, it also has to include the representation of cultural difference, the way people live as well as the way they think. Biases that marginalize or misrepresent individuals or groups effectively deny influence and status to those people. They cease to be full participants or citizens. The other adverse effect that results from bias is misinformation. If people use the mass media to inform themselves about their society and about the performance of their politicians, and if they use this information to direct their political choices and participation, then inadequate or inaccurate information is liable to result in misconceived political acts.

For reasons of both representation and information, therefore, it seems that a democratic society requires unbiased media. But this raises two sets of very difficult questions. The first concerns the possibility of removing 'bias'. It may be reasonable to expect the media to provide factual information. They can get the details right: what a peace agreement says, or who the signatories were, for example. But such criteria do not take us far. There are an infinite number of details to any story; the problem is identifying the salient detail. Relevance can be defined by the way a particular detail fits into an explanation of an event (an irrelevant detail – 'the president is a Taurean' – contributes nothing to our understanding) or determined by the interests of the audience (such as the priority given to national news over international news). What should media say in reporting disputes about the evidence for the human causes of climate change? Should it privilege the overwhelming consensus in favour of this view, or should it given prominence to the few dissenting voices – the so-called climate change sceptics? Either way, there will be no settled view as to what constitutes relevant information (whether or not it is accurate). The problem does not necessarily disappear if the media simply seek to elicit different opinions – at least, not if it is assumed that beneath these competing views lies a 'right' answer or a consensus. Certainly such an approach is sometimes implied by the idea of balance, because it assumes a fulcrum, a central position around which to balance the 'extremes'; but this position can be seen as an arbitrarily selected point, or one that serves certain political interests. It does not represent any objective truth.

The logic of this argument does not lead to an uncritical relativism. Standards of accuracy and truthfulness still have validity in the assessment of media coverage. To this extent then, a liberal democratic media should aspire to represent events accurately, but beyond this there is a political debate to be had about the way the facts or events are represented. As we saw in discussion of the frames that are used in reporting politics, quite different perspectives and understandings can be introduced through the way the story is told. Political actions can be interpreted cynically or as the product of principle; events can be seen as episodic or the result of long-run processes. The appropriate frame is a matter of analysis and argument, but is it a matter for regulation, and if so what standards should be set?

Equally, consider the problem of ensuring 'representativeness' in coverage and content. To represent the people may mean to provide a mirror image of them, one in which the mix of men and women, young and old, sexualities and ethnic backgrounds, are those of the population at large. The problem here is to determine which characteristics need to be recognized and which ignored, given that there are limits to the time and space available in the media. There is also the question of how these characteristics should be portrayed: how should nationalities or sexualities be represented? And what of political representativeness? Should the media give due weight to the range of opinions and attitudes people have? This was the kind of problem that the BBC confronted in 2009 when deciding whether to include the recently elected Member of the European Parliament and leader of the British National Party, Nick Griffin, on its political discussion programme *Question Time*. On the one hand, Griffin was a legitimately elected representative of a legal party. On the other, his party was seen by many as racist and as a cause of racial tension.

Even if it is believed that a democratically regulated media should include the full range of political views, there remains the question as to how this range might be mapped or discerned. Are opinion polls or interest groups or elections sufficient guides? To counter these problems some might argue for 'enlightened representation', where others speak on behalf of the rest. It was this kind of representation that Edmund Burke (1975) famously claimed for himself in his address to the electors of Bristol in 1774, but it is also present in public service broadcasting commitments to 'education'. This version of representation involves *anticipating* people's interests, rather than reflecting them (Schudson, 2008).

One final problem is the danger of eliding 'the people' with the 'audience' or the 'readership'. In thinking about representativeness, should media reflect those who watch and read them, or should they refer to a nation or region (including those who do not buy the paper or watch that channel)? This is not to argue against all attempts at representativeness, only to draw attention to the difficulties – both practical and theoretical – in making it work. Any answer will be open to criticism, but the liberal democratic notion of a free press requires some judgement to be made about media content. The problem is finding the right criteria and the right process for implementing them.

Access

The problems posed by identifying the appropriate principles for coverage can lead to the adoption of a different approach. Instead of focusing on the content of the media, attention can be shifted to who has access to the public sphere created by media. Who should have access to the means of communication, and how should this access be used? Popular participation may, for example, help to improve the standards of accuracy, which are important to democratic media. This is what has been dubbed 'the wisdom of crowds' (Surwiecki, 2004). The more voices, the wider the range of experiences that participate in the production of media texts, the closer we will come to achieving an accurate account of what is happening and the easier it is to correct inaccurate reporting. This might be dubbed the Wikipedia phenomenon, whereby multiple contributions produce an ever more accurate and up-to-date resource. Put another way, relying on a single source risks the possibility of both inaccurate reporting and a lack of accountability. The guiding thought is that, in a liberal democracy, the media should in some sense be 'open', making it possible for these diverse views and experiences to appear and for redress and correction to be provided where standards of accuracy lapse. As with representativeness, there are various ways in which openness can be measured. Here we sketch two different forms of access, which can be labelled indirect and direct.

Indirect access involves the opportunity for people to express their views about what is written or broadcast, but does not guarantee them control over the product. Letter columns, email addresses and websites hosted by press and broadcasters, 'right to reply' programmes and readers/ viewers polls, all are examples of this kind of access. This media-based participation is supplemented by institutions whose job it is to monitor codes of media conduct and to rule on abuses of it. These forms of access allow people with an interest or view to respond to news stories and other kinds of coverage. There are limits, however, to this monitoring because it is by definition retrospective and because it does not guarantee any change in media behaviour. Another form of indirect participation is the political interview. The connection with the public is made explicitly or implicitly by the interviewer who claims to speak on behalf of the voters. But while the interviewer appears to speak on behalf of his or her audience, this is more a matter of rhetoric than reality. Interviewers do not have any formal links, and very few informal ones, with those they represent.

Direct participation, by contrast, shifts the balance of power from television producers and journalists, towards audiences. The phone-in or television's equivalent ('Meet the public') allow members of the public to interrogate politicians. Because the ordinary citizen is unschooled in interview techniques, or the codes that constrain professional interviewer–interviewee relations, they can speak from personal experience, they can persist (where the professional might move on to another subject) and they can unsettle politicians who cannot easily resort to typical answer-avoidance techniques. On the other hand, such participation is closely mediated, and the amateur's opportunity to probe is limited by the professional intermediary. The politician has, furthermore, the resources of status and experience with which to 'handle' awkward questions and questioners. There is, in short, likely to be an uneven (and undemocratic) distribution of cultural and social capital in this relationship, which, as John Mickler (2004) shows in his analysis of talkback radio in Australia, can play into the hands of elite political coalitions, rather than give voice to the ordinary citizen.

Certain types of user-generated content represents a further development of this kind of popular participation (Kelly, 2009). But this, like the examples above, may be confined to existing media structures. The terms and opportunities of participation are determined by those at the top of established media hierarchies. There are forms of user-generated content that emerge outside the established order. The political blog is one example; YouTube and Twitter are others. While much of this engagement may have an explicit or implicit political agenda, it does not form part of some deliberate political strategy, at least not of the kind that has organized community radio or groups such as Small World Media. The latter produced the alternative news series, *Undercurrents*. One of their film-makers explained their simple rationale: 'If what you see on TV were fair, there'd be no need for *Undercurrents*' (quoted in *New Statesman*, 24 March 1995: 24). Small World Media forms part of a larger phenomenon known as Indymedia. Formed in 1999 out of the anti-globalization movement, Indymedia presents itself as a global network offering 'radical, accurate and passionate tellings of the truth' (http://www.indymedia.org). Scholars disagree about the viability and impact of such a model of activist journalism, but it remains an important indicator of the options that a 'democratic media' might entail (Pickard, 2006; Platon and Deuze, 2003).

Democratic journalism

What organizations like Indymedia, and indeed other forms of popular participation, call into question is the role of the journalist. While radical claims have been made for the impact of new media on its traditional forerunner, it is reasonable to assume that for the short to medium term the press and broadcasting will continue to resemble their current forms, and audiences and readers will continue to rely on them for news and entertainment. If so, the professional journalist, however pressured and diminished their role, will continue to constitute a key intermediary, acting as a representative of audiences and readers. Such a role, as Onora O'Neill (2002) suggests, depends on trust, and trust depends upon accountability. Unlike other professions, journalism, O'Neill argues, has never been properly regulated: 'the media, in particular the print media – while deeply preoccupied with others' untrustworthiness – have escaped demands for accountability' (2002: 89).

Citizens need to be able to rely on journalists, and media outlets need to reassure their consumers of the reliability of their product and the integrity of those who produce it. This trust is bolstered by the codes to which media outlets commit, and to the punishments meted out to those who break them. But these are not in themselves sufficient guarantees. The opportunity to give expression to a set of ideas or accounts of the world, argues O'Neill, must be matched by the opportunity on the part of the readers and viewers to *assess* or *evaluate* what is being claimed. As she writes, 'Good public debate must not only be *accessible* to but *assessable* by its audiences. The press are skilled at making material accessible, but erratic about making it assessable' (2002: 95; her emphasis). For O'Neill, the capacity to make an assessment is inextricably linked to the question of trust. Trust, in this instance, is established through a degree of transparency, achieved by making clear the sources upon the information is based and the interests of those involved in producing that information.

Whether we agree or not with O'Neill's particular emphasis, her general argument is hard to ignore. It lies behind the widespread debate about the need to protect privacy and to regulate journalistic behaviour in relation to it (Whittle and Cooper, 2009). Democratic media – media, that is, that serve democracy – must address the question of how trust in journalism can be assured and maintained. Some might suggest that this is a matter of a more fully regulated professionalism, borrowing from systems used to license doctor and lawyers. Others might contend that it depends on legislative frameworks that separate and demarcate political and media power (Media Standards Trust, 2009). Whatever strategy is favoured, the issue remains: the role and regulation of journalism is a necessary component of democratic media.

Public sphere and public service

In ending this brief survey of the issues prompted by the notion of democratic media, we need to turn to the matter of the public sphere. For some, the media's democratic role is capsulated in this single idea. Following from Jurgen Habermas's (1989) hugely influential historical tracing of the idea, and his subsequent refinement (1996) of it, it has been assumed that the media must serve to create a space for dialogue and deliberation within which citizens can come to realize their common identity and purpose. Subsequent discussion (Fraser, 1992; Warner, 2005) has qualified the original idea, but it still assumes a central place in discourses around media and democracy. In particular, it remains as a challenge to those who offer uncritical support to the fragmentation of traditional media and their replacement by the multiple forms of narrow and mass self-communication of the new media era. Like Cass Sunstein (2001), Kari Karpinnen worries about the impact of new media's celebration of diversity; he asks, 'is there not a point at which healthy diversity turns into unhealthy dissonance?' (2007: 15). He argues for the need for political intervention to counter fragmentary trends.

By contrast Elizabeth Jacka argues that such battles are lost, and that we need to begin by reflecting on what democracy now means and involves:

> If ... we see democracy as pluralized, as marked by new kinds of communities of identity, as a system in which the traditional public–private divide does not apply, and as a system in which there is no universal visions of the 'common good' but, rather, pragmatic and negotiated exchanges about ethical behaviour and ethically inspired courses of action, then we will be able to countenance a plurality of communication media and modes in which a diverse set of exchanges will occur.
>
> (Jacka, 2003: 183)

In such a world, public service broadcasting is not a central or necessary component. Jacka's views are not universally shared, and Nicholas Garnham (2003) argues against her counsel of despair.

What Jacka is challenging are the assumptions that have organized traditional political and media debates, ones that have typically been captured in the ideological spectrum between left and right, or between state and market orders, or between liberal representative and direct participative democracy. Such divides are seen by some to no longer reflect adequately the world we inhabit (Castells, 2009; Giddens, 1998; Hirst, 1994). Rather than the state or the market (or some mix of the two) as the means of political management, their attention is turned to networks and associative organizations. In this reconfiguration of democracy, the key term ceases to be power (and propaganda) and becomes information (and communication) (Hirst, 1994). Democracy, according to Paul Hirst (ibid.: 34–40), is to be defined in terms of communication; it is this that allows associations to coordinate their actions and register their demands. The state's responsibility is primarily to enable this communication to occur. Apart from the constraints imposed by laws of libel, racial incitement and the like, there would be no pressure on these media outlets to present themselves as impartial or authoritative, but rather they would be expected to make explicit their own political perspective in order to advance the debate about shared goals and purposes. This is what Nicholas Garnham means when he argued that the media 'needs to be more highly politicized, with political parties and other major organized social movements having access to the screen on their own terms' (1986: 50).

The argument about media democracy shifts from either state-centric or market-centric models. The key term becomes 'pluralism', albeit rescued from its traditional meanings and associations (Connolly, 2005b). In matters of media content, the idea is not that 'bias' can be replaced by 'truth', but that bias is to be acknowledged as a necessary and desirable part of political discourse. The logic of this is that we need a plurality of points of view and perspective, but the overarching purpose remains that of finding some agreed notion of the good life and some method for resolving the conflicting claims it generates. The emphasis shifts from direct democracy's old concern with power to a version of democracy more oriented to deliberation and dialogue (Miller, 1992). As a consequence, emphasis is placed on the conditions which allow people to reflect collectively on questions of public policy. Again the intention is not to make decisions based on the aggregation of individual preferences, but rather to allow for deliberation about common purposes. The implications for mass media lie not in state control, but in the state enabling or facilitating independent media enterprises. Keane (1992: 120) writes of the need for 'the establishment of media enterprise boards to fund alternative ownership of divested media .... Freedom of communication undoubtedly requires the establishment of publicly owned printing and broadcasting enterprises.'

A similar logic animates John Thompson's (1995) arguments for mass media's role in a deliberative democracy. He too is sceptical about the possibility and desirability of the two models that have tended to dominate discussion: the traditional liberal and direct versions. The reason for his scepticism stems from his understanding of the emerging world order. Both of the old models, he argues, appeal to a world of discrete nation states and a managed (or manageable) media corporate structure. The reality is one of globalized political economy, in which the powers of nation states are attenuated and the powers of media corporations extended. Thompson argues that mass media now operate within a framework that makes the previous models of democracy irrelevant. The traditional notion of the free press depended upon competition between relatively small corporations. The new conglomerates represent major power blocs. Furthermore, the state, one possible source of regulation, is now dwarfed by these conglomerates and is in a dependency relationship with them. These developments compromise the capacity of the system to provide a forum within which deliberation about political concerns and interests can take place. In these circumstances, Thompson argues, we need a new sense of 'publicness' and a new kind of infrastructure.

Thompson favours what he calls 'regulated pluralism'. Regulated pluralism entails the decentralization of resources and the separation of the state from media institutions. Regulated pluralism, as he explains,

> is the establishment of an institutional framework which would both accommodate and secure the existence of a plurality of independent media organizations. It is a principle which takes seriously the traditional liberal emphasis on the freedom of expression and on the importance of sustaining media institutions which are independent of state power. But it is a principle which also recognizes that the market left to itself will not necessarily secure the conditions of freedom of expression

and promote diversity and pluralism in the sphere of communication.

(Thompson, 1995: 240–1)

The market, he concludes, has to be managed. This means limiting the concentration of media corporations and encouraging
the development of new ones. But such intervention must itself
operate independently of the state.

Thompson himself further distances the state by requiring it to
play an 'enabling' function, along the lines proposed by
Garnham. But where Thompson's argument differs from those
of Garnham is in his emphasis on deliberative democracy
(rather than on direct democracy). His view is that regulated
pluralism does not make for direct involvement or dialogue,
but for a more distant relationship. This is what he means by a
new version of 'publicness', which (unlike the dialogic publicness of Rousseau's General Will) is a mediated one that is not
confined to a particular locale and is not dialogical. Instead it is
open-ended and provides the citizen with a new 'space of the
visible' which politicizes the everyday, and allows citizens to
form their own judgements through their interactions with the
media. The media provide the resources through which citizens
come to construct their identities and to deliberate about the
realization of their interests. This is not a matter of controlling
the media in the name of particular interests; it is about a
process of discovery and construction. Democratic media are
not, therefore, marked just by the systems of control that organize them, but also by the way in which their content, and the
accessibility of this content, allows for people to know and
comprehend each other.

One critic of public broadcasting in the United States pointed
to the way it was organized 'for' the people, not by them, and this
was evident in the Olympian attitude whereby audiences were
offered education from on high. 'Rational thinking' was
preferred over 'emotionally and bodily invested political participation, such as women's consciousness raising groups, boisterous
union meetings and bar-room debates' (Ouellette, 1999: 76).
Curran (2000: 148) echoes this argument when he writes that a
democratic media system 'should empower people by enabling
them to explore where their interests lie'. He goes further by
offering a 'working model' for democratic media, where he

argues for the creation of different media sectors, each of which provides space for particular skills and expertise (ibid.: 142ff). These include a 'civic media sector' for parties, social movements and interest groups, and a 'professional media sector' for journalists and others to produce work that is committed to 'truth telling', whether in fiction or in news. Curran's model is an attempt to combine elements of public service media and private sector media, and to combine principles of advocacy and impartiality.

Both Thompson and Curran may be accused of being idealistic in their proposals, and far too readily to uncritically adopt deliberative democracy (Schudson, 2008). But they do at least force us to focus on the central issues that should concern anyone intent upon creating a democratic media system. And for writers like Castells (2009: 298), their agenda is a matter of urgency rather than idle reflection: 'Democracy can only be reconstructed in the specific conditions of the network society if civil society, in its diversity, can break through the corporate, bureaucratic, and technological barriers of societal image-making.' For Castells (ibid.: 413), the key lies less in the formal structures of power described by Curran and Thompson, and more in the 'reprogramming of networks of meaning', but the effect is the same: to provide mechanisms whereby systems of communication engage directly with systems of political power.

In ending here, it is important to recall that the arguments in the latter part of the chapter have been rooted in a break from traditional liberal theories of press freedom and of democracy itself. This has been done for two reasons. The first was to acknowledge the logic of this revisionist liberalism, and to explore its implications for the role of mass media in a democracy. If we do adopt the notion of a 'situated self', if we do embrace a form of 'deliberative democracy', if we are seeing the emergence of 'network society', there are important implications for the operation and organization of mass media. The second reason is that, even if this alternative approach is unattractive and unpersuasive, the fact of its existence does at least draw attention to the politics that underpins the discussion of mass media's place in a democracy. We are not just dealing with competing notions of media power but also with contested concepts of the person, politics and civil society.

Conclusion

In thinking about the ways in which the media might be changed in order better to serve democracy, there is a danger that we will overlook other aspects of the problem. However democratic the media, they cannot fulfil their allotted function if, for example, they confront a wall of official secrecy. Freedom of information is a fundamental feature of a democratic society, as are laws of defamation that are even-handed between the rights of individuals and media. Equally, the conditions under which politics is conducted affect the media's capacity to fulfil a useful role. Ronald Dworkin argues, for instance, that restrictions on campaign spending are a necessary corollary of media effectiveness:

> If politicians had much less to spend on aggressive, simple-minded television spots ... political campaigns would have to rely more on reporters and on events directed by non-partisan groups, like television debates, and political argument might become less negative and more constructive.
>
> (Dworkin, 1996: 19)

Dworkin's faith in media coverage may be misplaced, but his argument does recognize the link between political life and its media representation. The other side to this general argument is that restrictions on the media are not in themselves restrictions on democracy. It would be perfectly possible to defend, for example, stricter privacy laws in the name of democracy. The German media are prevented (albeit not always effectively) from publishing photos that 'violate the dignity' of an individual, a policy that is entirely in keeping with Sandel's notion of civic republicanism. Democratic media do not, in and of themselves, create democracy. Democratic media need a democratic polity, and vice versa.

This chapter has tried to illustrate some of the issues that need to be addressed in deciding what kind of contribution the mass media can make to democracy. It does not follow that democratic media are unexciting or worthy. There is no reason why coverage of politics needs to be treated with the solemnity and earnestness of a funeral. It could as well be treated like a branch of showbusiness, and subjected to the same pressures and demands that we apply to that. Democratic media must, after all, serve to keep our rulers in their place, and as Andrew Marr (1996: 299) notes, 'Laughter is the secret weapon of democrats.'

The thought that satire has a valid place in a democracy, and that the formal boundaries that mark the divide between politics and entertainment are permeable, returns us to an earlier discussion in this book. Reflections on the relationship between democracy and mass media cannot be divorced from the character and content of the programmes and papers themselves. The debates about bias, about the way politics is represented, are crucial to the question of what constitutes democratic media, as are arguments about ownership and control, about state regulation and about accountability. If there is one theme that underpins much that has gone before, it is that we cannot draw neat dividing lines between news and entertainment. What we understand by 'politics' is not defined by the formal prescriptions of constitutions; equally, our view of the world and of ourselves does not exist independently of communications media. In the end, it is not a matter of politics and mass media, of two separate entities, but rather of a complex network of relations, in which politics and mass media cease to occupy discrete categories but form part of multiple networks, bringing into conflict and alliance the seemingly firm distinctions between public and private, politics and pleasure, individual and communal.

Conclusion

This book began by reflecting upon the dramatic changes that have marked modern forms of communication, and about how many of these had been harnessed by Barack Obama's campaign to become the 44th president of the United States. Together these changes and Obama's success lead to the thought that politics is being transformed, and that the key agent of this transformation are the mass media in both their traditional and new guises. It is certainly true that the forms of political communication now in use are dramatically different from those deployed fifty or so years ago; it is also true that the issues faced by those who make (or debate) media policy could not have been anticipated in the days of the press baron. To this extent, there are clear signs of transformation, but there is, too, evidence of continuity.

We should not be surprised by this, even as we are bombarded by rhetoric about the brave new world around the corner. The relationship of media and politics is a power relationship. It is about the processes that determine who gets what, when, and how. However much the technologies change, and whatever new opportunities they open up or close down, our concern is with the circulation of the resources and capacities that causes some interests to win and others to lose out. Media as a source of meaning and of money has a particularly vital role in the story of power. So while this book has tried to trace and reflect the rapidly developments in media technology and the claims about the transformation of politics that they have engendered, it has also tried to put these into context, to see how they are to be understood and analysed in relation to the current exercise of political power and to some possible future in which that power is distributed differently.

These larger themes have been addressed through the particular stories to be told about the politics embedded in media texts and about how we get at the political meaning through concepts like 'bias' and 'frames'. Whose interests are served by the ideas and images contained within news reports and in popular entertainment? What kind of world do they imagine for us? Concern with the text leads to questions about its effects – how do we know if people are influenced politically by what they see and read? To the extent that media affect what we think and do, the question then becomes who determines the way those media outlets behave, what they cover and how they cover it. Hence, our attention turned to the power exercised by conglomerates, governments and journalists in determining the form of political communication. And from there, we went on to consider the new forms of political communication made possible both by new technology and by new approaches to the marketing of parties and politicians. We ended with questions about the power wielded by media and about the issues raised by any attempt to re-distribute that power more equitably.

Answers to these questions have, I hope, emerged during the course of the book. I will not repeat them here. Instead, let me summarize the working assumptions that have organized my approach. My first assumption is, 'don't believe the hype'. While much is often claimed for the impact of this or that technology, this or that event or trend, the reality turns out to be less exciting. Or put differently, the key to change is the constellation of political forces and political values organized around media. It is important that we concentrate upon these if we want to be able to pronounce upon the changes that define our immediate impressions and sensations. My second assumption is, always compare. There is a strong temptation to generalize, if only because wherever we look the same (or similar) media technologies are in use, or the same newspaper and programme formats are being consumed. In fact, the same technologies are organized differently and impact differently because there are any number of intermediary variables. Which leads to a third assumption: never underestimate the role of the state. The rhetoric of globalization has tended to marginalize discussion of the state, but it is a key actor in determining many aspects of the relationship between politics and media. A fourth suggestion, one that echoes its predecessor, is never underestimate the importance of political values. They are key to the practices and policies that constitute the routines of media's political engagement. One final assumption or injunction is, don't ignore the pleasure. There is a tendency, when dealing with serious matters such as politics, that we associate it only with other forms of seriousness. Forms of pleasure matter too, not just for the portrayals of politics that they offer, but also for the forms of engagement they engender.

But if we stop looking back at the topics covered and the lessons learnt, and instead look forward; what do we see? I make no apology for returning to the same writers that I quoted in the first edition of this book. Their wisdom and insights seem as valid now as they did then. The transformation of political life and ordinary life, and the blurring of the two, has led some writers to perceive a bleak future, one in which politics becomes demeaned (literally, de-meaned, deprived of meaning). Politics, it is suggested, is fast becoming just another game show, another docusoap. Danilo Zolo writes:

> The real electors see themselves replaced by their own demo-scopic and televisual projection, which anticipates them and leaves them the passive observers of themselves. Individual citizens, despite being the true holders of the right to vote, find themselves subjected to the pressure of public predictions which tend circularly to be self-fulfilling by edging them out of the electoral event.
>
> (Zolo, 1992: 163–4)

In a similarly despondent tone, Michael Sandel worries that 'the narrative resources' that are essential to a functioning civic republic are being 'strained' by the prevalence of 'the soundbites, factoids and disconnected images of our media-saturated culture' (1998: 350). The proliferation of channels, the generation of interactive systems, the sheer explosion of information, have created a world in which the media are the only reality, and in which the demands of sponsors and advertisers create pressure for ever more spectacular or humiliating shows. The world is constantly being made and remade, as facts and fictions become entwined. News and politics are reduced to slogans and sound bites, mimicking the aesthetics of the pop video and of YouTube. It is a world in which newscasters are celebrities, and celebrities become politicians. In 2010, Tiger Woods, the world's most famous sportsman, delivered an apology to his wife and family for the many affairs he had had during his marriage. He did not offer this apology in the privacy of his home, but instead to a small invited audience of friends, family and associates. It was carried live on all the main US television channels. It led the news on British television. This is, you might suppose, the new media order.

Others, though, offer a less bleak picture of the future, seeing, in the blending of the private and public, of the cultural and the political, a new politics emerging. They celebrate the birth of the blogosphere and the 'Twitterati' as a new public sphere, in which we are all engaged in ongoing deliberation. They delight in the ways in which formal mechanisms of regulation no longer constrain public comment; they relish the spontaneous collective action that can be organized via texting.

Certainly, we cannot ignore the greater choice and control that media consumers have, at least within the developed world. We can create our own viewing schedules from an ever-expanding range of alternatives. The days of mass consumption and mass viewing have given way to individual choice and niche markets, to many private worlds. It is just this prospect that prompts another scenario to appear over the horizon. This is a world of isolated individuals, disconnected from communities and groups, vulnerable and manipulable. The new technologies do not necessarily represent choice and devolved power; they represent surveillance and centralized suppression. The emerging systems of communication provide conglomerates and state authorities with the ability to monitor movement and thought in ways that were never possible previously. Every cash transaction, every electronic communication, provides data on the desires and actions of citizens. Political parties now no longer lead, they merely follow the swerves and switches of populist opinion. As they acquire more and more data on their constituents, so their policies become ever shallower responses to the twitch of public opinion.

Elements of each of these scenarios are already with us, and will probably become much more pronounced with each passing year, but there will be consequences that are beyond our best imaginings. What can be certain is that, just as the relationship between politics and mass media has changed dramatically in the last decades, so it will in the future. It is important, though, to think critically about these changes.

We will no doubt see political parties devise ever more sophisticated ways of exploiting the opportunities offered by the media. We will see politicians increasingly taking on the guise of popular culture's celebrities. The point, however, is not to move automatically to the conclusion that we are seeing the 'dumbing down' of politics. We need to assess what is happening in terms that are sensitive to the processes involved. Rather than dismiss such a state of affairs as a sign of cultural and political terminal decline, we should understand it first as part of a wider set of factors and changes. This is not to foreclose any judgement we may subsequently make, but rather to set such judgements within a realistic appraisal of the process being judged. After all, to dismiss modern political campaigning as mere artifice and show is simply to connect it to many other cultural forms which are also artifice and show. We need to discriminate between artifices, not to imagine that we can go beyond them to some authentic reality. The culture of politics, as with all forms of culture, is a product of a complicated set of interests, regulations and institutions, which organize, reproduce and police that culture.

We need also to be aware of the profoundly important stakes that are being played out in the way media are organized and used. While it has been fashionable to make fun of 'media studies' and dismiss its concerns as the pseudo-scientific pursuit of trivia, our mass media are a vital element in the way we live our lives and come to know ourselves and our world. They contain our memories and our histories; their resources provide for the stories people tell each other. And Sandel argues:

> Political community depends on the narratives by which people make sense of their condition and interpret the common life they share; at its best political deliberation is not only about competing policies but also about competing interpretations of the character of the community, of its purpose and ends.
>
> (Sandel, 1998: 350)

This is why we should both value and criticize the forms taken by media culture. We should value them because of the role they have in constructing those narratives; we should criticize them for their failure to enrich them. Sandel makes a direct connection between the quality of political and cultural discourse and the well-being of the democratic order.

It may be that political life is being damaged by a media obsessed with ratings and politicians desperate for votes; it may be that the commercial interests of multimedia corporations are putting a price on everything (and selling it cheap), but to complain is not enough. We need to be clear about what is to be valued in politics and in media culture. John Keane has suggested that we now inhabit an era of 'monitory democracy', in which elections are less important in ensuring the accountability of the powerful (2009: 688ff). Instead, those with power are constantly monitored – or at least can be monitored – through modern media. He writes, 'Representative democracy sprang up in the era of print culture .... By contrast, monitory democracy is tied closely to the growth of multi-media-saturated societies' (ibid.: 737). As a result, he continues, 'Every nook and cranny of power becomes the potential target of "publicity" and "public exposure"; monitory democracy threatens to expose the quiet discriminations and injustices that happen behind closed doors and in the world of everyday life' (ibid.: 740). In the last few weeks, as I was finishing this book, the British prime minister was heard, from the supposed privacy of his car, to describe a voter as a 'bigot'; a leading football administrator was recorded in private conversation casting aspersions on rival countries; and the Duchess of York was caught on camera offering to sell access to the Royal Family. Each case was brutally exposed in the media. Each was a raw example of monitory democracy at work. In such a world, analysing the relationship of media and politics remains a vital task for anyway who wants to understand our societies and the distribution of power within them.

Bibliography

Aaronovitch, D. (2009) *Voodoo Histories: The Role of the Conspiracy Theory in Shaping Modern History*, London: Jonathan Cape.

Aarts, K. and H. Semetko (2003) 'The divided electorate: media use and political involvement', *Journal of Politics*, 65(3), pp. 759–84.

Abramson, J. B., F. C. Arterton and G. R. Orren (1988) *The Electronic Commonwealth: The Impact of New Media Technologies on Democratic Politics*, New York: Basic Books.

Adonis, A. and G. Mulgan (1994) 'Back to Greece: the scope for direct democracy', *Demos Quarterly*, 3, pp. 2–9.

Adorno, T. and M. Horkheimer (1979) 'The culture industry: enlightenment as mass deception', in *Dialectic of Enlightenment*, London: Verso, pp. 120–67.

Allan, S. (2003) 'Mediating citizenship: on-line journalism and the public sphere new voices', *Development*, 46(1), pp. 30–40.

Anderson, P. and A. Weymouth (1999) *Insulting the Public? The British Press and the European Union*, London: Longman.

Ang, I. (1996) *Living Room Wars: Rethinking Media Audiences for a Postmodern World*, London: Routledge.

Ankersmit, F. R. (1996) *Aesthetic Politics*, Stanford, Calif.: Stanford University Press.

Ankersmit, F. R. (2002) *Political Representation*, Stanford, Calif.: Stanford University Press.

Anstead, N. and W. Straw (2009) 'Introduction' in N. Anstead and W. Straw (eds), *The Change We Need: What Britain can Learn from Obama's Victory*, London: Fabian Society, pp. 1–6.

Arblaster, A. (1987) *Democracy*, Milton Keynes: Open University Press.

Arterton, C. (1987) *Teledemocracy*, London: Sage.

Asp, K. and P. Esaiasson (1996) 'The modernization of Swedish campaigns: individualization, professionalization, and medialization', in D. Swanson and P. Mancini (eds), *Politics, Media, and Modern Democracy*, New York: Praeger, pp. 73–90.

Atton, C. (2002) 'New cultures and new social movements: radical journalism and the mainstream media', *Journalism Studies*, 3(2), pp. 491–505.

Austin, E. W., R. Vord, B. Pinkleton and E. Epstein (2008) 'Celebrity endorsements and their potential to motivate young voters', *Mass Communication and Society*, 11, pp. 420–36.

335

Bailey, D. (1999) 'Politics on the internet', *American Voices,* September.

Baker, C. E. (2002) *Media, Markets and Democracy,* Cambridge: Cambridge University Press.

Baker, C. E. (2007) *Media Concentration and Democracy: Why Ownership Matters,* Cambridge: Cambridge University Press

Barber, B. (1984) *Strong Democracy: Participatory Politics for a New Age,* San Francisco, Calif.: University of California Press.

Barber, B. (1997) *Jihad vs McWorld: How Globalism and Tribalism are Reshaping the World,* New York: Ballantine.

Barker, M. and J. Petley (2001) *Ill Effects: The Media Violence Debate,* London: Routledge.

Barnett, S. (1993) 'Sliding down the market slope', *British Journalism Review,* 4(1), pp. 67–9.

Barnett, S. (2002) 'Will the crisis in journalism provoke a crisis in democracy?', *Political Quarterly,* 73(4), pp. 400–8.

Barnett, S., E. Seymour and I. Gaber (2000) *From Callaghan to Kosovo: Changing Trends in British Television News 1975–1999,* Harrow: University of Westminister.

Barthes, R. (1967) *Elements of Semiology,* London: Jonathan Cape.

Bartle, J. and D. Griffiths (eds) (2001) *Political Communication Transformed: From Morrison to Mandelson,* Basingstoke: Palgrave Macmillan.

Bartle, J., S. Atkinson and P. Mortimore (2002) *The General Election Campaign of 2001,* London: Frank Cass.

Baum, M. (2005) 'Talking the vote: why presidential candidates hit the talk show circuit', *American Journal of Political Science,* 49(2), pp. 149–67.

Baym, G. (2005) '*The Daily Show*: Discursive integration and the reinvention of political journalism', *Political Communication,* 22, pp. 259–76.

Becker, J. (2004) 'Lessons from Russia: a neo-authoritarian media system', *European Journal of Communication,* 19(2), pp. 139–63.

Beesley, M (ed.) (1996) *Markets and the Media,* London: Institute of Economic Affairs.

Belfield, R., C. Hird and S. Kelly (1991) *Murdoch: The Decline of an Empire,* London: Macdonald.

Bellamy, R. (2007) *Political Constitutionalism: A Republican Defence of the Constitutionality of Democracy,* Cambridge: Cambridge University Press

Bellamy, R. and M. Hollis (1995) 'Liberal justice: political and metaphysical', *Philosophy Quarterly,* 45(178), pp. 1–19.

Bennett, T. (1982a) 'Media, "reality", signification', in M. Gurevitch, T. Bennett, J. Curran and J. Woollacott (eds), *Culture, Society and the Media,* London: Routledge, pp. 287–308.

Bennett, T. (1982b) 'Theories of the media, theories of society', in M. Gurevitch, T. Bennett, J. Curran and J. Woollacott (eds), *Culture, Society and the Media,* London: Routledge, pp. 30–55.

Bennett, W. and D. Paletz (eds) (1994) *Taken by Storm: The Media, Public Opinion and US Foreign Policy in the Gulf War,* Chicago, Ill.: University of Chicago Press.

Bennett, W. and R. Entman (eds) (2001) *Mediated Politics: Communication in the Future of Democracy,* Cambridge: Cambridge University Press.

Benton, S. (1997) 'Political news', *Soundings,* 5, Spring, pp. 137–48.

Berlin, I. (1969) *Four Essays on Liberty,* Oxford: Oxford University Press.

Besley, J. (2006) 'The role of entertainment television and its interaction with individual values in explaining political participation', *Harvard International Journal of Press/Politics,* 11(2), pp. 41–63.

Besley, T. (2007) *Principled Agents? The Political Economy of Good Government,* Oxford: Oxford University Press.

Besley, T. and A. Prat (2006) 'Handcuffs for the grabbing hand? Media capture and government accountability', *American Economic Review,* 96(3), pp. 720–36.

Billig, M., D. Deacon, P. Golding and S. Middleton (1993) 'In the hands of the spin–doctors: television politics, and the 1992 General Election', in N. Miller and R. Allen (eds), *It's Live – But Is It Real?,* London: John Libbey, pp. 111–21.

Bin, Z. (1998) 'Popular family television and party ideology: the spring festival eve happy gathering', *Media, Culture and Society,* 20, pp. 43–58.

Birch, A. H. (1964) *Representative and Responsible Government,* London: George Allen & Unwin.

Blain, N., R. Boyle and H. O'Donnell (1993) *Sport and National Identity in the European Media,* Leicester: Leicester University Press.

Blanning, T. (2008) *The Triumph of Music,* London: Allen Lane.

Blumler, J. and S. Coleman (2001) *Realising Democracy Online: A Civic Commons in Cyberspace,* London: Institute for Public Policy Research (IPPR).

Blumler, J. and M. Gurevitch (1995) *The Crisis of Public Communication,* London: Routledge.

Blumler, J. and M. Gurevitch (2002) 'Public service in transition? Campaign journalism at the BBC, 2001', in J. Bartle, S. Atkinson and P. Mortimore (eds), *Political Communications: The General Election Campaign of 2001,* London: Frank Cass, pp. 215–35.

Blumler, J. and E. Katz (1974) *The Uses of Mass Communications,* Beverly Hills, Calif.: Sage.

Blumler, J. and D. McQuail (1968) *Television in Politics: Its Uses and Influences,* London: Faber & Faber.

Bourdieu, P. (1986) *Distinction: A Social Critique of the Judgement of Taste,* London: Routledge.

Bourdieu, P. (1998) *On Television and Journalism,* London: Pluto Press.

Bower, T. (1988) *Maxwell: The Outsider,* London: Aurum.

Bowes, M. (1990) 'Only when I laugh', in A. Goodwin and G. Whannel, *Understanding Television,* London: Routledge, pp. 128–40.

Boyd-Barrett, O. and T. Rantanen (1998) 'The globalization of news', in O. Boyd-Barrett and T. Rantanen (eds), *The Globalization of News,* London: Sage, pp. 1–14.

Brants, K., M. Huizenga and R. van Meerten (1996) 'The new canals of Amsterdam: an exercise in local electronic democracy', *Media, Culture and Society,* 18(2), pp. 185–212.

Braudy, L. (1997) *The Frenzy of Renown,* New York: Oxford University Press.

Brennan, G. and A. Hamlin (2000) *Democratic Devices and Desires,* Cambridge: Cambridge University Press.

Brown, R. (2003) 'Spinning the war: political communications, information operations and public diplomacy in the war on terrorism', in D. Thussu and D. Freedman (eds), *War and the Media,* London: Sage, pp. 87–100.

Bruns, A. (2008) 'Life beyond the public sphere: towards a networked model for political deliberation', *Information Polity,* 13(1–2), pp. 71–85.

Bryan, C., R. Tsagarousianou and D. Tambini (1998) 'Electronic democracy and the civic networking movement in context', in R. Tsagarousianou, D. Tambini and C. Bryan (eds), *Cyberdemocracy: Technology, Cities and Civic Networks,* London: Routledge, pp. 1–17.

Bua, A. (2009) *Realising Online Democracy: A Critical Appraisal of 'Online Civic Commons',* London: Compass.

Budge, I. (1996) *The New Challenge of Direct Democracy,* Cambridge: Polity.

Budge, I. and K. Newton (1998) *The Politics of the New Europe,* London: Longman.

Burke, E. (1975) 'Speech to the electors of Bristol', in B. Hill (ed.), *Edmund Burke on Government, Politics and Society,* London: Fontana, pp. 156–8.

Burston, J. (2003) 'War and entertainment: New research priorities in an age of cyber–patriotism', in D. Thussu and D. Freedman (eds), *War and the Media,* London: Sage, pp. 163–75.

Buxton, D. (1990) *From The Avengers to Miami Vice: Form and Ideology in Television Series,* Manchester: Manchester University Press.

Calabrese, A. and M. Borchert (1996) 'Prospects for electronic democracy in the United States: rethinking communication and social policy', *Media, Culture and Society,* 18(2), pp. 249–68.

Campbell, A. (2007) *The Blair Years: Extracts from the Alastair Campbell Diaries,* London: Hutchinson.

Campbell, D. and S. Connor (1986) *On the Record,* London: Michael Joseph.

Cantor, P. (2001) *Gilligan Unbound: Pop Culture in the Age of Globalization,* New York: Rowman & Littlefield.

Cantwell, R. (1996) *When We Were Good: The Folk Revival,* Boston, Mass.: Harvard University Press.

Cappella, J. and K. Jamieson (1997) *Spiral of Cynicism,* New York: Oxford University Press.

Cardo, V. (2009) 'A new citizenship? The politics of reality TV', unpublished PhD, University of East Anglia.

Carlson, M. (2007) 'Blogs and journalistic authority: the role of blogs in US Election Day 2004 coverage', *Journalism Studies,* 8(2), pp. 264–79.

CARMA (2006) *Western Media Coverage of Humanitarian Disasters,* London: CARMA.

Carpenter, H. (2000) *That Was Satire That Was: The Satire Boom of the 1960s,* London: Victor Gollancz.

Carruthers, S. (1998) '"The Manchurian Candidate" (1962) and the cold war brainwashing scare', *Historical Journal of Film, Radio and Television,* 18(1), pp. 75–94.

Carruthers, S. (2000) *The Media at War,* Basingstoke: Macmillan Palgrave.

Castells, M. (1996) *The Rise of the Network Society,* Oxford: Blackwell.

Castells, M. (2009) *Communication Power,* Oxford: Oxford University Press.

Cave, M. and R. W. Crandall (2001) 'Sports rights and the broadcast industry', *Economic Journal,* 111, pp. 4–26

Chadwick, A. (2006) *Internet Politics: States, Citizens and New Communication Technologies,* Oxford: Oxford University Press.

Chalaby, J. (1998) 'A charismatic leader's use of the media: De Gaulle and television', *Harvard International Journal of Press/Politics,* 3(4), pp. 44–61.

Chilton, P. (2003) *Analysing Political Discourse: Theory and Practice,* London: Routledge.

Christensen, T. (1987) *Reel Politics: American Political Movies from Birth of a Nation to Platoon,* Oxford: Basil Blackwell.

Clark, C. (1997) 'In favour of civic journalism', *Harvard International Journal of Press/Politics,* 2(3), pp. 118–24.

Clark, T. N. and V. Hoffman-Marinot (eds) (1998) *The New Political Culture*, Boulder, Colo.: Westview.

Clark, T. N. and Inglehart, R. (1998) 'The new political culture: changing dynamics of support for the welfare state and other policies in postindustrial societies', in T. N. Clark and V. Hoffman-Marinot (eds), *The New Political Culture*, Boulder, Colo.: Westview, pp. 9–72.

Cloonan, M. (1996) *Banned! Censorship of Popular Music in Britain*, Aldershot: Arena.

Cloonan, M. (1999) 'Popular music and the nation–state: towards a theorisation', *Popular Music*, 18(2), pp. 193–207.

Cloonan, M. (2007) *Popular Music and the State in the UK*, Aldershot: Ashgate.

Cloonan, M. and S. Frith (eds) (2008) Special Issue on Music Policy, *Popular Music*, 27(2).

Cockerell, M. (1988) *Live From Number 10*, London: Faber & Faber.

Cockerell, M, P. Hennessy and D. Walker (1985) *Sources Close to the Prime Minister*, London: Papermac.

Cole, J. (2005) 'Playing with politics', *British Journalism Review*, 16(4), pp. 31–7.

Coleman, S. (1998) 'Interactive media and the 1997 UK General Election', *Media, Culture and Society*, 20, pp. 687–94.

Coleman, S. (2003) 'A tale of two houses: the House of Commons, the Big Brother house and the people at home', *Parliamentary Affairs*, 56, pp. 733–58.

Coleman, S. (2002) 'Election Call 2001: how politicians and the public interacted', *Parliamentary Affairs* 55(4), pp. 731–42.

Coleman, S. (2005) 'Blogs and the new politics of listening', *Political Quarterly* 76(2), pp. 272–80.

Coleman, S. (2007) *Beyond the West(Minister) Wing: The Depiction of Politicians and Politics in British Soaps*, Research Report, Institute of Communications Studies, University of Leeds.

Coleman, S. and Blumler, J. G. (2009) *The Internet and Democratic Citizenship: Theory, Practice and Policy*, Cambridge: Cambridge University Press.

Coleman, S. and J. Gotze (2001) *Bowling Together: Online Public Engagement in Policy Deliberation*, London: Hansard Society.

Coleman, S., A. Kuik and L. Van Zoonen (2009a) 'Laughter and liability: the politics of British and Dutch television satire', *British Journal of Politics & International Relations*, 11(4), pp. 652–66.

Coleman, S., S. Anthony and D.E. Morrison (2009b) *Public Trust in the News. A Constructivist Study of the Social Life of the News*, Oxford: Reuters Institute for the Study of Journalism.

Collins, R. and C. Murroni (1996) *New Media, New Policies*, Cambridge: Polity.

Connolly, W. E. (2005a) 'The evangelical–capitalist resonance machine', *Political Theory*, 33(6), pp. 869–86.

Connolly, W. E. (2005b) *Pluralism*, Durham, N.C.: Duke University Press.

Corner, J. (1995) *Television Form and Public Address,* London: Edward Arnold.

Corner, J. (2000) 'Mediated persona and political culture: dimensions of structure and process', *European Journal of Cultural Studies*, 3(3), pp. 389–405.

Corner, J. (2003) 'Mediated persona and political culture', in J. Corner and D. Pels (eds), *Media and the Restyling of Politics*, London: Sage, pp. 67–84.

Corner, J. and D. Pels (eds) (2003) *Media and the Restyling of Politics*, London: Sage.

Corner, J. and P. Robinson (2006) 'Politics and mass media: a response to John Street', *Political Studies Review*, 4, pp. 48–54.

Couldry, N., S. Livingstone and T. Markham (2007) *Media Consumption and Public Engagement: Beyond the Presumption of Attention*, Basingstoke: Palgrave Macmillan.

Couldry, N. and T. Markham (2007) 'Celebrity culture and public connection: bridge or chasm?', *International Journal of Cultural Studies*, 10(4), pp. 403–21.

Crewe, I., B. Grosschalk and J. Bartle (eds) (1998) *Political Communication: Why Labour Won the General Election of 1997*, London: Frank Cass.

Crewe, I. and B. Sarlvik (1983) *The Decade of Dealignment*, Cambridge: Cambridge University Press.

Crick, B. (2002) *Democracy: A Very Short Introduction*, Oxford: Oxford University Press.

Crissell, A. (1991) 'Filth, sedition and blasphemy: the rise and fall of satire', in J. Comer (ed.), *Popular Television in Britain,* London: BFI Publishing, pp. 145–58.

Crook, T. (2009) *Comparative Media Law and Ethics*, London: Routledge.

Crouch, C. (2004) *Post-Democracy*, Cambridge: Polity.

Cumberbatch, G. (1998) 'Media effects: the continuing controversy', in A. Briggs and P. Cobley (eds), *The Media: An Introduction,* London: Longman, pp. 262–74.

Curran, J. (1986) 'The impact of advertising on the British mass media', in R. Collins, J. Curran, N. Garnham, P. Scannell, P. Schlesinger and C. Sparks (eds), *Media, Culture and Society: A Critical Reader,* London: Sage, pp. 309–35.

Curran, J. (1991) 'Mass media and democracy: a reappraisal', in J. Curran and M. Gurevitch (eds), *Mass Media and Society,* London: Edward Arnold, pp. 82–117.

Curran, J. (2000) 'Rethinking media and democracy', in J. Curran and M. Gurevitch (eds), *Mass Media and Society*, 3rd edn, London: Arnold, pp. 120–54.

Curran, J. (2002) *Media and Power*, London: Routledge.

Curran, J. and J. Seaton (2010) *Power without Responsibility: Press, Broadcasting and the Internet in Britain*, 7th edn, London: Routledge.

Curran, J. and C. Sparks (1991) 'Press and popular culture,' *Media, Culture and Society*, 13(2), pp. 215–37.

Curtice, J. and H. Semetko (1994) 'Does it matter what the papers say?', in A. Heath, R. Jowell, J. Curtice and B. Taylor, *Labour's last Chance? The 1992 Election and Beyond*, London: Dartmouth, pp. 43–63.

Curtis, L. and M. Jempson (1993) *Interference on the Airwaves*, London: Campaign for Press and Broadcasting Freedom.

Dahl, R. (1956) *A Preface to Democratic Theory*, Chicago, Ill.: University of Chicago Press.

Dahlgren, P. (2001) 'The public sphere and the net: structure, space, and communication', in W. Bennett and R. Entman (eds), *Mediated Politics: Communication in the Future of Democracy*, Cambridge: Cambridge University Press, pp. 33–55.

Daloz, J.-P. (2003) 'Political representation and the connection between symbols of distinction and symbols of likeness', paper to ECPR Workshop on Political Representation, Edinburgh.

Davies, N. (2008) *Flat Earth News*, London: Chatto & Windus.

Davis, A. (2002) *Public Relations Democracy: Politics, Public Relations and the Mass Media in Britain*, Manchester: Manchester University Press.

Davis, A. (2003) 'Whither mass media and power? Evidence for a critical elite theory alternative', *Media, Culture and Society*, 25, pp. 669–90.

Davis, A. (2007) *The Mediation of Power*, London: Routledge.

Day, R. (1991) 'Interviewing politicians', in I. Crewe and M. Harrop (eds), *Political Communications: The General Election Campaign of 1987*, Cambridge: Cambridge University Press, pp. 126–36.

De Sola Pool, I. (1990) *Technologies without Boundaries*, Cambridge, Mass.: Harvard University Press.

De Tocqueville, A. (1988) *Democracy in America*, New York: HarperPerennial.

Deacon, D., P. Golding and M. Billig (1998) 'Between fear and loathing: national press coverage of the 1997 British General Election', in D. Denver, J. Fisher, P. Cowley and C. Pattie (eds), *British Elections and Parties Review*, 8, London: Frank Cass, pp. 135–49.

Deacon, D., P. Golding and M. Billig (2001) 'Press and broadcasting: "real issues" and real coverage', in P. Norris (ed.), *Britain Votes 2001*, Oxford: Oxford University Press, pp. 102–13.

Deacon, D., M. Pickering, P. Golding and G. Murdock (2007) *Researching Communications*, London: Hodder Arnold.

Deacon, D. and D. Wring (2002) 'Partisan dealignment and the British press', in J. Bartle, S. Atkinson and P. Mortimore (eds), *Political Communications: The General Election Campaign of 2001*, London: Frank Cass, pp. 197–211.

De Launey, G. (1995) 'Not-so-big in Japan: Western pop music in the Japanese market', *Popular Music*, 14(2), pp. 203–26.

DellaVigna, S. and E. Kaplan (2007) 'The Fox News effect: media bias and voting', *Quarterly Journal of Economics*, 122(3), pp. 1187–234.

Delli Carpini, M. and B. Williams (2001) 'Let us entertain you: politics in the new media environment', in W. Bennett and R. Entman (eds), *Mediated Politics: Communication in the Future of Democracy*, Cambridge: Cambridge University Press, pp. 160–81.

Dennett, D. (1986) 'Information, technology, and the virtues of ignorance', *Daedalus*, 115(3), pp. 135–53.

Denning, M. (1997) *The Cultural Front*, London: Verso.

Doig, A. (1997) 'The decline of investigative journalism', in M. Bromley and T. O'Malley (eds), *A Journalism Reader*, London: Routledge, pp. 189–213.

Dooley, P. and P. Grosswiler (1997) '"Turf wars": journalists, new media and the struggle for control of political news', *Harvard International Journal of Press/Politics*, 2(3), pp. 31–51.

Dowding, K. (1994) 'The compatibility of behaviouralism, rational choice and "new institutionalism"', *Journal of Theoretical Politics*, 6(1), 105–17.

Downs, A. (1957) *An Economic Theory of Democracy*, New York: Harper & Row.

Dover, K. (2008) *Rupert Murdoch's China Adventures*, Vermont: Tuttle.

Doyle, G. (2002) 'What's "new" about the future of communications? An evaluation of recent shifts in UK media ownership policy', *Media, Culture and Society*, 24, pp. 715–24.

Drezner, D. (2007) 'Foreign policy goes glam', *The National Interest*, November/December, pp. 22–8.

Druckman, (2003) 'The power of television images: the first Kennedy–Nixon debate revisited', *Journal of Politics*, 65(2), pp. 559–71.

Dunleavy, P. and C. Husbands (1985) *Democracy at the Crossroads*, London: Allen & Unwin.

Dunleavy, P. and B. O'Leary (1987) *Theories of the State: the Politics of Liberal Democracy*, London: Palgrave.

Dunn, M. (2007) 'How to survive Rupert Murdoch', *Guardian*, 3 December.

Dworkin, R. (1978) 'Liberalism', in S. Hampshire (ed.), *Public and Private Morality*, Cambridge: Cambridge University Press, pp. 114–43.

Dworkin, R. (1996) 'The curse of American politics', *New York Review of Books*, 17 October, pp. 19–24.

Dyson, K. and P. Humphreys (eds) (1988) *Broadcasting and New Media Policies in Western Europe*, London: Routledge.

ECN (Eastern Counties Newspapers) (n.d.) *Editorial Policy*, Norwich: ECN.

Edwards, D. and D. Cromwell (2006) *Guardians of Power*, London: Pluto.

Eldridge, J. (1993) 'News, truth and power', in Glasgow University Media Group (ed.), *Getting the Message: News, Truth and Power*, London: Routledge, pp. 3–33.

Electoral Commission (2005) *Election 2005: Engaging the Public in Great Britain. An Analysis of Campaigns and Media Coverage*, London: Electoral Commission.

Ellul, J. (1964) *The Technological Society*, New York: Vintage.

Ellul, J. (1972/1965) *The Political Illusion*, New York: Vintage.

Elshtain, J. B. (1982) 'Democracy and the QUBE tube', *The Nation*, 7–14 August, pp. 108–9.

Entman, R. M. (1993) 'Framing: toward clarification of a fractured paradigm', *Journal of Communications*, 43(4), pp. 51–8.

Entman, R. M. (1996) 'Reporting environmental policy debate: the real media biases', *Harvard International Journal of Press/Politics*, 1(3), pp. 77–92.

Entman, R. M. (1997) 'Manufacturing discord: media in the affirmative action debate', *Harvard International Journal of Press/Politics*, 2(4), pp. 32–51.

Entman, R. M. (2003) 'Cascading activation: contesting the White House's frame after 9/11', *Political Communication*, 20, pp. 415–32.

Entman, R. M. and S. Herbst (2001) 'Reframing public opinion as we have known it', in W. L. Bennett and R. M. Entman (eds), *Mediated Politics: Communication in the Future of Democracy*, Cambridge: Cambridge University Press, pp. 203–25.

Ess, C. (ed.) (1996) *Philosophical Perspectives on Computer-Mediated Communication*, Albany, N.Y.: State University of New York Press.

Esser, F., C. Reinemann and D. Fau (2000) 'Spin doctoring in British and German election campaigns', *European Journal of Communication*, 15(2), pp. 209–39.

Euromedia Research Group (1986) *New Media Politics,* London: Sage.

Eyerman, R. and A. Jamison (1998) *Music and Social Movements,* Cambridge: Cambridge University Press.

Farnsworth, S. J. and S. R. Lichter (2003) *The Nightly News Nightmare Network Television Coverage of US Presidential Elections, 1988–2000,* New York: Rowman & Littlefield.

Fenchurch, R. (1994) 'Network wonderland', *Demos Quarterly*, 4, pp. 11.

Feynoe, A. (2010) *The World Online: How UK Citizens Use the Internet to Find Out about the Wider World,* London: International Broadcasting Trust (IBT)/Department for International Development (DFID).

Fishkin, J. (1991) *Democracy and Deliberation,* New Haven, Conn.: Yale University Press.

Fischoff, B., S. Lichtenstein, P. Slovic, S. Derby and R. Keeney (1983) *Acceptable Risk*, Cambridge: Cambridge University Press.

Flyvberg, B. (1998) *Rationality and Power: Democracy in Practice,* Chicago, Ill.: University of Chicago Press.

Foucault, M. (1984) *The Foucault Reader,* ed. P. Rabinow, New York: Pantheon.

Fowler, R. (1991) *Language in the News: Discourse and Ideology in the Press*, London: Routeldge.

Franklin, B. (ed.) (1992) *Televising Democracies,* London: Arnold.

Franklin, B. (1994) *Packaging Politics: Political Communications in Britain's Media Democracy,* London: Edward Arnold.

Franklin, B. (2004) *Packaging Politics: Political Communications in Britain's Media Democracy,* 2nd edn, London: Arnold.

Franklin, B. (1998) *Newszak and News Media,* London: Arnold.

Fraser, N. (1992) 'Rethinking the public sphere: a contribution to the critique of actually existing democracy', in C. Calhoun (ed.), *Habermas and the Public Sphere*, Cambridge, Mass.: MIT Press, pp.109–42.

Freedman, D. (2008) *The Politics of Media Policy*, Cambridge: Polity.

Friedland, L. (1996) 'Electronic democracy and the new citizenship,' *Media, Culture and Society,* 18(2), pp. 185–212.

Frith, S. (1988) 'The pleasures of the hearth: the making of BBC Light Entertainment', in S. Frith, *Music for Pleasure,* Cambridge: Polity, pp. 24–44.

Fuchs, C. (2009) 'Some reflections on Manuel Castells' book *Communication Power*', *tripleC*, 7(1), pp. 94–108.

Gaber, I. (2000) 'Government by spin: an analysis of the process', *Media, Culture and Society*, 22, pp. 507–18.

Gallagher, R. (1989) 'American Television: fact and fantasy', in C. Veljanovski (ed.), *Freedom in Broadcasting*, London: Institute of Economic Affairs, pp. 178–207.

Gamson, W. A. and A. Modigliani (1989) 'Media discourse and public opinion on nuclear power: a constructionist approach', *American Journal of Sociology*, 95(1), pp. 1–37.

Garnham, N. (1986) 'The media and the public sphere', in P. Golding, G. Murdock and P. Schlesinger (eds), *Communicating Politics*, Leicester: Leicester University Press, pp. 55–67.

Garnham, N. (2000) *Emancipation, the Media, and Modernity*, Oxford: Oxford University Press.

Garnham, N. (2003) 'A response to Elizabeth Jacka's "Democracy as Defeat"', *Television and New Media*, 4(2), pp. 193–200.

Garthwaite, C. and T. Moore (2008) 'The role of celebrity endorsements in politics: Oprah, Obama and the 2008 Democratic Primary', available at: http://econweb.umd.edu/~garthwaite/celebrityendorsements_garthwaitemoore.pdf (accessed 16 July 2010).

Garton Ash, T. (2009) *The File: A Personal History*, New York: Atlantic.

Gavin, N. and D. Sanders (2003) 'The press and its influence on British political attitudes under New Labour', *Political Studies*, 51(3), pp. 573–91.

Genovese, E. (1976) *Roll, Jordan, Roll: The World the Slaves Made*, New York: Vintage.

George, N. (1999) *Hip Hop America*, London: Penguin.

Gentzkhow, M. and J. Shapiro (2006) 'What drives media slant? Evidence from US daily newspapers', Working Paper 12707, Cambridge, Mass.: National Bureau of Economic Research.

Geraghty, C. (1992) 'British soaps in the 1980s', in D. Strinati and S. Wagg (eds), *Come On Down? Popular Media Culture in Postwar Britain*, London: Routledge, pp. 133–49.

Gibson, R. and S. Ward (2002) 'Virtual campaigning: Australian parties and the impact of the internet', *Australian Journal of Political Science*, 37(1), pp. 99–129.

Giddens, A. (1979) *Central Problems in Social Theory*, London: Macmillan.

Giddens, A. (1998) *The Third Way*, Cambridge: Polity.

Gilboa, E. (2005) 'Global television news and foreign policy: debating the CNN Effect', *International Studies Perspectives*, 6, pp. 325–41.

Gillespie, M. and J. Toynbee (2006) *Analysing Media Texts*, Milton Keynes: Open University.

Gilliam, F., S. Iyengar, A. Simon and O. Wright (1996) 'Crime in black and white: the violent, scary world of local news', *Harvard International Journal of Press/Politics*, 1(3), pp. 6–25.

Gillmoor, D. (2006) *We the Media: Grassroots Journalism By the People, For the People*, Sebastopol, Calif.: O'Reilly Media.

Ginsborg, P. (2005) *Silvio Berlusconi: Television, Power and Patrimony*, London: Verso.

Gitlin, T. (1991) 'Bites and blips: chunk news, savvy talk and the bifur-cation of American politics', in P. Dahlgren and C. Sparks (eds), *Communication and Citizenship: Journalism and the Public Sphere,* London: Routledge, pp. 119–36.

Glasgow University Media Group (GUMG) (1976) *Bad News,* London: Routledge.

GUMG (1980) *More Bad News,* London: Routledge.

GUMG (1985) *War and Peace News,* Milton Keynes: Open University Press.

GUMG (1993) *Getting the Message: News, Truth and Power,* London: Routledge.

GUMG (2004) *Bad News from Israel,* London: Pluto.

Glencross, D. (1993) 'Convergence at Aspen', *Spectrum,* Autumn, 3.

Golding, P and G. Murdock (2000) 'Culture communication and polit-ical economy', in J. Curran and M. Gurevitch (eds), *Mass Media and Society,* London: Arnold, pp. 70–92.

Goodwin, A. (1990) 'TV news: striking the right balance?', *Understanding Television,* London: Routledge, pp. 42–59.

Gray, H. (1995) *Watching Race: Television and the Struggle for 'Blackness',* Minneapolis, Minn.: University of Minnesota Press.

Gray, H. (2005) *Cultural Moves: African Americans and the Politics of Representation,* Berkeley, Calif.: University of California Press.

Green, P. (1998) 'American television and consumer democracy', *Dissent,* Spring, pp. 49–57.

Greenslade, R. (2005) *Seeking Scapegoats: The Coverage of Asylum Seekers in the UK Press,* Asylum and Migration Working Papers, No, 5, London: IPPR.

Greenslade, R. (2004) *Press Gang: How Newspapers Make Profits from Propaganda,* London: Pan.

Griffin, D. (1994) *Satire: A Critical Reintroduction,* Lexington, Ky: University Press of Kentucky.

Griffin, M. (2001) *Reaping the Whirlwind,* London: Pluto.

Grimes, C. (1997) 'Whither the civic journalism bandwagon?', *Harvard International Journal of Press/Politics,* 2(3), pp. 125–30.

Grossberg, L. (1992) *We've Gotta Get Out of This Place,* London: Routledge.

Habermas, J. (1971) *Towards a Rational Society,* London: Heinemann.

Habermas, J. (1989/1962) *The Structural Transformation of the Public Sphere,* Cambridge: Polity.

Habermas, J. (1996) *Between Facts and Norms,* Cambridge: Polity.

Hacker, K. L. and J. van Dijk (eds) (2000) *Digital Democracy: Issues of Theory and Practice,* London: Sage.

Hall, P. (1999) 'Social capital in Britain', *British Journal of Political Science,* 29, pp. 417–61.

Hall, S. (1980) 'Encoding/decoding', in S. Hall, D. Hobson, A. Lowe and P. Willis (eds), *Culture, Media, Language,* London: Hutchinson, pp. 128–38.

Hall, S. (1982) 'The rediscovery of "ideology": return of the repressed in media studies', in M. Gurevitch, T. Bennett, J. Curran and J. Woollacott (eds), *Culture, Society and the Media,* London: Routledge, pp. 56–90.

Hallin, D. (2000) 'Commercialism and professionalism in the American news media', in J. Curran and M. Gurevitch (eds), *Mass Media and Society,* London: Arnold, pp. 218–37.

Hallin, D. and P. Mancini (2004) *Comparing Media Systems: Three Models of Media and Politics,* Cambridge: Cambridge University Press.

Hamilton, J. T. (2004) *All the News That's Fit to Sell: How the Market Transforms Information into News,* Princeton, N.J.: Princeton University Press.

Hardy, J. (2008) *Western Media Systems,* London: Routledge.

Hargreaves, I (2003) *Journalism: Truth or Dare?,* Oxford: Oxford University Press.

Harrabin, R., A. Coote and J. Allen (2003) *Health in the News: Risk, Reporting and Media Influence,* London: King's Fund.

Harris, J. (2003) *The Last Party: Britpop, Blair and the Demise of English Rock,* London: Fourth Estate.

Harris, R. (1983) *Gotcha! The Media, the Government and the Falklands Crisis,* London: Faber & Faber.

Harris, R. (1990) *Good and Faithful Servant,* London: Faber & Faber.

Harris, S. (1991) 'Evasive action: how politicians respond to questions in political interviews', in P. Scannel (ed.), *Broadcast Talk,* London: Sage.

Harrison, M. (1985) *TV News: Whose Bias?,* London: Policy Journals.

Harrison, M. (1994) 'Exploring the information superhighway: political science and the internet', Keele Research paper, no. 6.

Harrop, M. (1986) 'The press and post–war elections', in I. Crewe and M. Harrop (eds), *Political Communications: The General Election Campaign of 1983,* Cambridge: Cambridge University Press, pp. 137–49.

Harrop, M. (1987) 'Voters', in J. Seaton and B. Pimlott (eds), *The Media in British Politics,* Aldershot: Gower, pp. 45–63.

Hart, R. (1999) *Seducing America: How Television Charms the Modern Voter,* New York: Oxford University Press.

Hay, C. (1997) 'Divided by a common language: political theory and the concept of power', *Politics,* 17(1), pp. 45–52.

Hay, C. (2007) *Why We Hate Politics,* Cambridge: Polity.

Heath, A., J. Curtice, R. Jowell, G. Evans, J. Field and S. Witherspoon (1991) *Understanding Political Change,* Oxford: Pergamon.

Held, D. (1980) *Introduction to Critical Theory*, London: Hutchinson.

Held, D. (2006) *Models of Democracy*, Cambridge: Polity.

Held, D., A. McGrew, D. Goldblatt and J. Perraton (1999) *Global Transformations*, Cambridge: Polity.

Helms, L. (2008) 'Governing in the media age: the impact of the mass media on executive leadership in contemporary democracies', *Government and Opposition*, 43(1), pp. 26–54.

Hennessy, P. (1990) *Whitehall*, London: Fontana.

Henningham, J. (1998) 'Ideological differences between Australian journalists and their public', *Harvard International Journal of Press/Politics*, 3(1), pp. 92–101.

Herman, E. and N. Chomsky (1988) *Manufacturing Consent: The Political Economy of the Mass Media*, New York: Pantheon.

Herman, E. and R. McChesney (1997) *The Global Media: The New Missionaries of Corporate Capitalism*, London: Cassell.

Herman, E. and R. McChesney (1999) 'The global media in the late 1990s', in H. Mackay and T. O'Sullivan (eds), *The Media Reader: Continuity and Transformation*, London: Sage, pp. 178–210.

Hermanns, H. (2008) 'Mobile democracy: mobile phones as democratic tools', *Politics*, 28(2), pp. 74–82.

Hermes, J. and C. Stello (2000) 'Cultural citizenship and crime fiction', *European Journal of Cultural Studies*, 3(2), pp. 215–32.

Herzog, H. (1998) 'More than a looking glass: women in Israeli local politics and the media', *Harvard International Journal of Press/Politics*, 3(1), pp. 26–47.

Hesmondalgh, D. (2007) *The Cultural Industries*, 2nd edn, London: Sage.

Hewison, R. (1988) *Too Much: Art and Society in the Sixties*, London: Methuen.

Hindess, B. (1996) *Discourses of Power*, Oxford: Blackwell.

Hindman, M. (2009) *The Myth of Digital Democracy*, Princeton, N.J.: Princeton University Press.

Hirst, P. (1994) *Associative Democracy: New Forms of Economic and Social Governance*, Cambridge: Polity.

Hollis, M. and S. Smith (1991a) *Explaining and Understanding International Relations*, Oxford: Clarendon Press.

Hollis, M. and S. Smith (1991b) 'Beware of gurus: structure and action in international relations', *Review of International Studies*, 17, pp. 393–410.

Holmes, S. (1990) 'Liberal constraints on private power? Reflections on the origins and rationale of access regulation', in J. Lichtenberg (ed.), *Democracy and the Mass Media*, Cambridge: Cambridge University Press, pp. 21–65.

Hong, L. (1998) 'Profit or ideology? The Chinese press between party and market', *Media, Culture and Society*, 20, pp. 31–41.

Hooghe, M. (2002) 'Watching television and civic engagement', *Harvard International Journal of Press/Politics*, 7(2), pp. 84–104.

Hornby, N. (2000) *Fever Pitch*, London: Penguin.

Hughes, T. (1983) *Networks of Power*, Baltimore, Md.: Johns Hopkins Press.

Humphreys, P. (1996) *Mass Media and Media Policy in Western Europe*, Manchester: Manchester University Press.

Hutton Report (2004) available at: http://www.the–hutton–inquiry. org.uk/content/report/index.htm (accessed 16 July 2010).

Hutton, W. (2008) *The Writing on the Wall: China and the West in the 21st Century*, London: Abacus.

Hyde, M. (2009) *Celebrity: How Entertainers Took Over the World and Why We Need an Exit Strategy*, London: Harvill Secker.

Illich, I. (1975) *Tools for Conviviality*, London: Fontana.

Index on Censorship (2000) *Manufacturing Monsters*, 5, London: Index on Censorship.

Irons, P. (ed.) (1997) *The First Amendment*, New York: New Press.

Islamic Human Rights Commission (2007) *Annual Report 2007*, available at: http://www.ihrc.org/ (accessed 16 July 2010).

Iyengar, S. (1991) *Is Anyone Responsible? How Television Frames Political Issues*, Chicago, Ill.: University of Chicago Press.

Jacka, E. (2003) '"Democracy as defeat": the impotence of arguments for public service broadcasting', *Television and New Media*, 4(2), pp. 177–91.

Jackson, D. (2007) Selling politics: the impact of celebrities' political beliefs on young Americans', *Journal of Political Marketing*, 6, pp. 67–83.

Jackson, D. and T. Darrow (2005) 'The influence of celebrity endorsements on young adults' political opinions', *Harvard International Journal of Press/Politics*, 10(3), pp. 80–98.

Jackson, W. (1997) 'Save democracy from civic journalism: North Carolina's odd experiment', *Harvard International Journal of Press/Politics*, 2(3), pp. 102–17.

Jakubovicz, K. (1996) 'Television and elections in post-1989 Poland: how powerful is the medium?', in D. Swanson and P. Mancini (eds), *Politics, Media and Modern Democracy*, New York: Praeger, pp. 129–54.

Jamieson, K. (1984) *Packaging the Presidency*, Oxford: Oxford University Press.

Jamieson, K. H. (1992) *Dirty Politics: Deception, Distraction, and Democracy*, Oxford: Oxford University Press.

Jones, D. (2004) 'Why Americans don't trust the media', *Harvard International Journal of Press/Politics*, 9(2), pp. 60–75.

Jones, J. (2005) *Entertaining Politics: New Political Television and Civic Culture*, New York: Rowman & Littlefield.

Jones, N. (1995) *Soundbites and Spin Doctors,* London: Cassell.

Jones, S. (ed.) (1995) *Cybersociety,* London: Sage.

Kahn, R. and D. Kellner (2004) 'New media and internet activism: from the 'Battle of Seattle' to blogging', *New Media and Society,* 6(1), pp. 87–95.

Karpinnen, K. (2007) 'Against naïve pluralism', *Centre for the Study of Democracy Bulletin,* 14(1&2), pp. 15–16, and 22.

Kavanagh, D. (1995) *Election Campaigning: The New Marketing of Politics,* Oxford: Basil Blackwell.

Keane, J. (1991) *The Media and Democracy,* Cambridge: Polity.

Keane, J. (1992) 'Democracy and the media – without foundations', *Political Studies,* 40, special issue, pp. 116–29.

Keane, J. (2002) *Whatever Happened to Democracy?* London: IPPR.

Keane, J. (2009) *The Life and Death of Democacy,* London: Simon & Schuster.

Kellner, D. (1995) *Media Culture,* London: Routledge.

Kelly, J. (2009) *Red Kayaks and Hidden Gold: The Rise, Challenges and Value of Citizen Journalism,* London: Reuters Institute for the Study of Journalism.

Khazen, J. (1999) 'Censorship and state control of the press in the Arab world', *Harvard International Journal of Press/Politics,* 4(3), pp. 87–92.

Kiousus, S. (2001) 'Public trust or mistrust? Perceptions of med credibility in the information age', *Mass Communication and Society,* 4(4), pp. 381–403.

Klaehn, J. (2002) 'A critical review and assessment of Herman and Chomsky's "propaganda model"', *European Journal of Communication,* 17(2), pp. 147–82.

Klapper, J. (1960) *The Effects of Mass Communication,* New York: Free Press.

Knopper, S. (2009) *Appetite for Self Destruction: The Spectacular Crash of the Record Industry in the Digital Age,* London: Simon & Schuster.

Kohring, M. and J. Matthes (2007) 'Trust in news media', *Communication Research,* 34(2), pp. 231–55.

Kohut, A. and R. Toth (1998) 'The central conundrum: how can the people like what they distrust?', *Harvard International Journal of Press/Politics,* 3(1), pp. 110–17.

Krugman, P. (2007) 'The Murdoch factor', *Guardian,* 29 June.

Kurtz, H. (1998) *Spin Cycle: Inside the Clinton Propaganda Machine,* London: Pan.

Kwenda, S. (2009) 'In the shadow of Mugabe', *Index on Censorship,* 38(4), pp. 103–9.

Labour Party (1995) *The Net Effect,* London: Labour Party.

Lanchester, J. (2010) *Whoops! Why Everyone Owes Everyone and No One Can Pay*, London: Penguin

Landtsheer, C. de, P. de Vries and D. Vertessen (2008) 'Political impression management: how metaphors, sound bites, appearance effectiveness, and personality traits can win elections', *Journal of Political Marketing*, 7(3/4), pp. 217–38.

Langer, A. (forthcoming) *Personality Politics in the UK*, Manchester: Manchester University Press.

Ledbetter, J. (1997) *Made Possible By … The Death of Public Broadcasting in the United States*, London: Verso.

Lee, C.–C. (1998) 'Press self-censorship and the political transition in Hong Kong', *Harvard International Journal of Press/Politics*, 3(2), pp. 55–73.

Lee, L. F., J. Chan and C. So (2004) 'Press freedom and politics of objective journalism in post-handover Hong Kong', paper presented at the International Communications Conference, New Orleans, 27 May.

Lee, S. (1990) *The Cost of Free Speech*, London: Faber & Faber.

Lees-Marshment, J. (2001) 'The marriage of politics and marketing', *Political Studies*, 49(4), pp. 692–713.

Lees-Marshment, J. (2004) *The Political Marketing Revolution: Transforming the Government of the UK*, Manchester: Manchester University Press.

Leigh, D. (1979) *The Frontiers of Secrecy*, London: Junction Books.

Levine, P. (2002) 'Building the electronic commons', *The Good Society*, 11(3), pp. 1–9.

Levy, D. (1999) *Europe's Digital Revolution: Broadcasting Regulation, the EU and the Nation State*, London: Routledge.

Lewis, J., S. Inthorn and K. Wahl–Jorgensen (2005) *Citizens or Consumers? What the Media Tells Us about Political Participation*, Maidenhead: Open University Press.

Lewis, P. and J. Booth (1989) *The Invisible Medium: Public, Commercial and Community Radio*, Basingstoke: Palgrave Macmillan.

Leys, C. (2001) *Market-Driven Politics: Neoliberal Democracy and the Public Interest*, London: Verso.

Lichtenberg, J. (ed.) (1990) *Democracy and the Mass Media*, Cambridge: Cambridge University Press.

Lichter, R. and T. Smith (1996) 'Why elections are bad news: media and candidate discourse in the 1996 presidential primaries', *Harvard International Journal of Press/Politics*, 1(4), pp. 15–35.

Liebes, T. and A. First (2003) 'Framing the Palestinian–Israeli conflict', in P. Norris, M. Kern and M. Just (eds), *Framing Terrorism: The New Media, the Government and the Public*, New York: Routledge, pp. 59–74.

Lippmann, W. (1922) *Public Opinion*, New York: Dover.

Littlewood, J. and M. Pickering (1998) 'Heard the one about the white middle-class heterosexual father-in-law? Gender, ethnicity and political correctness in comedy', in S. Wagg (ed.), *Because I Tell a Joke or Two: Comedy, Politics and Social Difference*, London: Routledge, pp. 291–312.

Lively, J. (1975) *Democracy*, Oxford: Basil Blackwell.

Lloyd, J. (2004) *What the Media are Doing to our Politics?* London: Constable.

Loader, B. (ed.) (1997) *The Governance of Cyberspace*, London: Routledge.

Lockyer, S. and M. Pickering (eds) (2005) *Beyond a Joke: The Limits of Humour*, Basingstoke: Palgrave Macmillan.

Louw, E. (2001) *The Media and Cultural Production*, London: Sage.

Louw, E. (2005) *The Media and Political Process*, London: Sage.

Lukes, S. (2005) *Power: A Radical View*, 2nd edn, London: Palgrave Macmillan.

Lumley, R. (2001) 'The last laugh: Cuore and the vicissitudes of satire', in L. Cheles and L. Sponza (eds), *The Art of Persuasion: Political Communication in Italy from 1945 to the 1990s*, Manchester: Manchester University Press, pp. 248–77.

Lynch, D. (1999) *After the Propaganda State: Media, Politics, and "Thought Work" in Reformed China*, Stanford, Calif.: Stanford University Press.

Lyon, D. (1988) *The Information Society*, Cambridge: Polity.

Lyon, D. (1994) *The Electronic Eye: The Rise of Surveillance Society*, Cambridge: Polity.

Lyon, D. (2001) *Surveillance Society: Monitoring Everyday Life*, Milton Keynes: Open University Press.

Lyon, D. (2003) *Surveillance after September 11*, Cambridge: Polity.

Malm, K. and R. Wallis (1993) *Media Policy and Music Activity*, London: Routledge.

Mancini, P. and D. Swanson (1996) 'Politics, media, and modem democracy: introduction', in D. Swanson and P. Mancini (eds), *Politics, Media, and Modern Democracy*, New York: Praeger, pp. 1–26.

Mansell, R. (2004) 'Political economy, power and new media', *New Media & Society*, 6(1), pp. 74–83.

Marnham, P. (1982) *The Private Eye Story: The First 21 Years*, London: André Deutsch.

Marquand, D. (2004) *The Decline of the Public: The Hollowing Out of Citizenship*, Cambridge: Polity.

Marqusee, M. (1994) *Anyone But England: Cricket and the National Malaise*, London: Verso.

Marr, A. (1996) *Ruling Britannia*, London: Penguin.

Marr, A. (2004) *My Trade*, London: Macmillan.

Marshall, P.D. (1997) *Celebrity and Power: Fame in Contemporary Culture*, Minneapolis, Minn.: University of Minnesota Press.

Masters, R., S. Frey and G. Bente (1991) 'Dominance and attention: images of leaders in German, French and American TV news', *Polity*, 23(3), pp. 373–94.

Matheson, D. (2004) 'Weblogs and the epistemology of the news: some trends in online journalism', *New Media & Society*, 6(4), pp. 443–68.

Mathews, T. D. (1994) *Censored!* London: Chatto & Windus.

McEnteer, J. (1996) 'Guns, goons, gold, and glitz: Philippine press coverage of the 1995 national elections', *Harvard International Journal of Press/Politics*, 1(1), pp. 113–20.

McGinniss, J. (1969) *The Selling of a President,* New York: Trident Press.

McGuigan, J. (1996) *Culture and the Public Sphere,* London: Routledge.

McLean, I. (1986) 'Mechanisms for democracy', in D. Held and C. Pollitt (eds) *New Forms of Democracy*, London: Sage, pp. 135–57.

McLean, I. (1989) *Democracy and the New Technology,* Cambridge: Polity.

McLeod, J., D. Scheufele and P. Moy (1999) 'Community, communication, and participation: the role of mass media and interpersonal discussion in local political participation', *Political Communication*, 16, pp. 315–36.

McLuhan, M. (1964/1994) *Understanding Media: The Extensions of Man,* London: Routledge.

McNair, B. (1995) *An Introduction to Political Communication,* London: Routledge.

McNair, B. (2000) *Journalism and Democracy*, London: Routledge.

McQuail, D. (1992) *Media Performance,* London: Sage.

McQuail, D. (1994) *Mass Communication Theory,* 3rd edn, London: Sage.

Media Standards Trust (2009) *A More Accountable Press*, available at: http://www.mediastandardstrust.org/home.aspx (accessed 16 July 2010).

Merelman, R. (1991) *Partial Visions: Culture and Politics in Britain, Canada and the United States,* Madison, Wis.: University of Wisconsin Press.

Meyer, T. (with L. Hinchman) (2002) *Media Democracy: How Media Colonize Politics*, Cambridge: Polity.

Meyrowitz, J. (1985) *No Sense of Place: The Effect of Electronic Media on Social Behavior,* New York: Oxford University Press.

Mickiewicz, E. and A. Richter (1996) 'Television, campaigning, and elections in the Soviet Union and post-Soviet Russia', in D. Swanson and P. Mancini (eds), *Politics, Media, and Modern Democracy*, London: Praeger, pp. 107–28.

Mickler, (2004) 'Talkback radio, anti-elitism and moral decline: a fatal paradox', in M. Sawer and B. Hindess (eds), *Us and Them: Anti-Elitism in Australia*, Perth: Api Network, pp. 97–116.

Mill, J. (1992) *Political Writings*, Cambridge: Cambridge University Press.

Mill, J. S. (1972) *On Liberty*, London: J. M. Dent.

Miller, D. (1992) 'Deliberative democracy and social choice', *Political Studies*, Vol. 40, Special Issue, pp. 54–67.

Miller, D. (1993) 'The Northern Ireland Information Service and the media: aims, strategy, tactics', in GUMG (ed. J. Eldridge), *Getting the Message: News, Truth and Power*, London: Routledge, pp. 73–103.

Miller, W. (1991) *Media and Voters*, Oxford: Oxford University Press.

Miller, W., N. Sonntag and D. Broughton (1989) 'Television in the 1987 British election campaign: its content and influence', *Political Studies*, 37(4), pp. 626–51.

Mills, B. (2005) *Television Sitcom*, London: BFI Publishing.

Mills, B. (2008) '"Paranoia, paranoia, everybody's coming to get me": peep show, sitcom, and the surveillance society', *Screen*, 49(1), 1–14.

Mills, C. W. (1956) *The Power Elite*, New York: Oxford University Press.

Modleski, T. (1987) 'The search for tomorrow in today's soap operas', in D. Lazere (ed.), *American Media and Mass Culture*, Berkeley, Calif.: University of California Press, pp. 266–79.

Morgan, P. (2005) *The Insider: The Private Diaries of a Scandalous Decade*, London: Ebury Press.

Morley, D. (1986) *Family Television: Cultural Power and Domestic Leisure*, London: Routledge.

Morley, D. (1992) *Television, Audiences and Cultural Studies*, London: Routledge.

Morozov, E. (2009) 'How dictators watch us on the web', *Prospect*, Issue 165, December, pp. 34–9.

Morris, J. (2005) 'The Fox News factor', *Harvard International Journal of Press/Politics*, 10(3), pp. 56–79.

Morrison, D. and H. Tumber (1988) *Journalists at War: the Dynamic of News Reporting During the Falklands Conflict*, London: Sage.

Morriss, P. (1987) *Power: A Philosophical Analysis*, Manchester: Manchester University Press.

Moy, P., D. Scheufele and R. Holbert (1999) 'Television use and social capital: testing Putnam's time displacement hypothesis', *Mass Communication and Society*, 2(1), pp. 25–43.

Muir, K. (2005) 'Media darlings and falling stars: celebrity and the reporting of political leaders', *Westminster Papers in Communication*, 2(2), pp. 54–71.

Murdock, G. (1982) 'Large corporations and the control of communications industries', in M. Gurevitch, T. Bennett, J. Curran and J. Woollacott (eds), *Culture, Society and the Media,* London: Routledge, pp. 118–50.

Mutz, D. and B. Reeves (2005) 'The new videomalaise: effects of televised incivility on political trust', *American Political Science Review*, 99(1), pp. 1–15.

Nash, K. (2000) *Contemporary Political Sociology: Globalization, Politics and Power,* Oxford: Blackwell.

Naughton, J. (2000) *A Brief History of the Future: The Origins of the Internet*, London: Phoenix.

Neale, S. (1980) *Genre,* London: British Film Institute.

Needham, C. (2004) 'Citizens or consumers? Electronic government in the USA and UK', in R. Gibson, A. Roemelle and S. Ward (eds), *Electronic Democracy*, London: Routledge, pp. 43–69.

Negrine, R. (1994) *Politics and the Mass Media in Britain,* 2nd edn, London: Routledge.

Negrine, R. (1996) *The Communication of Politics,* London: Sage.

Negrine, R. (2008) *The Transformation of Political Communication: Continuities and Changes in Media and Politics*, Basingstoke: Palgrave Macmillan.

Negus, K. (1999) *Music Genres and Corporate Cultures,* London: Routledge.

Neil, A. (1997) *Full Disclosure*, London: Pan.

Neve, B. (2000) 'Frames of presidential and candidate politics in American films of the 1990s', *The Public/Javnost*, 7(2), pp. 19–32.

Newton, K. (1989) 'Media bias', in R. Goodin and A. Reeve (eds), *Liberal Neutrality,* London: Routledge, pp. 130–55.

Newton, K. (2006) 'May the weak force be with you: the power of mass media in modern politics', *European Journal of Political Research*, 45, pp. 209–34.

Newton, K. and M. Brynin (2001) 'The national press and party voting in the UK', *Political Studies*, 49(2), pp. 265–85.

Nicholson, J. (2000) 'The rise of the "e-precinct"', *Harvard International Journal of Press/Politics*, 5(1), pp. 78–81.

Nimmo, D. (1996) 'Politics, media, and modern democracy: the United States', in D. Swanson and P. Mancini (eds), *Politics, Media, and Modern Democracy,* New York: Praeger, pp. 29–48.

Norris, P. (1996) *Electoral Change Since 1945,* Oxford: Blackwell.

Norris, P. (ed.) (1997a) *Women, Media, and Politics,* New York and Oxford: Oxford University Press.

Norris, P. (1997b) 'Women leaders worldwide: a splash of color in the photo op,' in P. Norris (ed.), *Women, Media, and Politics,* New York and Oxford: Oxford University Press, pp. 149–65.

Norris, P. (2000) *Virtuous Circle: Political Communications in Post-Industrial Societies,* Cambridge: Cambridge University Press.

Norris, P. (ed) (2001a) *Britain Votes 2001,* Oxford: Oxford University Press.

Norris, P. (2001b) *Digital Divide: Civic Engagement, Information Poverty, and the Internet Worldwide,* Cambridge: Cambridge University Press

Norris, P. (2002) *Democratic Phoenix: Reinventing Political Activism,* Cambridge: Cambridge University Press.

Norris, P., J. Curtice, D. Sanders, M. Scammell and H. Semetko (1999) *On Message: Communicating the Campaign,* London: Sage.

Norris, P., M. Kern and M. Just (eds) (2003) *Framing Terrorism: The News Media, the Government, and the Public,* New York: Routledge.

North, R. D. (2007) *'Scrap the BBC!' Ten Years to Set Broadcasters Free,* London: Social Affairs Unit.

O'Donnell, H. (1999) *Good Times, Bad Times: Soap Operas and Society in Western Europe,* London: Leicester University Press.

O'Neill, O. (1990) 'Practice of toleration', in J. Lichtenberg (ed.), *Democracy and the Mass Media,* Cambridge: Cambridge University Press, pp. 155–85.

O'Neill, O. (2002) *A Question of Trust: The Reith Lectures 2002,* Cambridge: Cambridge University Press.

Oates, S., D. Owen and R. Gibson (eds) (2005) *The Internet and Politics: Citizens, Voters and Activists,* London: Routledge.

Oborne, P. (2005) *Basil D'Oliveira: Controversy and Cricket,* London: Sphere.

Ofcom (2005) *Viewer and Voters: Attitudes to Television Coverage of the 2005 General Election,* http://www.ofcom.org.uk/research/tv/reports/election/ (accessed 16 July 2010).

Ofcom (2008) *The First and Second Review of Public Service Broadcasting Television,* http://www.ofcom.org.uk/tv/psb_review/ (accessed 16 July 2010).

Olson, M. (1971) *The Logic of Collective Action: Public Goods and the Theory of Groups,* 2nd edn, Cambridge, Mass.: Harvard University Press.

Ouellette, L. (1999) 'TV viewing as good citizenship? Political rationality, enlightened democracy and PBS', *Cultural Studies,* 13(1), pp. 62–90.

Pandania, S., S. Coleman and M. Georgiou (2006) *Reflecting the Real World 2: How We Connect with the Wider World,* London: CBA/IBT/Concern Worldwide/One World Broadcasting Trust.

Page, B. (2003) *The Murdoch Archipelago*, London: Simon & Schuster.

Paterson, C. (1998) 'Global battlefields', in O. Boyd-Barrett and T. Rantanen (eds), *The Globalization of News*, London: Sage, pp. 79–103.

Pease, A. and P. Brewer (2008) 'The Oprah factor: the effects of a celebrity endorsement in a presidential primary campaign', *International Journal of Press/Politics*, 13(4), pp. 386–400.

Pels, D. (2003) 'Aesthetic Representation and political style: re-balancing identity and difference in media democracy', in J. Corner and D. Pels (eds), *Media and the Resyling of Politics*, London: Sage, pp. 41–66.

Philo, G. (1990) *Seeing and Believing: The Influence of Television*, London: Routledge.

Pickard, V. (2006) 'United yet autonomous: Indymedia and the struggle to sustain a radical democratic network', *Media, Culture and Society*, 28(3), pp. 315–36.

Pickerill, J (2000) 'Environmentalists and the net: pressure groups, new social movements and new ICTs', in S. Ward (ed.), *Reinvigorating Government? British Politics and the Internet*, Aldershot: Ashgate.

Pickerill, J. (2004) 'Rethinking political participation: experiments in internet activism in Australia and Britain', in R. Gibson, A. Roemmele and S. Ward, *Electronic Democracy: Mobilisation, Organisation and Participation via new ICTs*, Routledge: London, pp. 170–93.

Pilger, J. (2003) *New Rulers of the World*, London: Verso.

Pilger, J. (2006) 'East Timor: the coup the world missed', *New Statesman*, 22 June.

Pitkin, H. (1967) *The Concept of Representation*, Berkeley, Calif.: University of California Press

Platon, S. and M. Deuze (2003) 'Indymedia journalism', *Journalism*, 4(3), pp. 336–55.

Ponting, C. (1985) *The Right to Know: The Inside Story of the Belgrano Affair*, London: Sphere.

Ponting, C. (1986) *Whitehall: Tragedy and Farce*, London: Hamish Hamilton.

Postman, N. (1987) *Amusing Ourselves to Death*, London: Methuen.

Pringle, H. (2004) *Celebrity Sells*, Chichester: John Wiley.

Prior, M. (2005) 'News vs entertainment: how increasing media choice widens gaps in political knowledge', *American Political Science Review*, 49(3), pp. 577–92.

Putnam, R. (1995) 'Tuning in, tuning out: the strange disappearance of social capital in America', *PS: Political Science and Politics*, December, pp. 664–83.

Putnam, R. (2000) *Bowling Alone: The Collapse and Revival of American Community*, New York: Simon & Schuster.

Radway, J. (1991) *Reading the Romance: Women, Patriarchy and Popular Literature,* London: University of North Carolina Press.

Rawls, R. (1971) *A Theory of Justice,* Oxford: Oxford University Press.

Read, D. (1992) *The Power of News: The History of Reuters 1849–1989,* Oxford: Oxford University Press.

Reporters Sans Frontières (1993) *1993 Report: Freedom of the Press Throughout the World,* London: John Libbey.

Rheingold, H. (1992) *Virtual Community,* London: Mandarin.

Riddell, P. (1999) 'A shift of power – and influence', *British Journalism Review,* 10(3), pp. 26–33.

Ridout, J., A. Grosse ands A. Appleton (2008) 'News media use and Americans' perceptions of global threat', *British Journal of Political Science,* 38, pp. 575–93.

Riegart, K. (ed.) (2007) *Politicotainment,* New York: Peter Lang

Robertson, R. (1995) 'Glocalization: time–space and homogeneity–heterogeneity', in M. Featherstone, S. Lash and R. Robertson (eds), *Global Modernities,* London: Sage, pp. 25–44.

Robinson, M. (1976) 'Public affairs television and the growth of political malaise: the case of "The Selling of the Pentagon"', *American Political Science Review,* 70(2), pp. 409–32.

Robinson, P. (2002) *The CNN Effect: The Myth of News, Foreign Policy and Intervention,* London: Routledge.

Rogin, M. (1987) *Ronald Reagan, the Movie and Other Episodes in Political Demonology,* Berkeley, Calif.: University of California Press.

Romer, R. (2000) 'An "interactive" opportunity', *Harvard International Journal of Press/Politics,* 5(1), pp. 82–5.

Rose, T. (1994) *Black Noise: Rap Music and Black Culture in Contemporary America,* London: Wesleyan University Press.

Rosen, J., S. Davis and C. Campbell (2000) 'Debate: public journalism', *Journalism Studies,* 1(4), pp. 679–94.

Rosenbaum, M. (1997) *From Soapbox to Soundbite,* London: Macmillan.

Rospir, J. (1996) 'Political communication and electoral campaigns in the young Spanish democracy', in D. Swanson and P. Mancini (eds), *Politics, Media, and Modern Democracy,* London: Praeger, pp. 155–69.

Said, E. (2000) 'Apocalypse now', *Index on Censorship,* 5, London: Index on Censorship, pp. 49–53.

Sandel, M. (1998) *Democracy's Discontent: America in Search of a Public Philosophy,* Cambridge, Mass.: Belknap Press/Harvard University Press.

Sanders, D. (1996) 'Economic performance, management competence and the outcome of the next general election', *Political Studies,* 44(2), pp. 203–31.

Sanders, K. (2009) *Communicating Politics in the Twenty-First Century*, Basingstoke: Palgrave Macmillan.

Sartori, C. (1996) 'The media in Italy', in T. Weymouth and B. Lamizet (eds), *Markets and Myths: Forces for Change in the European Media*, London: Longman, pp. 134–70.

Sartori, G. (1989) 'Video power', *Government and Opposition*, 24(1), pp. 39–53.

Savigny, H. (2009) *The Problem of Political Marketing*, New York: Continuum.

Saward, M. (2006) 'The representative claim', *Contemporary Political Theory*, 5(3), pp. 297–318.

Scammell, M. (1995) *Designer Politics: How Elections are Won*, London: Palgrave Macmillan.

Scammell, M. (1999) 'Political marketing: lesson for political science', *Political Studies*, 47, pp. 718–39.

Scannell, P. (1991) 'Introduction: the relevance of talk', in P. Scannell (ed.), *Broadcast Talk*, London: Sage.

Schickler, E. (1994) 'Democratizing technology: hierarchy and innovation in public life', *Polity*, 27(2), pp. 175–99.

Schlesinger, P. (1987) *Putting 'Reality' Together*, London: Methuen.

Schlesinger, P. (2006) 'Is there a crisis in British journalism?', *Media, Culture and Society*, 28(2), pp. 299–307.

Schlesinger, P., G. Murdock and P. Elliott (1983) *Televising 'Terrorism': Political Violence in Popular Culture*, London: Comedia.

Schoenbach, K. (1996) 'The "Americanization" of German election campaigns: any impact on the voters?', in D. Swanson and P. Mancini (eds), *Politics, Media, and Modern Democracy*, New York: Praeger, pp. 91–104.

Schudson, M. (2000) 'The sociology of news production revisited (again)', in J. Curran and M. Gurevitch (eds), *Mass Media and Society*, London: Arnold, pp. 175–200.

Schudson, M. (2001) 'The objectivity norm in American journalism', *Journalism*, 2(2), pp. 149–70.

Schudson, M. (2008) *Why Democracies Need an Unlovable Press*, Cambridge: Polity.

Schultz, J. (1998) *Reviving the Fourth Estate: Democracy, Accountability and the Media*, Cambridge: Cambridge University Press.

Schumpeter, J. (1976/1943) *Capitalism, Socialism and Democracy*, London: Allen & Unwin.

Scott, A. (1997) 'Introduction – globalization: social process or political rhetoric?', in A. Scott (ed.), *The Limits of Globalization*, London: Routledge, pp. 1–24.

Scott, A. (1999) 'War and the public intellectual: cosmopolitanism and anti-cosmopolitanism in the Kosovo debate in Germany', *Sociological Research Online*, 4(2): http//www.socresonline.org.uk/4/2/scott.html (accessed 16 July 2010).

Scott, J. (1990) *Domination and the Arts of Resistance*, New Haven, Conn.: Yale University Press.

Scott, M. (2008) *Screening the World: How UK Broadcasters Portrayed the Wider World in 2007/8*, London: IBT/DFID.

Scott, M. (2009) *The World in Focus: How UK Audiences Connect with the Wider World and the International Content of News in 2009*, London and Norwich: Commonwealth Broadcasting Association (CBA)/DFID/IBT.

Scott, M., S. Inthorn and J. Street (forthcoming) 'From entertainment to citizenship: a comparative study of the political uses of popular culture', *International Journal of Cultural Studies*.

Selb, P. (2004) *Beyond the Front Lines: How the News Media Cover a World Shaped by War*, Basingstoke: Palgrave Macmillan.

Semetko, H. (1996) 'Political balance on television: campaigns in the United States, Britain, and Germany', *Harvard International Journal of Press/Politics*, 1(1), pp. 51–71.

Semetko, H., J. Blumler, M. Gurevitch and D. Weaver (1991) *The Formation of Campaign Agendas: A Comparative Analysis of Party and Media Roles in Recent American and British Elections*, Hillsdale, N.J.: Lawrence Erlbaum.

Seymour, E. and S. Barnett (2005) *Bringing the World to the UK: Factual International Programming on UK Public Service TV*, London: 3WE.

Seymour-Ure, C. (1974) *The Political Impact of Mass Media*, London: Constable.

Shawcross, W. (1992) *Rupert Murdoch*, London: Chatto & Windus.

Sheeran, P. (2001) *Cultural Politics in International Relations*, Aldershot: Ashgate.

Shen, F. (2009) 'An economic theory of political communication effects: how the economy conditions political learning', *Communication Theory*, 19(4), pp. 374–96.

Siebert, F., T. Peterson and W. Schramm (1956) *Four Theories of the Press*, Urbana, Ill.: University of Illinois Press.

Silverstone, R. (1994) *Television and Everyday Life*, London: Routledge.

Slaatta, T. (1998) 'Media and democracy in the global order', *Media, Culture and Society*, 20, pp. 335–44.

Smith, J., L. Edge and V. Morris (2006) *Reflecting the Real World? How British TV Portrayed Developing Countries in 2005*, London: CBA/DFID/IBT/Open University/Voluntary Service Overseas (VSO).

Snoddy, R. (1992) *The Good, the Bad and the Unacceptable*, London: Faber & Faber.

Solop, F. (2001) 'Digital democracy comes of age: internet voting and the 2000 Arizona Democratic primary election', *Political Science and Politics*, 34(2), pp. 289–93.

Sparks, C. (1998) *Communism, Capitalism and the Mass Media*, London: Sage.

Sparks, C. (2000) 'From dead trees to live wires: the internet's challenge to the traditional newspaper', in J. Curran and M. Gurevitch (eds), *Mass Media and Society*, London: Arnold, pp. 268–92.

Sreberny, A. (2000) 'The global and the local in international communications', in J. Curran and M. Gurevitch (eds), *Mass Media and Society*, London: Arnold, pp. 93–119.

Sreberny-Mohammadi, A. (1990) 'US media covers the world', in J. Downing, A. Mohammadi and A. Sreberny-Mohammadi (eds), *Questioning the Media: A Critical Introduction*, London: Sage, pp. 296–307.

Stanyer, J. (2003) 'Politics and the media: a breakdown in relations for New Labour', *Parliamentary Affairs*, 56, pp. 309–21.

Stanyer, J. (2004) 'Politics and the media: a crisis of trust?', *Parliamentary Affairs*, 57(2), pp. 420–34.

Stanyer, J. (2006) 'Levelling the electoral communication playing field? The hype and the reality of campaign blogging', paper presented at the annual meeting of the American Political Science Association, Philadelphia.

Stanyer, J. (2007) *Modern Political Communication*, Cambridge: Polity.

Stanyer, J. and D. Wring (2004) 'Public images, private lives: the mediation of politicians around the globe', *Parliamentary Affairs*, 57(1), pp. 1–8.

Starkey, G. (2007) *Balance and Bias in Journalism: Representation, Regulation and Democracy*, Basingstoke: Palgrave Macmillan.

Starr, S. F. (1983) *Red & Hot: The Fate of Jazz in the Soviet Union*, Oxford: Oxford University Press.

Statham, P. (1996) 'Berlusconi, the media and the new right in Italy', *Harvard International Journal Press/Politics*, 1(1), pp. 87–106.

Staton, C. D. (1994) 'Democracy's quantum leap', *Demos Quarterly*, 3, pp. 31–2.

Stonor Saunders, F. (2000) *Who Paid the Piper? The CIA and the Cultural Cold War*, London: Granta.

Stolle, D. and M. Hooghe (2005) 'Inaccurate, exceptional, one-sided or irrelevant? The debate about the alleged decline of social capital and civic engagement in Western societies', *British Journal of Political Science*, 35(1), pp. 149–67.

Street, J. (1986) *Rebel Rock: The Politics of Popular Music,* Oxford: Blackwell.

Street, J. (1992) *Politics and Technology,* London: Macmillan.

Street, J., S. Hague and H. Savigny (2008) 'Playing to the crowd: the role of music and musicians in political participation', *British Journal of Politics & International Relations,* 10(2), pp. 269–85.

Strömbäck, J. and Dimitrov, D.V. (2006) 'Political and media systems matter: a comparison of election news coverage in Sweden and the United States', *Harvard International Journal of Press/Politics,* 11(4), pp. 131–47.

Stromer-Galley, J. (2009) 'The web 2.0 election', in N. Anstead and W. Straw (eds), *The Change We Need: What Britain Can Learn from Obama's victory,* London: Fabian Society, pp. 49–58.

Sullivan, K. (2005) 'Women, speech and experience', *The Good Society,* 14(1–2), pp. 35–9.

Sunstein, C. (2001) *Republic.com,* Princeton, N.J.: Princeton University Press.

Surowiecki, J. (2004) *The Wisdom of Crowds: Why the Many are Smarter than the Few,* London: Abacus.

Sussman, G. (1997) *Communication, Technology, and Politics in the Information Age,* London: Sage.

Swanson, D. and P. Mancini (eds) (1996) *Politics, Media, and Modern Democracy,* New York: Praeger.

Tannsjo, T. (1985) 'Against freedom of expression', *Political Studies,* 33(4), pp. 547–59.

Taylor, L. and B. Mullan (1986) *Uninvited Guests: The Intimate Secrets of Television and Radio,* London: Coronet.

Temple, M. (2006) 'Dumbing down is good for you', *British Politics,* 1(2), pp. 257–73.

Teneboim–Weinblatt, K. (2009) '"Where is Jack Bauer when you need him?" The uses of television drama in mediated political discourse', *Political Communication,* 26(4), pp. 367–87.

Thompson, D. (1998), 'Privacy, politics and the press', *Harvard International Journal of Press/Politics,* 3(4), pp. 103–13.

Thompson, E. (1968) *The Making of the English Working Class,* Harmondsworth: Penguin.

Thompson, H. S. (1973) *Fear and Loathing on the Campaign Trail '72,* New York: Popular Library.

Thompson, J. (1988) 'Mass communication and modern culture: contribution to a critical theory of ideology', *Sociology,* 22(3), pp. 359–83.

Thompson, J. (1995) *The Media and Modernity: A Social Theory of the Media,* Cambridge: Polity.

Thompson, J. (1997) 'Scandal and social theory', in J. Lull and S. Hinerman (eds), *Media Scandals,* Cambridge: Polity, pp. 34–64.

Thrall, A.T., J. Lollio-Fakherddine, J. Berent, L. Donnelly, W. Herrin, Z. Paquette, R. Wenglinski and A. Wyatt (2008) 'Star power: celebrity advocacy and the evolution of the public sphere', *International Journal of Press/Politics*, 13(4), pp. 362–85.

Thussu, D. (2003) 'Live TV and bloodless deaths: war, infotainment and 24/7 news', in D. Thussu and D. Freedman (eds.) *War and the Media: Reporting Conflict 24/7*, London: Sage, pp. 117–32.

Thussu, D. and D. Freedman (eds) (2003) *War and the Media: Reporting Conflict 24/7*, London: Sage.

Tiffen, R. (1989) *News and Power*, Sydney: Allen & Unwin.

Time Warner, *Annual Report* 2009: available at http://ir.timewarner.com/phoenix.zhtml?c=70972&p=irol-reportsAnnual (last accessed 16 July 2010).

Tolson, A. (1991) 'Televised chat and the synthetic personality', in P. Scannell (ed.), *Broadcast Talk*, London: Sage, pp. 178–201.

Tomlinson, J. (1999) 'Cultural globalisation: placing and displacing the West', in H. MacKay and T. O'Sullivan (eds), *The Media Reader: Continuity and Transformation*, London: Sage, pp. 165–77.

Tracey, M. (1985) 'The poisoned chalice? International television and the idea of dominance', *Daedalus*, 114(4), pp. 17–56.

Tsagarousianou, R., D. Tambini and C. Bryan (1998) *Cyberdemocracy: Technology, Cities and Civic Networks*, London: Routledge.

Tunstall, J. (1996) *Newspaper Power: The New National Press in Britain*, Oxford: Oxford University Press.

Tunstall, J. (2008) *The Media were American: US Media in Decline*, Oxford: Oxford University Press.

Tunstall, J. and D. Machin (1999) *The Anglo-American Media Connection*, Oxford: Oxford University Press.

Tunstall, J. and M. Palmer (1991) *Media Moguls*, London: Routledge.

Tutt, B. (1992) 'Televising the Commons: a full, balanced and fair account of the work of the House', in B. Franklin (ed.), *Televising Democracies*, London: Routledge, pp. 129–48.

Van de Donk, W., I. Snellen and P. Tops (1995) *Orwell in Athens*, Amsterdam: IOS Press.

Van Noije, L. J. Kleinnijenhuis and D. Oegema (2008) 'Loss of parliamentary control due to mediatization and Europeanization: a longitudinal and cross-sectional analysis of agenda building in the United Kingdom and the Netherlands', *British Journal of Political Science*, 38, pp. 455–78.

Van Zoonen, L. (1998a) '"Finally, I have my mother back": politicians and their families in popular culture', *Harvard International Journal of Press/Politics*, 3(1), pp. 48–64.

Van Zoonen, L. (1998b) 'A day at the zoo: political communication, pigs and popular culture', *Media, Culture and Society,* 20(2), pp. 183–200.

Van Zoonen, L. (2005) *Entertaining the Citizen,* New York: Rowman & Littlefield.

Veljanovski, C. (1989) *Freedom in Broadcasting,* London: Institute of Economic Affairs.

Vickers, G. (1965) *The Art of Judgment,* London: Chapman & Hall.

Vilches, L. (1996) 'The media in Spain', in T. Weymouth and B. Lamizet (eds), *Markets and Myths: Forces for Change in the European Media,* London: Longman, pp. 173–201.

Wagg, S. (1992) '"You've never had it so silly": the politics of British satirical comedy from *Beyond the Fringe* to *Spitting Image*', in D. Strinati and S. Wagg (eds), *Come On Down? Popular Media Culture in Postwar Britain,* London: Routledge, pp. 254–84.

Wagg, S. (1998) '"They've already got a comedian for governor": comedians and politics in the United States and Great Britain', in S. Wagg (ed.), *Because I Tell a Joke or Two: Comedy, Politics and Social Difference,* London: Routledge, pp. 244–72.

Wajcman, J. (1991) *Feminism Confronts Technology,* Cambridge: Polity.

Wallis, R. and S. Baran (1990) *The Known World of Broadcast News,* London: Routledge.

Walzer, M. (1985) *Spheres of Justice,* Oxford: Basil Blackwell.

Wang, H. (2010) 'Investigative journalism and political power in China', Working Paper, January, Oxford: Reuters Institute for the Study of Journalism.

Ward, I. (2006) ''The media, power and politics', in A. Parkin, J. Summers and D. Woodward (eds), *Government, Politics, Power and Policy in Australia,* Frenchs Forest: Pearson, pp. 363–79.

Warner, M. (2005) *Publics and Counterpublics,* New York: Zone.

Washbourne, N. (1999) 'New forms of organizing? Translocalism, networks and organizing in FoE', paper to 'A New Politics?' conference, University of Birmingham.

Washbourne, N. (2010) *Mediating Politics,* Milton Keynes: Open University Press.

Weale, A. (1999) *Democracy,* Basingstoke: Palgrave.

Webster, F. (2001) *Culture and Politics in the Information Age: A New Politics?* London: Routledge.

Weizenbaum, J. (1984) *Computer Power and Human Reason,* London: Penguin.

West, D. and J. Orman (2003) *Celebrity Politics,* New Jersey: Prentice-Hall.

Whannel, G. (1992) 'The price is right but the moments are sticky: television, quiz and game shows, and popular culture', in D. Strinati and

S. Wagg (eds), *Come On Down? Popular Media Culture in Postwar Britain*, London: Routledge, pp. 179–201.

Wheeler, M. (2006) *Hollywood: Politics and Society*, London: BFI Publishing.

Whittle, S. and G. Cooper (2009) *Privacy, Probity and Public Interest*, Oxford: Reuters Institute for the Study of Journalism.

Wicke, P. (1992) '"The times they are a-changing": rock music and political change in Eastern Germany', in R. Garofalo (ed.), *Rockin' the Boat. Mass Music and Mass Movements*, Boston, Mass.: South End Press, pp. 81–93.

Wiener, J. (1984) *Come Together: John Lennon in His Time,* New York: Random House.

Williams, R. (1981) *Culture,* London: Fontana.

Winder, R. (1999) *Hell for Leather: A Modern Cricket Journey,* London: Indigo.

Winner, L. (1986) *The Whale and the Reactor,* Chicago: University of Chicago Press.

Winner, L. (1994) 'Three paradoxes of the information age', in G. Bender and T. Druckrey (eds), *Culture on the Brink: Ideologies of Technology,* Seattle, Wash.: Bay Press, pp. 191–7.

Winston, B. (1998) *Media Technology and Society,* London: Routledge.

Wober, M., M. Svennevig and B. Gunter (1986) 'The television audience and the 1983 General Election', in I. Crewe and M. Harrop (eds), *Political Communications: The General Election Campaign of 1983,* Cambridge: Cambridge University Press, pp. 95–103.

Wright, S. (2002) 'Dogma or dialogue? The politics of the Downing Street website', *Politics,* 22(3), pp. 135–42.

Wright, S. (2005) 'A comparative analysis of government-run online discussion forums at the local, national and European levels', unpublished Ph.D. thesis, University of East Anglia.

Wright, S. (2006) 'Government-run discussion fora: moderation, censorship and the shadow of control', *British Journal of Politics and International Relations,* 8(4), pp. 550–68.

Wright, S. (2009) 'Political blogs, representation and the public sphere', *Aslib Proceedings: New Information Perspectives,* 61(2), pp. 155–69.

Wright, S. and J. Street (2007) 'Democracy, deliberation and design: the case of online discussion forums', *New Media & Society,* 9(5), pp. 849–69.

Wring, D. (2005) *The Politics of Marketing the Labour Party,* Basingstoke: Palgrave Macmillan.

Wring D. and Horrocks (2001) 'The transformation of political parties', in B. Axford and R. Huggins (eds), *New Media and Politics,* London: sage, pp. 191–209.

Young, S. (2007) 'The regulation of government advertising in Australia: the politicisation of a public policy issue', *Australian Journal of Public Administration*, 66(4), pp. 438–52.

Young, S., S. Bourne and S. Younane (2007) 'Contemporary political communications: audiences, politicians and the media in international research', *Sociology Compass*, 1(1), pp. 41–59.

Zaller, J. (1992) *The Nature and Origins of Mass Opinion*, Cambridge: Cambridge University Press.

Zasurskii, I. (2002) 'Control by other means', *Index on Censorship*, Issue 203, 31(2), pp. 18–23.

Zhao, B. and G. Murdock (1996) 'Young pioneers: children and the making of Chinese communism', *Cultural Studies,* 10(2), pp. 201–17.

Zhao, X. and G. Bleske (1998) 'Horse-race polls and audience issue learning', *Harvard International Journal of Press/Politics*, 3(4), pp. 13–34.

Zolo, D. (1992) *Democracy and Complexity,* Cambridge: Polity.

Index

Manufactured by Amazon.ca
Bolton, ON

14602699R00221